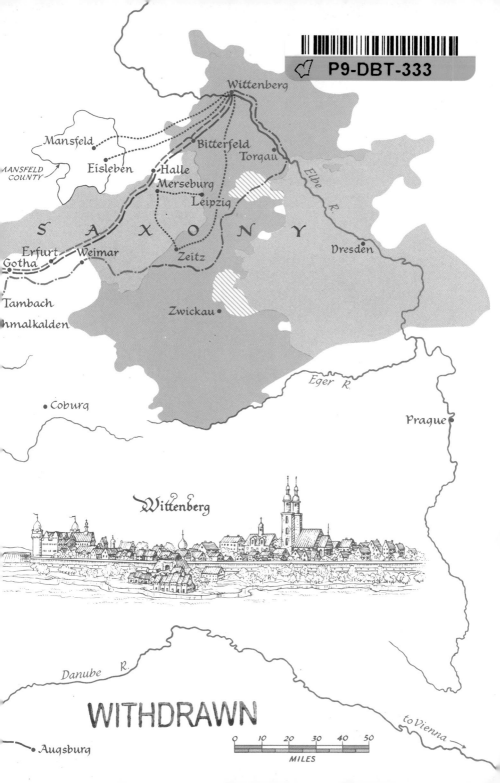

Mansfeld

MANSFELD
COUNTY

Eisleben

Mansfeld

Wittenberg

Bitterfeld

Torgau

Halle
Merseburg

Leipzig

S A X O N Y

Elbe R.

Erfurt Weimar

Gotha

Zeitz

Dresden

Tambach

Schmalkalden

Zwickau

Eger R.

Coburg

Prague

Wittenberg

Danube R.

WITHDRAWN

Augsburg

0 10 20 30 40 50

MILES

to Vienna

LUTHER

LUTHER
An Experiment in Biography

H. G. HAILE

1980   Doubleday & Company, Inc., Garden City, New York

Grateful acknowledgment is made for permission to excerpt the essay "Algorithm and Epikeia" by H. G. Haile now incorporated in "Reconciliation" in this volume, which first appeared in the Winter 1978 edition of *Soundings*, An Interdisciplinary Journal, © copyright 1978 by Vanderbilt University and the Society for Values in Higher Education.

This religious attitude, so to speak, toward truth is not without its influence on the total personality of scientific man. Aside from what presents itself to his experience, and the rules of thinking itself, the researcher recognizes as a matter of principle no authority whose decisions or utterances can lay claim to "truth." This gives rise to the paradox that a man who dedicates his best powers to things outside himself becomes, from the social point of view, an extreme individualist who, in principle at least, relies on nothing but his own judgment. One can even argue the position that intellectual individualism and scientific aspiration appeared at the same moment in history and have remained inseparable.

ALBERT EINSTEIN, 1950

CONTENTS

ACKNOWLEDGMENTS

Many generations of pious labors have erected, in Luther scholarship, one of the major monuments to learning in modern times. It is certainly parochial, the views expressed sometimes seem quaint, and biased—but the endless devotion and meticulous care of all those good men have made my own, more detached presentation possible (if such it be). I am conscious this Luther portrait would seem impious to many of them, so I confess here both my immense debt, and my doubt that I have become any less captive to conscience than they.

I was privileged to work at one of the world's noblest libraries, with an unusually large collection of imprints from that early era of the book so much influenced by Martin Luther, and including original issues not yet catalogued, even though Luther is surely the most bibliographed of authors. Thus I was able to do all my work here in the American Middle West, although I am grateful to the University of Illinois Research Board for sending me to Saxony to get the lay of the land. The Board has been generous with me over the years, from matching large sums with the library for rare Luther imprints, to wages for assistants. In a day when aid is preferably channeled into projects conceived to pay off in grants to the institution, so that efforts are encouraged to resonate with accepted philosophies, we in the humanities must be happy with any help whatsoever. How thankful must I therefore be for the long, worthy tradition at the University of Illinois, of gleaning science and engineering grants to support the humane studies. My university also gives me time for research and, beyond that, has allowed me to wander off to guest appointments at other great German departments. At Georgia and at

Michigan I was given all freedom and facilities for writing. Thus I am indebted to many department heads, deans, directors, secretaries, and—at the top of the heap—students who have put a lot into this book. I have enjoyed advantages rare in the venerable history of Luther scholarship.

Colleagues who volunteered to go over my manuscript and whose suggestions made it more readable, John Howard at Georgia and Mark McCulloh at Illinois, deserve thanks. William Carey Moore of Doubleday showed me how to make crucial additions which brought the sense of the book to the fore, the ideal function of an editor. Through his good offices then I gained the benefit of thoughtful commentary by the dean of Luther studies in America, Roland Bainton. Correspondence with this generous scholar (whose gentle demurrals moderated some of my claims for Luther) has been a precious reward for my efforts. As any writer knows, the support of our family goes without saying, but this time I must record that my wife, Mary Elizabeth, served like Kate as research assistant to Doctor Luther.

H. G. HAILE
Champaign, Illinois
Fall 1979

IMPORTANT EVENTS

FOR

	LUTHER	HIS CONTEMPORARIES	EUROPE
1483	Martin Luther born on 10 November, in Eisleben.		Richard III murders Edward, to become king of England.
			Charles VIII succeeds to rule in France.
			Portugal denies Columbus support in his quest for a sea route to India. He petitions Spain instead.
1484	The family moves to Mansfeld, where Luther spends his boyhood.	Ulrich Zwingli, the Swiss reformer, is born.	
1485			The House of Saxony is divided between Ernest and Albert.
			Henry VII deposes Richard III.
1486		John Eck, great Dominican opponent of Luther, is born.	

IMPORTANT EVENTS

	LUTHER	FOR HIS CONTEMPORARIES	EUROPE
1488		Ulrich von Hutten, militant humanist, is born.	Bartholomeu Dias rounds the Cape of Good Hope.
1489		Thomas Cranmer, English reformer, is born.	
1490		Albert of Brandenburg, later cardinal, is born.	
1491		Henry VIII of England and Ignatius Loyola are born.	Botticelli completes his drawings to accompany Dante's *Divine Comedy*.
1492		Margaret of Navarre, French novelist, is born.	Alexander VI, father of Cesare and Lucretia Borgia, is elected pope.
		Ludwig Senfl, German composer, is born.	The Inquisition drives the Jews out of Spain.

1493

William Tyndale is born.

Behaim in Nuremberg manufactures the first globe.

Columbus lands in Cuba.

Cesare Borgia becomes cardinal.

Paracelsus, German physician and thinker, is born.

Pope Alexander, dividing the New World between Spain and Portugal, reveals Europe's near total ignorance of the western hemisphere.

Maximilian I becomes emperor of the Holy Roman Empire.

1494

François Rabelais is born.

Hans Sachs is born.

Sebastian Brant's *Ship of Fools* is published.

1495

Albrecht Dürer makes his first trip to Italy.

Syphilis appears as a new disease in Naples.

1496

Michelangelo makes his first journey to Rome.

IMPORTANT EVENTS

FOR
HIS CONTEMPORARIES

EUROPE

LUTHER

1497 Young Martin goes away to school, first to Magdeburg,

Philip Melanchthon is born.

Leonardo da Vinci completes his fresco *The Last Supper*.

Pope Alexander confers the title of Catholic Majesty upon the Spanish crown.

Tobacco is first reported in Europe.

Savonarola is burned in Florence.

1498 then to Eisenach.

1500

Emperor Charles V is born.

Michelangelo completes the *Pietà*.

Benvenuto Cellini, Italian sculptor, is born.

1501	Enrolls at the University of Erfurt, takes the Bachelor of Arts degree.
1502	Erasmus publishes the *Enchiridion*.	The University of Wittenberg is founded.
		Titian paints the *Gypsy Madonna*.
		The first pocket watches are produced, in Nuremberg.
1503	Nostradamus, the French astrologer, is born.	Julius II is elected pope, known for his military prowess.
	John Frederick of Saxony is born.	Construction begins on Canterbury Cathedral.
	Michelangelo's *David* is completed.	
1504	Philip of Hesse is born.	
	Filippino Lippi dies.	

IMPORTANT EVENTS

FOR

LUTHER	HIS CONTEMPORARIES	EUROPE
	Raphael comes to Florence.	
	Götz von Berlichingen loses his right hand while besieging Nuremberg.	
1505 In January Luther takes the Master of Arts degree.	Michelangelo is called to Rome by Julius II.	
On 17 July he enters the Augustinian monastery in Erfurt.		
1506	Columbus dies in the belief he has discovered a sea route to India.	Julius II begins construction of Saint Peter's Cathedral, and the Dominican John Tetzel brings indulgence sales into German lands.

1507	Brother Martin a priest, says his first mass.	Da Vinci's *Mona Lisa* is painted.
1508	Called to Wittenberg to teach for a semester.	Michelangelo begins the ceiling of the Sistine Chapel. Andrea Palladio, Italian architect, is born.
1509	Returns to Erfurt in October.	John Calvin is born. Erasmus publishes his *Praise of Folly*. Henry VIII becomes king, marries Catherine of Aragon, aunt of the future emperor. Jacob Fugger lends Emperor Maximilian 170,000 ducats to wage his war against Venice.
1510	Journeys to Rome in the company of a fellow Augustinian, on business for the order.	Geiler von Kaisersberg, powerful reform preacher of Strasbourg, dies.

IMPORTANT EVENTS

FOR

HIS CONTEMPORARIES	EUROPE		LUTHER

		John Reuchlin, eminent Hebraicist, defends himself against charge of heresy.		
	1511	Returns to Erfurt, is transferred to Wittenberg.	Miguel Servetus, the antitrinitarian burned at the stake by John Calvin (1553), is born.	
The last general council of the church, the Fifth Lateran, is convoked by Julius II.	1512	October 19, takes the degree of Doctor of Theology.	Gerhard Mercator, the cartographer, is born.	
Leo X is elected pope. Balboa discovers the Pacific.	1513	Begins his first lectures, on Psalms.	Dürer completes *Knight, Death, and the Devil.*	

1514   Andreas Vesalius is born.

        Albert of Brandenburg is
        named archbishop of
        Mainz.

        The financial house of Fugger in
        Augsburg acquires the German
        indulgence sales.

1515   Lectures on Romans.

        Francis I succeeds to the French
        crown and begins his successful
        campaigns in Italy.

        Baldung-Grien paints *Rest on the
        Flight into Egypt*.

        Correggio paints the *Madonna of
        Saint Francis*.

1516   Lectures on Galatians.

        Ariosto writes *Orlando
        furioso*.

        Erasmus publishes his
        Greek New Testament.

        Thomas More's *Utopia*
        appears.

        Charles, later emperor, succeeds
        to the crown of Spain.

IMPORTANT EVENTS

LUTHER	FOR HIS CONTEMPORARIES	EUROPE
1517 Makes appeal to his bishops against the indulgence sales (95 Theses).	Hans Sachs writes his first Lenten farce.	Ulrich von Hutten is crowned poet laureate by Emperor Maximilian; publishes (anonymously) the *Letters of Obscure Men*, a satire in defense of John Reuchlin.
		Cardinal Ximenes concludes the Complutensian Polyglot Bible (Hebrew, Greek, Latin, Aramaic).
1518 Sylvester Prierias writes against Luther.	Philip Melanchthon becomes professor in Wittenberg.	Albert of Mainz is elevated to cardinal.
Luther is cited to Rome, but is permitted to come before Cardinal Cajetan instead, at the imperial diet in Augsburg. He makes appeal to a general council of the church.		

1519	A papal emissary is sent to Wittenberg to effect reconciliation.	Ulrich Zwingli begins his reforms in Switzerland.
	At the celebrated debate with John Eck in Leipzig, Luther questions papal infallibility and is accused of Hussitism.	Maximilian dies. Charles V is elected emperor.
		Leonardo da Vinci dies.
1520	The three great reform tracts appear: *Address to the Christian Nobility of the German Nation*, *The Babylonian Captivity of the Church*, and *Freedom of the Christian*.	Magellan reaches Cape Horn.
	The papal bull *Exsurge Domine* threatens Luther with excommunication.	
	Luther burns canon law publicly, and a copy of the bull for good measure.	

IMPORTANT EVENTS

FOR

LUTHER	HIS CONTEMPORARIES	EUROPE
1521 The bull *Decet Romanum* announces Luther's excommunication.	Sebastian Brant dies.	Radical church reforms begin while Luther is in hiding.
In April, Luther makes his stand before the imperial diet at Worms, will not recant until refuted.	Josquin Desprez, eminent French composer much admired by Luther, dies.	Henry VIII writes an anti-Luther tract, for which the pope rewards him with the title Defender of the Faith.
In early May, Luther is taken covertly to the Fortress Wartburg in the Thuringian hills.		
The Edict of *Worms* outlaws Luther.		
In December, Luther makes a stealthy trip to Wittenberg to moderate the reforms there, returns to the Wartburg.		

Year			
1522	At the Wartburg, the New Testament is translated into German, published in Wittenberg in September.	Justus Jonas, priest at the castle church and Luther's old friend, marries. John Reuchlin dies.	Adrian VI is elected pope. Favors reform. Remnants of Magellan's expedition complete the circumnavigation of the globe.
1523	Writes his first song, in commemoration of the martyrdom of two Augustinian brothers in Brussels.	Ulrich von Hutten dies.	The Zurich City Council adopts Zwingli's reforms. Clement VII elected pope.
1524		Erasmus writes the anti-Luther tract *Concerning Free Will.*	The Peasants' War begins. Zwingli abolishes the mass.
1525	Tracts against religious enthusiasts, against the rebellious peasants, and against Erasmus (*Concerning the Bondage of the Will*).	Thomas Müntzer is executed. Jacob Fugger dies.	Charles V defeats France at Pavia and captures Francis I. Frederick the Wise of Saxony dies, is succeeded by his brother, John.

IMPORTANT EVENTS

FOR

	LUTHER	HIS CONTEMPORARIES	EUROPE
	In June, marriage with Catherine von Bora.		
1526	The first son, Hans, is born in June.		The imperial diet at Speier decrees religious observance to be a matter determined on territorial basis pending a council.
1527	Luther's first severe illness (heart?) is accompanied by acute depression.	Machiavelli dies.	Lutheran reforms spread significantly, Hesse, Sweden.
	In December a daughter is born, Elizabeth, who dies in the following summer.		

1528   Albrecht Dürer dies.

1529   German protestants convene at Marburg, where their first attempt at concord fails—Luther's famous exchange with Zwingli.

        "Protestant" estates walk out of the (2nd) imperial diet at Speier, calling the territorial arrangements affecting church usage inequitable.

        Turkish forces besiege Vienna.

        Another daughter, Magdalene, is born in May.

1530   Spends the spring and summer at the Fortress Coburg, to be nearer the diet at Augsburg.

        The Augsburg Confession, a definitive formulation of Lutheran doctrine, is read at the imperial diet. It is rejected both by south German protestants and by delegates from Rome.

1531   A second son, Martin, is born in November.

        Ulrich Zwingli falls in battle.

        Tillmann Riemenschneider, beloved German woodcarver, dies.

        Philip of Hesse forms the League of Schmalkalden, powerful military alliance among the protestant principalities.

IMPORTANT EVENTS

| | FOR | |
LUTHER	HIS CONTEMPORARIES	EUROPE
		Halley's comet confirms approaching end of the world.
1532	John Frederick, who grew up under the influence of Luther, becomes elector of Saxony.	Machiavelli's *The Prince* appears in print for the first time (written in 1513). The Peace of Nuremberg defers the Edict of Worms, establishes a tranquil Germany for more than a decade.
1533 Another son, Paul, is born in January.	Ariosto dies. Montaigne is born.	Henry VIII marries Anne Boleyn, and a daughter is born, later Elizabeth I of England.
1534 The complete German Bible is published. The last child, Margaret, is born in December.	Rabelais's *Gargantua and Pantagruel* is published.	Paul III is elected pope. Interested in a general council.

		Henry VIII, by his Act of Supremacy, dissolves English ties to the papacy.
		Loyola forms the Society of Jesus (to become the Jesuit order in 1540).
		The Kingdom of Zion is established in Münster, bloodily put down in the following year.
		Michael Kohlhaas, later immortalized in the novella by Heinrich von Kleist, declares his private war against electoral Saxony.
		In Paris, Vesalius performs public dissections (on four hanged criminals).
1535	Pietro Paolo Vergerio seeks Luther's commitment to a general council.	Thomas More is beheaded.
1536	South German protestants visit Luther, establish the Wittenberg Concord.	Anne Boleyn beheaded. Erasmus dies.
		Pope Paul III calls a council to be held in Mantua at Pentecost of 1537.

IMPORTANT EVENTS

	LUTHER	FOR HIS CONTEMPORARIES	EUROPE
1537	Luther draws up that testament later known as the Articles of Schmalkalden.	John Bugenhagen carries the Lutheran reform to Denmark.	Pope Paul III must defer the council because of disagreements with the duke of Mantua.
	Attends the conference at Schmalkalden, where he suffers a severe attack of the stone.		
1539		George of Saxony dies.	
1540		Doctor Faustus said to be fetched away by the devil.	Protestantism loses its most powerful leader when Philip of Hesse commits bigamy.

1541

Luther writes three terrible anti-Semitic tracts.

Paracelsus dies.

Michelangelo paints the Judgment Day fresco in the Sistine Chapel.

John Knox introduces the Calvinist reform into Scotland.

Conferences in Worms and Regensburg achieve extensive agreement between protestant and Roman theologians.

1543

Osiander in Nuremberg publishes Copernicus's *De Revolutionibus*.

Vesalius's *De Humani Corporis Fabrica* appears.

1545

Luther's last revision of his Bible. His most vitriolic tract against the papacy.

Albert of Mainz dies.

The Council of Trent is convoked.

1546

Luther dies in February.

Shortly before Luther's death, the Council of Trent meets, no protestant delegates in attendance.

In the War of Schmalkalden, the emperor invades Saxony.

IMPORTANT EVENTS

FOR

LUTHER	HIS CONTEMPORARIES	EUROPE
1547	Henry VIII dies. Francis I dies. Michelangelo assumes direction of construction at Saint Peter's.	In January, John Frederick is defeated at Mühlhausen, imprisoned for five years. Philip of Hesse suffers the same fate. The Saxon electoral crown is transferred to John Frederick's cousin Maurice.

To bring the dead to life
Is no great magic.
Few are wholly dead:
Blow on a dead man's embers
And a live flame will start.

ROBERT GRAVES

LUTHER

PROLOGUE

What does the typical, educated reader know about Martin Luther? The child of harsh circumstances and tensions with a severe father, he experienced a crisis in young manhood. Caught in a thunderstorm, at a critical juncture in his university studies, he was so terrified by a lightning bolt that he uttered a compulsive vow to become a monk. His years in the monastery were fraught with brooding about how he might become justified in the eyes of an angry God. At last came his evangelical breakthrough, the Tower Experience, when he discovered his doctrine of salvation by grace alone. On All Saints' Day in 1517, Martin Luther nailed upon the door of the castle church in Wittenberg his 95 Theses against papal indulgences, thus initiating the Protestant Reformation. When called before the Diet of Worms in April of 1521, he held steadfast in his faith, declaring before emperor and the assembled imperial estates, "Here I stand, I can do no other. God help me. Amen."

Every one of the statements above may well be false. Most of them almost surely are. None can be proved by contemporary documents (or disproved).

How can this be? No man's life has been more thoroughly documented by contemporaries than was Martin Luther's. Yet documents give testimony, first of all, to the attitudes of those who produced them; our reading of the documents is profoundly influenced by those who pass them down to us. Reformation history was long dominated by rigid denominationalism. In our own day a new zealotry has been added to those ancient partisanships, the Marxist image of Luther as helpless or cynical instrument in the hands of feudal and capitalist powers. Successive vogues in history writing have seldom returned to the original documentation at all, but prefer to reshape and reapply the commonplaces of earlier interpretations.

In Luther's case, even the original evidence wants skeptical, loving evaluation. Largely, it stems from the older man himself, as he looked back on that heroic legend I recounted in the first paragraph. A great mass of most persuasive records, his *Table Talks*, was taken down by pupils who had better understanding, naturally, for Luther's ever shifting irony and raucous humor than did later, staid and stolid church historians. While these writers have been at pains to extract details of Luther's thoughts and actions in his middle thirties (1517–21), they shunned and were frequently embarrassed by the man in his forties, fifties, and sixties whom they had to thank for most of their information. What is a biographer to do?

Shall I patiently set forth my reexamination of that "Protestant Revolt"—a colorful phrase historians apply to events which occurred a dozen years before the term "protestant" emerged, and to some events which may never have occurred at all? To do so would hopelessly encumber my Luther portrait with learned banter, and defeat the greatest service biography can provide Luther scholars: an authentic impression of that man who is their main source, but who remains little known or understood, the mature and aging Martin Luther. As biographer, I have tried to present no more than the character of the man in his later years.

Focus on one particular time in a subject's life is nothing new in biography, and it is certainly not new in Luther studies. Much of our present-day Luther image—as in the Luther movie or in the play *Luther* by John Osborne—goes back to a book by a psychiatrist of the 1950s, Erik Erikson's *Young Man Luther: A Study in Psychoanalysis and History*. Erikson was rightly skeptical about chief Luther interpretations before him, but not a historian himself, much less a philologist, he was not inclined to be very critical of the documents, or of the well-accepted "factual" account of Luther's career. Naturally, he was taken to task by the professionals, no doubt justifiably. To the art of biography, however, Erikson and his pupils have made a major contribution.

By calling attention to the phases of adult life, how "each man in his time plays many parts," they have shown that we must approach the unique character and problems of each time of life on its own terms. I am introducing my reader to Martin Luther in his fifties, a grand personality in its own right, one of the most pungently alive in all history. Without quibbling over the legends surrounding the younger man (or otherwise departing into the intellectual history of ages *after* Luther's), I would go straight to the Wittenberg of 1535, where the source of those legends, an articulate and prolific professor, was probably the most influential figure in Renaissance Europe.

It is quite impossible for any of us to approach this Doctor Luther without our preconceptions. Rather, however, than going with our minds full of the ideas developed by Protestant and Catholic (denominations which arose only after his death), let us seek out the viewpoint of one of his informed contemporaries. Perhaps my reader will be patient with me as we try to glimpse Renaissance Europe through the eyes of a churchman as he approaches Wittenberg.

ONE

WITTENBERG

Approach from
the South

The Renaissance church was corrupt. An organization with a very long history, however, it had been able to rediscover its essential justification in earlier epochs and still nurtured the germ for its self-renewal. A reform was under way. The growing concern with reform in the 1520s and 1530s was apparent in successive meetings between high officials of the church and Doctor Martin Luther of Wittenberg, Augustinian and professor.

They had handled him first in that offhand, brutalizing fashion of mammoth bureaucracies, later—as political expediency dictated—with generous condescension. But his reform writings became so trenchant (and popular) as to bring down his excommunication, a rash measure which quickly polarized sentiments. When neither harsh nor friendly persuasion would budge him from his anti-papal stand, a general council of the church became inevitable. For some years the papacy resisted it as diminishing supreme Roman authority, but eventually a papal legate came to Wittenberg to obtain Doctor Luther's cooperation.

This last meeting of a high Roman emissary with the reform advocate was remarkable enough in itself. In the life of the papal nuncio it had a mysteriously symbolic quality. Pietro Paolo Vergerio had felt Luther's influence while still a student in Padua, but his career placed him in the service of Rome. The meeting with Luther affected him little at the time. Yet his later career was sucked up entirely into furthering the cause of that man whom he never saw again.

Vergerio came from the Capo d'Istria on the Gulf of Trieste, a part of the Republic of Venice. He had been a student when Luther first disputed papal commercialization of the church. Since his own ancient university of Padua was popular with law students from the north, he naturally heard about the new university at Wittenberg and its refractory professor. Nevertheless, it was somewhat surprising that he resolved to forsake one of Europe's most prestigious institutions in favor of continuing his studies in that remote German corner.

Had this youth somehow sensed Europe's intellectual center of gravity shifting northward? Would a young Venetian applaud any or every dissent with rival Rome? Our only sure knowledge is that he obtained a recommendation from a Venetian merchant to George Spalatin, the influential confessor to Frederick the Wise of Saxony, who had protected Luther during the early, dangerous defiance of Rome. The letter was dated 29 October 1521, or just about a year after Luther had become—and been officially declared—notorious for a ceremonious public burning of canon law (intriguing for a Padua law graduate). If it was Luther's activity attracting the young Vergerio, it was precisely Luther's teachings that also frustrated his ambition to study in Wittenberg.

His sponsor, with whom he planned to make his journey north, and the author of his letter of recommendation, was one of the suppliers of relics to Frederick the Wise, whose collection was famous throughout the world. Unfortunately, by the time the company was prepared to depart Venice, the reform spirit had radically damaged Saxony's relic market.

I am returning herewith the relics [Spalatin wrote to the merchant] as well as the crucifix, in hopes you will sell them as advantageously as possible, for in Venice they probably cost more and are valued more highly than here. Here the common man is so well instructed that he thinks (and rightly so) only faith and confidence toward God, and brotherly love, are enough.[1]

The trip was canceled and the young Capodistrian's wish to visit Wittenberg would not be fulfilled for many years yet, not until the faculty there had become illustrious in the north and infamous in his own land. Nor would he at last go there as a student to learn, but as a negotiator to interpret and to persuade.

Vergerio's career became that of a routine, ambitious Italian. He toured France, became established in the legal profession in Verona and Padua, taught a bit of law at the university (which also crowned him *poetus laureatus*), went on to serve the Republic of Venice, Europe's principal maritime force and one of its most powerful governments. A grander court was to be found only in Rome. Pietro Paolo's brother Aurelio, secretary to Pope Clement VII, obtained an audience for him. The magnetism of the young man's personality, no doubt his vigorous presence as well, won him the pope's trust. In 1533, Vergerio was appointed nuncio to the court of King Ferdinand in Vienna and dispatched there so promptly his credentials had to be prepared and sent along after him. One of his prime responsibilities in the empire would be to help Clement avoid the council the Germans were demanding.

Upon Clement's death the next year, one might have expected Vergerio to be replaced, because Paul III wished to pursue a different line toward the church in the north and was prepared to accept a council. But Paul settled on the same proud, intensely ambitious, good-natured and winning young Venetian for a second and quite different mission to Germany. This time he was to visit the principal courts with an ambiguous task. He must arouse interest in a council where German national issues were not to be paramount, and which was not to be held in Germany. His diplomacy would be complicated by the lack of any clear council agenda to offer his suspicious hosts. It was thus in a salesman's role, though with nothing very specific to sell, that Pietro Paolo Vergerio at last came to Wittenberg.

Was his mission successful? Upon his return to Italy he received an ambivalent reward, the bishop's miter in his home town. When we consider proposals he had made for his own future—that he be sent to Constantinople to sue for peace with the Turk, or that he be dispatched to the court of Henry VIII to resolve that schism—together with the fact that his correspondence with Rome had never failed to mention diplomatic advancement, we recognize that pastoral duties were not entirely in accord with the dynamic fellow's estimate of his abilities. Yet here on the Gulf of Trieste he remained during those years while the church struggled to hold itself together, and failed.

The council toward which he had worked was still to be a catholic one in the sense that it included representatives from the whole empire. As the 1530s drew to a close, the Inquisition was waxing in power; even in Italy reform doctrines were spreading, especially in Vergerio's own northeast. For the first time in his life the bishop began to read Lutheran tracts, began to acquire some first authentic intellectual acquaintance with the man he had met face to face in Wittenberg. These reform works constituted the bishop's first introduction to theology.

At the same time, he was being deeply touched by victims of the Inquisition. One especially moving case constituted a kind of turning point in his career. By the end of the 1540s Bishop Vergerio was openly sympathizing with protestants in his diocese. In 1549 he was himself excommunicated and fled into German-speaking lands. He became a vigorous anti-Romanist. In the service of the duke of Württemberg during the last dozen years of his life, he remained an active and articulate traveler and writer, operating his own printing press against Rome.

Thus the career of Pietro Paolo Vergerio, born on the Istrian cape which shelters Trieste from the Adriatic Sea, had begun like that of any gifted and ambitious jurist. As a compass senses a powerful though distant magnet, it was affected early by the energies of Martin Luther. His confrontation with Luther at mid-career brought no immediate religious awakening. The young man in his thirties returned from Germany convinced the only way to bring the Germans to heel was by force of arms. Yet his subsequent life was profoundly influenced by the protestant problem, eventually all his efforts being drawn up into the cause. His confrontation in Wittenberg in 1535 became symbolic, a kind of figure for his entire life. Perhaps he came to think so himself—after Luther's death.

At the time it appeared a young diplomat's dream. From his permanent base in Vienna the papal nuncio had undertaken a tour up the Danube, down the Main and Rhine, then back across the quiltwork of sovereign fiefdoms in the middle of the Holy Roman Empire, from Cologne through Paderborn to Halle and thus into the Lutheran heartland, calling on major courts and attempting to extract individual commitments, but satisfied if he could establish good will and a communality of interest. The protestant princes preferred to put him off until their conference, scheduled to begin in Schmalkalden at the end of the year. Vergerio suspected he might, prior to that conference, pluck in Wittenberg a most brilliant feather for his diplomatic cap.

The king of France had a delegation in Schmalkalden at the moment. Robert Barnes and others from London were in Wittenberg, and Vergerio was intensely curious about their mission. Luther stood practically alone among theologians outside Rome in firm refusal to declare the sixteen-year-old marriage between Henry VIII and Catherine, the emperor's aunt, invalid (and therewith Catherine's daughter, Mary, illegitimate). He had been unmoved, so the rumor, by Henry's substantial bribe.[2] Here Vergerio glimpsed one point of agreement. The desire for a council was presumably another. What a tremendous diplomatic coup if on the eve of the Schmalkalden meeting, where the northern powers sought a common front against Rome, he could obtain the agreement of Luther himself on the point his pope considered most important: the location of the council!

His troop arrived in Halle, the seat of Germany's most powerful prince and Luther's most irresolute archbishop, Cardinal Albert of Mainz, on 2 November. Perhaps it was in conversations here that Vergerio had hit upon the stratagem of approaching Luther directly (the nuncio was so devious in his communications that his authorization for doing so, if any, remains as obscure as the foggy time and place of their meeting). His letter requesting passage to Wittenberg was not sent off to that city until the fourth. It announced his departure for the next day, the fifth.

He knew Elector John Frederick of Saxony was absent from Wittenberg at the moment, but addressed the letter to him anyway. He said he was confident he would not be denied safe-conduct, "since, with the permission and protection of both his imperial and his royal majesties, I bring such business and affairs as are pleasing to all pious people."[3] The missive was delivered to that prefect of Wittenberg whom Luther constantly scolded for notorious adultery, Hans Metzsch. The messenger could inform Metzsch that the papal party consisted of twenty members.

The prefect had to act fast. Vergerio traveled by horseback and was remembered in Germany for his rapid movements across the land. Undetained by the axle-breaking German roads, he was quite capable of making it all the way to Wittenberg in less than two days, and he had given scarcely one day's notice. His caravan was received, however, on its first day out by a welcoming party in Bitterfeld, where Metzsch had already provided rooms at the inn. On 6 November, Metzsch himself rode out to meet his guests. He and Vergerio hit it off well from the start, both men skilled in dealing with people and experienced in the manipulation of power. He took the company straight to the castle, had sumptuous meals served, and even accompanied the nuncio and his entourage halfway to Potsdam the next day.

The stopover in Wittenberg was in one way a disappointment for Vergerio. Robert Barnes declined an invitation to a convivial bath, a Renaissance delight usually taken with a consort of music, and dinner afterward. Nor had it been possible to glean intelligence about the English presence in any other way. But Doctor Luther did come over to the castle for breakfast on the morning of the seventh, bringing along the superintendent of Wittenberg churches and schools, John Bugenhagen, called Pomeranus. There was leisurely conversation, and the Germans had shown the courtesy of accompanying their visitors to the horses.[4]

The most immediate source of information we have on the substance of the nuncio's talk with Luther may be certain words he spoke toward the end of the month in Prague, where he at last intercepted John Frederick, elector of Saxony. This prince, just a few years younger than Vergerio, had grown up in profound admiration of Martin Luther and was the most devoutly protestant of the pious Saxon line. Looking forward to meeting with the other princes in Schmalkalden just a fortnight hence, he had declined to receive the papal nuncio while visiting Vienna, but suggested that written communication would be fine with him. Nor did he wish to be detained on his way to Schmalkalden, but Vergerio, supremely self-confident, rushed to meet him anyway. John Frederick sent aides to hear the papal presentation, but the nuncio insisted on waiting until the elector himself should pass through Prague. Audience was at last granted him in

the Hradschin on the last day of November. Our record is that
kept by the spiritual and temporal counsel to John Frederick
himself and to his father and uncle before him: George Spalatin,
sometime recipient of a letter recommending this same Vergerio.
Vladislavski Hall was new and fashionable in those days, when
the nuncio opened his address beneath its sinuous arabesque
vaultings.

Inasmuch as events had not permitted him (he began in florid
Renaissance Latin) to wait upon the prince elector in Saxony,
but had transferred his good fortune here to Bohemia, he would
set forth his business in behalf of the Roman curia in all the
greater brevity. This turned out to be far from the truth. The
nuncio's oratory bore him along on great vacuous waves, where
he floated the names of eminent personages whose approval he
had already obtained. He vowed the pope had sent him not as a
mere formality and ruse, as if he were merely pretending he
wished a council and did not really mean it. The pope did not
merely wish to keep everyone quiet, peaceful, and docile. Vergerio alluded to the previous papal policy of making offers
which were not followed through, and he marveled at the great
seriousness and urgency with which the present pope pursued his
purpose. For this reason the nuncio now wished to come to the
point in the most brief and direct manner.

Thus he continued for some time, John Frederick really able
to appreciate neither his eloquence nor the lack of substance. At
last Spalatin used his notes to translate the speech into German.
John Frederick made a terse reply which might have been
formulated in advance. The German princes had long desired a
council, he said, and the issue was to be treated in Schmalkalden.
As had long since been agreed, holding the council outside of
Germany would be out of the question.

Once these remarks had been translated into Latin for Vergerio, he began to explain how the pope was not really considering, at this time, any other location than Mantua (a city in
northern Italy whose magnificent Ducal Palace would accommodate a large assembly). During these preliminaries John Frederick scribbled a note to the effect he would not discuss these
matters further, got up and left the hall.

In the elector's absence Vergerio became relatively succinct.

He continued his speech before the remaining officials only long enough to devise a stratagem for regaining the prince's presence: he had a secret message, he said, which must be concealed from his own aides as well as from German ears other than John Frederick's most intimate advisers.

And so it came to a private meeting between the two young men, the Italian glib and importunate, the Saxon brusque and now openly contemptuous. What were the "secret" messages? The king of France, hitherto insistent the council must meet in Savoy, had agreed, according to communication just received from the pope himself, to Mantua. Secondly, his imperial majesty was also in accord, insofar as the pope could agree with the princes of the German nation. And lastly, the nuncio did not wish to conceal from his grace the prince elector that he had visited Wittenberg. He wished to express his most dutiful thanks for the honorable and cordial reception he had enjoyed there. He reported, furthermore, extending an invitation to Doctor Martin Luther, who (he said) had dined with him. Luther had stated his position on the council thus:

I hold a general free and Christian council such as the pope proposes to be highly necessary. I personally desire it, not for our sake. By God's grace we have no need whatsoever for a council, for we already have the pure word of God and teachings which lead to salvation, as well as churches where the ceremonies are conducted in accordance with God's word. The council will be healthful for other, foreign nations to whom our teaching might thus be spread.

To this, the nuncio said he had replied:

Martine, quid dices nunc? What are you saying, my dear fellow? Look to it that you be not too conceited, for you are mortal, and can err. Do you think you are cleverer, wiser, more learned and holier than so many church councils and holy fathers—than so many men of great learning throughout the whole world, who also honestly confess themselves to be Christians?

One must admire the Italian for his spunk, not only to quote Doctor Luther before his liege lord, but to report how he had himself called the learned man to order, and schoolmastered him.

Of course, when Vergerio quoted himself, he no doubt did so with considerable charm and even a touch of buffoonery—such a truism were those words of his, and so eminently reasonable within his own circle, that he felt no need of gravity or pomp to back them up. With his cosmopolitan manners and sound Venetian practicality, he was but appealing to the healthy respect he was sure the prince must have for opinions universally held in Rome. A man of the world like John Frederick would not, he hoped, limit himself to the views of a few provincial theologians. In taking his rather prolix leave, therefore, Pietro Paolo went ahead to draw a clear demarcation between the prince elector's interests and those of that proud doctor of his, whose opinions were so at variance with the rest of the world.

At last Vergerio had succeeded in arousing the young elector, who delayed his return to table (for he had been called away from dinner) long enough to deliver his most extensive statement to the nuncio. He took pains to endorse each point which Luther was reported to have uttered.[5]

Vergerio's report to John Frederick contained but one paltry error—an excusable one. Luther had not come to *dine* with him. Vergerio had invited him to dinner, true. He had also invited Robert Barnes, who declined. It would be unreasonable to expect the courtly Italian, in the presence of majesty, to use such a modest word as "breakfast." As to the gist of Luther's statement, three other sources report he did say words exactly to that effect. There is no independent confirmation of Vergerio's riposte, but since he knew John Frederick would be seeing Luther soon, this seems a most credible part of his account. As to what else went on at the breakfast table in Wittenberg, extensive materials are available.

The principals
1. Vergerio

Just a few days after the Wittenberg meeting, he sent his report to Ambrogio Ricalcati, private secretary to Pope Paul. It gave a colorful visual impression of Martin Luther at age fifty-one but trying to look younger (and succeeding). Ricalcati was not provided a detailed account of the conversation. Vergerio assumed Rome's main interests to be in the English intrigues, and

he was eager to tell the influential secretary what ⟨...⟩ to hear. He relayed, for example, a slanderous ac⟨...⟩ ther's "illegitimate" parentage of the sort one might ⟨...⟩ have picked up in Rome than in Wittenberg.

There is one problem with this report to Ricalcati. V⟨...⟩ would have him believe the meeting with Luther had been a⟨...⟩ of accident. The road to Potsdam led past Wittenberg, he ⟨...⟩ plained. He accepted lodgings at the castle there solely becaus⟨...⟩ the plague had rendered public accommodations unsafe. Here the prefect Metzsch had overwhelmed his party with hospitality, as a token of which Luther had been summoned to entertain the nuncio, other Latin speakers having retired to Thuringia to escape the plague. Vergerio had no choice but to put up with the heretic—who was quite deferential, standing before the pope's emissary cap in hand—while his party took breakfast and the horses were being saddled. According to this written testimony, he had said just as little as possible to Luther. Nevertheless, Ricalcati is told of substantially the same exchange as that reported to John Frederick.[6]

This is all that comes down to us from Vergerio, save occasional mention of Luther in letters he wrote much later in life. He defended the Waldensian movement in France, for example, as a doctrine no different from "that approved by Luther, Melanchthon and other great and good men." By this time, Vergerio was himself a protestant.[7]

2. Luther

Several letters make casual mention of Vergerio, both before and shortly after his visit. There is confirmation of the original invitation extended him, a hint as to Luther's own attitude and demeanor, a few additional snatches of the conversation. Also, the prospect of a council had been a source of humor at the Luther table for years.

"Herr Doctor, when you come to Mantua you'll probably be the pope's favorite," roared the portly scholar from Pomerania one day in December of 1536, for example. "He'll welcome you and not let you leave, but dispose of you for the rest of your life." In such contexts, various recollections of Vergerio occurred.[8]

Observers

Our fullest reports of the meeting do not come from Luther
and Vergerio, but from onlookers. Two anonymous accounts
contain utterances so true to the characters of both men as to be
quite convincing. One appears to be from a member of Luther's
party who was with him from early in the morning. He might
have been one of the numerous lodgers in the Luther household,
but most of the students and scholars among these were, as Vergerio said, away at the time. Whoever it was seems to have accompanied the doctor to the castle for breakfast, not to have
been privy to all that was said there, but to have gone along with
those who saw the nuncio's party off. He gives us a vivid picture
of the lively emissary hurling his final, good-natured admonition
to Luther as he swings onto his horse.[9]

The other anonymous account is probably from one of those
on the papal side of the table, most likely Vergerio's aide, Ot-
tonello Vida. Some investigators have declared it utterly reliable
—and the remarks it attributes to Vergerio and Luther do ring
true. Others have questioned this source on two grounds. In the
first place, it comes down to us only in the form used by Paolo
Sarpi, the distinguished historian of the Council of Trent, who
wrote in the seventeenth century. While a Catholic himself, he
was a decidedly anti-Roman Venetian who disapproved of papal
power and policy. For that reason it is possible to accuse him of
bias. In the second place, Sarpi's version states that Vergerio
brought explicit instructions from Paul III to call on Luther and
to broach the issue of the council. There is no other record of
any such instructions, and their existence would contradict Vergerio's own statement to Ricalcati that he had encountered Luther quite by chance, even against his will. If Pope Paul had
given specific instructions to Vergerio to deal with Luther,
would not his own private secretary have known?[10]

Perhaps this contradiction impugns Sarpi's source. Or perhaps
it tells us something about the atmosphere at the court of Rome.
The events of the past have existence now only in whatever
image we are able to form of them. Our documents are subject
to interpretation. We weigh the one judiciously against the

other, much as an optician carefully adjusts his lenses. Our wish is to bring into focus one of the most colorful scenes of the dramatic Renaissance age.

So let us groom the principal actor.

Invitation to Breakfast

Andreas Engelhard was a frequent visitor to Wittenberg's great Black Cloister where dwelled the large Luther household. He came often on a Sunday, because the learned doctor liked to have his hair dressed and his beard shaved before climbing up to his rostrum to deliver the sermon. But when Andreas was called well before sunrise on the first Sunday in November 1535, he did not really expect to groom Luther, who had been having his headaches, dizzy spells, and ringing in the ears again. Of late he had been especially subject to those characteristic vacillations of his, "now sound, now sickly, now happy, now depressed," which he sometimes complained made him "completely useless for morning tasks." So it was more likely that he wished to have Andreas restore the delicate balance between his bad head and his phlebitic leg by reopening a vein in the latter, and Andreas was pleasantly surprised to discover his friend in high spirits.[1]

"How is it, Herr Doctor, that you've called for your barber so early in the morning?"

"I have been summoned by our holy father the pope, to wait upon his emissary and entertain him. If I am able to come upon the scene as a man young in years, he will think to himself: '*Pfui Diaboli!* If a Luther who is not yet an old man has already caused all this tumult among us, what shall become of us, what might he yet undertake, before he has reached the fullness of years?'"

While Andreas performed the cosmetic ministrations, the doctor's finery was brought in. The German equivalent of "When in Rome, do as the Romans do" is: "When among wolves, one must howl." In the irony typical of his race, Luther costumed himself to go before the representative of the papal court as a Renaissance dandy: a jacket of dark camlet (a heavy oriental fabric of goat hair woven in intricate pattern), the sleeves with a showy ballooning of satin. Over it he slipped a coat of cretonne, richly lined with fox fur. We, accustomed to thinking of Luther in somber academic robes which reach to his feet, must take particular note that this garment was, in Vergerio's words, *assai corta* (pretty short), so that we have to imagine the venerable doctor in tight Renaissance hose to match the jacket and—if I mistake him not—the most gorgeous codpiece available to him. Vergerio was impressed by the numerous rings on his fingers.

Master Andreas was delighted. As Luther topped his array by hanging a magnificent gold medallion around his neck, Andreas observed:

"Herr Doctor, you are going to be a bit of an offense to them."

"I do so with the good cause that we have taken sufficient offense from them. This is the way to deal with foxes and snakes."

Andreas, bidding goodbye with a papal gesture, made a show of his Latin: "*Abi in pace, et Dominus sit tecum.* May they be converted by your actions." Like all the rest in Wittenberg, Andreas confidently expected miracles of Doctor Luther. He could sometimes perform them.

"I am going to do that—but perhaps I will just give them a good talking to and send them on their way."[2]

The main street of Wittenberg ran parallel with a bend in the Elbe River, from the gate in the west wall where the castle was a part of the fortification, over across the marketplace in front of the Rathaus and church, on to the other side of town where the Black Cloister was also built into the wall. The whole distance was only a few minutes' walk, but Luther's festive little party rode down in a coach. Their spirits were high, and Luther announced:

"Behold the German pope and Cardinal Pomeranus, witnesses and instruments of God!"[3] It was an expression of passionate contempt.

When younger, Luther had looked up to Pope Leo X as to a brother in Christ and a reverend father in the church. But he had

been appalled, frightened, hurt, and eventually calloused by the
tactics of Roman bureaucracy. Now he was irreconcilably preju-
diced against all Italians. They excelled the Germans, he
confessed readily, "in pompousness, quickness, agility and sub-
tlety. With their show and gestures they can bend the minds of
their audience at will."[4]

In his many remarks along these lines there was always a bit of
the country boy, marveling at the city slicker, e.g.,

> We Germans and other simple folk are clean slates, while the
> Italians are so inscribed with false opinions it's hard for them
> to give them up—it's easier for them just to add worse ones.
> They look down on all other peoples, but they are themselves
> just abominable. Their fasts are more splendid than our great
> banquets. They adorn themselves sumptuously. Where we
> spend a gulden for satin they need ten. Their chastity is sod-
> omy, as they themselves declare. Betrayed by a perverse intel-
> ligence, they do violence to natural and divine law by despot-
> ically forbidding matrimony. I guess they'll ban shitting next.[5]

He made frequent reference to "Italian nuptials" ("Thank God
no mother tongue in German lands has a word for it"[6]). We can
imagine his expectation of the proposed council if he said of the
last one, the Lateran Council of 1515: "Here they decreed it permissible to believe in the resurrection of the dead, and for each
cardinal to have five boys for his Ganymedes. But Leo took that
back."[7] He thought the Italians were "very clever fellows." If
you wanted to confuse them, you'd have to remember the German proverb, "A hard knot wants a hard wedge."[8]

It may be that Master Andreas was in the coach, and that he
was the anonymous note-taker. Aside from John Bugenhagen
(whom Luther called Pomeranus, after his homeland), most of
the well-known associates were absent from Wittenberg this November, having retired with the whole university to Jena in fear
of the plague. Vergerio was disappointed not to be able to greet
Robert Barnes among his guests, for he knew that Englishman
was living with Luther. It is difficult to say whether the chance
to meet an emissary of Henry VIII may not have seemed more
exciting to him than talking to Luther.

Yet we must not underestimate the astute young Venetian or

suppose him merely pragmatic or superficial. Of all the Italians of his day, he was among those most open to a balanced perception of affairs here in Wittenberg. Not least among his qualifications was precisely his diplomatic detachment. Even in small talk he kept an eye on the main issues. Asked about his trip, he admitted having been treated somewhat threateningly by the populace around Halle.⁹ A major argument against bringing a council to Germany was that the safety of delegates could not be guaranteed here. In this very year the "Kingdom of Zion"—the Anabaptist occupation of the town of Münster—had been bloodily put down, and was on everybody's mind.

Hans Metzsch, eager to provide an impressive reception, pleased Vergerio with a lavish "collation" of wine and meats, to which the large company was set down. The traveler assured Luther he was finding protestant lands indeed greatly different from what he "had been led to expect." It may have been no more than the usual diplomatic way of emphasizing the benefit of face-to-face discussions to clear away misapprehensions, but Luther long remembered the remark.¹⁰ For his own part, he just could not resist the abrasive humor typical of him, but sometimes lost on the smooth Venetian, because it was so outrageous he would not believe his ears. Nevertheless, the report to Ricalcati did preserve at least two unmistakable Lutherisms:

> He said some words in praise of His Holiness, having understood him to be a wise and good man, at least up until that time when he [Luther] had visited Rome. "At which time," the beast added, grinning, "I celebrated several masses."¹¹

This cut was indeed a vicious one. When Luther was in Rome as an Augustinian monk on an errand for his order, nearly a quarter century earlier, the present pope had been a well-known cardinal, Alessandro Farnesi, notorious for his rich and hedonistic life. He was censured, for example, for sponsorship of "pagan" art. In all fairness, it ought to be added that he forbade Michelangelo to paint nudes on the Sistine ceiling (and as a consequence himself appears on the chapel wall among the damned, with an ass's ear). As Pope Paul III, he is treated favorably by historians precisely because of his efforts in behalf of a council, which led to the Luther-Vergerio meeting, but his more frivolous younger years, to which Luther was wickedly referring, were well known, as was his lifelong favoritism toward his bastard progeny. Luther's humor might be rendered less subtly, "Oh yes, I heard about Alessandro Farnesi back in the days when I was an obscure but devout monk and he a notorious Epicurean."

Poor Vergerio began to receive even unbarbed humor warily. Luther, poking a little fun at himself, wondered whether Vergerio had heard anything in Rome of his reputation as a drunken German.

"Just note, if you please," he wrote to Ricalcati, "the intent of this arrogant and imprudent remark, which certainly shows that he has acted and continues to act out of resentment and ill will, as if on some kind of vendetta."[12]

As repast and small talk drew to a close, Vergerio's diplomatic mind was rapidly reviewing the presentation he planned to make, and calculating just which points might best appeal to this grinning but hostile creature before him. Some of the company retired, not to return until the Italians were about to take their leave. Our anonymous protestant note-taker had to admit that much was transacted to which he was not party, but Vergerio's aide left record of his nuncio's address to Luther and Bugenhagen.[13]

Vergerio began with compliments, assuring Luther of the highest esteem (*grandissima estimatione*) in which the present pope and college of cardinals held Luther, then went directly into a strongly worded denunciation of the policy pursued by the Roman church in the early days, specifically of the rigidity of Cajetan (*la durezza del Gaetano*)—that cardinal who had met Luther at the Augsburg imperial diet in 1518—and *il rigore* of Leo X, who must have been acting "at the instigation of others, not of his own disposition." Our informant assures us that Vergerio had been authorized by Paul III to make these statements, and there can be no doubt that the nuncio expected them to have great effect—provided Luther believed him. He had therefore calculated the further course of his speech to dispel any suspicions about his sincerity. He was willing to arouse the well-known irascibility of his vis-à-vis, because he planned to conclude his delivery with bright personal prospects for Luther.

Disclaiming theological background and denying intention of

disputing about such matters, Vergerio wished to appeal to common sense (*raggioni communi*). The numerous sects who so abominated one another, not even to speak of all the uprisings of the past eighteen years (*tante seditioni populari, con morte & esterminatio d'innumerabili persone*—that was sure to get a rise out of Luther) could not possibly come from God. Warming to his delivery, Vergerio insisted that what was so destructive (*perniciosa al mondo*) had to be wicked, and he accused Luther of self-love and egotism thus to trouble the world.

> If it was for your own conscience and salvation's sake you tampered with the faith in which you were born and educated for thirty-five years—why, then you could have kept it to yourself. If love of neighbor moved you, why did you disturb the whole world unnecessarily, seeing that without you men did live in tranquillity and serve God?

He bore not in vain the title *Pontificii Orator*.

Vergerio now felt himself at the peripeteia of his address, at that brink where passions had been sufficiently heightened and it was time to turn about. Confusion, he continued in a tone which bespoke all sanity and reasonableness, had gone so far that remedy could no longer be deferred. Hence the pope was resolved to call a council where all the learned men of Europe would bring truth to the church, and disperse the unquiet spirits. As for the site, the pope had designated the city of Mantua,

> And while principal hope lies in the grace of God, we must also take into account the good works of man. It is in the power of Martin Luther, by his personal presence and charitable collaboration, to hasten the remedy, thereby incurring the debt also of the pope, a munificent prince who accords to merit recognition.

He called to mind the example of Eneas Silvius, who so long as he clung to his own convictions was, with much devotion and labor, able to advance no further than canon at Trent; but, changing for the better, he became bishop, cardinal, and finally Pope Pius II. He recalled Bessarion of Nice, who from a miserable collier of Trebizond became such a great and renowned cardinal, not lacking much of succeeding to pope.

Can the papal nuncio really have so miscalculated Martin Luther? Was this Venetian courtier so blinded by personal ambition as to project love of worldly honor also into Luther, and hold out material reward to this aging God-seeker? Why, these had been the very temptations which Luther had fled as a youth, and which he had so brutally and eloquently condemned when a man. Did Vergerio truly conclude his prepared oration with arch reference to a "successful" churchman whose "miserable" background was so reminiscent of Luther's own? Is it possible for real events to produce such an absurd parody of life as to be quite incredible were they presented as fiction? The sober realities of the Saxon plain were very different from the bright, busy shores of the Adriatic.

If Vergerio thought Luther winced beneath the stick of his reproaches, he erred. But the carrot he held out did not fail of its effect. Vehement and fierce, quite in accord with his natural tendencies, we are told, was Luther's answer. He said he took no account of the esteem he might enjoy at the court of Rome; he neither feared their hate nor regarded their benevolence. He only served the divine will as best he was able, and when he had done all he could he was still but a useless servant. He did not see how Christian efforts could be joined to those of the papacy, any more than darkness might be joined to light.

Nothing in his life had been more profitable to him than *il rigore* of Leo and *la durezza* of Cajetan, which he did not attribute to them at all, but to divine providence. In those days he had not yet been illuminated by the entire truth of the Christian faith, but had merely discovered some abuses in the matter of indulgences. He had been ready to keep his silence, had his adversaries done likewise. But the writings of the Master of the Sacred Palace, Cajetan's insults and Leo's inflexibility had compelled him to study, so that he discovered many other abuses and less tolerable errors in the papacy, of a sort which he could not in good conscience dissemble or conceal from the world. The nuncio had been honest enough to admit he knew nothing of theology—well, that was obvious from the reasoning he offered. No one could call Luther's teachings new, except someone who thought that Christ, the apostles, and Saint Peter had lived the way the pope, cardinals, and bishops did in the present age. Nor would any cite the recent unrest in Germany as an argument against his teachings, unless they had not read the Bible and did not know it to be the nature of the word of God and of the gospel to cause disturbances and tumults, even to setting father against son wherever it was preached. This was its virtue: to bring life to them that hearken unto it, and greater damnation to whoever rejects it.

After this first torrent, Luther fell into his eternal optimism and made a sincere attempt to appeal to the young man before him by remarking pointedly that it had been the universal failing of the Roman brethren to predicate the government of the church on human reason, just as if it were some temporal state. He quoted Saint Paul's equation of human wisdom with folly before God, and he denied it to be within his power to further the council. Indeed, he expressed his profound distrust of all the learning being assembled there, doubting that there were any error so absurd it would not be embraced by these wise men, "By the wise sooner than by others, because since they think they know so much, it pleases God to confound them." He confessed himself unimpressed by the examples of Eneas Silvius and Bessarion, although he did refer to them respectfully as *splendori tenebrosi* (twinklings in the darkness). As concerned his own advancement, he quoted Erasmus to the effect that poor, humble Luther had brought riches and power to many, and he named—with somewhat less deference—the late John Fisher, bishop of Rochester, and Nicholas Schomberg, both of whom had been elevated to cardinals because, he implied, of their opposition to the protestant cause.

Thus ended the formal portion of the meeting, for Vergerio could not resist trying to draw Luther out, at the mention of Fisher, on his connection with the English court. This occasioned a dialogue more unguarded than at the breakfast table, where they had been parrying before a good-sized audience.

Vergerio clowned it up a bit, using pantomime to indicate the feelings of Rome toward Henry VIII, who had executed Fisher despite the pope's attempt to protect him by the elevation to cardinal. Luther allowed that Fisher had got no less than he deserved, but he would not be enticed to discuss what business had brought Robert Barnes to Wittenberg. Detecting Vergerio's curiosity, he played the deliberate tease. The tone of conversation became lighter—even friendly. Luther spoke of his wife and children, Vergerio permitted himself a joke about this Lutheran heresy being the worst of all, the excommunication costing an annual three thousand gulden in Thuringia, and eighteen hundred in Meissen (in lost revenues).[14]

About this time the rest of the company returned, so that the protestant record now also includes that much repeated exchange on the trifling nature of the council in Luther's view. The protestant set down with relish that Luther had ceased using the traditional honorific titles while addressing the nuncio, whom he accused of not being serious about the council, but only toying. And even if the pope did actually convoke the council it would be to treat externals only, not Christian teachings. The Roman insincerity was of no consequence, however—

> We who are certain of these things through the Holy Spirit need no council. You wretched men led astray by your godless teachings are the ones who need a council. Your faith is futile and uncertain.[15]

These are the stinging words which Vergerio was still able to recall at the end of the month in Prague, when he told how he had rebuked Luther for them. Here is his reply as he penned it shortly after the meeting:

> "Certainly this is too much arrogance, Martin. You think that if most of the good, wise, and learned men in the world come together in a council (and upon them the Holy Spirit will surely descend), their only purpose will be to corroborate your opinions."
>
> Luther interrupted me with his usual bestial temerity, saying: "You may be sure I will attend the council, and may I lose my head if I do not there defend my opinions against all the world." Saying this he was, by my faith, all changed in the face, and he ejaculated: *"Haec quae exit ab ore meo non est ira mei, sed ira dei:*—What you hear from my mouth is not my wrath, but the wrath of God."[16]

Far from being intimidated by Luther's passion, Vergerio promptly took him up on his agreement to attend the council:

"Where, in what city would you have the council held? Just let us know."

"Let it be in Mantua or Padua or Florence, wherever you like."

"Would you come to Bologna?"

"Who rules Bologna?" Luther asked, falling easily into the role of provincial bumpkin. He well knew that Julius II had incorporated Bologna into the papal states back when Vergerio was but a schoolboy, and he himself a student at the university.

"The pope does."

"Good God! And has the pope gobbled up that city too? All right, I'll come to you there as well."

"Nor would the pope refuse to come to you here, in Wittenberg."

"Good. Let him come. We are looking forward eagerly to seeing him."

The nuncio's wits, dulled by the routine cordiality of diplomatic life, were growing sharper in the acerbic atmosphere of this old doctor. An appreciative listener copied conscientiously and rapidly.

"Are you looking forward to the pope's coming with an armed hand, or unarmed?"

"However it may please him to come, we shall look forward to his coming and gladly receive him."[17]

The banter had elevated their spirits. Years later, Luther recalled Vergerio's turning to an aide during a part of Luther's scoldings and saying, "He's hit the nail on the head."[18] Some interest was expressed in the management of church affairs in Saxony, and Vergerio made bold to ask:

"Do you ordain priests?" He knew this was a ceremony to be performed only by an ordained bishop, upon whom hands had been laid reaching back through the church, eventually to Saint Peter, who had been given the keys to the kingdom by Christ himself.

"Indeed we do ordain." Again Luther spoke words which struck Vergerio as sufficiently important that he found himself able to reproduce the direct quotation: *"Nos cogimur ita facere et ordinantur viri qui sunt communiter approbati—*We are compelled to do so; men receive ordination who have general approval."

Vergerio asked what Luther meant by saying he was "compelled," and received reminder that the pope had cut the Saxons off from apostolic succession.

"*Ecce, hic sedet episcopus ordinatus*—Behold, there sits our ordained bishop." Luther nodded toward the smiling Pomeranus, from whom Vergerio now got some further details as to how the clergy were being chosen and passed upon by respected members of the cloth. But Luther became restless as conversation settled down to seriousness. He broke in to assert that there ought to be two fast days every week, not just one. And on the fast days people should abstain from food entirely, not just from meat. Of course, he added, this would have to be incorporated into law by the emperor, because Germans would not obey the pope.[19]

Vergerio was able to understand this sally only as further evidence of the man's unstable judgment. He had been much impressed by the flashing eyes, which reminded him of those he had observed in other men possessed of an evil spirit.[20] As he walked with Luther to the waiting horses he congratulated himself for the coolness with which he had handled this quite unpredictable fellow. It would be a good thing now if his triumph could be made explicit here in the presence of his own company, with the assembled Saxons looking on. Rising to the saddle, the nuncio called out:

"*Vide, ut sis instructus ad concilium*—Be sure, Martin, that you're prepared for the council."

"*Veniam, domine, cum isto collo meo*—I'll be there, my lord, holding my neck out."[21]

The Calm After a Storm

"It is generally thought, and with some considerable justification," says one of Luther's best recent biographers when speaking of the period after 1530, "that Luther deteriorated in these years." A Danish psychiatrist, who wrote a two-volume medical study of Martin Luther just at the time when our own century was much taken by that approach, found his subject had entered senility around the year 1530 (Luther was born in 1483). Even the admiring compiler of the still standard nineteenth-century biography, the great scholar Julius Köstlin, spoke of Luther's *Lebensabend*, his "declining years," as beginning at about this time—in his forty-seventh year! What wonder if other biographers, once the dramatic events of around 1520 are told, begin to round off their work and waste few words on the older Luther who, in a calmer Europe, strove to hold the catholic church together.[1]

He was aging, it is true, but still in command of his best powers. The sharp, measuring eye of Vergerio saw a fellow

> a bit more than fifty years old, but robust and strong, so that he does not appear to be forty. His features are rather coarse, but he tries to lend them a suffering and tender expression. He has a rather quick articulation, and not too harsh—for a German.[2]

Granted that Luther was trying to impress the papal emissary with his youthfulness, still, in this Venetian he had a tough and skeptical audience. What can account for the difference between the perception of this eyewitness and that of later writers? Can it be that the exhausting struggles of the 1520s have left the biographers with less vigor than their subject retained?

Perhaps. But unlike Vergerio, his judgment swayed by the commanding presence of the man himself, biographers have been guided by Luther's own testimony. He loved to say, "I know I don't have long to live, and my head is like a knife that has had its steel honed entirely off it, so that nothing is left but iron. The iron won't cut any more, and neither will my head."[3] He got in the habit of saying things like that during his long, lonely stay at the Fortress Coburg in the summer of 1530, while the imperial diet was being conducted in Augsburg. An outlaw of the empire, he had not been permitted to accompany the Saxon delegation all the way there. The best alternative to personal presence at the important negotiations seemed to be waiting at this mountain keep just inside Saxon territory and within two days of Augsburg by messenger. He had a secretary with him, George Rörer, and a beloved young assistant, Veit Dietrich, with whom he could take occasional outings (they tried to learn archery), but Luther felt alone, nevertheless, exiled for the first time since his celibate days. In a letter to Melanchthon he fell out of the accustomed Latin to sigh in German, "I just don't have it in me any more, that's clear. The years are piling up on me." Then he reverted to Latin for a word play on *caput* ("head") and its diminutive, *capitulum* ("chapter"): "My *caput* has become just a *capitulum*. I guess it will go ahead and become a paragraph, and finally just a sentence."[4] He was missing the company and all the attention focused on him at the Black Cloister. But he had quite real ailments, too.

By modern standards he was overweight, his heart had already shown alarming signs of weakness. Accustomed to the rich, too abundant diet of the upper classes during the Renaissance, he was familiar with all those afflictions we know from the lives of his contemporaries: the stone, sciatica, and gout from excessive consumption of protein and alcohol; varicose veins and hemorrhoids from want of sufficient exercise; poor circulation and high blood pressure were already producing dizzy spells and ringing in the ears. All such routine ailments of the era were quite beyond Renaissance medicine. Its most efficacious treatment for Luther was maintenance of open ulceration in his left leg so he could bleed himself at will: it helped against vertigo.

Such a plethora of afflictions could not fail of its effect on his biographers, especially after both preventive and curative medicine began to flourish. Luther spoke and wrote freely about his infirmities, often embarrassingly so. In a way typical of the age but also revealing of this openhearted man, he regularly begged for the prayers of his friends. The modern psychiatrist, nonplussed, quotes such passages as sure evidence of a pathological mental condition.

Childishly open about his characteristic, often violent oscillations in mood, especially during attacks of depression, Luther's ready references to death can shock a modern reader. He found it not at all improper in an exhausting illness to say, "Ah, how I'd like to die now, I'm so weak and worn down—and this is a moment when my heart is happy and tranquil."[5] In the solitude of the Coburg, news of his father's death made him intensely aware of his own mortality. The preoccupation continued for the rest of his life, but it was by no means morbid. In a beautiful letter he had sent to his father he made clear that death is not to be feared, "for our faith is certain, and we do not doubt that we shall meet again soon in Christ."[6] He looked around in the fortress yard to find a spot where he'd like to be buried, and he mentioned it from time to time in later years. His exquisitely sensitive self-awareness might have inclined Luther toward hypochondria, had he not been so strenuously occupied. "I'd give a hundred gulden, if I had them, just not to be able to count my pulse beats—every time I do it, I make myself sicker than I am."[7] What wonder if such a man's correspondence contains fairly full treatment of physical and mental sufferings? One must be careful to read them in sympathy with his character and in the spirit of their times, not our own, which, uncomforted by faith, so fears death and longs for youth.

Old age, in agrarian societies like Renaissance Europe's, enjoyed great deference. If Luther, who had undergone extremely traumatic conflicts with authority, began to refer to himself as an "ancient" at the earliest possible time in his life, he was not complaining, but rather laying claim to that respected status.

The words he used were German *Greis* and Latin *senex,* applicable to anyone with gray in his temples (the Renaissance had not developed our concept of "middle-aged"). Many of Luther's century spoke of being "old" while still in their forties—Shakespeare, Tasso, Michelangelo, Luther. Although some lived into their eighties—Hans Sachs, Lucas Cranach, Pope Paul III—death in one's fifties or sixties was sooner considered the rule than the exception—insofar as people paid much attention to chronological age, and they were less conscious of it and specific about it than we. In any case, when Luther referred to himself as an "ancient," he was in no way admitting to "senility," as his modern psychiatrist believed.[8]

The problem of aging was certainly a major theme of his life, as of any man's. Yet, when we begin to scrutinize his many remarks about his advancing years, we discover that they every one turn out to be statements as to how youthfully busy and productive he was compelled to be. Shortly before his fifty-fifth birthday he began a letter, typically, alluding to his "plight of business, labors, aging and trials." He went on to complain,

> An old man, exhausted and tired by so many labors, I am rejuvenated daily, which is to say that the new sects arising require a new youth of me if I am to resist them.[9]

He was a full-time administrator in church and university, where he took the office of *Dekan* ("president") in 1535. As professor he usually lectured three times a week. He was a regular preacher, often delivering several sermons in one day. His correspondence was staggering, the torrent of his publications unabating. When one compares his mountainous output with Julius Köstlin's allegation of flagging productivity during these very years, one recalls with delight that ironical twinkle in Doctor Luther's eye, and such gleeful remarks as,

> It is enough. I have worked myself to death. For one person, I have done enough. I'll go lie down in the sand and sleep now. It is over for me, except for just an occasional little thwack at the pope.[10]

He was fifty-five. His most crushing deprecations of the papacy, so outrageous both in word and stark drawing that one might indeed seek to excuse them as senile, were all yet to come. Some thwacks.

The problem of Luther's "deterioration," alleged to have begun in his late forties, is one which we must keep before us. Let us begin by accepting his own word for his condition in 1535. He began a letter to a friend,

> I wanted to write you the long letter you asked for, but I have had a cough and a cold in the head. Actually, the worst sickness, in my case, is just now beginning: the sun has shone on me too long. As you well know, this ailment is widespread, and many die of it. Why, some people eventually go blind from lengthy exposure; some turn gray, black, wrinkled. Who knows, that may be what is wrong with your leg . . . But it isn't the dear sun's fault if, beneath its rays, dung gets hard and wax grows soft. The nature of a thing, its true quality, becomes manifest at last.

He turned to business matters, but in closing became personal and jocular again—

> Tell my brother that my cough and his silence have forbidden me to write to him. Convey my regards to his black hen and the chicks . . . My lord Kate [so Luther referred to his wife] sends greetings to you and requests that, while the sun is shining down so hard on me you mustn't let it shine any harder on you—insofar as that is within your power . . . Don't be offended by my manner (you know me), for I am so tough and gross, fat, gray, green, overworked, overloaded, overwhelmed with stuff that I have to take a few little unwarranted jabs from time to time, just for the sake of my poor cadaver. A man's a man, for all that—except that God can do with a man what he will (with our unction, of course).

The definitive edition of Luther's works prints this letter under the synopsis, "Luther, with a cold, longs for the spring sunshine." When they come to Kate's wish that the sun may spare the friend, the editors explain how Luther means the friend must "not jealously take the warmth of the sun away from me."[11] This is not the only time Luther's humor has been lost on no-

nonsense scholars. Dour literal-mindedness explains part of the discrepancy between modern inferences about Luther's senescence and the vivid impression Vergerio took away with him as he rode out that Sunday morning.

He thought he had encountered a man in his best years—and they were beyond doubt Luther's most influential ones. He presided at a table full of disciples who had begun openly to record his remarks, thus eliciting sententious nuggets useful for their careers in the pulpit. Of course they preserved most eagerly the improprieties and outrageous candor which, though they sometimes arose from black despair, usually bespoke the man's supreme confidence. This was the period when even the slick portraits by Lucas Cranach, despite his workshop's stereotype of its most regularly painted celebrity, still cannot suppress a humorous gleam in the eye and the fugitive smirk on lips which have just put one past you, or are about to. No longer the lean, intense idealist of the early Cranachs, but now sleek and full, jowly before long, here is the sardonic Luther who escaped his biographers.

A reform demanded for generations had at last begun in his name. By the time he reached his fifties it had acquired a life and a will of its own. He was pleased that there was no turning back now. Neither the inevitability nor the finality of Rome's rejection (after his death, at the Council of Trent) could yet be apparent. On the contrary, Luther looked forward to that general council where he would be vindicated as his gospel spread throughout the church. Not that he felt reform was contingent on the council. Had it not already taken place? Seven years before the Vergerio visit he had been able to specify:

> In the first place, I have hounded the papists into their books, especially into scripture . . . In the second place, I put a quietus to the hullabaloo and carnival of corrupt indulgence sales, which no council had been able to touch. In the third place, I have almost blockaded the pilgrimages and the heathen altars.[12]

The introduction of evangelical reforms even in lands still nominally papist was of enormous satisfaction to him—"They are about as much in awe of the pope as they are of the King of Hearts."[13]

His consciousness of being a historical figure was at the same time both lofty and humble. Counting himself a modern Jeremiah, he said he wanted to stand in that line beginning with the Old Testament patriarchs and continuing through the judges, prophets, and church fathers, through whom God had preserved his gospel.[14] Yet he consistently spurned any authoritative role in administrative or in doctrinal matters—

> Who is Luther? This is not my doctrine. I have not been crucified for anybody . . . How did a poor, stinking bag of worms like me come to have the children of Christ called by his wretched name? Do not do it, dear friends. Let us wipe out the partisan name and call ourselves Christians after him whose teachings we follow.[15]

This insistence that his doctrine was as old as Adam may be regarded as pride, of course, too. Indeed, it held potential dangers. His experience over the years had taught Luther to be most chary of opinions of others, to avoid general approval, to suspect precisely those convictions in which all men believed. How often had the learned and the powerful combined against him! As instrument of a higher power, he had not scorned such opposition, but regarded it as heaven-sent to confirm and refine his teachings. Although he gratefully, even childishly accepted personal comfort from friends as the counsel of God, he assembled many a biblical word of caution against the approval of the world,

> for we are called to another life, and do not belong in this one. The world loveth its own—we have to accept that. I am happy when my own pupils as well as outsiders reject me: I do not want their approval. "Woe unto you when all men shall speak well of you."[16]

By his middle years, Luther had given up his earlier hope and expectation to die a martyr's death. He had resigned himself to living as "the German prophet," a sobriquet he defiantly accepted from his opponents in 1530, not unmindful that a prophet must suffer and rail.

Like the prophet of old, he had been sent to revive and maintain his ancient faith despite the complacent world. The revival of the early 1520s was now a proud accomplishment. The religious and social ferment which had marked the first decade under young Emperor Charles V appeared settled by agreements reached at Augsburg in 1530 and in Nuremberg in 1532. Here the "protestant estates," as they were called, had achieved formal consolidation and been granted recognition within the established frameworks of church and empire. These were all-embracing structures, their monumental stability scarcely imaginable in our era (ushered in by the statement that governments are instituted to secure liberty and justice for all—more: that they must be abolished if found destructive of those ends). The Holy Roman Empire, like the church, was regarded as quite permanent.

These structures did in fact constitute the most stable government known to the Western world. If judged by its ability to maintain the public peace and the ancient, established order of things, it was a sound government, and that was the way it was judged for nearly a thousand years. When Pope Clement VII in 1530 ceremoniously placed the crown of empire on the head of Charles V (who had at that time been reigning for over a decade), they were repeating a ritual performed for Charlemagne in A.D. 800. It symbolized the fundamental political truth of most of human history: worldly authority implied divine sanction. These temporal structures were admittedly transitory, enduring only until judgment day, but in the meantime they were not to be tampered with. Disobedience of one's liege lord violated the Fourth Commandment, to honor thy father, and by implication the First Commandment as well. Luther freely admitted he could think of no better governmental arrangement than that established by the Golden Bull of Charles IV (in 1350), "where the emperor is elected by seven men . . . It gave them the power of the sword: let them therefore use it." He praised his own elector Frederick the Wise for having refused the imperial crown in 1519. Frederick had known, Luther said,

> that practically no one would be able to stand up to the king of France. And finally they did elect Charles—not in his capacity as king of Spain, but as German prince, for he is, you know, archduke of Austria. It would be better if all the electors were temporal lords.[17]

Three of the electors of the empire were archbishops, and Luther did not like to see church and state thus intermingled—but he was proposing no change.

However characteristic change might be in our imperfect vale here below, no one expected any good to come out of change. From the point of view of mortal man, history was a willy-nilly, at best cyclical sequence which would acquire meaning only in the eyes of God. The lifelong efforts of Charles V to maintain the faith of his fathers reflected the obligation he had assumed right along with his seven-hundred-year-old empire. Luther, for his part, firmly denied making any innovations whatsoever. As he told Vergerio, he was but holding to the practice of the primitive church, older and more sacred than the empire. His idea of the council's purpose was to reform the recent, corrupting innovations by the papacy. He felt sure the Romans themselves were at last recognizing how their preoccupation with externals had no legitimation in Christianity. Other protestants, to a greater or lesser degree, shared his hopes, so that all were trying to pull their ranks together in time to make the best use of a council when it came about.

The great benchmark had been presentation, at the emperor's request, of their own conscientious statement in 1530: the Augsburg Confession. Many even in Rome thought it a full, indeed a somewhat conciliatory summation of the Christian faith. Since the more radical protestants, especially those in the German southwest, had declined to subscribe to such a middle-of-the-road document, obtaining union with them remained a major Wittenberg desideratum. The death of Ulrich Zwingli in 1531, the militant Swiss reformer, removed a formidable hindrance to concord ("If God took him to heaven," Luther speculated, "it was by a special dispensation").[18] At the same time, protestant self-awareness was growing so strong that the two major protestant principalities, Hesse and Saxony, entered into the alliance of Schmalkalden. The emperor negotiated the Peace of Nuremberg with this league in 1532. It guaranteed a peaceful *status quo* in German lands, permitting the mobilization of a large and successful force against the Turk. The empire remained tranquil within, and protestantism spread both officially and unofficially.

Religion had become a territorial affair. When a ruler was

converted, as in Anhalt, or when a Lutheran ruler assumed office, as in the powerful duchy of Württemberg, his subjects also became "protestant"—a word which gained currency after some had "protested" territorial arrangements proposed in Speier in 1529 as inequitable. Even traditionalists welcomed the simpler church service in their own language and the communion in which all partook equally—hallmarks of the reform. Emphasis on the personal side of religion had become popular. No complex bureaucracy of the sort which had encrusted the church is beloved among the people. Luther, so long as he lived, minimized all ceremony, rules, and regulations.

The church districts for which he was responsible became ever more manageable in the 1530s, as the often refractory older generation gradually retired in favor of preachers who had studied under him. By now, he had been a professor in Wittenberg for some twenty years. Even a few of the princes recently succeeding to power were his old students, as the young dukes of Pomerania. John Frederick, who became elector of Saxony in 1532, had grown up in an atmosphere dominated by Luther.

Also the once radical university had calmed. Evangelical deemphasis of externalities had almost brought extinction to the doctorate, but beginning in 1533 several of the established theologians became doctors. The graduation formula spoken over Caspar Cruciger, preacher at the castle church and skillful editor of Luther's sermons, and John Bugenhagen, preacher at the city church except for an interval devoted to the reform in Denmark, was Luther's own improvisation. Its ingenuous pomp preserves some intimation of how exalted the calling to the doctorate was:

By apostolic and divine power, as well as by power of imperial and provincial authority—both powers divine: the one heavenly and the other earthly—I do call, pronounce and declare thee Doctor of Sacred Theology in the name of the Father, the Son and the Holy Ghost. This I say unto thee that thou mayest remember who, of what sort and how great is he who hath called thee; and also against whom thou art called, of what sort and how great they are. That thou mayest be a leader, messenger and emissary of God against the adversaries of him who sends thee, as I am sent.

Now, may the Lord strengthen thee, and may thou be strong. Fear not, for the Lord is with thee. Amen.[19]

Two more of Luther's close associates took the doctorate in 1535. Just a fortnight before Vergerio's visit the banquet for them—an all-male affair of seven to eight tables—had been held at the Black Cloister, and each had received the traditional thick gold ring from his "doctor father." Luther called upon John Frederick for a gift of game (such meat being the prerogative of royalty). He turned to an old friend who held the chair in theology, Justus Jonas, for his help as well—

I hope, dear Jonas, you received my letter in which the sow instructs Minerva on what is to be said at the graduation exercise. The Grand Wizard our lord Kate [Luther's wife] is sending you several pieces of silver with which you are to purchase birds, fowl and flying creatures together with whatever else (edible) from that airy kingdom of the feathered may be subject to the dominion of man—except ravens. Sparrows, for example, we will gobble up in any quantity. If you need to spend more, you will be reimbursed. Then if you can buy or bag some rabbits for love or money, or other such tidbits, send them along, too. We are looking to fill up everybody's stomach, if only that beverage they call zythum turns out all right. My Master Kate has cooked up seven of what they call quarts, into which she has mixed thirty-two bushels of malt, because she wants to tickle my palate. She hopes it will turn into good beer. Whatever it is, you shall all taste it.[20]

"Zythum" was a classical word for ancient Egyptian beer, but the absurd recipe Luther attributed to poor Kate was entirely his own—like the numerous other quips, puns, and allusions which continue to puzzle earnest interpreters.

Guests coming to the banquet had to stroll through the academic quarter of Wittenberg, past university buildings and faculty residences—the door of Philip Melanchthon's handsome house—to arrive at the gate of the Black Cloister. It opened onto a broad courtyard, not unlike many another in that agrarian epoch. From the gate the large building on the opposite side was visible, a rather austere three-story structure which had housed

forty monks in the old days. The windows on the ground floor
to the kitchen and storage rooms were somewhat smaller than
those of the dwelling and sleeping compartments above. Ob-
structing the view of the convent's left wing was a dilapidated
church supported in various makeshift ways pending the com-
pletion of a new one. Future foundations lay complete around
the old building, but no further progress was as yet apparent on
the new. It symbolized Luther's mission, and kept his past constantly before him.

On the other side of the yard stretched stalls for a half-dozen
cows and their calves, a goat or two, and a lot of pigsties and
chicken sheds. The Luthers had a swineherd who drove the animals out beyond the city gates of a morning, but the yard retained its chickens, peahens, and other fowl, which kept it picked
clean of grass. Once Luther came upon Kate's sows wallowing
near the old church. "This should be a sacred structure," he
remarked wistfully. "This is the church where I preached for the
first time." He recalled how from its pulpit he had exhorted the
congregation not to purchase the papal indulgences being sold in
nearby towns. His desire to prove the indulgence sales fraudulent
had prompted him to comb the church fathers, to weigh canon
law, and at last to send his letter of protest to the bishops,

> not to attack the pope, but to counter the blasphemous voices
> of the hucksters. Then the whole world under Emperor Max-
> imilian's rule was disturbed, the pope grumbled, the bishops
> raged that the sacrament of confession was being abolished,
> the Carthusians cried out.[21]

The Black Cloister and its grounds were a constant evocation of
memories.

Wagon ruts led across its court to a corner on the right of the
main building, for there was much coming and going at Kate's
brewery there. The Augustinian order had possessed a city fran-
chise to produce its own beer, and that was passed on to her
when the Saxon electors gave Luther the building. Brewing was
but one of the ways she had made her enterprise self-sufficient.
In addition to the large cloister garden where the doctor liked to
putter and stroll, Kate leased and purchased various plots around
town. It was expected of university professors to make provision

for their protégés, and some of Luther's boarders brought their own students for whom they were responsible. With the help of servants and female relatives Kate ran a large household of rural stamp which, because of her husband's responsibilities and his profligate openhandedness, was always overflowing with "a motley and indifferent crowd of young fellows, students, girls, widows, old women, children and therefore confusion," according to a contemporary report.[22]

But from without the aspect was idyllic, the Black Cloister symbolic of a peaceful land in a rural age. There were fruit trees in the courtyard, one of them that tall pear to which the doctor frequently referred when reminiscing. In his mind the pear tree spanned the years of turbulence so recently subsided, and recalled the serenity of the monastery, in the days when silent brothers walked there. Beneath those branches where his own nine-year-old climbed, brother Martin as celibate son of the church had once stood in earnest dialogue with his father superior, John Staupitz. Staupitz had persuaded the young monk to become Doctor of the Bible, an awesomely high and responsible calling which the young man in his twenties, most concerned with his own peace of mind, stoutly resisted. But under the pear tree he had given in, and the stormy years became inevitable. His responsibility as doctor had left him no choice but to teach the truth as he found it in scripture, for who else but a Doctor of the Bible would do so? In the matter of indulgences he gave provocation to those in high places. It plunged him into personal danger and, incomparably more excruciating, questioning his own beliefs and uncertainty about his own irreversible deeds.

Students and colleagues going in and out at the Black Cloister knew the professor's past from the copious records they kept of his private remarks—more than have been recorded for any other man. They carefully recopied them and passed them around. They had sat in his lectures. He had taught them to debate. They had read, religiously, all the writings of this most prolific author in history. Are we ready to follow them into the convent to seek out his presence?

Paralipomena

The bells ringing sound very different when they toll for one you love [Elector John died in 1532]. The swashbucklers wanted power—well, they have it now.

The bird flying through the air makes a hole in it that closes up behind him. That's the way mice swim underground as easily as frogs in water [during a mouse plague in Wittenberg].

The world demands six qualities of a preacher:

1. that he have a good speaking voice,
2. that he be learned,
3. that he be eloquent,
4. that he have a handsome exterior,
5. that he take no money, but give money to preach,
6. that he say what they like to hear.

There was a time when many journeyed to the saints in Rome, Jerusalem, Campostella . . . but we are able to make true pilgrimages in faith by reading the psalms, prophets, and gospels diligently. That is to take a stroll not through holy cities, but through hearts and minds, to visit the true promised land, the paradise of eternal life.

Duke Philip of Mecklenburg to the duke of Lüneburg: We have drunk heavily, Franz.
Doctor Luther: The princes should take measures.
Ernest of Mecklenburg: We *are* taking measures.

The Germans can bear up under any labors—oh, could they but bear thirst. The princes and the nobility will found a new order and dub it the Order of Ignorance. The cowls will be of silk and satin.

Good Lord, let thy word persevere, for once our faith in it is gone, we will believe anything. Without it, there is nothing so absurd we won't fall down and worship it, just as the Romans worshiped Priapus.

TWO

PUBLICIST

Song and Devotion

Before we advance beyond the dreamy courtyard of Luther's semi-rural residence, we must try to form an image of the master as he was known to those going in and out there. He was famous far beyond Wittenberg, and they were aware of that: Martin Luther was the first in the long line of media celebrities.

The technology assembled at the middle of the previous century, and by Luther's time the major and prototype capitalistic enterprise, the printing press, had made him a familiar personal presence to millions who never saw him. One had some dim awareness of the fantastic power he wielded, but it was such a new phenomenon that he did not really comprehend it himself. His fellow citizens would scarcely have found words to frame their impression of the public Luther. We can, of course, so let us first consider Luther for what he was: a writer.

That sounds simple enough. Is it not merely to accept him on the basis of what he himself had to say? Luther was the most prolific author Germany has ever produced. When he looked back on his lifetime's production he found it "such a rude and undigested chaos" that he despaired of ever putting it in order.[1] He wrote so much that any discussion of it must be severely selective just in order to remain comprehensible.

Consider the early 1530s. Here is a most serene and reflective interval in a hitherto turbulent life. Would not the work of these few years constitute a fair sample? When we count the published works from the six years preceding the Vergerio visit, 1530–35, excluding sermons and other utterances not published until later—also excluding his major work, the German Bible translation, which was at last complete in 1534—we come up with one hundred fifty-six publications. This imposing figure may confirm us in our hunch that it is right to approach Martin Luther first of all in his capacity as a writer. But it also humbles us in the recognition that we must select only a tiny portion of his works as characteristic—and that even the most conscientious judgment is likely to be biased and subjective.

His literary output is mountainous not only in sheer volume, but also in the baffling variety of faces it presents to an explorer. Where shall we discover an approach to this formidable and rugged natural monument which will lead most directly to the veins of ore at its heart? I have the impression that the literary mother lode surfaces most plainly in his songs. Here is the spontaneous, the intimate Luther. He himself argued that the most important quality in writing, the quality he found most woefully lacking in the scholarship of his predecessors and contemporaries, was sincerity. Thus the songs may offer a touchstone for applying to his other compositions, too.

In the year of Vergerio's visit to Wittenberg, the second edition of a popular songbook appeared with two new songs by Luther. They had not been in the earlier edition of two years before, so we can accept them as the work of the man in his fifties. The two compositions are very different from one another. One is that simple children's song "From Heaven on High," *Von Himmel hoch*, still sung throughout the world on Christmas; the other, a complex arrangement with powerful imagery, may have seemed papish and was soon dropped from Lutheran hymnals.

In the years immediately following his Coburg stay, the Black Cloister began (literally) to crawl with little children. By 1535, Hans was nine, Elizabeth eight, Magdalene six, Martin four, Paul two, and Margaret completing her first year. Papa wrote a Christmas song for them. It is in various ways typical of this particular fond father, but by now it has gone to the hearts of many generations of children the world over. The melody speaks for itself:

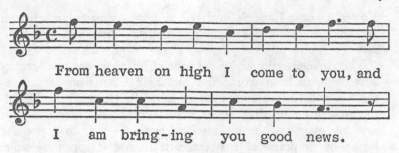

From heaven on high I come to you, and
I am bring-ing you good news.

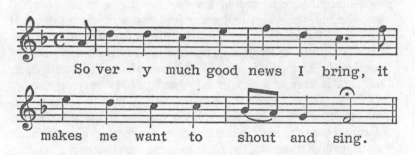

So ver - y much good news I bring, it
makes me want to shout and sing.

There are sixteen strophes, each a very simple little sentence about the baby Jesus, put together out of two couplets with pretty obvious rhymes. They tell the story in accordance with a Christmas play performed in German churches since time out of mind. Here is Luther at his best, proving in deed what he so frequently argued in theory: that the highest theology is the simplest, so that one must become as a little child in order to grasp the really important things, e.g.:

> Ah, Lord and Creator of all,
> How art Thou now become so small—
> Lying there upon the grass,
> Where munch a cow, and an ass! . . .
>
> So this is what most pleaseth thee:
> To make the truth quite clear to me
> That all men's honor, wealth and might
> Amount to nothing in thy sight.[2]

To test Doctor Luther's declared purpose of matching sense to melodic line, the reader might just sing these little verses to himself.

The timeless simplicity of the Christmas song contrasts strongly with both words and music of a Renaissance masterpiece which Luther composed at about the same time: "She is my love, that dear girl," *Sie ist mir lieb, die werde Magd*. As this first line suggests, the melody was taken over from a popular love song in praise of a sweetheart. Luther retains its simple, good-hearted tone to sing of his own love for a woman clothed with the sun, the moon under her feet, and wearing a crown of stars (as in Revelation 12). Thus the Virgin Mary appears in medieval sculpture and painting, but she is also "the Lord's bride," the church. The song is put together out of only three strophes, but each is very complex, rhythm and melody varying considerably within the strophe. It is not for singing in a congregation, as are most of Luther's hymns. One must imagine Doctor Martinus himself, having meticulously tuned that most difficult of stringed instruments, the lute, and now demonstrating the virtuosity of his tender alto in the florid coloraturas at the end of each line: the old roué as Renaissance lover, courting his heavenly girlfriend.

We need not quibble about the melody of "From Heaven on High." There has been much ink spilled over whether Luther's compositions are "original." It is an argument which distracts from the crucial point. He was not trying to create anything distinctive or new. On the contrary, the composer was deliberately probing for the most intimately familiar chords in the heart. The only true medium of communication, he thought, is shared experience. He liked to say of the Bible that we understand it only in that moment when we feel from within what we hear from without, so that we are constrained to sigh, "Ah, verily, that is the way it is!"[3] The air of "From Heaven on High" is strongly reminiscent of Luther's most famous hymn, "A Mighty Fortress Is Our God," and it is also closely related to his very first known composition, written when he was forty, "A New Song We Raise." One music critic has declared that this "melody type" must actually reach back into prehistoric times.

Luther as songwriter was trying to give voice to some of his own ideas, of course. But he was at the same time singing with the familiar voice of his people. Unacquainted with our (post-Romantic) idea of the "artist" as distinct from the artisan, he probably would not have admitted mortals to be capable of original creation, anyhow. He said his main purpose was just to match the words to melody and beat.[4] He liked to talk about this problem, calculating it to be at basis a "literary" skill which he had learned from Virgil. He seemed to think that drawing on native materials was the only really sincere kind of songwriting, saying that both text and music must arise "from our mother tongue and voice, otherwise it's all imitation—like monkeys."[5]

Singing was the regular way of concluding a meal at the populous table there on the second floor of the Black Cloister.[6] The head of the household had played his lute since student days, sang his alto with precision but apologized for an occasional false note. He claimed that music is second only to theology as a comfort to the human soul,[7] and spoke admiringly of contemporary composers. He vowed that God preached his gospel of grace through compositions like those of Josquin Desprez, which "flow happily, willingly, sweetly—are never forced or violated by the rules—it's like the song of the finch."[8] He wrote to Ludwig Senfl asking the famous Munich composer to do him a favor despite his bad reputation down in papist lands. He would like to have a polyphonic arrangement of an antiphon which he had loved since childhood.[9] It was evidence that the singing at Luther's table was not in unison, but harmony. When two people began to speak at the same time, he liked to admonish them that two people can sing, but not talk, together. Actually, he was himself capable of the kind of composition he asked of Senfl. While at the Coburg he had sent off to the friends in Augsburg a song in three voices which he claimed he had found. The idea was that they should send it right back to him. He planned to present it to George Rörer (his secretary) as the latest hit from the city.[10] Obviously, he composed more music than has come down to us.

In all, there survive some thirty-six songs, including less than a dozen melodies definitely ascribed to him—a paltry output to justify his reputation as "father of the German hymn."[11] He earned the title partly by the many songs erroneously attributed to him, but truly through his warm espousal of singing by congregations in their native tongue (instead of by the choir only, in Latin). Such general hymn singing had been associated with dissident gróups like the Hussites. In Wittenberg now song became a regular part of devotion, and the practice spread. Two hundred years later a young Englishman on the interminable voyage from his native isle to Georgia, John Wesley, listened to the singing of Moravian Brethren and was motivated to learn the German language. He discussed theology with them then, but as a proper high churchman could not approve their Lutheran reliance on grace alone to justify man, in God's eyes. Yet he could not resist their singing. He translated some thirty-three German hymns; he and his brother became prolific hymn writers. Song became characteristic of Methodism, indeed of religion in the colonies. There in Savannah, 1735, was a living link between Luther's singing congregations and song throughout America.[12]

Like his songs, every other item in the long list of Luther's writings—save his Bible—is an occasional piece, written to meet some need of the moment, often a quite personal one. Almost every one of his works became immensely popular. We are able to judge this by the large number of imprints issued and reissued all over Germany. Consider, for example, the short work written in 1535 for a friend of many years, Peter the Barber.

Peter was an old man, garrulous like many in his profession and at his age, so that Luther knew about his personal problems. There was reason to be especially concerned about his irritability and quick temper.[18] But he was also beset by some crazy ideas, his preoccupation with the devil being one. It was not particularly unusual to explain the malice of the world by personifying it—Luther took the devil quite seriously—but Peter had got the idea into his head he must launch a frontal attack upon Satan. When he confided his plan to his eminent patron, Doctor Martinus scratched out one of those rough and ready jingles of his, warning his friend that the devil might prove too clever for him. The concluding lines:

> If you pray, you'll be all right,
> Though Satan rage in envy and spite.

He was serious in this advice, for the old man was clearly disturbed. Later on, Luther prepared *A Simple Way to Pray* especially for Peter. It is a short devotional book in the tradition of Thomas à Kempis, later taken up by Ignatius Loyola. Luther's method is to hew closely to his own catechism (consisting of the Ten Commandments, the Lord's Prayer, and the Creed).

"Sweet Master Peter," he begins, "I'll help you all I can, and tell you how I practice my own prayers. May our Lord help you and others to do better than I." When the business of the day has distracted him, he says, leaving his heart "cold and disinclined to pray," he takes his little Psalter and flees to his own room. There he goes over his catechism "the same way my children do."[14] Morning and bedtime are the best times for prayer, and during the day one must not forget what Saint Jerome says, that "all works of the faithful are prayer." On the other hand, Luther cautions against doing anything whatsoever, be it in deed or word, mechanically. With this in mind he goes through the Lord's Prayer to show how each word is full of meaning and requires much reflection. This consumes several pages, and awakens Luther's typical concern:

> Now you must know that I do not intend you to *say* all this when you pray. That would amount to babble and empty chatter, based on the book or its letters—like telling beads or reading the Breviary. I mean for you to wake up your heart and teach it what kind of thoughts to think while saying the Lord's Prayer.

He assures Peter that he does not himself ever repeat the same words. "Today I say it one way, tomorrow another, depending on how warm and eager I am." Perhaps he will dwell long on one particular idea.

> When such an abundance of good ideas comes to us we ought to forget other prayers and make plenty of room for our reveries, listening to them quietly and by no means interfering with them. Because that is the Holy Ghost himself preaching to us, and just one word of his sermon is better than a thousand of our prayers.

The goal is to warm up one's heart and mind, so that one is free and eager toward God. "To let your face blabber one thing while your heart dwells on another is just tempting God." After the manner of a preacher, Luther dramatizes his point by depicting a priest saying his prayers while ordering servants to go about their various chores, and then by asking Peter to consider a barber chattering away, allowing his attention to be distracted —and cutting his patron's throat. "Any and every thing, if it is to be done well, demands the entire man, all his mind and faculties."[15]

The author of the little work discovered at this point that he was not entirely in sympathy with the very task he had set himself. The method of prayer, he realized, was not important, anyhow. Genuine prayer is spontaneous. Might not his recommendations actually interfere? He went ahead, nonetheless.

If contemplation of the Lord's Prayer has not yet made the heart "free and eager," then one may proceed to the Ten Commandments. This section becomes quite specific, recommending that one stir the heart with each Commandment by "plaiting a wreath of four strands." Imagine the Commandment first as instruction, then as a reminder of all we should be grateful for, third as confession of our failings, and finally as prayer. This is the longest part of the tract. Luther enjoys his little medieval game, and sets us an example by plaiting ten separate wreaths of his own. It requires considerable space and when he is done, he finds he is only two thirds through with his original plan. The Creed still remains, but he is weary—

> This ought to be enough for the heart to come to itself, and warm up to praying. Look to it that you do not try to do all of it, don't try to do too much, lest your spirit grow weary. Besides, a good prayer mustn't be too long. Don't draw it out. Prayer ought to be frequent and fervent.[16]

He admits he just isn't going to get around to the third part— "This is not the place to go into the Creed, or the Bible, that would be an endless task."[17]

A Simple Way to Pray had scarcely been published before printers in Nuremberg and Augsburg got hold of it and reproduced it in those cities. When the author saw it in print he was unhappy with its abrupt end. He had modeled it, after all, on his own catechism, which consisted of *three* parts, not two—and he had called his catechism his best work. So, still in 1535, he added two sheets to the second Wittenberg imprint. This augmented edition was now reprinted many times, all over Germany, right on into the eighteenth century. It was translated into Latin, Low German, and at last into English (1840). What Luther added was really pretty short, about a page for each of the three Articles of Faith. His remarks on the first are in no way limited to Luther's particular epoch, or even to one particular faith—

"I believe in God the Father Almighty, Creator of heaven and earth." A great insight illuminates your heart right here, if you will accept it. It teaches you in few words what cannot be expressed in all the languages, or with many books. Namely, what you are, where you come from, and where heaven and earth come from: you are God's creature, nature and work. Of yourself and in yourself you are nothing. You have no skill, don't know anything and can't do anything. Well, where were you a thousand years ago? . . . You were just as much nothing as those things are nothing which never are going to be created. What you are, however, what you know, your skills and abilities—these are things God made, just as you say very plainly in the Creed . . . Many learned people have tried to find out what man and nature are, and they have not found it. Here it says, the Creed says, that God made everything out of nothing. Here is the pleasure garden of the soul, where we can promenade among God's works—but it would take too long to write about all that.[18]

This was the mature Luther speaking as simply as he could on the most profound issue he knew. It was his feeling that less significant matters might be treated in a more learned fashion, drawing on an author's ratiocinative powers and appealing to the intellect. What was to sink into the heart, on the other hand, must come from the heart, he believed. Hence he tried to be, and to help others to be, as spontaneous and genuine as possible.

Scholarship

To our own way of thinking, there is a vast difference between the popular, devotional writing exemplified by *A Simple Way to Pray* and serious scholarship. Luther was not unacquainted with this point of view. He associated it with Scholasticism, which he contemptuously called "sophistry." He consciously broke away from this kind of scholarship.

As our own era gained a more balanced view of the Reformation, many Roman Catholic writers have found sympathy with that view Luther represented to Vergerio: that he had by no means broken with the church, but was holding close to its authentic traditions. Modern historians are inclined to place Luther in a long line of reform movements, even to characterize Christianity as a reform religion.[1] At the same time, there can be no doubt that Luther as a scholar was making a clear and conscious break with professional scholarship of a certain stamp. He accused contemporaries and predecessors of being remote, recondite, and insincere. The kind of writing he offered in *A Simple Way to Pray* merged imperceptibly into the most austere and demanding erudition.

Among the advances in learning accomplished during the Renaissance, those in the linguistic sciences ranked high. In the early sixteenth century, the liveliest of these was Hebrew studies, and the little group centered about Martin Luther, Philip Melanchthon, and Matthew Aurogallus, all professors at the University of Wittenberg, were among the most intense devotees of the new research. Perhaps the most difficult portion of the Old Testament—still full of problems today—was the Book of Psalms. Their work on its translation into German, culminating in the early 1530s, is most characteristic of Luther's scholarship, where commonness, simplicity, and—above all—sincerity were his criteria for scholarly success.

Despite that biting reference to mechanical reading of the Breviary, Luther had himself observed this daily, routine reading of Psalms since the time he became a monk in his own early twenties. It was the portion of the Bible he had been best acquainted with even before that, for his request of Ludwig Senfl really did reflect childhood memories. The line of music in question was the plainsong for Holy Saturday,

I will both lay me down in peace, and sleep: (Ps. 4:8)

In our own busy day we can probably no longer grasp such a degree of intimacy with any literary work as that to which Luther had long since attained with these ancient, passionate songs, the Psalms.

The first lectures he had held after graduating as Doctor of the Bible in 1513 had been on Psalms. He knew no Hebrew at the time. Few in Europe did. One of the great benefits he drew from brilliant young Philip Melanchthon's arrival in Wittenberg in 1518 was the opportunity it afforded for linguistic help with his favorite, but most difficult part of the Bible. Now he undertook another series of lectures on Psalms. It was interrupted by that historic trip to the imperial diet at Worms in 1521. After that, the rapidly developing reform movement curtailed his lectures entirely. Outlawed and excommunicated, Luther had been seized by friends and hidden at the remote Thuringian fortress Wartburg. He spent most of a year there, champing at the bit. It turned out to be a momentous exile, because here he began the major work of his lifetime, the German Bible translation. It became not only the greatest classic of the German language, but also the model for similar efforts in other lands. The New Testament appeared in September of 1522, and he immediately plunged with his Wittenberg colleagues into work on the Old. The energy they brought to the task seems, when we look back upon it, phenomenal. In addition to the earlier books of the Old Testament, the Psalter was available at the book dealers by 1524.

Luther continued to interpret and revise it. He thought it the central book in the Bible, a summation of all the rest and better than any of the others—not just telling *about* the "saints," but giving us their very own words,

how they talked and prayed to God, how they are still speaking and praying—so that other legends and examples present us, as compared with the Psalter, with silent saints. The Psalter creates in our minds good sturdy living saints. Why, a silent man compared with a speaking man is the same as dead, there being no more powerful, no nobler gift in man than speech. Consider how man is distinguished from other animals more by speech than in any other way, more than by his physical form or by any other gift.[2]

This is from the 1528 preface to his new translation of Psalms. The year after that, he put out a revision of the Latin Psalter (according to the Vulgate). This gave him an idea which has struck modern writers as peculiar.

Gathering together the notes he had made on his favorite psalm, the 118th, he sent them off to an old chum from his student days at Erfurt, Helius Eobanus Hessus (his real name seems to have been Koch, but he dubbed himself after the sun—he was born on a Sunday—after his patron saint, and after his homeland of Hesse). He was Germany's most celebrated poet, but quite unknown today: he never found a medium appropriate to his own era, so remained captive to traditional forms, and to the Latin language. At a time when learning was spreading among the middle class, many now able to read German, it was his ambition to take his place beside Terence and Virgil and Erasmus. He could find no poetic tradition in the German language. To this master of classical prosody Luther sent his notes on Psalm 118, along with the suggestion that he put the psalm into correct and eloquent Latin verses.

A modern biographer of Hessus finds "only technical merit" in the work.[3] Hessus knew no Hebrew, and his classical Roman distichs quite ignore the spirit of the original. The sixteenth century, clothing its biblical figures in Renaissance garb, was entirely unhistorical, to our way of thinking. But Luther was just delighted with Hessus's classical version of his psalm. He probably had more antiquarian interest in ancient Hebrew civilization than anyone else in his day, but he had the strong feeling that great literature must remain ever present. Just as before God there was no before and after, all things being present in his eyes, inspiration was essentially the same from one epoch to the next.

Luther's theory of literature was of a piece with his theology. In his letter to Hessus, used later as a preface to Hessus's Latin Psalter of 1537, he praised the work highly, then went ahead to reject "incursion of Jewish darkness into the clear light of Psalms." No matter that these were originally Jewish works, Eoban had shown "how a spirit from aetherial realms resides in poets." He had become a modern David,

> being genuinely moved by the substance itself, beyond the powers of the intellect, as we call them. It is an emotion that does not come from nature or from the ordinary powers of the muses. Nor is it received as their usual inspiration. It is truly a new gift of the spirit, and a higher inspiration from heaven.

Such remarks are truly noteworthy, coming as they do from a man who had so long labored to reproduce "the powers of that royal poet," David. Luther went on with great candor,

> I confess myself to be among those whom poetry moves more deeply, delights more profoundly, and affects more permanently than the prose even of a Demosthenes or a Cicero. This being my reaction to ordinary writings, how much more must you imagine me to be affected by the Psalter, the book which has been my companion, my delight, and my exercise from youth.

While apologizing for his obvious lack of humility, he confessed to

> that holy arrogance, before all the thrones and kingdoms of earth to boast of what I have gained . . . from enjoyment and meditation of the Psalms. In God, pride is certainly permitted. One ought to rejoice, triumph and glory in his gifts, as I do in my German Psalter.[4]

He had found in the Hessus distichs precisely his own original purpose for his German translation: to make the ancient material present and immediate for his own generation.

His delight with Hessus's version of Psalm 118 moved him to write a line-by-line commentary. The method was the same as we observed in *A Simple Way to Pray*. The great abundance of meaning that dwells in each word must be brought before the reader's mind—"They are not words to read, but to live."[5] Finding time on his hands during those months at Coburg, he filled 120 quarto pages with his own fine hand (the manuscript survives), later—as usual—regretting his verbosity. His first ten pages go to the first words, "O give thanks unto the Lord, for he is good: because his mercy endureth forever." Luther does not want us to "read or glance over it coldly and crudely." We must "think how these are living, excellent and abundant words which contain and convey everything—to wit: that God is merciful (not like men), from the bottom of his heart desiring to help and do good." Only for about half a page is Luther able to remain so succinct, then he plunges into his beloved specifics—

> "His mercy endureth forever"—that is, incessantly, he keeps on and on, doing the best for us, creates our body and soul, protects us day and night, keeps us alive and well, makes sun and moon to shine upon us, heaven, fire, air and water to serve us, wine, grain, feed, food, clothes, wood, and all necessities to grow out of the earth; provides gold and silver, house and hearth, wife and child, cattle, birds, fish—in sum, who can name them all? And everything in abundance and superabundance, every year, every day, every hour, every moment. Why, who can calculate his mercy in giving and maintaining just one healthy eye, or hand? When we are ill, or have to lose a member, then we discover for the first time what a kindness it is to have a healthy eye, a healthy hand, foot, leg, head, nose, finger, and what a benefit lies in bread, clothing, water, fire, home, etc.[6]

If we would but admit it, he argues, any one of our gifts is greater than a whole kingdom, for we wouldn't exchange a one of them, nor accept "all the malmsey in the world if we had to give up water just for a day,"[7] yet how devilishly ungrateful we are! No one takes thought—

> Just tell me, how many people are there on earth who understand this verse? I'll grant you that there is not a single little

boy so wicked not to have sung it in church, or heard it somewhere. He thinks he understands it so well he has drunk it dry.
Yet not one time in his life has he given a thought to the milk
he sucked from his mother, or given thanks for that—much
less for all the mercy God has shown him his whole life long
in such infinite, ineffable ways. Why, I guess he has sinned
more times per minute in ingratitude alone than there are
leaves in the woods, and grass—if God were a moneylender
and kept strict accounts.[8]

Luther could go on like this in the solitude of his study pretty
much indefinitely. He argued the importance of remembering
God's many kindnesses in the face of misfortune, which should
really serve us as a lamp to illuminate those words, "His mercy
endureth forever." He said when he had translated this psalm he
had not wanted to stray too far from the Hebrew, but those
words really mean: "What a good, faithful, kindhearted Lord
God you are, the way you just keep on doing good for me and
the whole world!"[9] He devoted a full paragraph to the two Hebrew words *hesed*, "kindness and mercy," and *olam*, "constantly,
eternally," which he said were important not only here but
throughout the Old Testament. Men, he reminded his reader, are
not capable of using *hesed* toward one another *olam*, yet that is
precisely what the psalm is attributing to God.

We would not follow Luther through his entire exposition as
he follows "David," word for word and verse by verse. He was
right to look back and complain he had been far too prolix. "It's
a lot of chatter," he said some years later. "Why, I was able to
prattle more about a flower than I would now about a whole
meadow. I don't like verbosity."

"It comes from the Holy Spirit," interposed an admiring
friend, "and it pleases me."[10]

It pleased the rest of Germany, too. No author has ever
known such a large, eager readership. Nor was Luther right to
suggest he ever had overcome his volubility. He responded very
powerfully to great literature. Once he began to write, his pen
was propelled by the fear that other readers of the Bible might
not be affected by it if he did not keep admonishing them.

"I called upon the Lord." *Call* is what you have to learn. You
heard it. Don't just sit there by yourself or off to one side and
hang your head, and shake it and gnaw your knuckles and
worry and look for a way out, nothing on your mind except
how bad *you* feel, how *you* hurt, what a poor guy you are.
Get up, you lazy scamp! Down on your knees! Up with your
hands and eyes toward heaven! Use a psalm or the Lord's
Prayer to cry out your distress to the Lord![11]

But Luther treasured Psalm 118 not merely as an eloquent expression of his own passion. He read the final verses as a prophecy of Christ. For him the entire Bible had one central theme:
Christ lived and died to redeem each individual human. He heard
Christ's voice ringing clearly throughout the Psalter,[12] perhaps
more clearly than in the Gospels themselves. As a consequence,
he had a sure sense of their meaning and was able to focus his attention on just how to couch the same emotions in his native
German. Later scholars are, ironically, hindered by their very
wealth of linguistic and archaeological data, and almost never
find such felicitous expression as Luther did.

Luther's personal copy of his 1528 translation survives, as it
happens, so that we are able to look over the marginal notes he
made. He planned yet a further revision of Psalms, so some entries pertain to correct translation. Others are simply witness to
his emotions at the time of reading. For example, he wrote beside
"I love the Lord" (Ps. 116:1): "How fine that is! I really like
that!" Beside Psalm 119:1–2:

> The greatest comfort is to be sure that what you are doing is
> God's command, because that is what will endure, and take
> hold. The man who knows that will persist and win out in the
> end against all the devils, the world and its wickedness, just by
> standing fast.[13]

The "old and tattered" tome, which so obviously bore the marks
of its owner's passion and devotion, eventually attracted the eye
of a pious souvenir hunter, who offered Luther a new Psalter.
When the gift was accepted and the sly giver tried to make
quietly away with the well-leafed old one, Luther protested he
had to have it for reference purposes. He explained how *me-*

moria localis, facility in finding a particular passage, was worth a lot to him. "I ruined my *memoria localis* when I made the new translation."[14]

He was referring to his final revision of Psalms, which appeared in 1531. It constitutes one of our best examples of what he meant by "sincere" scholarship: the most exacting research and the highest standards were to be guaranteed by the popularity and commonness of the product.

In the early months of 1531 the close associates who had been poring together over the Old Testament for a decade now began to meet regularly on Psalms. Their purpose was to discuss their translation line by line. Aside from Luther himself the most active participant was Philip Melanchthon. He was the man who knew Luther best. He never made the error so fatal to many writers at a greater remove who supposed Luther to have been a man like any other, interpretable by the same motives as you or I—or they themselves. For Philip, the great doctor exemplified the psalmist, and at Psalm 119:53, he timidly observed, "You have that same kind of wrath within you. It is a heroic virtue."[15] They relied on Professor Matthew Aurogallus for precision in the Hebrew, Luther confessing he could not himself "bear the chains" of its grammar.[16] His contribution to the team, he thought, was his familiarity with usage throughout the Old Testament, and the facility with which his mind associated one passage with another—his *memoria localis*—so he did most of the talking.

This was to be a relatively brief seminar of only a month or so, to put the final polish on the language of a translation which the scholars, having already revised it once, thought was as close to the meaning as they were likely to get. "It is one thing to understand the Psalms," Luther observed at one point, "but finding the most effective words to communicate it is quite another."[17] The course of their discussions proved him wrong there: "understanding" could not be so nicely distinguished from wording. Trying to come up with the most felicitous German phrasing demanded, they discovered, rethinking and reexperiencing the psalmist's intent. For example, they had been just about as wordy at Psalm 4:7 as the King James Version is: "Thou hast put gladness in my heart more than in the time that their corn and wine increased." Here Luther tried to formulate, in German, the message of the entire psalm, then was able to return to the verse and put it into terse, lucid German.

He opened the discussion by testing a few ways German might have for saying "put gladness in my heart." Then, as he surveyed the rest of the verse, he wondered just who the psalmist might have had in mind when he said *their* corn and wine increased.

> *They* scorn that gladness of heart that comes from faith, and from the word, and from good conscience in grace. *They* want to be big in the pleasures of the belly. *They* see not the glory of God, only riches and power. *They* want to fly high, have plenty to eat and drink. The papists applied this verse to their mass, and were right to do so, because all they were concerned with was their bellies—and they filled them.

He went back to the preceding verse: "Lord, lift thou up the light of thy countenance upon us." Luther experimented: "Don't wrinkle your brow . . . smile at me, comfort me, speak kindly to me." He looked down at the succeeding verse, that plainsong which he said had been his favorite since childhood: "I will both lay me down in peace and sleep: for thou, Lord, only makest me dwell in safety." The Lord, Luther explained to his colleagues, is the sole comfort there is. Now what would be some ways of saying that in German? After thinking of a few German idioms, they returned to their original problem, Psalm 4:7.

> Here we have [Luther began] the people who want to have plenty of grain and wine. They aren't interested in the joys of the heart, only in the joys of the belly. "Thou gladdenest my heart and givest a good conscience." They scorn such comfort as that. "Grain and wine increase"—that would sound like timid Philip [Melanchthon].

Luther warmed himself to boldness by thinking of some papists, John Eck, against whom he had debated, and the duke of Brunswick, for whom he could usually come up with a slanderous sobriquet—

> Doctor Eck wants to be pope, Duke Slaychild would like to be emperor, the Turkish emperor. Now if they were, they

would have bread and wine enough and to spare, in and out, round about. In a word, what they want is to get their bellyful of grub and suds, power, wealth. They want to lord it over others. What the psalm is saying is that while good people suffer want, the wicked flourish and abound in all good things. Thou, O Lord, wilt comfort our hearts; they have confidence in present things, and they worship and believe in Mammon.[18]

By making the psalm come round to his own experience, Luther had arrived at a succinct statement: "You gladden my heart, even though they have a lot of wine and grain."

Compare that with what current scholarship does with the same verse. The Anchor Bible volume for Psalms reads: "Put happiness in my heart; now let their wheat and wine increase." A lengthy note makes the somewhat awkward English more understandable by explaining that the verbs are in the "precative perfect, so that the psalm is actually a prayer for rain rather than a hymn of thanksgiving for blessings bestowed." This authoritative translation, applying archaeological research and linguistic evidence from other Semitic cultures, perceives no such contrast as Luther did. The Revised Standard Version, it should be added, agrees with Luther.

Clearly, Luther interpreted and translated subjectively, but he knew it. More recent scholars strive for complete objectivity. Of Psalm 63:5, the Anchor Bible says, for example: "In the Masoretic phrase *hēlēb wadesen*, 'fat and fatness,' the latter is often deleted here as contributing little to the thought and disrupting the meter. The difficulty can be resolved by the vocalization *hālāb*, 'milk.'" So the Anchor translates: "Yonder with milk and fatness may my desire be satisfied; while my lips shout for joy, my mouth will praise you." Luther explained the Wittenberg scholars' approach to the same verse thus:

Here is the way we had translated it before: "Let my soul be sated with lard and fat, that my mouth may praise thee with happy lips." No German can understand that, so the Hebrew words "lard and fat" had to go. They indicate joy. A healthy, fat animal grows happy, and a happy one, fat. A sorrowful animal falls off and grows lean, a lean animal, sorrowful. We now speak clear German: "That would be my joy and delight, to praise thee with a happy mouth." That's what David meant.[19]

He said he and his co-workers had been "bold enough to reproduce the sense and let the words go, something for which many pedants will censure us." Characteristically, he faced right up to them: "What is the point in being unnecessarily rigid and cold in reproducing the words when they cannot be understood?" His formula was entirely intuitive: "If you can understand the Hebrew man speaking, then grasp that sense, and say to yourself, 'Now look here, how does a German say something like that?' Once you have found German words for it, then let the Hebrew go, open up, and speak the best German you are able." The idea of free translation was so novel in the early sixteenth century that one is tempted to say Luther was centuries ahead of his time. The fact is, his intuitive grasp of language remains centuries, aeons removed from literal-minded scholarship of any age—and each bears its pedants anew.

His intuition frequently led Luther to hold quite slavishly to his original. In Psalm 91:5-6, he rendered the Hebrew literally:

Thou shalt not be afraid for the terror by night; nor for the arrow that flieth by day; nor for the pestilence that walketh in darkness; nor for the destruction that wasteth at noonday.

He explained that these verses, "obscure and spoken with ambiguous words, may well be interpreted differently by one reader than by another. So we have given leeway for each to understand them in accord with the gifts and limits of his own mind. Else we would have translated them in such a way as to display our own intellect."[20] Rare the scholar who can let pass an opportunity to display his own intellect—but Luther was enough of a poet himself to shy away from imposing concrete references on figurative speech. In our modern Anchor Bible, we find extensive annotation to the same lines, thorough enumeration of their possible allusions, and an explanation for dropping "terror by night" in favor of (Ugaritic) "pack of night": "Namely, the pack of wild dogs that marauds at night."

In the great majority of instances, Luther would no doubt have welcomed the data accumulated by modern research. Yet it is surprising how often he comes to precisely the same conclusions as does twentieth-century work, but by following his quite "unscholarly" pathways.[21] Anticipating the objections that would be raised to his interpretive brand of translation, he lashed out at the nigglers in advance, "He is a shameful and disgusting fellow, Sir Pedant is."[22] He loved to remind the sticklers for accuracy in detail that they were dependent on him for an understanding of the entirety they'd never have arrived at alone. He said he did not want or seek scholarly approval.

Over the centuries, assiduous researchers have examined Luther's every utterance so closely, and been so successful in deriving virtually every one of his doctrinal tenets from some scholiast before him, that he has been left with very little that one would call original. In fact, one of the men who knew Luther best, Philip Melanchthon, praised him for hewing to tradition. Melanchthon said Luther had "only clarified the common and quite necessary doctrine of penance, forgiveness of sins, faith, and comfort in the cross." Referring to Luther's most immediate predecessors, he found no innovations by his friend and mentor, save a stronger emphasis on grace. In this regard, Philip did attribute to Luther a kind of revisionism. He admitted he had insisted on the distinction "between philosophy and the gospel, something which is actually not present in Scotus, Thomas, and their fellows."[23]

By "philosophy," Melanchthon meant speculative studies, in a detached, objective frame of mind. One can and must treat philosophical questions with disinterest, as if they did not affect us. "Gospel," on the other hand, being inaccessible to human reason and often confuting it, requires personal involvement precisely of the sort we have seen Luther bring to the final revision of Psalms. His great objection to his scholarly predecessors was what he called a lack of sincerity in treating "rationally" those subjects which are revealed to passion alone. He had never met the great Humanist whose Greek New Testament he had used for his own translation, Desiderius Erasmus. After the anti-Erasmus treatise *Concerning the Bondage of the Will* (1525), he had no further exchange with him—but Erasmus remained an astonishingly frequent reference in conversation and writing. The urbane classical scholar embodied for Luther that superficiality which "thinks the Christian religion is a comedy or tragedy. It contains not real events, but fictions conceived to teach good behavior."[24] The sharpest condemnation may be Luther's simple, "He is not committed." How can you deal with people who have no firm belief to which you might appeal? "You can't refute them by scripture, because it doesn't mean anything to them."[25]

What Luther liked to call "sincerity" is precisely that quality in his scholarship which both separated him from many churchmen of his day, and which also continues into the present to be unacceptable even to Catholics who admire him and who freely recognize the abuses of the Renaissance church which he corrected. Those abuses needed to be reformed, they were reformed —and the modern, ecumenically minded Catholic scholar agrees with moderates of Luther's day like Cardinal Contarini: the schism is therefore unfortunate and unnecessary. Luther, on the other hand, insisted that the issue was not abuses at all, but a matter of doctrine. The most eminent twentieth-century church historian, Joseph Lortz, called this Luther's "subjectivism," which could not be reconciled with the church. Luther was subconsciously, Lortz said, acting on the *false* assumption "that the transformation in us, whereby we are justified, must be experienced with such emotion and immediacy as to be certain."[26] Here the man of the twentieth century has at last found his common ground with Luther, where their fundamental disagreement can be stated in terms which both men could understand and accept. It is a difference in scholarly ethos: shall priority be given to intellectual understanding, or to subjective experience?

Gloss

The figure of Martin Luther stands upon a divide in the history of communications, astride two quite different traditions. On the one side, he is history's most voluble representative of the spoken word, dominant in human culture until the invention of printing, and for a good while thereafter. Sermon and debate—these were the forms in which Luther felt most at home. Whether he wrote Latin or German, he remained in the medieval, oral tradition. Yet at the same time he is the author who developed his written style in closest collaboration with the embryonic printing industry. As a consequence, the future of publishing in Europe bore the mark of his character for centuries to come.

We must imagine a world as yet little influenced by the printing press. Information fixed in print constantly reinforces our own notion of objective truth. We can, after all, look it up when in doubt. The facts are stored in books, libraries, and computers. The factuality sustained in print dominates our education. Luther, on the other hand, learned by oral methods, by rote: factuality seemed dependent on memory. He liked to marvel at how unfamiliar the Bible had been even among the learned. He had not seen one himself until his university days, and *it* had been nailed down! There was some truth to his implication that the great enlightenment had come through his reforms. Perhaps he exaggerated, but his depiction of his own bookless education is reliable. He had not drawn his early learning from the printed word, as he observed his children doing.

He and his fellows had been taught to establish the truth by means of the *disputatio:* academic debate. "Truth" was what could be maintained in the minds of an audience by eloquent delivery, colorful formulations, memorable phraseology, devastating irony. Those many writers who speak of Luther as "thundering" not only forget his alto singing voice, they also disregard the incisive qualities needed in debate. "I have a small voice," he lamented, "with little resonance."

"It carries well, nonetheless," Melanchthon interposed.[1]

Listeners were not easily gulled. They were themselves practiced in the rhetorical arts, so that mere bombast would not impress, nor sophistry beguile them. Fallacies must eventually be driven out by the inexorability of logic, the main content of university education. The *disputatio* was the central academic exercise and a primary form of entertainment for the student body. The conclusion of one's studies was not a doctoral dissertation, but a public debate. How natural for the young Doctor Luther in 1517 to formulate his objections to papal indulgences in the standard form of theses to be debated! How understandable for those who came after, beginning with Melanchthon, to assume he had "posted" those theses, too, as was the academic custom.

Recent research has cast some doubt on that famous legend. It seems likely that these particular theses may have been merely forwarded to the bishops in the immediate area, one of whom was responsible for the indulgence sales. In later years Luther referred to All Saints' Day, 1517, as "when I began to *write* against indulgences," and certainly the fuss over his 95 Theses did transform him into a writer and publicist. The theses were answered —or Luther was called to order—by the Master of the Sacred Palace in Rome, Sylvester Prierias, in 1518. Prierias did not speak to Luther's arguments against indulgence sales at all, but merely invoked the authority of the pope. Such pompousness struck Luther as blatant self-indictment, and his reaction was characteristic of a debater before a public forum. He simply handed the pamphlet over to a local printer to be published for all to read. There followed an exchange of pamphlets during the course of the year, a kind of *disputatio* in print (Latin, of course), Prierias even using the form of dialogue in which he and his adversary confronted one another. In this new medium for debate, however, Luther was by far the more adept.

This was to be expected. Prierias was of the older generation. The faculty at the young University of Wittenberg was accustomed to doing things the modern way. Early in Luther's professorial career he had enlisted the printing press as lecture aid. Now it was a mere matter of adapting familiar techniques to reach an audience beyond the lecture hall.

The organization of his lectures was not much different from what we encounter in his writings, a fairly pedestrian progress from one Bible verse to the next, enlivened mainly by professorial wit and a wealth of rhetorical devices. Before his students lay copies of the biblical passages under discussion. The university printer had prepared them especially for this purpose, leaving a wide margin and plenty of room for entering Doctor Luther's interpretations, his "glosses." It had become for Luther second nature to develop his thoughts in close interaction with a text. The gloss therefore symbolizes a basic pattern in his thinking.

A most entertaining document, showing how the old oral tradition with its debater's flourishes and posturings carried over into the new universe of print, arose out of that continuing exchange with the Master of the Sacred Palace. In 1519, Prierias announced his return to the fray:

> A pugilist both robust and strong has arisen, instructed in the use of mortal weapons, to lay [Luther] low before the eyes of all Christendom. Lest he call it a surprise attack, here is a list of my weapons.[2]

Now followed Sylvester's *Epitome of a* [forthcoming] *Response to Luther*. Its braggadocio cried out for marginal glossing. The extravagant claims for authority had to fall of themselves if merely placed alongside impertinences. It became the first of Luther's reprintings with glosses.

Where Prierias referred to the pope as "head" of the church, in the margin was added: "Not the foot or the elbow." Glossing was more fun than debate, because it permitted interrupting one's opponent. Prierias' statement that he would now review how he had refuted Luther endured the polite comment, "Let the reader note this figure of speech, past tense for future action."[3] Prierias vaunted papal authority on earth. Luther added, "In heaven too, Christ and God being deposed."[4] If Prierias climbed oratorical heights to declare that papal authority must still prevail even should the pope lead whole "nations, one after the other, to the devil," Luther could rise along with him: "Tremble, heavens, and reel, earth. O ye Christians, behold what Rome is!"[5]

It was all great fun, the gladiators never suspecting any dangerous implications in their mock combat. In his afterword, Luther retained the martial imagery of Prierias's introduction to set down the often quoted words:

> If thieves upon the gallows and highwaymen by the sword, if heretics by fire be punished, shall we not all the more seize these teachers of perdition, these cardinals, these popes, and this whole ferment of Roman Sodom which endlessly corrupts the church of God, and wash our hands in their blood?[6]

Amplified through a powerful new technology, the printing press, the debater's rhetoric pealed out a thousand times over all Europe. That old ceremonial battleground of the *disputatio* was to become, after Luther's death, a field where real blood was shed.

Those who blame Luther for his inflammatory language must avoid hyperbole themselves. This first example of his glossing was in Latin, the elite language of academic debate, where such trumpetings were routine. As he shifted to the vernacular, Luther had to leave the martial brandishings of the Latin tradition behind him. But popular language expanded the audience which the new pamphlet medium could reach. And Luther was still the debater. He published the Sorbonne's judgment of his famous debate with John Eck, in 1519.

> So that Germans, too, may observe how theologians, as if infected by an epidemic, have gone crazy not only in Germany but in all lands, I have myself translated the judgment of Paris against me, not deeming it necessary to answer it.[7]

Of course not: he glossed it. In 1522, he did the same with the papal bull *Coena Dominia*, where he had found his own name included for the first time on the pope's annual list of heretics. And so it went, through the years.[8]

The merriest example of his use of the gloss to focus public ridicule involved the powerful prince elector Joachim, margrave of Brandenburg. It was a tale of violence, passion, and that Renaissance license scarcely exceeded by any other epoch. Joachim, called *Cicero teutonicus* by those who admired his eloquence before imperial assemblages, was about Luther's age. He had been a major contender for the imperial crown in 1519—that is to say, one of the highest bidders. Luther was fortunate that the Spanish monarch, Charles, had produced a larger sum, because Joachim was among those who, at Worms in 1521, urged Charles to dispose of the heretic Luther forthwith. It was to the credit of the young Emperor Charles V that he insisted on honoring the safe-conduct he had granted. Luther never forgot Joachim's advice, and whenever godless despotism came up for discussion at his table the margrave of Brandenburg was among those he cited as examples. Even after the margrave's death, Luther related how

> exhausted from debauchery, he still said: "If I could but enjoy the eternal pleasure of being carried from the bed of one whore to another, I'd forgo heaven." Oh, dear Lord, what depravity and godlessness. You'd think one would grow weary at last, such an old man as that.[9]

In 1527, Joachim used armed cavalry to round up forty of the Brandenburg clergy whom he suspected of Lutheran leanings. About this time his own wife, Elizabeth, had taken the Lord's Supper in both kinds, after the Lutheran fashion. Of the Danish royal family, she had long favored the evangelical movement. Joachim had been away in Breslau, with a mistress, but Elizabeth's daughter tattled when her father returned. He laid down an ultimatum that Elizabeth must take the Roman communion by Easter of 1528, or submit to lifelong imprisonment. She was as headstrong as her brother, that brilliant but vengeful monarch recently driven from the throne of Denmark, Christian II. On a March evening Elizabeth slipped out of the castle, crossed the moat, and plunged into a daredevil ride in a coach with a broken wheel (mended by wrapping her skirts around it) to the Saxon border, where Christian met her. John of Saxony (Luther's prince in these years) was their uncle. He gave her asylum until after Joachim's death. She liked to visit Luther, so she and her daughter figure in some of his later problems.

Luther was at this time already involved in another of Joa-

chim's notorious scandals. One of the margrave's more prominent subjects, Wolf Hornung, had married the former mayor's
daughter in Berlin, sister of the archbishop of Riga, Catherine
Blankenfeld. She soon presented Wolf with a baby daughter, and
as a young mother must have been especially attractive. Catherine was only in her early twenties when she met Joachim at an
affair of state. He was forty, at that dangerous age when an old
roué may seem intriguing to a young woman. A liaison developed which the grand lord made little effort to conceal. When
Hornung dared approach him, he openly demanded his rights to
a subject's spouse, and impatiently asked not to be bothered.

The young Hornung was indecisive. For Catherine to be mistress to the margrave of Brandenburg need certainly bring no dis-
advantage to a discreet husband. But Renaissance Berlin was not
only given to its passions; it was terrified by its sermons. One
Sunday after Wolf and Catherine had heard an especially moving exhortation against adultery, a disagreement arose between
them which culminated in his lashing out at her with a table
knife (Luther later said it was a blunt one). She fled to her
margrave.

Joachim used young Hornung's embarrassment to compel him
to renounce all rights to Catherine, to her dowry, and to any
debts the Blankenfelds might owe him. He was banished from
Brandenburg under pain of death, in accordance with formal
agreements laid before him by Joachim's lawyers and signed by
the exile. Needless to say, it was not long before Catherine regretted her infatuation with the great man and its consequences,
but she was quite literally in the margrave's clutches. Her father
was dead, her powerful brother far away. An ignorant woman in
a misogynist age, she was helpless. Since Catherine had never
learned to write, she depended on venal go-betweens. Even communications with her mother were not safe from her lover's sur-
veillance. And what could her mother do?

There was another daughter, married to a citizen in Wittenberg. Together with Hornung, they enlisted Luther's aid in behalf of Catherine. His attempts to arrange a meeting for the es-
tranged couple went on for years. Catherine at times genuinely
desired a reconciliation, but she was not always cooperative. Disguised as a page, for example, it had been she who accompanied

Joachim to Breslau on that occasion when Elizabeth took her decisive step toward Lutheranism. Any contact whatsoever with Luther became as daring for Joachim's mistress as for his wife. But Luther continued to support Wolf Hornung, at one time helping him compose an appeal to Joachim. In the grand fashion appropriate to his station, the margrave rejected all petitions, returning some unopened. He had an addition built to Hornung's house to facilitate his visits there. Catherine bore him a son.

Finally, Luther resorted to the public forum with open letters to Joachim as well as to both clerical and temporal powers in Brandenburg, pleading the injustice done, the illegality of the documents Hornung had been compelled to sign, and the peril to the soul of such a young fellow deprived of his wife. This brought a strongly worded letter to Hornung from "Catherine Blankenfeld" (his wife's maiden name).

Until now Luther had observed all proprieties, but this missive was too much. Its true author was clearly Joachim himself. Luther published it with a foreword which cited the biblical admonition that a man shall not put on a woman's garment,

and may God protect every man's wife from *this* Madame Catherine Blankenfeld—until a good hog gelder has first had at her with his gelding shears and made a barrow of her. Else she would turn all our wives into Catherine Blankenfelds.[10]

By glossing the letter now, Luther could playfully tug at the great lord's unseemly mask.

One of the first glosses exclaimed, "Gracious, she is truly wrathful and speaks to her husband like a great prince!"[11] The letter had made personal attacks on Luther himself, but these were most readily disarmed by a gloss. For example, Joachim had pictured Luther as a lover unfaithful to his renegade nun, "strolling upon the streets of an evening, playing his lute." Luther: "I would vow upon Sir and Madame Catherine's chastity that it was no lute, but a bagpipe."[12] The author of the letter disclaimed any wrongdoing, but a gloss mentions the illegitimate offspring.[13] Appeal made in the letter to depositions signed by Wolf Hornung evoked Luther's sneer that they were "sealed with a sausage," i.e., quite illegal.[14]

Since he was glossing a fictional lady and not a real one, certain indelicacies may be forgiven Luther. When "Catherine" laid claim to her property, he asked if she meant that one upon which she sat. "Now, should a division be in order, then one half must be consigned to Hornung, and the other half to your sweetheart. I think that would be appropriate."[15] The glosser was able to maintain his detached, ironical tone right up to the end. But here the offer of safe-conduct for Hornung to return to Brandenburg awakened Luther's old grudge and moved him to a forgivable lapse: "Let the devil believe your safe-conduct, not me."[16]

After this publication, Joachim moved Catherine and her children to remote Frankfurt on the Oder, where the notoriety was less. It did not help Hornung, nor was he able to obtain satisfaction by appealing to the imperial diet at Augsburg in 1530. He served as messenger there between the Saxon delegation and Luther at the Coburg, and Luther afterward helped him settle down in a village south of Wittenberg.[17] Did Catherine ever join him there? A note taken by a theology student in Luther's garden in May of 1532 may be evidence that she did. Among random remarks presumably made by Luther we find, "Jacob Krach abducted the margrave's whore."[18] We cannot say who Jacob Krach was, but it might appear that Catherine was at last removed by force or by stealth. As for Joachim, Luther reported that he had not changed his ways when he died in 1535, "going from one whore to another."[19]

Throughout his life the gloss continued to be a favorite technique for Luther, but it reached its culmination here with the Hornung affair.[20] The gloss was not important writing, but it does offer us an instructive element in the author's development. It affords insight into his early motives for publication, but especially into the relationship between his experience at academic debate and his career as that publicist who first used the new medium of print to mobilize public opinion. The frequency with which he used the gloss tends also to confirm Luther's repeated declaration that he placed no value at all on his own writings, but wished they might all perish. Few literary forms are so ephemeral as the gloss. Nevertheless, Luther's glosses are valuable to us as an example of how his scholarly habits and methods carried over into his popular appeal.

On Behalf of
Children and Youth

Immediately after his friends had left him at the Coburg in that spring of 1530, themselves to journey on to Augsburg, Luther began a letter to them:

> I have nothing to do but write this, my trunk and effects not yet having arrived . . . We have everything that solitude might require: an entire huge wing of the castle and keys to all the rooms. Thirty men are said to eat bread here, twelve watchmen by night and two buglers in opposite towers by day. But what is all that to you? I just don't have anything else to do but write. [greetings to our friends] from the empire of the birds, at the third hour, Martinus Luther.[1]

Luther's admiring young companion, Veit Dietrich, wrote that this first day in the great fortress above the town was a restless one. An hour after his first letter, the doctor began another— "Here we sit among the clouds in the empire of the birds." This time he had nothing to tell about except the loud noise and chatter of the jackdaws, which he compared with the self-satisfied banter of those "sophists" with whom his colleagues would soon have to contend.

> You see, I have nothing to write—but rather than write nothing, I preferred nonsense over silence. Especially among these screaming jackdaws who fill the heavens and earth with their yakking. To remain timidly silent would seem remiss, in one whose profession is words.[2]

This was dated at four o'clock. By five, he had turned out yet another letter on the birds, a little masterpiece in the venerable German tradition of the animal tale (though his language in writing to a learned friend was Latin): "You are not the only ones, dear Spalatin, who have gone off to an imperial diet. We came to one just as soon as we left you—so we are way ahead of you by now." His party did not have to wait around for the arrival of the principals, as Spalatin will—and there are other differences:

> Here you would get to see kings, dukes, and other lords who are sincerely concerned about their affairs and their subjects. With untiring voice they hurl decrees and pronouncements into the air. By no means are they shut up in those courtly antrums and spelunks which you call (with little justification) palaces.

He describes the glorious sylvan abode of this populous nation, then speaks of their admirable dress:

> They despise that foolish display of gold and silk. All follow the same custom, the same colors, the same style, and the same language. The uniformity and equality of their regalia are unbelievable: all in the same deep black, with cerulean eyes, and in musical harmony (save the happy distinction between voices of young and old).

Luther reports the mobility of their forces and their military prowess as superior. From their interpreter he has been given to understand that war has been declared on every variety of grain. This nation's cunning in thievery and pillage prompts more explicit comparison between the jackdaws and the German nobility. He wishes these "fathers and preservers of our country" might be freed of that hateful name *monedula* (Latin for "jackdaw"). They really ought to be called "lancers," or "pikemen," he feels, playing with Latin in such a way as to say at the same time that they really deserve to be impaled and skewered. As a matter of fact, he observes, if you but reverse the two parts of the (Latin) word for jackdaw, *mon-edul*, you clearly come up with the German word for nobleman: *edel-man*. "But now I have gone too far, because your *edel-man* is much too adroit at *monedulan* virtue. Our *monedulae* boast but one superiority: their forum is much less expensive than yours at Augsburg."[3] Luther was so well content with his animal allegory that he told it just one more time: for the table at the Black Cloister, in German. Its style betrays his immense pleasure, for it was a composition, after all, in a German tradition.

The years of work translating the Old Testament had made him sensitive to the timeless qualities of literature as well as to its intimate bond with the peoples who produce it—as modern Bible critics say, its *Sitz im Leben*. This interest had sharpened his awareness of his own native traditions, and we have various examples of his fondness for the animal tale. Perhaps his best, and one of the merriest fables of all time, is his narrative of how the sly fox duped the animal kingdom into accepting the jackass (naturally endowed with the emblem of a cross on its back) as their new sovereign. On another occasion, he drew up an eloquent bill of complaint by the birds against his faithful old servant Wolf Seburg, who had set up nets to trap them.

Luther edited the *Liber Vagatorum*, or *Beggar's Book* of the Middle Ages, appending his glossary of the argot; he undertook a private collection of German "proverbs," nearly five hundred colorful sayings and idioms; he was familiar with those tales at last collected three hundred years later by the brothers Grimm, and he liked to draw on them to illustrate a point.[4] Among the most charming documents to this cultivation of popular literature is a letter to an old friend from monastery days, now active in Nuremberg. It begins in the usual Latin, but suddenly leaps into Rabelaisian vernacular chatter to beg help in collecting all kinds of

> German pictures, songs, books, and *Meistersänge* which in recent years have been painted, written, produced, or printed by your German poets and artisans—for I have good cause to want them: Latin books we can make all right; as to German books, we are but learning. We are hoping to do it just about well enough (if we have not already succeeded) to displease everybody.[5]

Good simple German, he felt, required sure footing in his native culture.

Transferring the ancient Hebrew tales into popular idiom had given him enormous satisfaction, and during the early, idle hours at the Coburg he resolved to do the same with another collection, the fables of Aesop. As master of the humorous German animal tale, Luther felt a strong sympathy with the Aesopic tradition and was one of the early scholars to recognize that here, just as in the Old Testament, he was not dealing with the work of a single hand, but with a disparate accumulation by many generations of collectors, all motivated as he was by love of the fable. While at the Coburg he put a dozen of them into such charming German that they are still enjoyed by children today. We know that he told one (but do not know which) to Martin Bucer when that south German divine visited the Coburg in May; and from time to time in subsequent years he accorded Aesop his highest praise, comparison with the Bible.[6] Hoping eventually to publish his own Aesop, he wrote a preface, but the plan did not immediately materialize. By the middle 1530s he was trying to interest others in the task.[7] His own manuscript was not published during his lifetime, but some of the remarks from his preface bear quoting:

> This book of fables, or tales, has been highly acclaimed by the most learned men on earth, especially in pagan times. Even today I would have to admit that, aside from Holy Scripture, I could name few books superior to it—for anyone who values practicality, artistry, and wisdom more highly than calculated ballyhoo.[8]

He was most impressed by the simplicity of the fables and their pedagogical effectiveness. His concept of the history of Aesop's fables had arisen from his ponderings over the Old Testament. "Aesop" was in his opinion a fiction—

> I maintain that many wise people drew the collection together, bit by bit, over the years. Finally, a scholar probably arranged it in the present order, pretty much the same way people might collect the fables and sayings circulating among us in the German language and arrange them nicely in a book.[9]

Since it was unlikely that any one man could have collected them all, he assumed a great variation in age among them. He

thought he understood why their compiler had invented a
fictional author. It had to do with the dangerous and awkward
nature of truth.

> Not only children, but also great lords, are best beguiled into
> truth, in their own best interest, by conveying it to them
> through foolishness. Fools are tolerated and listened to by
> those who cannot suffer the truth from a wise man. Ah, all the
> world hates the truth when it strikes home.[10]

Some years after he had written these lines Luther pulled forth
the old manuscript and read aloud from it. Pleased perhaps with
his own German, but ostensibly in praise of Aesop, he exclaimed, "He who can speak well—now that's the man. *Sermo
est sapientia, sapientia est sermo.*"[11] He went ahead to observe
(correctly) the kinship of the German words for "speech" and
for "counsel."

His Latin adage might be rendered: "Communication is understanding, and to understand is to communicate." It is in accord
with a remark he made at quite different periods in his life to the
effect that he, like Saint Augustine, was one of those persons
who progress was not by inspiration, but in the process of writing and reading.[12] This self-characterization contrasts strongly
with the traditional, very dramatic presentations of Luther's life
as determined by sudden insights and revelations. Let us bear it
in mind as we come to know him better.

The first hours at the Coburg revealed in a most touching way
that Martin Luther was a natural and compulsive writer. Entirely aside from his work on the Bible translation (Psalms and
the prophets), he turned out nearly half a hundred publications,
among them several substantial works, during his stay there of
less than six months. As a man who relied on his writing to
develop his thinking, he was often guilty of prolixity. He frequently deplored his own verbosity, and it certainly has damaged
his reputation as an author. He seldom reread or revised his own
treatises (this in sharp contrast with his tedious review and re-
working of his translations). While he praised succinctness as the
cardinal literary virtue, he never abbreviated or compressed. It
was partly the fault of the printers, who on occasion actually set
up his manuscripts while he was still writing on them, so that the

first sheets were drying before the last pages had been written. It was because he sold so well, of course. Throughout the 1520s he had been far and away the most widely read publicist on all aspects of contemporary life. By 1530, his quill had made him the most influential man in Europe. None had ever attained to power by that instrument before.

Let us single out just one of the works from the Coburg to see if we can understand his appeal. One of his main concerns had long been education. He had very ambivalent feelings about the emptying of the monasteries, for centuries the traditional centers of learning. The prospect of monastic life for their children had motivated parents to send them to Latin school. Luther was less pleased that his own proliferation of German publications had increased literacy than he was troubled by the decline of classical studies. Why learn Latin, parents asked. Were there not plenty of German books for all to read? As early as 1524, Luther wrote *To the Councilmen of All Cities in German Lands: That They Establish and Maintain Christian Schools*, a spirited defense of liberal studies. But the problem continued to prey on his mind, and he attacked it from the pulpit sporadically over the next few years. During the summer of 1530, he drew the ideas together in a *Sermon: That Children Should Be Sent to School*. It serves as a good example of how far a "sermon" might depart from strictly religious issues.

The earlier admonition *To the Councilmen* had urged the education of boys and girls alike. Now Luther's emphasis goes to the community's dependence on the schools for leadership, and to the importance of the learned professions. The main obstacle, he finds, is the common man's preoccupation with material wealth. Therefore he dwells on the central argument, that arts and letters alone can assure the kind of stable society in which a businessman can survive and prosper. Luther is quite sensitive to the suspicion such talk may arouse.

"Aha," so you say, "how is that? Suppose it does not turn out so well, and my son becomes a heretic or some such varlet? We have heard of being 'mad with too much learning.'" Well, that is true, but it is just a risk you have to take. Your toil and tears will not be lost in any case. God will recognize your faithful effort, and count it the same as if your son had turned out well. You run the same risk whatever career he chooses.[13]

Not surprisingly, Luther recommends the cloth as the most rewarding profession. He calls attention to the number of livings available in German principalities—"What else are they than a kitchen and cellar already filled by God for your son, his sustenance prepared for him before he even needs it, or has earned it?"[14] We now read a strikingly modern statistical estimate as to the number of positions which must become available annually as a result of retirements.

Here is one of the rare occasions where Doctor Martinus even finds a gentle word for the law, which he commends as second in importance to the clergy. When he considers parents who would not even support their sons in training for this profession, the old fire flickers forth:

> You must be a crass, ungrateful bumpkin, and men should drive you out among the beasts, if you know your son can help the emperor maintain his empire, sword, and crown; help the prince to rule his land; advise cities and districts; help many a man guard his person, his wife, child, property, and honor; and you still will not make the investment necessary for his study and advancement . . . Ah, it is a shameful disrespect for God when we begrudge our children such fine, godly works, and plunge them instead into the service of the belly, and of avarice, let them learn nothing but to seek sustenance, just like a hog to root away in filth, and do not raise them up to that worthy estate and condition. We surely must be crazy, or we do not really love our children.[15]

But since learning is so very dear to Luther's heart, gentler strains return almost immediately, as he depicts the joys of reading, of discussions with the erudite, of travels into foreign lands, and the commerce thus opened. He fondly quotes Justinian to the effect that a proud nation must have the ornament not merely of arms, but of laws, and he extols the good sense of that remark.

But Luther had his middle-class audience too clearly in mind to rest his case on intangibles. Rather, he emphasized the posi-

tions available in the power structure for men of learning. Here
he fully merited that epithet of "German prophet," for he was
quite explicit about the rise of the bourgeoisie. We, with the advantage of hindsight, know he was right in saying they would
attain to power through education.

> Chancellors, city clerks, jurists, and the people in office have to
> make their voices heard, they must give advice, and help rule
> . . . They are the lords on earth, in fact, even though in per-
> son, birth, or estate they do not have that title . . . Who rules
> the land and its people in peacetime, when there is no war?
> Why, I say it is the quill.[16]

Here the temptation to digress became too great. Luther could
not refrain from a long excursion on the nobility of the pen. He
admitted the swashbucklers at court speak contemptuously of
"scribes,"

> but don't let that worry you. Those big fellows have to have
> their fun, too. Grant them their little pleasures, and go ahead
> and be a scribe, before God and the world. When they bluster
> and swagger, you will observe that they honor above all else
> the quill, placing one upon their hat or war helmet, thus to
> proclaim in very deed that the quill rules the world. Without
> it, they could neither perform their feats of arms nor live in
> peace, much less swashbuckle. So, you see where they elevate
> the tool of our trade, the sweet feather—and rightly so—while
> they hang their own implement, the sword, down around their
> loins. That is the right place for it. It would not fit their heads.
> Up there must flutter—the quill![17]

He contrasts the heroism of the pen with feats of the sword,
insisting that the former makes the greatest demands on the
body, especially "its best part (the head), the noblest member
(the tongue), and its highest accomplishment (language)."[18] The
prophetic, sociologically accurate element in this outburst is the
emphasis Luther places on the social mobility made possible by
the pen.

> Look around among all the royal courts, city councils and par-
> sonages . . . There you will find the jurists, doctors, council-

men, scribes, and preachers were in most cases poor, and in all cases schoolboys who have advanced themselves to their present heights by means of the quill.[19]

God, he asserts flatly, never intended the world to be ruled by the nobility alone. He cites his own case, in which a hard-working father "enabled me to get where I am, by the sweat of his brow."[20] (Hans Luther had died just a month or two earlier.) Luther concludes that he would not exchange his own condition now for that of a sultan.

So let your son go to the university. Perhaps he'll suffer want, for a time, but you will be providing our Lord with a sturdy piece of wood to carve an important man. And that is the way it will go on: your son and my son, the children of common people, will have to rule the world both in spiritual and temporal callings.

The wealthy can certainly not be relied on, for they are captive to Mammon, he says. By themselves, the nobility cannot even manage their temporal affairs, and in spiritual matters they are helpless. Therefore, the responsibility for both realms devolves upon "the poor, ordinary, common people, and on their children."[21]

As he came to the end of his tract, Luther felt himself inspired like an Old Testament prophet. He had a vision of a barren epoch when the gospel would be rejected by some, ignored by others, so that posterity "will neither support pastors and preachers, nor give anything to maintain them," when "young people will turn away and let these professions decline."

If that is the way it is to be in German lands, then I shall grieve that I was born a German or ever spoke or wrote German. And if I could defend it before my conscience I would aid and abet reinstatement of the pope with all his abominations, to press, shame, and waste us even more viciously than he did before.[22]

The Renaissance was indeed a calculating and materialistic age, and Luther concluded with some appropriate reproaches. A real Moses, he said, was needed to pray for Germany, for "I feel, when I try to pray for my dear German land, that my prayer bounces back and will not rise up, as it does when I pray for other things."[28] The powerful prayer of Doctor Luther was known, sought, and feared far and wide. He could be sure such black remarks would not fail of their effect. Can we therefore suspect him of calculated emotionalism in behalf of schooling? Well, perhaps. But it is also fair to remember that the lonely man at Coburg was a young father, with two children at home.

In these same days he sent off a letter to his firstborn, Hans, who had just celebrated his fourth birthday. Demonstrating as it does Luther's great fluency in native fairy-tale motif and metaphor, it is a fine way to close a chapter that began with animal tales.

Grace and peace in Christ, my beloved son:

I am happy to learn that you are studying hard and praying regularly. You do that, my son, and keep it up. When I come home, I'll bring you a fine fairing.

I know where there's a nice garden, pretty and merry. Lots of children go there. They wear golden dresses and gather apples from under the trees—pears too, cherries, berries, and plums. They sing and dance and have fun. They've got nice little ponies, too, with golden bridles and silver saddles.

So I said, "Nice man, I have a son myself, and his name is Hänschen Luther. Couldn't he come to your garden, too, so he could eat some of those good apples and pears, and ride those pretty ponies, and play with these children?"

Then the man said: "If he likes to pray, studies, and is good, why then he must come to the garden. Send Lippus and Jost, too [four-year-old sons of Melanchthon and Jonas]. And when they all come, there'll be flutes and drums, lutes and all kinds of fiddles. They can dance and shoot my little silver crossbows."

And he showed me a lovely lawn in the garden for dancing. And there were hanging all golden flutes and drums, and fine, silver crossbows. But it was still early. The children had not eaten yet. So I could not stay to see them dance.

I said to the man: "Oh, my dear fellow, I am going to go straight and write this to my dear son Hänschen, so he will get busy studying and praying and being good. Then he can come to the garden, too. But he has an Aunt Lena [Kate's aunt], she will have to come with him."

The man replied: "Then that is the way it shall be. Go and write that to him."

So, my dear son Hänschen, you study and pray as much as you like. And tell Lippus and Jost, so they will study and pray. Then every one of you will go to the garden. Now I leave you in God's care. Say hello to Aunt Lena and give her a kiss from me.

> Your loving father,
> Martinus Luther[24]

The German Machiavelli

The mature Luther was a churchman with an unswerving sense of mission. Reform meant to him preserving the teachings of his great predecessors. Had not faith by grace been the simple core of Christianity since the beginning? Paul, Augustine, even moderns like Gabriel Biel († 1495) had made this abundantly clear. Only those ignorant of the Bible and the fathers would find anything new in Luther, he was fond of saying. Yet there was a new element. No previous reform had occurred within a church so tightly intertwined with political and economic institutions. At an early point Luther had therefore been compelled to take a more comprehensive view of the church in society than had hitherto been attempted. He accomplished this, characteristically, in the process of writing.

His first political tract had taken the form of an address *To the Christian Nobility of the German Nation*. It was an attempt to disentangle the temporal affairs of Germany from the meshes of the Roman church establishment. In the same year, 1520, he followed this German work with one in Latin, for a scholarly and theological audience: *Concerning the Babylonian Captivity of the Church—A Prelude*. It was a clear and detailed statement of how the Roman bureaucracy had instituted practices and ceremonies which interfered with religion. This was where he reduced the sacraments back to those two connected directly with Christ and implying, so Luther argued, "promises" from God. The third great tract of the year 1520 was one he wrote both in German and in Latin (an exceptional solicitude, for Luther): *Concerning the Liberty of a Christian*. Here he struck that fundamental distinction between the inner man, by faith an

utterly free child of God, and the external man who is totally
subject to the powers of this world, during the brief sojourn
here. Widely circulated in Europe, this work became especially
well known in English translations. Its teaching eventuated, in
America, in the powerful doctrine of separation of church and
state.

Luther had drawn a somewhat similar conclusion himself. His
own formulation was the doctrine of "two realms," one temporal
and the other spiritual, which must on no account be permitted
to encroach on one another. His contemporaries had some
difficulty comprehending it, and he enunciated the teaching
many times over the years. To Luther it seemed obvious, perhaps
because of his debater's mentality, accustomed to operating with
clear opposites, but also because of the great influence of Frederick the Wise on his political understanding. During the somewhat threatening religious disputes around 1520, Frederick judiciously dodged involvement. He even succeeded in dissuading
young Emperor Charles V from sending him the Edict of
Worms, which outlawed Luther (1521). Luther admired Frederick enormously, and felt he owed the survival of his cause to
that prince's determination that religion be left to the theologians. In general, when considering Luther's political views, we
must remember that they took form under the benign and
deeply conscientious reign of the Saxon princes Frederick, his
brother John, who succeeded him (1525–32), and the latter's son
John Frederick, who looked to Luther as mentor.[1]

All conceived the state as God's agent in worldly affairs, and
counted theologians among their chief advisers. Thus Martin Luther, while he argued the strict exclusion of the church from
worldly rule, was himself deeply embroiled in both. That tract
of 1520 was but the first in a long series of publications on
strictly secular topics. Their drift was generally conservative. He
consistently excoriated any form of "mob" rule. He wrote repeatedly against interest charges, "usury." He opposed the peasants' uprisings in 1525, and he opposed the ensuing reprisals
against the peasants. He was originally against enlistment of German help in campaigns against the Turks, calling it a mere papal
ruse for extracting money. The Christians should set their own
house in order, he allowed, before flying off to foreign wars.

After the stinging defeat of imperial forces at Mohacz in 1528, followed by the Turkish siege of Vienna in 1529, he felt constrained to modify that earlier judgment, and claimed his objection had been based on his doctrine of the two realms: while the Turk ought to be opposed, the pope—as church leader—had no business raising the army. At table, he liked to tell the story of a certain bishop in Hungary who promised "supper in heaven with the Lord" to any Christian who might die in an impending battle with the Turks—but the bishop declined to take the risk himself, having vowed to fast that day.[2] The gibe is illustrative of Luther's political assumptions. He knew very well that expediency would always dictate worldly affairs. Yet his logical mind could conceive expediency only as the most effective means to some end in view—some animating vision. Expediency cut loose from faith struck him as an absurd joke.

This attitude consigned his finest political writing to oblivion. A new age of pragmatism in politics had already dawned in Italy. It would be reinforced from England as soon as Baconian science began to focus "serious" men's attention on tangible, measurable reality. Centuries would have to pass before ethical and moral referents could be reinstated as *sine qua non* either in science or in politics. The most important political tract of Luther's day is still assumed to be *The Prince*, by Niccolò Machiavelli. Luther's *Interpretation of Psalm 101* is an ideal companion piece to that more famous work. Although it is Martin Luther's best and most general political treatise, it is little known.

Niccolò Machiavelli (1469–1527) and Martin Luther (1483–1546) present an interesting contrast in Renaissance potential. Both men had a sardonic temperament; both loved vulgarisms, the one by way of showing his aristocratic contempt for piety, the other to express his contempt for the flesh. Both were brilliant minds, and each in his own way managed to acquire learning without falling into that frivolity and superficiality which was the intellectual vogue of the day. The thinking of each was characterized by commitment to the inexorability of logic: they followed where it led, regardless of the consequences. There the similarity ends.

Machiavelli was of aristocratic stock come upon hard times; Luther's parents had risen out of penury by dint of hard work.

Machiavelli followed precisely the kind of career Luther's father had envisaged for his son. Fourteen years Luther's senior, he was a respected counselor and diplomat in Florentine service while young Martin was still studying at Erfurt. Luther's agonizing over whether he should pursue the law and a worldly career occurred when Niccolò was already the observant envoy to Cesare Borgia, and conceiving a lifelong admiration for that tyrant's audacity and ruthlessness. While the younger man was a neophyte monk, the older was accompanying the warrior pope, Julius II, on successful military campaigns.

The young Luther's fortunes were good. He rose rapidly in the Augustinian order, was urged by his mentor, John Staupitz, to take the doctorate, and went on to become professor of the Bible. He delivered his first lectures on Psalms in 1513. Even while young Professor Luther stood there in the lecture hall, an imprisoned Machiavelli, his Florentine patron having been deposed, writhed upon the rack under torture. When released, he retired to his farm near San Casciano. He did not particularly enjoy writing, but in his enforced leisure the man of action nonetheless produced that masterpiece of Renaissance political theory and of calculating self-aggrandizement, *Il Principe* (1513). A classic espoused by virtually all seventeenth- and eighteenth-century autocrats, it has served as the handbook of *Realpolitik* right into modern times, for dictators and revolutionaries alike. Various attempts have been made to refute it, some by ruling princes like Frederick the Great, with his *Antimachiavell* (1759). They must fall short of the mark, simply because the Machiavellian assumptions have come more and more to be accepted by men in all walks of life since the Renaissance, including Machiavelli's would-be rebutters. Machiavelli's strictly secular view strips the power seeker of all pretensions to moral mission, heeds no divine calling. He draws the unavoidable political consequences for any ruler unfettered by religious scruples or uninspired by a transcendent vision, and he makes them explicit.

While *Il Principe* is a prince in the abstract, calculating his optimum strategy and tactics, the *Interpretation of Psalm 101* is advice to one particular prince, John Frederick, who had just acceded to the throne in 1532. It is not, strictly speaking, Luther's advice. The organization is not at all what Machiavelli might regard as systematic, i.e., in accord with the theory being propounded. Rather, it takes its structure from Psalm 101. Luther offers a verse by verse commentary (there are eight verses). Where, the author might seem to be asking, could one find a more appropriate form? Psalm 101 had been accepted throughout the Middle Ages as King David's own statement of his royal duties—modern scholarship, by the way, does not disagree. Hence Luther, in his translation of the Bible, entitled this psalm "The Princely Mirror."

The very form, in short, in which Luther embeds his political counsel already constitutes his fundamental premise: any political act is predicated on the ultimate sense and purpose it is presumed to serve. The form also states that Luther will find this sense in the ethical and moral tradition of Judeo-Christianity. At the same time, he would himself admit, I suspect, that the relationship which individual parts of this long treatise bear to the verse being "interpreted" at the moment may not always be apparent. The first verse, for example, "I will sing of mercy and judgment . . ." is found to contrast the inadequacy of human reason with the pompousness of one who would presume to give advice to a ruling prince. Such advisers think, "It is just as clear as seven and three make ten. That is right, the calculation . . . is correct. But in the real world God may melt the seven into one . . . and multiply the three into thirty." Luther claims (here and elsewhere) he is himself unfamiliar with goings-on at court, but he can imagine how it must be:

> There sits the king or the prince, wise and clever in his own right. He has grasped the matter by all five corners. Up comes the jerkist—pardon me, jurist—with his books and reveals an abundance of law all certain, clear, and infallible. Then comes an intellectual whose head is much too small for his grand intelligence and wisdom. His argument is so firmly based and profoundly rooted in natural law that the whole world could not overthrow it. When at last all chime together, the big bell in the church accompanies them . . . All the while, our Lord God has to sit above idle, and is not admitted into the counsel of the well informed. So, he just passes the time chatting with

Gabriel. He says, "What do you suppose those wise men are doing in the counsel chamber, that they do not draw us into their deliberations? They're probably going to build another tower in Babylon. Listen, Gabriel, go down there and take Isaiah with you. Read a private lesson to them through the window, and say: 'With seeing eyes ye shall see naught; with hearing ears ye shall hear naught; and with understanding heart comprehend naught. Take counsel with one another, and all will come to naught; speak the word, and it shall not stand.' "[3]

Luther hastens to make clear that he approves of due process, and is only spoofing the notion "that it is enough to be in the right, and that we are competent to see our good cause through." He explains that such self-righteousness and self-confidence violate the First Commandment.[4] Precisely when we think we are most in the right, that is when we should most fear the Lord, "who takes pleasure in spoiling the prettiest righteousness and in dashing our best causes."[5]

He could scarcely make it clearer that his "The Princely Mirror" is not going to offer any neat formula for government. That would be silly, for "the world is a sick creature. It is a furpiece with neither hide nor hair that is sound." Good men are rare and God sells them dear. True, we must have government, but we can expect no more than "pure patchwork and beggary. It's a true sickroom where princes, lords, and rulers want wisdom and courage . . . much as the sick want vitality and strength."[6] Even if reasoned strategies could be devised, they would plainly be counterproductive, for "all kings and princes, when they follow nature and its best wisdom, must needs oppose God and persecute his word."[7] If reason then is so inadequate—even inappropriate—in managing the affairs of the world, wherein does Luther's (or David's) advice to the prince consist?

As Luther regarded the situation of his own young prince, he saw the major problem to be that of coping with his officers of state, counselors, and courtiers. From private remarks, we know that Luther worried about their influence even while John Frederick's father was still alive.[8] Here he does not state flatly that they are the prince's enemies, but he does—twice—quote the margrave of Meissen to the effect that a ruler need not fear his distant foes, while the supporters who follow at his heel would really like to be treading upon his head.[9] We suspect Luther of having a better acquaintance of life at court than he admits. A prince, he says,

> rides upon great, extravagant stallions, who have to be filled with the best fodder. They want a long, free rein, and they will not suffer the spur. They like to move down the street sideways, kick up at the heels, shove and bite, all the while being much admired and feared beneath the saddle and livery of their lord. Finally, when the mood and mettle strike them, they will lay the lord himself upon the cobblestones.[10]

The utter dependence of the sovereign on his high-blooded aides, who are not really concerned about his best interests, but pursue their own, strikes Luther as the central problem of government. The prince is unable to see into their hearts, therefore he is in a real sense governing in the dark.

> He is as in a coach by night, which he must drive by intuition, often not knowing whither. When he thinks he wants to go gee, it goes haw—turns over, harness and wheels asunder.[11]

He must therefore be a truly heroic and patient man, looking to God for inspiration yet dealing quite cold-bloodedly with his advisers. In this context, Luther does recommend a kind of Machiavellian approach. The prince, he says,

> must in God's name despise and deploy useful, clever, competent people, who accomplish much good and are highly meritorious in kingdom and court, while they are at the same time godless, wicked knaves.[12]

This requires the "heart of a lion," but it is not the prince's heaviest burden. He must also accept and live with the fact that many a deserving servant will go unrewarded—or worse.

Nor can the prince expect any reward for himself. In solitude he patches the shabby, thankless furpiece here and there. Why is the body politic such a hopeless mass? Why, because so few people believe in God, and "to have no God is to believe neither this nor that, and to remain unaffected by any teaching or sermon that might occur in God's name."[13] Just as his complaints about scholarship in his time went back to "Erasmian" relativism, he confesses now that just such a supercilious attitude is widespread among the people. That leaves it up to the prince alone to try to steer a right course, despite self-seeking advisers. "Be David whoever can, and follow his example so far as you can, especially princes and lords who do have sufficient power and property."[14]

But David was after all a temporal ruler. How is it that Luther is setting him up as an example of godly conduct? Is that not a confusion of the "two realms"? Why, Luther replies, such a charge as that would be tantamount to objecting when he, a man of the church, offers such political counsel as he is now giving. He welcomes this opportunity to refine the doctrine of the two kingdoms, temporal and spiritual. One must not forget that while both are separate here below, they emanate from the one authority above. Therefore when the prince commands that God's word be obeyed, he is but acting as a servant of the word, "for toward God and in the service of his kingdom all men are equal, and there is no distinction, not between spiritual and temporal, pope and emperor, or between lord and servant."[15] Luther knows he has got onto some thin ice. He skirts the problem of how the prince, God's faithful servant who must also "teach and command" in accordance with the word, is to be sure he interprets the word aright. He does not say how his subjects (equal to him before God) are supposed to react if the prince should teach and command *against* God's word. Eventually, of course, Luther had to face up to such questions, but here he has John Frederick in mind, whom he knows to be staunch in the faith. He pursues the issue no further than reaffirmation of his teaching that the churches may not meddle in temporal affairs.

Marxist writers suspect Luther of conspiracy on this point, or at least of connivance at tyranny. It is difficult for the progressive mentality to believe that such conservatism as Luther's could be sincere. He simply did not believe he could take a political stand without jeopardizing the integrity of religion—and religion was clearly the more important, he argued, for where else would politics find sense and direction? "I sometimes think," he said, "that the government and the lawyers need a Luther, but I am afraid they might get a Müntzer." Thomas Müntzer was that revolutionary preacher who had drawn the political implications of all men's equality before God, and who is, as a consequence, much honored by Marxist historians. But Luther went on,

> For God does not think so much of his temporal realm as he does of his spiritual realm . . . So I would not advise that any changes be made. We just have to patch and darn as best we can while we live, punish the abuses and lay bandages and poultices over the sores.[16]

If Luther is not himself prepared to advise his prince in behalf of the poor, suffering people, and if he argues that the nobility and other counsel are quite selfish, why does he not allow that the people themselves be entrusted with their own welfare? Such a question might not be at all comprehended by Luther. By way of a rhetorical flourish, he raises the possibility that all might be equally endowed with knowledge and understanding—

> Why, then the fools, children, and women could govern and wage war just as well as David, Augustus, and Hannibal . . . Nay, all humans would be equal, and none rule over the other. What a revolution and chaos that would be! But God has arranged things so that men are unequal, and one shall govern the other, and obey the other.[17]

The man who had spread throughout the world the doctrine that all souls are equal before God (*Concerning the Liberty of a Christian*) rejected drawing political implications from it.

The prince must not look for approval, much less popularity among the "crazy mob." Luther reminds John Frederick of Alexander's remark, "Ah, when we do right and all men speak evil of us, we are being treated like a king." Luther interprets that as meaning "the royal virtue is too noble for the crazy mob to understand it, and too excellent to merit praise from useless people. Alexander learned that from his prophet, Homer."[18] This brings Luther to confess he cannot hold with that Greek heritage of free speech, but prefers the biblical admonition to punish those who speak ill of the prince. The topic of slander leads back into the central theme, the problem of a prince's immediate personal surroundings at court. Here the strongest admonitions, against flattery, against influence-mongering, seem in order. Luther feels that the fundamental political problem is one of moral character.

He was deeply impressed by the corrupting influence of power on those in office, *nam honores mutant mores*, he intoned once at table—"high office alters behavior, never for the better."[19] Here he uses another of his favorite sayings:

> There is no office so petty, but it merits hanging. Office in itself is divinely instituted, and it is good, be it the office of prince or that of his ministers. But those who occupy these offices are usually put there by the devil.[20]

Mankind, he stipulates, simply cannot bear up under any kind of good fortune. Hence it is next to impossible for anyone elevated into a position of authority, however petty, to use it well. Luther was quite sincere in his conviction that advancement corrupts, hence he distrusted the hereditary ruler less than functionaries who had been elevated to power.

The only sovereign, however, for whom he had unqualified praise was John Frederick's uncle, Frederick the Wise. He had never spoken to the old duke face-to-face, but had merely looked on while Frederick astutely avoided confrontation during the early conflict with Roman power, which seemed so dangerous for Luther. Frederick's shrewd tactics to protect him appeared all the more remarkable in retrospect, so that here seemed to be the ideal figure to hold up as a model for the nephew.

> I have heard Doctor Staupitz tell how Duke Frederick complained from time to time that the longer he reigned the less able he was to do so, because people had become so unpredictable. He no longer knew whom he could trust. I thought that was a strange saying, because I could not understand how the regime of a powerful and clever prince could suffer hindrance or interference.

But Frederick's saying was eventually confirmed by Luther's own efforts in governing the church. There he discovered that one must not blame individuals for being untrustworthy. The cause lies with God, who treats us all as one dough, makes of us what he will. Sometimes he gives wisdom and virtue to a nobleman more than to three princes, or more to a commoner than to six of the nobility.[21]

Luther clearly feels John Frederick to be most imperiled by his fellow noblemen in Saxony.

On this heading, the most delicate treated so far, Luther casts about for a yet higher authority than Frederick the Wise, and finds it in the most popular of emperors, Maximilian, "the last knight," who had died in recent memory (1519), to be succeeded by the Romish-minded Spaniard Charles V. According to Luther, Maximilian attributed the immense amount of hard work which the prince must personally invest in good government to the fact that the German nobility was unwilling or unable to perform well. This passage is of interest as a most severe commentary on the lamentable condition of the German nobility in the sixteenth century, even though Luther fails to make it entirely clear where Maximilian's opinions cease and his own begin—

> It may very well be that Maximilian recognized how they were not only unwilling, but incompetent as well. Not only after they come to court, but already in their youth the nobility debauch themselves with carousing, gaming, and churlishness, so that they grow up willfully unskilled, untamed, and inexperienced. It is not possible for them to produce many competent men—especially in the wine country.[22]

Now in the typical Luther combination of tenderness with the very grossest expressions, he deplores John Frederick's own greatest weakness:

> Every country just has to have its peculiar devil. Italy has one, so does France. Our German devil is surely a stout wineskin, and his name is Chugalug.[23]

"The Princely Mirror" reflects even the blemishes on John Frederick's own face.

Luther strives to conclude on a positive note. The Germans, he admits, do have one important virtue. When they lie, they are at least ashamed of it. They do not make a joke out of sincerity "like Italians and Greeks."[24] This, he urges, is no small matter, because good faith is of cardinal importance in the prince's dealings. Here at the end, Luther becomes quite personal. The last verse of Psalm 101 begins, "I will early destroy all the wicked out of the land." Luther stresses the word "early," for John Frederick is just beginning his reign. He must avoid all bad faith from the outset. The "wicked" are interpreted as the untrustworthy: "Right now certain Italian virtues are taking hold in Germany, especially in government."[25] The prince must pull out the weeds before they can take root, kill the caterpillars before the good leaves are consumed.

He returns to David at last, to show how miserable even the best of reigns must be. He details all the crimes and tribulations, then scoffs,

> Now, sweet David, come ahead and boast of your good government, and praise God for it. Why, the government of that wretched Herod can scarcely have been worse![26]

While David deserved no personal satisfaction as king, God was satisfied with David—

> If he suffered many misfortunes, then that was because he ruled well and sincerely. If he sinned, well, he did not defend his sins, the way Saul and other kings do, but he gave them up and desisted.[27]

Viewed from a modern vantage, Machiavelli and Luther certainly do share certain views. Neither of these Renaissance minds, for example, anticipated our democratic ideal of government for the people. Even Luther, while benign as compared with the Florentine, does not hold up before John Frederick any obligations toward his Saxon subjects. It is they who owe duties to their lord. The Renaissance political problem was not conceived as concerning the people at all, but the prince. In Luther's favor we might note that he expects no benefits to accrue *to* the prince, only trials. But he explicitly removes himself from the likes of a Thomas Müntzer, who would draw from government some material benefits for the governed.

One might also argue that the people stand to gain at least indirectly from the high calling Luther envisages for the prince.

His insistence that the temporal power is subject to God inescapably imposes Christian ethics on a ruler—and the "crazy mob" was clearly, in his view, incapable of looking after its own long-range interests. But it would be improper to seek to defend Luther's views. His final paragraph begins, in typical insolence:

> Here I close. I hope it is good. By "good," I mean pleasing to few and sorely vexing to many . . . If it pleases everyone, it is surely a wicked, shameful piece of work I have done.[28]

Satire

> I'll just begin by talking about myself, and I'll make a little
> confession to you holy fathers—it won't hurt you to absolve
> me of my sins. Not long ago I awoke at midnight, for the
> devil had challenged me to a debate in my heart (ah, he knows
> how to render many a night bitter and sleepless).[1]

Thus Luther begins that treatise on "the very heart of the Christian faith," the mass.[2] It is also a fine piece of satirical writing which holds special interest for Luther biography. The early notes survive to show how the author's thoughts developed in the process of writing. The work began as an objection to the priesthood, but before it was finished it had become a statement *Against the Private Mass*. As such it eventually had a positive influence on the Roman church (which today disavows the private mass).

Luther regarded the priesthood (which he called an innovation by Pope Gregory I) as an intrusion on the direct relationship between God and man. He had long objected to the priest's role, especially in administering holy communion or, as the reformers preferred to say, the Lord's Supper.[3] That was the direction his thoughts were taking as he began organizing them on paper in 1533. He speculated that, since the ordination of priests is not a divine (biblical) institution, but a design by man, then actually anyone *not* anointed must be *more* competent to perform the sacraments than someone sullied by the chrism. Pleased by this paradox, Luther shifted from his usual Latin to growl, "You cake consecrators, eat crud and cake."[4] Buoyed now by insolence, he wondered whether priests are so debased that consecration cannot occur under their hands at all (so that the bread and wine would not even be the body and blood of Christ), but he did not pursue the point—"Let them answer for that."[5]

That was a typical debater's ploy. Although Luther did not himself doubt the real presence of Christ in the Eucharist, he had come upon a useful question to raise as devil's advocate. Answering it would compel an adversary to affirm the purely spiritual quality of the priesthood. If it were spiritual, could it not be shared by any believer? In order to appreciate how diabolical he felt he was being to impugn the validity of the sacrament we must remember that this was precisely the issue with the Anabaptists and the Zwinglians. They questioned the real presence of Christ in the bread and wine of the Lord's Supper, and Luther opposed them more bitterly than he did even the papists.

In a later set of notes he came back to his mischievous suggestion again. He confirmed the presence of Christ in the bread and wine, writing that even an unbelieving priest cannot harm what Christ himself instituted. But is he a priest at all, he asked. Since the papal church is wicked, does that not invalidate the priest's vocation? He worked out his problems on paper by means of questions and answers. Beginning with Paul in 2 Thessalonians 2:4, he came to the question,

> What if I am created a priest under the rule of the pope—am I still a priest? I answer that I am, because although I may be a servant of the Antichrist, I am still in the church.[6]

He tried various attacks and various defenses (it was a problem he knew well from Saint Augustine, who had tackled it as the Donatist heresy more than a thousand years earlier) but in every case found that the church was a guarantor of the sacrament's integrity—

> Therefore, to sum up, you cannot avoid finally saying: I did not institute the sacrament. God did. There is no other logical conclusion. Now, that means: since it derives from God, it is correct.[7]

How might the devil's advocate attack that conclusion, he wondered.

A third set of notes, the lengthiest, finally took on the form of a little drama, a debate. Luther began by setting down the proposition,

> It is *not* a sacrament.
> Here the rejoinder is possible: oh, yes it is, because the priest is called to this office and anointed by his bishop. Also, another answer would be: he is acting in good faith.
> Here one can argue: simple vocation is not enough. Among the Turks, too, they are called to their holy works.
> But that is different!
> I answer: even if both doer and deed differ, the fact remains that both are godless. And the godlessness is greater among Christian priests, because they are wickedly and godlessly defiling a divine institution—and the Turks aren't.[8]

Luther had made progress while writing. He was no longer treating the general issue of priesthood, but had drawn his bead on the priest's function at mass. He was testing his assumption that the sacrament itself, divinely ordained, must remain valid however wicked the participants. Involved in a phantom debate, he had been drawn into the first person, "*I* answer." As the exchange became hotter, he designated one side "the argument of the devil," presenting it, too, in the first person.[9] He had been touched by the dramatic muse, sincerely articulating two opposing, but logically coherent viewpoints. The words he finally set down to introduce the exchange were probably quite true: "Not long ago I awoke at midnight, for the devil had challenged me to a debate in my heart."

His finished pamphlet made the midnight debate famous throughout Germany and (in Latin translation) all Europe. The devil preens himself as a polished academician and begins thus:

> I submit, my learned colleague, that you will recall having conducted private masses for fifteen years. And I ask you to suppose those masses to have been pure idolatry, to suppose that you, far from revering Christ's body and blood, were in fact worshiping mere bread and wine, and teaching others to do the same.
> But I am an ordained priest [Luther replied]! I received or-

dination and blessing from the bishop! Besides, I act in sincere
obedience to orders. How can you impugn my blessing? I
spoke the words sincerely and performed mass with all possible devotion. You know that to be a fact.

Yes, he said, that is true. But the Turks and the heathens in
their churches also act in sincere obedience to orders . . . Let
us suppose your ordination, anointment, and blessing were just
as un-Christian and false as the Turk's.

At this, I really broke out in a sweat. My heart fluttered and
throbbed.[10]

Luther describes the overwhelming power of the devil's logic,
the incredible celerity of charge and countercharge. Compelled
both by conscience and desire to defend the priesthood, he
found no escape from the grueling debate. We can be sure we
are getting the true account of a genuine midnight encounter, as
well as an accurate example of how the academic arts were practiced at the University of Wittenberg.

The devil feigns sympathy with the poor priest's lack of faith.
He tells sadly how all the devils firmly believe the Epistle of
James, how Christ was born, died, and ascended into heaven,

but none of us takes comfort and hope in him as our own savior. We fear him as our austere judge. This, and no other, was
your faith when you were ordained to perform mass . . . That
is why all of you turned from Christ to Mary and the saints.
You needed comfort and succor against Christ.[11]

Luther's notes had left the sacrament untainted, regardless of the
wrongheadedness of the priest. But the devil knows no such
compunctions. Christ instituted a *sharing* of the Lord's Supper,
he charges, and reproaches Luther with having ministered private masses: "What kind of a priest were you, ordained as a servant unto yourself and not to the church? Christ had no part in
your kind of ordination, that's for sure." Christ's apostles were
preachers, but there is no preaching at the private mass, he
gloats. "You just whisper to yourself. Was that Christ's intention? Is that being a good priest?"[12]

What began as a clever literary device yields to an overwhelming diabolic presence. The dialogue gets lost, its author

becoming so wrapped up in his polemic that he forgets considerations of literary form. The devil and Martin Luther merge into one personality carrying on a written argument, no longer with one another, but with the reader. Instead of waiting for the poor intimidated priest to answer, the devil speaks for him, and then answers himself, e.g.,

> Here you will say: although I do not give the sacrament to the church, I do give it to myself. There are many who take a sacrament, let us say baptism, who are not believers. Yet it remains the true sacrament of baptism. So why should not my mass contain the true sacrament? Ah, my dear fellow, that is not the same thing. In baptism there are always two people present.[13]

The work has lost the tension of drama. The witching hour has passed, and the devil has faded into the shadows. What began as an exciting literary gem has flattened into just another polemic. Why?

Luther is too involved in his subject matter to meet the demands of art. He freely admits he cannot keep his distance—

> Here's where the holy papists will mock me and say: are you the great doctor and cannot refute the devil? Don't you know he is a liar?
>
> Thanks a million, my lords, for your comforting absolution and rebuttal. I'd never have guessed the devil is a liar if you hadn't told me so.

The devil hones his lies with the truth, so that no human is a match for him, and no defense is possible. Luther cites the example of Judas and concludes,

> No, my brother, the devil is not lying when he holds our undeniable wicked deeds up before us. He has two witnesses on his side whom none can impugn: God's commandment, and our own conscience. I cannot say no to them. But if I say yes, then death and the devil have me.[14]

This is why the devil as debater has disappeared. It is Luther speaking for mankind in general when he lashes out at the private mass:

What kind of a carnival is that? It's thievery! The body and blood of Christ, which is properly mine, to be freely received, is taken from me, and then I am given back a godless, wretched, man-made sacrifice, for money. Why, that is the same as to take my food and sell it back to me as shit. It's the same as to steal the kingdom of heaven from me, and in return for my money to sell me hellfire. I already had that in the first place, had earned it without paying.[15]

Luther is too intense. Satire requires detachment. Convinced as he is of the priesthood of all believers, he simply cannot abide a priestly elite which imagines itself

a far, far higher and holier estate than that given by baptism. A priest ordained with chrism is, when compared with a common, baptized Christian, as the morning star to a smoking lampwick. Baptism . . . but a dirty lantern compared with the sun.[16]

Thus what had its beginnings in fine satire trails off into bitter sarcasm.

True satire may draw upon bitterness, but its effect must be merry, as the animal tales of which Luther was master. In 1534, he wrote at least two successful parodies on official Renaissance epistolary style. One was never published, but placed into the hands of that lazy old amanuensis, Wolf Seberger. Luther claimed it was one of the many pleas for intercession constantly coming to him. It began,

To our dear gracious lord, Doctor Martinus Luther,
Preacher in Wittenberg:
We thrushes, blackbirds, linnets, goldfinches, and other God-fearing, honorable birds desirous of journeying through Wittenberg this fall do herewith make known to your reverence how we have it on good report that one certain Wolfgang Seberger, in your employ, has committed a great, licentious arrogation, buying at a dear price a few ancient, worn-out nets, in wrath and hate against us to devise a bird trap, thereby not merely undertaking to deprive our dear friends and finches of the God-given freedom to fly the air and to pick little grains

from the earth, but also endangering life and limb, though we have incurred no guilt, nor do we in any way deserve of him such grave and malicious usurpation . . .[17]

So the letter continues, indulging in Rabelaisian abundance of animal and insect names, quoting the Bible, and aping stuffy chancellery usage.

In the same year Luther also tried out the style of papal bulls.[18] Pope Clement had in March postponed the calling of a council again. This dereliction, so we learn from a broadside, has now come to the attention of a higher instance,

THE HOLY GHOST, LORD OF HOSTS,
MASTER AND GOVERNOR
OF
THE HOLY CATHOLIC CHURCH

To our ears hath come the constant and grievous outcry from our many beloved children throughout our church, to the effect that a certain fellow, Pope Clement by name, who without our knowledge or authority and solely by his own presumption hath usurped the governance of our church by means of simony, perversion, and purchase of votes, much to the injury and contumely of God vaunting himself as God's vicar on earth and as head of our catholic church,

Who, together with his cardinals and bishops, so-called prelates in our church, continueth in godless teachings and multiple enormities of his wicked life to inflict numerous grave outrages upon the good and pious souls in Christ, to the peril of their salvation, and as it grieveth us to learn . . .

The subordinate clauses roll inexorably on, one after another, finally to aver that this certain Clement has

not only tergiversated shamefully, but haughtily and impudently refuseth to incline his ear to urgent prayers from so many of our children, fearing correction and reform of the enormities and evils perpetrated by him and his accomplices, preferring that our entire church perish before he permit interference with their wickedness and evil,

NOW THEREFORE, we who in our accustomed clemency have tolerated all these enormities long enough, giving him ample opportunity for repentence and indulging him for the sake of his salvation, while deferring the continual outcry from our children, mindful of Solomon's admonition that a servant delicately handled will grow defiant . . .

After puffing up this clause until it matches the ones that went before, the Holy Ghost at last solemnly convokes a church council on his own. At this point it is revealed how the heavenly regime resembles Rome not only in its chancellery style, but also in its minions and subalterns jealous of their authority:

AND I, Archangel Gabriel, by divine authority appointed notary general and legate at the throne of God, having been present while all the aforementioned was accomplished, stated, and commanded, have drawn up the present document, requiring that it be faithfully copied by the hand of my subordinate, inscribed with my name and seal, witnessed by the blessed Lord Michael, Provost of Paradise, and by Raphael, God's Physician, together with many other blessed angels of God, all trustworthy, specially summoned and appointed for this purpose.[19]

Clement's successor, Paul III, rekindled general hopes for a council in May of 1536 by actually convoking it (abortively) for the subsequent year in Mantua (just as Vergerio had predicted). Luther released a broadside where this time not Gabriel in Latin, but Beelzebub in German expressed his concern that hell's own "loyal regent and counselors," the pope and his cardinals, may have fallen into "the Galilean, or Lutheran" heresy. Nevertheless, the demon assured the curia of his good will and trust, using the charming condescension of a Renaissance prince. This missive from hell to the Roman church gave assurance—

Our faithful legate Belial, reporting to us from the field, makes known that you are not at all serious with this reformation, and he confirms our long-standing gracious confidence in you to bamboozle the kings of the world and to cajole the Germans into eating horse apples for figs.[20]

About this same time, Luther's apprehension that the council, now called, would treat little but trivia gave rise to another brief satire. Although perhaps his best, it is not easily understandable today because it deals in terms of a somewhat low-class Renaissance card game called in German *Karnöffel* (=a swollen testicle caused by hernia).

The cards bore the names of various estates—citizens, peasants, popes, emperors, and so forth. The game represented a topsy-turvy world where the lower rank was the higher card, with the exception of the *Karnöffel* himself, who led a charmed life. Needless to say, the game turns up in the literature of the age as a favorite analogy to society at large. For Luther it had the added advantage of sounding just a bit like the religious order of the Carthusians, so he entitled this broadside *A Question from the Assembled Holy Order of the Cardsharks of Karnöffel, Addressed to the Council of Mantua*. It began,

> Having learned, O most holy father, how your holiness has made all preparations for the council by reforming the court at Rome, converting all the Romans, providing for all the churches everywhere, and driving out all the heresies, the Lutheran in particular, so that there is nothing left to do, we, in concern that your holiness have some business for the council, and lest you gather together for naught, do present this magnificent, supremely important question of great consequence for the entire world. Much great danger, homicide, bloodshed, violence, and injustice may be avoided if only serious attention can be given to this most urgent question— namely: why the *Karnöffel* takes the emperor and the pope, too, since he is after all, in the opinion of the most judicious, nothing but a common soldier, while the jack is a knight, the emperor an emperor, and the pope a pope?[21]

Now the argument becomes complex. Luther's detailed command of cardplayers' jargon dignifies his inquiries with that appearance of weightiness which has ever attached to scholarly prose, while a plodding style provides the final polish. Intricacies of the game permit constant digs at the curia, but the main point is of course that *Karnöffel* represents the level at which the council is sure to operate unless its organizers include central issues of church doctrine on the agenda.

Luther remained a satirist almost until the end. In 1542, he heard that the cardinal of Mainz was displaying some new relics. For his part, he published a little travesty entitled *News from the Rhine*, touting the following items:

1. A good piece of Moses' left horn.
2. Three flames from the burning bush upon Mount Sinai.
3. Two feathers and one egg from the Holy Ghost.
4. An entire corner of that banner with which Christ harrowed hell.
5. Also, one long hair from the beard of Beelzebub, as it clung to the above.
6. Half a wing from Saint Gabriel, the Archangel.
7. One full pound of the wind that passed by Samuel in the cave on Mount Sinai.
8. Two yards of the voice of the trumpet on Mount Sinai.
9. Thirty shakes of Miriam's timbrel heard at the Red Sea.
10. A big heavy chunk of the shout with which the children of Israel brought down the walls of Jericho.
11. Five fine bright chords from David's harp.
12. Three lovely locks of Absalom's hair, by which his head caught hold of the oak.[22]

From a literary point of view, these shorter squibs dealing with the proposed council and with the externalities of Roman worship were superior to the more gripping debate with the devil on the subject of private masses. The reason is obvious: in the later, shorter works, he was able to maintain his detached, sardonic posture. On the mass he had become too fervent to maintain irony for long. Furthermore, the devil himself was more than just a literary device for Luther. We recognize genuine experience in passages like the following:

In my fear and distress I tried to dismiss the devil with the old formulae, but he rebutted them with, "Tell me, my friend, where do you find that in the Bible? . . . where did God teach or command it? . . . If it is only man who teaches it, without God's word, then it is all a lie, and you are just tomcatting around in the name of the church."[23]

Modern Lutherans anxiously stress that the devil was no more than a literary adornment for this satirical piece.[24] It is a question which the reader should judge for himself as we proceed.

We have in any case seen how Doctor Luther was called upon to help people who felt themselves under assault by the very devil, like Master Peter the Barber (for whom *A Simple Way to Pray* was written). Just in the summer before Vergerio's visit, Peter stabbed his son-in-law to death. Perhaps they were drunk, but the son-in-law had boasted widely that he was charmed against knives. What was to be done with Peter? Renaissance society did not provide for incarceration of criminals except on a temporary basis, pending determination of guilt. There was no question Peter had done the deed, and the penalty for killing was death. But surely it was the devil had duped him, perhaps even guided his hand. Luther and others intervened for the old fellow, who was merely banished, taking refuge with friends in nearby Dessau.

Paralipomena

I wrote it after dining—but a Christian can speak better inebriated than a papist can sober.

I don't want my books published, especially the early writings. I'd rather they be destroyed. All the church is being filled with books. The Bible is being neglected. Many of Augustine's works don't amount to anything. The same is true of all Jerome's works, save his histories—and they could be collected on four quarto sheets. The world is vain, always wants something new and neglects the good. The bookstores draw a profit, and my example is used by others: everybody wants to write because Luther did.

If the peasants knew the subjects of our scholarship, they'd hoot us and hiss us.

The world can suffer no rulers but tyrants, nor ought it have any other. In the world, tyrants are called great men. That is just as it should be: let the flogged miscreant call his tormentor father.

Mere arithmetic is preposterous. If I were to drink as much as the elector [John Frederick], I'd drown. If he drank as much as I, he'd die of thirst.

Outright impious, blasphemous Sodomites, who want to reform the church in outward ceremony and usage! Until the teachings are reformed, the reform of practice is vain, for superstition and false piety are revealed only by the word and by faith. Piety is

of two sorts, substantial and incidental. Saint Francis was substantially, essentially pious by his faith in Jesus Christ, but then
he became enamored of incidental piety in the monk's cassock.
The cassock is non-essential, only incidental to piety . . . Ah,
dear Lord, shall we get to heaven by our clothing when this
flesh, hide and hair as they are, cannot get in? We need no cowl
and cord. We have plenty of cowls and orders right here in our
estates and callings: the preacher in his teaching, the magistrate
in his administration, the schoolmaster in his learning, the student
in his studies, the head of household in his affairs, the manser-
vants and maidservants in their chores. The Lord has filled the
whole world with this kind of cowl and orders, if we will but
don them. My cowl has more than 100,000 wrinkles in it.

THREE

CONTENDER

The Omnipresence
of God

The most serious weakness among the reformers, when one contemplated their prospects at the anticipated general church council, was the stigma attached to them as "protesters." If a splinter group themselves, were they not vulnerable to further defections? Luther had early been warned that his flouting of papal supremacy must eventually undermine all authority. Sure enough, proliferation of sects became a major plague of the 1520s. Vergerio had not failed, immediately upon being introduced at the castle, to thump upon this sore. Asked how his trip had been, he said he had been assaulted by rabid sectarians near Halle.

The confidence Luther exhibited on that occasion, and his eagerness to attend the council wherever the pope might convoke it, arose from his current correspondence with the most powerful of the sectarians, those in the wealthy cities of the German southwest. In the summer of 1535, emissaries from Augsburg had appeared in Wittenberg. Just shortly before Vergerio's arrival in the fall, Luther had dispatched letters to other south German cities proposing a high-level meeting. The nuncio had not long departed before another batch of assurances went off, in which Luther stressed the great personal satisfaction he would take in unity. He was at that time of life, he said, when all our duties have been discharged, and he felt exhausted by the trials. "Nothing lies so near my heart as the establishment of concord, insofar as possible, before my final sleep."[1]

Thus Vergerio had come upon him right in the midst of a project which held out great promise for agreement not only among protestants, but throughout the entire church. To appreciate the magnitude of the undertaking, we must remember that this was an age when not science, but the church expressed man's ultimate understanding of the world and his own destiny. Well might Luther rail at the papists' concern with mere ceremony, for the sense of his reform was renewal of the central teachings and symbols by which men lived. When dealing with fellow protestants, he was equally uncompromising in holding them to traditional interpretations.

The original bone of contention with the papal regime had been its commercialization of papal indulgences. In characteristic debater's posture, Luther had submitted that mortals cannot *do* anything whatsoever to deserve God's free gift of mercy, much less could a pope sell it to them. The papal response might have been reasoned argument, for the indulgence had a long history, but we have seen how Sylvester Prierias preferred to invoke absolute authority for the pope himself.

It was therefore not very surprising when many held with Luther, or when others went considerably further. Certain south Germans had long held notions more radical than his. Where Luther was interested in reforming the church for the sake of preserving its ancient sacred character, they hoped the movement might make the institution more appealing to human reason, in line with humanistic trends of recent decades. Luther was just scandalized to read how Ulrich Zwingli, the militant Swiss protestant and humanist, granted salvation even to eminent non-Christians of antiquity like Cato and Socrates. This south German tendency to elevate the intellect and Luther's profound distrust of human reason were bound to collide. The conflict did come on the central doctrines of the church: the sacraments and their nature.[2]

Under the papacy, sacraments were themselves good works which sanctified human life at each important station along its way: baptism, confirmation, penance, holy communion, matrimony or (alternatively) orders, and extreme unction. Luther allowed only two of these ceremonies to rank as immediate promises from God to his faithful: baptism and holy communion. But the more extreme protestants called even these remaining two "outward signs" only. The Anabaptists, for example, not comprehending how infant baptism could relate to the all-important inner change of being "born again," required *re*baptism. Widespread among the peasantry, Anabaptism was universally persecuted. The sect had become notorious when, in the summer of 1535, a group deposed the bishop of Münster and established a communal "Kingdom of Zion" for a short time in that city. When told free love was being practiced there, Luther said it was "clear as day: the devils are squatting one on top of the other like toads."[3] He had long since given up hope for such rabble.

At issue with the powerful protestant cities in southwest Germany was the nature of holy communion or, as they preferred to call it, the Lord's Supper. The enlightened Zwingli found something truly repulsive in the thought of eating Christ's body and drinking down his blood—cannibalism, he called it. Plainly, he said, Christ could not be in two places at one time, "at the right hand of the father" in heaven *and* in the bread and wine. These were merely tokens by which we "remember" our Lord. Such talk struck Luther as simply obtuse. Philip of Hesse, a prince who drew the political implications of the religious differences, called a conference in 1529 at Marburg, hoping the sides could agree. This was where Luther dramatically wrote down with chalk upon the table before him Christ's words, *hoc est corpus meum*, "This is my body," and ceremoniously laid a satin cloth over them. To Zwingli's exasperation, he punctuated later discussion by removing the cloth with a flourish, thus emphasizing how he clung to the text. When the two sides parted, neither willing to yield, Zwingli cried out in tears, "There are no people on earth with whom I would rather be at one than the Wittenbergers," but Luther affirmed, "Ye have another spirit than ours."[4]

Clearly, there was more at stake here than may meet a modern eye, accustomed to gazing confidently upon a tangible world. Both Luther and Zwingli accepted the palpability of material things, of course. But each peered on beyond such uncertain phenomena toward a surer reality in the spirit, and on past fleeting human life toward its source and larger frame, which their age took to be God. For Luther, the sacraments of baptism and the Lord's Supper were points where the mortal sphere does touch the divine, and opens to it. The ultimate ground of reality was at any time accessible to a Christian at the Lord's Supper.

He recognized that proliferation of the sacraments over the centuries had trivialized them until in his own age commercialization was able to debase them. With Zwingli, Luther also condemned the inroads of superstition and the doctrine of transubstantiation, whereby the priest was assumed to work a change in the elements. We have heard his biting satire on the private mass. Yet Martin Luther remained a stout defender of the real presence of God in body and blood at the Christian altar.

Papist corruption, he believed, bad as it was, could still be reformed if the reform itself were not to be undermined. This was the virulent threat of these ultra-rationalists of the southwest who claimed that God was not present in the "outward signs" of the Lord's Supper at all.[5] It was a view widespread among humanists, several of whom had become important leaders of the church in those regions. Wolfgang Capito of Strasbourg had been denying the real presence since 1512, long before the Lutheran issue arose. Capito's friend in Switzerland, John Oecolampadius, had gone so far as to aver that the words "This is my body" were a figure of speech!

Luther accepted the Lord's Supper as a symbol—but does not every symbol contain that which it symbolizes?

I pick up a wooden or a silver rose and ask: what is this? You answer: it is a rose. For I did not ask about its meaning, but about its being, so you told me what it was, not what it signified . . . "Is" always has to do with being. There is no other way to take it. But you say: it is not a rose, it is a piece of wood. Well, I answer, all right. But it is still a rose. Even if it is not a natural, organic rose out of my garden, it is still essentially a rose, in its own way. There are lots of roses—silver ones, gold ones, cloth, paper, stone, wooden. Nonetheless, each is in its own way, and essentially, a rose in its being. Not just a mere sign. Why, how could there be any *signifying* unless there were first a *being?* Whatever *is* nothing *signifies* nothing. Whatever signifies first has to be, and to be like that other thing.[6]

This difference between Luther and the rationalist in his own age continues to separate his approach from rationalism today. Linguistic science, for example, is committed to the concept of signs as things discrete from what they signify: precisely that distinction which Luther clearly illustrates with the rose—in order to reject it. But the division at Marburg was not over semantics. It went far beyond the nature of signs and symbols, beyond even the nature of the elements in the Lord's Supper.

At issue was the very substance of the outer world. Luther held to the mainstream of Christian thinking since its early epochs, in his confidence that God was close by. Jesus Christ, as God-man, was the realization of *the* essential quality of Luther's universe. The Lord's Supper was, for him, the ever present vouchsafe of reality, where heaven and flesh are joined. Christianity was the myth which enabled Luther to make sense of the world.

By "myth," I do not mean a fiction, of course, but rather the symbolic expression of a culture's most important insights, which can be expressed in no other way. Each individual soon learns from his own experience that man's conscious intellect is not always equal to the task of formulating even day-to-day problems. We draw on the mind's hidden ability also to form images and symbols, creating its own beauty where else there were chaos. Perhaps I would be going too far if I said we solve many of our problems while we are asleep, but we do regularly find conceptualization of them in dream imagery. Similarly, the really large questions, the imponderables for collective humanity, are quite beyond merely cognitive faculties, and take form as myths.

What, for example, is the relationship of humankind to its natural environment? It has given rise to some of our most beautiful myths. The scientific myth perceives nature not as capricious (as some myths do), certainly not as vicious or vindictive, but rather as a docile servant to her master, the intellect of man. The scientist's controlled experiments are held to be repeatable, documented experience reliable, and the future therefore absolutely predictable—in principle, at least. He who imagines nature to be intractable, in principle inscrutable, deceitful, or vengeful is unsuited to live rationally in the world of scientific myth. He would be—to borrow the word from church history—a heretic.

Just such a heresy confronted Christianity in its early centuries of growth in the Near East. Certain new converts conceived the true God as quite outside our world, leaving it a totally wicked place. The followers of Mani had been widespread in ancient Persia, the Manichaeans. Mani taught two principles: the light and the darkness. Existence was a struggle by the light to escape darkness. The world where we are is utterly dark, our souls alone holding to some faint glimmerings, still struggling to be free. Eventually these must also join the true God, who is far removed from our dismal world, which he did not create. As a Christian heresy, Manichaeism did not accept the creator Jehovah of the Old Testament as being that true, ultimate God. Nor was he the father of Christ. According to the Manichaean heresy Christ was a pure emanation from the true deity, and in no way human. He but dissembled a mortal exterior (Jesus) for our sake.

Like the early church fathers who rejected Manichaeism, Luther treasured the humanity of Christ as the essential guarantee for the integrity of creation. He understood Christianity as a holistic myth which suffered no split between God and nature, or between God and man. He frequently referred to the Manichaean error, and when Oecolampadius, at Marburg, begged him not to cling so fervently to the humanity of Christ, not to hang upon the flesh, but to elevate his mind to Christ's divinity, Luther burst forth, "I know of no God except the one who became man, and I want none other!"[7]

In Luther's logical brain, Manichaeism was not really different from its opposite, Arianism, which perceived Christ as mere man —or, for that matter, from Judaism. All missed the essential point of religion as nexus between man and an otherwise quite inaccessible, incomprehensible God. "God has no greater wrath than silence," he said once full of awe, "like that imposed on the Jews today . . . They cry out so vehemently and pray so ardently—I'd give goblets worth 200 fl. [fl.=gulden] if I could pray as they do! I wonder that God will not hear them." At last he folded his hands and prayed, "O heavenly father, let us stand by the son and let us not fall away from his word."[8] To Luther's mind, Christ was the vital connection which religion must provide, and the Lord's Supper its festive symbol. "The father is too sublime," he recalled Staupitz telling him, "so he said, 'I shall give you a way of coming to me, namely, Christ. Believe in him, hang upon Christ, then you will find out who I am, in good time.' "[9]

Through Christ, Luther's was a universe permeated with God. Just as he recognized the "essence" of the rose even in a wooden replica, he greeted God in every particle. He would not hear of a remote God—

> No sir, wherever you put God, there you must also place humankind. They cannot be cut apart and separated from one another. There came one being, from which humanity cannot be peeled off the way your ordinary citizen removes his jacket and lays it aside at bedtime. I'll give you a rough analogy, for the simple folk. Humanity is more closely joined with God than is our skin with the flesh, even than are body and soul . . . There is no spot, no space where the soul might reside without the body, like a shelled nut or flesh without skin or a pea out of the pod. Where the one is, the other has to be, as well. You cannot peel divinity off humanity and put it out there somewhere, where there are no humans.[10]

Here the issue of the Lord's Supper brought Luther to express the unique sense of Christianity as he understood it. He denied he was merely puffing up the idea of humanity until it appeared to touch the divine, for God was not some object, he said, with known dimensions which could be approached in that way, "but an imponderable essence beyond nature, entirely contained within every granule at all times, yet also above and outside all creation."[11] Such a concept of God was what the Lord's Supper meant—no: it was what the Lord's Supper *is:*

> If Christ was able to suffer and die on earth while at the same time he was a part of the godhead, one with God, well then, what is to prevent his suffering on earth today, even though he is in heaven? . . . Now, what if I should not only say that Christ was in heaven while walking upon the earth, but that

the apostles were, too—and all of us, even while we are mortal on earth, just as long as we have faith in Christ? Wouldn't that stir up a tempest in Zwingli's bag of tricks?[12]

This had been Luther's attitude when he and Zwingli disagreed in 1529 at Marburg.

The real presence of Christ in the Lord's Supper had then become one of the most important of the articles of faith in the Augsburg Confession, read before the assembled estates at the Diet of Augsburg in 1530. It was the article on the Lord's Supper which the Zwinglians found unacceptable. The principal author of the Augsburg Confession, Philip Melanchthon, had aimed at a centrist position, between Rome and the more extreme protestants. While his document pleased many on both sides as a summation of the Christian faith, he naturally offended others at the far ends of the spectrum. On the one hand, the emperor commissioned a refutation of the Augsburg Confession; on the other hand, four south German cities drew up their own articles, called the Tetrapolitan Confession because four cities subscribed to it instead of to Melanchthon's product.

The principal author of the Tetrapolitan Confession had been Martin Bucer of Strasbourg. This amiable Alsatian was to become the most important figure among the south German protestants after both Zwingli and Oecolampadius died in the same year, 1531. Luther imagined that the latter had "died by fiery darts and arrows of the devil."[13] Strasbourg was shortly accepted into the protestant League of Schmalkalden, and Bucer set busily about patching up the religious differences, first close to home, but before long with Wittenberg as well. By 1534, he had devised a formula for concord to which Swiss and south German cities subscribed. After much traveling in that part of Europe, he accepted an invitation from Philip of Hesse again, this time to meet with the great conciliator from Wittenberg, Melanchthon, at the landgrave's seat in Cassel. Melanchthon arrived at that middle German city on Christmas Eve, Bucer just a few days later. Before New Year's the two deft negotiators had produced a compact which both sides would, during coming months, approve.[14]

Their achievement was the more remarkable since Melanchthon had brought along strict written instructions from Luther forbidding any compromise whatsoever: "It would only make our cause more suspect and arouse doubt . . . if we should shift to a new, middle position."[15] The flexibility Bucer had shown in Marburg had struck Luther as suspect, and he advised Philip of Hesse to proceed cautiously now, making sure the Cassel agreement was genuinely intended and mutually understood. As the year 1535 drew to a close, plans for a gathering of all the major theologians had reached finality. Prospects for agreement were excellent.

Therefore Luther's enthusiastic acceptance of Vergerio's invitation to a general council was based on an optimistic view of his reform party's position. Representatives from the several protestant cities in Germany would come to Mantua speaking with an undivided voice. More than that: negotiations with the English, begun in Schmalkalden in December and continuing into early 1536, might even augment their strength. But yet more important than solidarity, when it came to accomplishing real success at the general council, would be just how palatable reform might be made to the traditionalists on the papal side. It was clearly worth Luther's best efforts to draw the southwest Germans back from their most radical doctrines, unacceptable even to the papal moderates—and there were many of these. His handling of the negotiations with the brethren from the German southwest was so very skillful that it appears to have been carefully calculated from the start.

Approach from the West

During the course of 1535, Martin Bucer tirelessly cajoled agreement to the Cassel compact from one south German city after another. By early 1536, all was prepared for the personal meeting with Luther, to seal these articles of concord. The last station was Augsburg, among whose theologians the winter had been one of squabbling. Bucer himself smoothed out an amicable settlement, and the sweet-smelling Swabian springtime now gave this traveler every reason for optimism. Only, he had as yet heard nothing from Luther himself, to whom he had written in early February. At last, on 11 April, a brief note reached him:

> I am compelled to write but little, dear Bucer, for these two weeks I have lain prostrated by unbearably excruciating pains in my left hip. I am scarcely recovered yet. Here is our decision about the meeting. Our prince has designated Eisenach, near Hesse, twenty-eight miles from Wittenberg, for the place.[1]

The much-traveled negotiator paid no heed to the fact that the conference would thus be twice as far removed from his home as from Wittenberg (a German mile was something over four English). Eisenach was in any case more convenient than Cassel, where he had met with Melanchthon. Luther's late response did worry him, though. Not that the illness seemed insufficient explanation. But the same letter set the meeting for the fourth Sunday after Easter—that left barely a month for the formidable task of drawing all participants together. Luther closed with the remark that he was not writing to anyone else. Arrangements were entirely up to Bucer.

Although Bucer immediately sent letters off, the Swiss brethren had to be contacted by relay (via Strasbourg). Their own parley did not then come about until the first of May, in Aarau. Here representatives from Zürich, Bern, Basel, Schaffhausen, St. Gallen, Mühlhausen, and Biel conferred and drew up a dispatch to Wittenberg. For them to send a delegate would be impossible, they said,

> on account of the great distance and the short notice. Hence it is our most kind request that ye be not offended, or think that some other consideration than lack of time prevents us.[2]

Luther had said all along he did not want a big assemblage. His letter asking John Frederick to appoint the meeting place had noted it was unnecessary "for a big bunch to congregate. That might bring a few restless troublemakers who could spoil things."[3] The absence of the doctrinaire Swiss now virtually guaranteed compliance by the more politic Swabians and Alsatians.

Even while the Aarau meeting was going on, Martin Bucer was already making his leisurely and convivial way across Swabian field and forests, among the most beautiful in the world, and dawdling in Renaissance towns which were the marvel of all Europe. Although his destination lay almost due north from Augsburg, he and the theologians from that city proceeded west, gathering up associates. At Ulm they were joined by the pastor there as well as another who came down the Aller River to meet them. They crossed over to the Neckar, and this loveliest of German streams took the party, by now grown to seven, on down to Frankfurt. The whole distance Augsburg–Frankfurt might be an afternoon's drive on the Autobahn. Bucer and his friends had spent ten of the gorgeous days in late April and early May on their excursion and its stopovers.

In Frankfurt, sad news awaited Bucer that the plague had visited Strasbourg. Three of his own household had succumbed, including a son. Of Bucer's thirteen offspring, only one survived childhood, a retarded boy. Bucer's treasures were not stored up in this world.

A stocky, dark Alsatian, Martin Bucer was a most learned theologian who placed love and harmony above all other tenets of doctrine. When Charles V exiled him from Strasbourg a dozen years later, he accepted an invitation from Thomas Cranmer to lecture at Cambridge, so that before his death he became an important figure in English protestantism, too. Like other scions of the busy southwestern cities, he tended to be more aware of political and economic implications to religious questions than were the theologians closer to Luther.[4] Born on a wine-rich tributary of the Rhine and educated in the Dominican cloister at Schlettstadt, he retained the good nature of that countryside. In this part of Germany the influence of Erasmus was strong, and Bucer was associated with two of the most eminent humanists among the protestants, John Oecolampadius and Wolfgang Capito. Their religiosity was milder than Luther's, and they showed an eagerness to compromise which Luther found suspect, but he had succumbed to Bucer's likeable presence. During the opening formalities at the Marburg colloquy, which included reading aloud certain letters praising the assembled delegates, Luther had wagged his finger and said to his old friend, with a smile, "*Thou art a scamp.*"[5]

Although eight years younger than Luther, Bucer was among his earliest admirers. He had met him in 1518, when the then still obscure professor had participated in a debate at Heidelberg and Bucer was in the Dominican order there. He obtained his release five years before Luther laid his own cowl aside. Married in 1522, Bucer drifted to Strasbourg, which had a long reputation of reform and of powerful voices from the pulpit, and was known as a religious asylum. The scholarly Wolfgang Capito became his patron here, and lifelong friend. With Capito, Bucer had drawn up the Tetrapolitan Confession in 1530. It was Capito who brought the sad news of his son's death to Frankfurt. These two men were to be the principal negotiators in Eisenach.

Bucer was not yet thirty-five, but Capito at sixty-four looked back on a distinguished career as a reformer long before Luther, and as a scholar who had made his mark in Hebrew studies. Though today he was a bearded, somewhat distracted insomniac, in his years as a smooth diplomat he had done much to protect Luther. Together with Erasmus, he had met with the newly crowned Emperor Charles V to urge deferral of imperial action against the young professor. By the time the papal bull *Exsurge*

Domine had been issued against Luther in 1520, Capito had become the influential adviser to the cardinal of German lands, Albert of Mainz, so that he could delay its publication in Germany. He was at work behind the scenes to gain Luther his hearing at Worms in 1521, and it was Capito who assured that the Edict of Worms, outlawing Luther, would never be effectively enforced (the essential signature, that of Cardinal Albert, was never affixed). In all this Capito was not acting as a Lutheran by any means—on the contrary, he became increasingly critical of Luther's pugnacity—but as an Erasmian, doubting that the truth in religious matters ever can be known, convinced only that maintaining the peace was of paramount importance.[6]

The very diplomacy which Capito used to protect Luther had made him suspect to its beneficiary. For example, when Luther wrote a devastating attack on Cardinal Albert in connection with relics and indulgence sales, Capito succeeded in squelching it. To do so required a special trip to Wittenberg to confer with Melanchthon (Luther was at the Wartburg). They made sure all correspondence between Albert and Luther would pass first through their mitigating hands. This remained possible so long as Luther remained in his "desert," as he dated one threat to Albert "to reveal to the entire world the difference between a bishop and a wolf."[7] In the same connection, Luther fired off a letter to George Spalatin, the friend whom he had entrusted with publishing the pamphlet against Albert: "Look to it you restrain that moderation and prudence of which I suspect you."[8] For Capito's mollifications he had harsher words.

Capito persuaded his cardinal to pen an incredibly humble missive thanking Luther for his "brotherly, Christian chiding," and promising to mend his ways.[9] It was a stunning piece of diplomacy, but Luther rewarded it with a lengthy, typically uncompromising condemnation of Capito's "untimely rhetoric . . . sweet servility and denial of Christian truth." He told Capito he should not have soothed Albert, for "Christianity is open and direct, acknowledges things as they are and admits to them." Even heathens, he reminded the classics scholar, denounced uncritical friendship, and as for Christ, he offended everyone, "not just some, but the whole world. So we know we ought to come right out and criticize, reprove, condemn everything, neither sparing, conniving at, nor excusing anything until truth carries the field, free, pure, and open." He quoted Jeremiah 48:10, "Cursed be he that doeth the work of the Lord deceitfully" (happily refraining from giving the entire verse). The letter found its way among the public, being printed in Strasbourg before the year was out (1522).[10]

Capito had not remained long in his post with Cardinal Albert, but used it to obtain an important living as vicar of Saint Thomas in Strasbourg. On a second good-will trip to Wittenberg, he had met Luther, and as time passed he came more and more to espouse Luther's cause. But he remained skeptical whether final truths can at all be known, hence he always gave peace and concord his first allegiance. As to the nature of the Lord's Supper, Capito had rejected the doctrine of transubstantiation years before Luther questioned indulgences. Communion was for him but a remembrance, and Capito remained, in the words of his biographer, "oddly unable to believe that anyone would be willing to quarrel over the exact nature of the elements in the Lord's Supper."[11]

To each of these old friends—to Capito as a sincere humanist, to Bucer as a man who placed love above dogma—agreement was more important than precision when it came to discussing the sacraments. Aside from their compliant temperaments, the two had taken on a considerable burden as leaders conducting their fellow townsmen on the long quest of a notoriously unbending Luther. The delegation in which these were the most important members was not likely to drive hard-nosed bargains.

The ride across Hesse was quick and businesslike. The party, now grown to a dozen, arrived in Eisenach on Saturday, 13 May, just before the Sunday appointed by Luther. He was not there. They dispatched a messenger to Wittenberg.

Next morning they attended the church of Pastor Justus Menius. They carefully noted how much popery had been retained here in remote Saxony. For the next few days they continued to wait in the mountains just below the castle Wartburg. Many the Luther associations—in Eisenach he had attended school as a boy, up there at the keep he had translated the New Testament—but no Luther. By Wednesday Bucer and Capito, responsible for bringing their friends thus far, could no longer wait passively. They set out together with the delegates from Augsburg, riding in the direction of Gotha. The pastor there, Frederick Myconius, might know something of the reverend father's intentions, might have news of his health.

Just outside Gotha they encountered a messenger from Wittenberg. Although the distance there could be covered in two days, he bore a letter which Luther had dated five days earlier, the twelfth. It had been Luther, of course, who had set the fourteenth as date for the Eisenach meeting, but the present letter began with a complaint that he had heard from Capito too late (Capito had written more than three weeks earlier) for him to make it to Eisenach at all, even if he were well. He therefore suggested that they

> deign to approach a little nearer—namely to Grimma, which is located three miles beyond Leipzig. I can either be there by next Sunday, or at least I shall be able to exchange letters with our side (should my health require it) in the space of a day. There is just no other course, or suggestion I can offer. It is God forcing those who wished and planned quite differently from what is now possible, to accommodate ourselves.[12]

Grimma, well off to the east, was scarcely more convenient for the journeyers than Wittenberg itself. Bucer immediately sent the courier back with word that the party would "take pains to meet the reverend father on Sunday in Wittenberg, if he did not object."[13] Gathering their little flock from Eisenach, together with the two local pastors, Justus Menius and Frederick Myconius, the Strasbourgers betook themselves on north, toward the Elbe. Luther can scarcely have expected them to do otherwise, but just in case they had gone on to Grimma, Melanchthon and Caspar Cruciger had been given instructions to fetch them in.[14]

So the last leg of the long ride out of Swabia and the Alsace led across the far-famed Golden Meadow, that fertile rolling country cradled between Thuringian mountains and the Erzgebirge. In May, full heads of wheat, dotted with bright poppies, declared the aptness of its name. The observers out of the German southwest were impressed by the foreignness of this expansive, treeless landscape. They were no longer in the fatherland of their ancestors, Swabians, Franks, Bavarians, but in territory colonized during the late Middle Ages, still sprinkled with Slavic names like Leipzig and (proceeding north from there) Wiederitzsch, Krostitz, Zschepptin, Pristablich, Kemnitz, Zschornewitz. Some villages still took the round, distinctively Slavic shape. Martin Bucer, native of a free imperial city and educated in Heidelberg, had spent his mature years in Europe's most cosmopolitan center. Wolfgang Capito, long accustomed to the sophistication of that same Alsatian capital, had cultivated his ways at a great court in the Rhine-Main basin, ancient crossroads of northern Europe. Now these amiable Rhinelanders, accustomed to good manners, common sense, and paved streets, trekked the windswept hills of Saxony all the way to a remote corner of that land, at last to gaze at a doubtful wooden bridge which must take them across the river, to Wittenberg.

The "wall" was not of masonry such as surrounded the wealthy cities of their homeland, but rather an immensely thick earthen dike. Within were a few hundred houses, mostly of clay, with thatched roofs. The streets were unpaved, during much of the year sluggish rivers of mud. Even the walks in front of the houses were perilous, for some Wittenbergers were so shameless as to bare their bottoms and relieve themselves there in broad daylight. Luther scolded them for it from his pulpit, as he did for their desecration of the graveyard beside the town church, which they had rendered a thoroughfare and commons.[15] At the center of town the newcomers beheld City Hall, under construction now for years. Right beside it stood the place of public execution—an institution removed to the outskirts of all imperial cities in their ken.[16] Proceeding in the direction of the university, the visitors passed structures displaying a more civil exterior, but the impression of being "at the end of the world," as Luther himself called this borderland, should have dispelled any lingering expectation of finding here a spirit of urbane compromise.[17] Capito, who had not seen Luther for a dozen years, may have been entitled still to some optimism, but Bucer well remembered their last meeting at the Coburg, and Luther's words, "Martin, if you are not sincere, it were better for us to remain enemies than to join in a fictional alliance."[18]

His anxieties were justified. After extensive peregrinations and dickering among south German friends, after the two-week journey across Swabia and up from Frankfurt culminating in that perplexity of finding no one at the meeting place appointed by Luther himself, after not only "deigning to approach a little nearer," but riding all the way now to the farthest side of Saxony, Bucer arrived with his followers on Sunday afternoon to learn that Luther did not wish to receive them at all. An edition of letters by Oecolampadius and Zwingli, printed up in January and carrying as preface an ancient letter by Bucer without his knowledge or authorization—a practice not so unusual in the early days of print—was said to have come to Luther's attention. He was reported to be in one of his notorious black humors, saying the Zwinglians were still teaching their old godlessness. He had let it be known no good results could be expected of a meeting with them now.[19] Myconius, the pastor from Gotha, did receive an invitation to sup with Luther—he expressed hope of putting the old warrior into a more congenial mood.

The two leaders of the south German party were granted an audience with Doctor Luther on the morning after their arrival, at seven o'clock. Bucer displayed his considerable experience as diplomatic agent by laying out all relevant documentation. Since this was a major conference which had cost the theologians enormous time and money, he felt it behooved them to make sure all points of importance would be brought forward for thorough discussion. He recommended that Luther likewise draw up his own comprehensive list of desiderata. The south Germans would then read it in private, testing his proposals against scripture. One or two members could subsequently present their collective opinion to Luther. This was an orderly way to assure clarification of each article. Luther said he would look through Bucer's materials and receive the two leaders again at three o'clock.

Bucer, cheerful by nature, had not yet grasped the purpose of his long pilgrimage. Doctor Martin Luther, after thirty years' grappling with religious problems, tireless study by day and wrestling by night with doubt and the devil, had not received this delegation with the thought of working out felicitous solutions by committee consensus. The south Germans had made their arduous journey for two reasons:

1. to entreat their orthodox Saxon brethren to accept a full and unreserved confession of agreement, and,

2. to carry back with them an impression so strong that it might in some degree offset their notorious lack of sincerity.

Luther's actions up to this point should have already made that clear to them.

That afternoon, Bucer and Capito again appeared alone, this time to find themselves facing a full-blown praesidium: the imposing John Bugenhagen, successful reformer of all Low Germany, just now being urgently summoned by Christian III to do the same for the Kingdom of Denmark; Professor Justus Jonas, whom Capito had met at the historic Diet of Worms, and Bucer at Marburg, the major pillar of Lutheran orthodoxy at the Diet of Augsburg; Caspar Cruciger, the brilliant young Hebrew scholar and editor of Luther's sermons, who had also faced them at Marburg. Present more as observers than as participants were those two pastors who had ridden in with them, as well as faces less familiar. The authoritative spokesman of Wittenberg theology, complaisant Philip Melanchthon, who had worked out the very agreement which brought them all here, was conspicuous by his absence.

Using accustomed aplomb, the undaunted Bucer opened with a lengthy statement of the pleasure he now took, together with all the churches he represented here, to come to Wittenberg at such an auspicious moment. After some display of eloquence, the practiced mediator went on to narrate his endeavors over the past four years, at last crowned by the present conference. He concluded with an enumeration of the main points upon which concord was now to be formalized and sat down to await introductory and welcoming remarks from his hosts.

Luther spoke. His address was also very long and well organized, under clear-cut headings—like a sermon. His manner was grave and earnest in the extreme.

There was absolutely no point, he began, in discussing anything at all if there were not full agreement on the Lord's Supper. They had feigned agreement with him, but they were still teaching error at home. They had represented the issue as one of mere semantics. There was nothing for it now, he said, until they explicitly renounced Zwingli's heresy and freely confessed, with the Saxons, that the bread of the Lord's Supper is the body of Christ, given and received into the hand and mouth of the faithful and of the unbeliever alike. Failure to do so would testify further to their insincerity.

Luther was laying bare the most sensitive point, which Bucer had taken pains to cover over with careful terminology. The experienced arbiter had correctly sensed a fundamental agreement: Luther's understanding of the Lord's Supper, being entirely spiritual, did not imply any elemental change at the hands of a priest. The south Germans' interpretation, also highly spiritualized, placed the sense of the ceremony in the faith of the communicant. They went so far as to consider it an invocation of magic to say that an unbeliever received the true sacrament. Luther, as we have seen, thought it crassly materialistic to deny the presence of Christ, and he said it was arrogant to imagine mere man, by belief or disbelief, could affect the Lord's Supper one way or another. He understood quite well, as he spoke to Bucer now, the embarrassment he was causing by being entirely explicit on this score.

We are told it was with a most aggrieved expression (no doubt that same look of "tender suffering" which had impressed Vergerio) that Luther went ahead to deplore Bucer's preface to the recently published Zwingli letters. Not only did it pain him for Bucer to make a show of agreement while teaching error behind his back, it was even more grievous to find himself partner in the guilt of others. Better matters had been left as they were than to make a bad situation worse by dissembling. "Even if we could deceive the world, we shall not be able to deceive the eyes and ears of the Lord."[20]

Bucer was dashed. Capito, near tears. They protested their innocence. Had they known Luther so distrusted them, they'd never have undertaken this difficult journey. Bucer explained he had had no part in the publication of those out-of-date Zwingli letters.

Luther helped them back onto the track by "repeating, very gravely, as is his custom,"[21] the two requirements: that they recant, and then confess that the real presence was not affected by any participant's "worthiness," or lack of it.

As to recantation, Bucer and Capito thought they could agree to that. They begged only that they not be asked publicly to take back statements they had never made in the first place. The

second demand might require more discussion. They had taught
that the faithful truly receive Christ's body and blood. As to
unbelievers, they had never made an issue of it. But they feared
there might be difficulty among their people if the point were
raised. A great weakness overcame Luther at this juncture, and
he adjourned the meeting. Nor was it reconvened the next morning. It was learned that Luther had not slept at all during the
night.

Bucer and Capito thus obtained an evening and a morning to
tell their colleagues about their hard reception, and of Luther's
willingness to send them all packing. Bucer had time to cast
about for remedies and to test them on his colleagues. Actually,
Luther had himself offered a hint when he referred to the
unbelievers as the "unworthy" (Paul's word in his first letter to
the Corinthians—11:27). Here, thought Bucer, was a word with
great potential. Were not *all* who came to the Lord's Supper, in
truth, "unworthy"? "Unworthy" did not *have* to mean "unbelieving."

On the second afternoon the entire south German delegation
was received by the Wittenberg praesidium, which now included Melanchthon—a good sign. Martin Bucer took the floor
and delivered an interpretation of the Lord's Supper which was
entirely satisfactory to the Saxons. He dwelled, to be sure, somewhat heavily on rejection of "crude papist" practices, but when
questioned by Bugenhagen about the unbelievers at the Lord's
Supper he answered deftly:

> Those who are quite without faith, but come with their intel-
> lects alone to the Lord's Supper—of these we hold that they
> receive bread and wine alone—

Here the audience hung anxiously—

> although with the bread and wine, in accordance with the in-
> stitution by our Lord and the mediation of the church, the
> true body and the true blood are placed before them.

This was satisfactory, but for Luther's sake he said further,

> For the institution of the Lord depends on no man's belief or
> disbelief, but solely upon itself, as God's word and sanction.[22]

Luther required the other delegates to speak up individually and let it be known whether Bucer's words reflected their convictions, too. Each did much more than that. They said they had ever taught thus, always intended to do so. Some reported the punishments inflicted on any in their districts who held otherwise. Luther and his advisers now solemnly withdrew from the room.

While the south German guests waited, he asked each member of his own party for an opinion. The visitors, it was decided, must be required once more to affirm their belief that the unworthy do also receive the body and the blood. Bucer and his associates were left to pass these tense moments as best they knew how.

The Luther who returned to them looked upon his brethren as if transfigured. His eloquent countenance beamed joy and pure kindness. Ignoring the decision just solemnly reached, he arbitrarily proclaimed concord. Both Capito and Bucer, ten days of anxiety behind them followed by yesterday's crisis and today's uncertain wait, found themselves weeping in the midst of the good doctor's emotional speech. On Wednesday, Luther assembled the theologians again by seven in the morning, and all other articles were dealt with smoothly. That afternoon Bugenhagen preached on John 17 (Jesus's prayer for his apostles), Thursday being Ascension Day. Beginning at 5 A.M., it was the turn of the visiting Saxons to preach, first Menius and then Myconius. All the theologians took communion together with about fifty citizens from the town. In the afternoon, Doctor Luther delivered a fine sermon on the final verses of Mark, where the risen Christ appeared to his eleven apostles,

> and upbraided them with their hardness of heart, because they believed not them which had seen him after he was risen. And he said unto them, "Go ye into all the world, and preach the gospel to every creature. He that believeth and is baptized shall be saved; but he that believeth not shall be damned."

Talks were resumed on Friday and Saturday, the Saxons and their south German friends indulging their curiosity about differences in usage and mutual problems. Schools were a subject of special interest, as was the question of just how far the magistracy could be entrusted with enforcement of church discipline. On Saturday, the regrets of the Swiss were conveyed, Luther apologizing for his own tardiness in the matter. "Back then, I had no idea so many of you were coming—I thought it would be just Strasbourg and Augsburg." At dinner he was in a "wonderfully good humor."[23]

A south German guest took the pulpit on Sunday morning at five o'clock. Luther suffered from vertigo later in the morning and could not join in communion, but he preached that afternoon. On Sunday night the entire company was invited to his table, and high spirits prevailed. With a cordial speech he saw Bucer and Capito off on Monday, but the Augsburgers could stay over for another day, because their return was shorter. They got to dine with the famous painter Lucas Cranach in his splendid home, and Melanchthon invited them in to inspect some ancient Greek manuscripts. Before they left, Luther let them know John Frederick would take care of their travel expenses.

How shall we regard Luther's magnificent performance in producing this Wittenberg Concord? As that of a calculating Machiavelli, at the same time a consummate actor? Before we accuse him of insincerity, we should recall that he was not dealing with gullible admirers, but with the most learned men in Europe and some of his most skeptical critics. Bucer and others had been observing him for years. None of these questioned the genuineness of his actions.

The convenience of his illnesses might certainly strike one as suspicious. They interfered so opportunely with his correspondence, preventing his coming to Eisenach, halted the session on Monday, and postponed resumption on Tuesday until the shock administered to Bucer and Capito had been imparted to their colleagues. Just as soon as the full effect of Luther's sternness had been achieved, he became pathetically kind, radiated good spirits, was strong enough to spend long hours in discussions, attended church, preached, and at last entertained the delegation along with local celebrities, drinking to the good fellowship of all.

Such radical oscillation in mood was a most characteristic feature of Martin Luther's genius. He was very much the victim of his momentary emotional state, over which he had little control.

Beyond question, his feelings altered his physical condition, and at his age he was always supplied with ailments. If heeded, they aggravated his desperate melancholy. But this is not to say he was a naive creature of his moods. Martin Luther's entire greatness arose from his ability to draw knowingly upon depths of his unconscious being, placing emotional powers at the disposal of an astute intellect.

The winter of 1535–36 had been a hard one for him. He did have a bad cough. His hip hurt. The Schmalkalden conference was dragging on vexingly while the English delegates, unbelievable toadies interested only in Henry VIII's marriage annulment, claimed their king would not permit them to make binding agreements in church doctrine.[24] The publication of Zwingli's letters was surely exasperating for Luther. He expressed quite genuine, black depression when he told everyone the conference with the south Germans would likely come to naught. He did not go to Eisenach as appointed because, from the bottom of his heart, he did not feel like it. Nor was he in any state to receive them when they arrived in Wittenberg. In addressing poor Bucer he allowed all his melancholy full sway. If it caused Bucer distress, so much the better.

Luther never doubted the south Germans would accept his doctrine. He only questioned their sincerity. As he had asked them in Marburg seven years earlier, how could he know *what* they would teach when they returned home? Why conceal from them this agonizing doubt? Was it not, after all, the optimum negotiating posture? If on Tuesday he overwhelmed his guests with good humor, became more and more jovial as their stay continued—why, he had been given cause to feel that way. His health improved. He was not unaware of the efficacy of his moodiness, had used it before this in dealing both with his children and with colleagues.[25] Twentieth-century psychology might describe his objective performance as a sophisticated behavior modification technique. Its subjective wellsprings were no less genuine for that.

Coping with depression in himself and others was one of Luther's major concerns, as we shall see, but he never achieved much control over his own mental and emotional turmoil. He appeared often to Melanchthon, who knew him best, simply to yield himself up to his fury. But he was as a rule able, at the same time, to direct it into productive channels. This was the case during the negotiations leading to the Wittenberg Concord of 1536. He was also long accustomed to drawing on his emotions for his songs, for some of his best writings, for the power of his passionate prayers. Emotionality was probably also the driving force in his penetrating thought about God and man.

Knocking the Grand Heads

Luther's proverbial wrath is a sin of which he is easily convicted by his own testimony. The fact is of course that his very candor enjoins us to caution in the use of such admissions. Few people ever examine their "sins" as exactingly as he did. Fewer then speak so openly about them. "I have a lot of spiritual failings," he might remark, "but I am about beyond my sins of the flesh. Avarice does not trouble me, because I have enough money. Lust doesn't trouble me either." He looked impishly over at Kate—

> I get plenty of what it takes to remedy that. But wrath just won't turn me loose. Why, I sometimes rage about a piddling thing not worthy of mention. Whoever crosses my path has to suffer for it—I won't say a kind word to anyone. Isn't that a shameful thing? I might be entitled to other sins, material comfort for example, but I let some trifle excite me![1]

Can a man like this have been slave to his emotions? Is he not likely to possess more self-control than others, who do not admit their emotionality?

Luther was entirely capable of using his anger, as he put it, to clear his head, to lend bite to his writings,[2] even to help him pray.[3] His artistic disposition was inclined to trust to its emotions and to follow them. Unlike many other scholars, he held reason in positive distrust. In his eyes it would therefore detract nothing from a sermon or treatise to call it passionate. Why should he conceal his feelings? He wore his heart on his sleeve for daws to peck at, his passions abundantly clear. Did they of themselves detract from the logical cogency of an argument or diminish its historical importance? Luther's emotional involvement in his work is a complex issue, and we must be wary of general statements about it.

His extreme language and the pathos it expresses certainly must concern any who are interested in the development of his personality. No man so long and so intensely involved in controversy can come away emotionally unscathed. Highly charged exchanges with the most illustrious figures of his day had imposed anguishing strains on him in an era which attached great importance to rank and station. That early polemic by the king of England, Henry VIII, vilifying Luther had an impact difficult for a modern, unintimidated by royalty, to assess. At first he stood up to the monarch, restating his positions so unabashedly that for many Germans "the sound contents paled beneath the impression of such a polemical tone."⁴ Just a few years later, however, he wrote an apologetic letter to the king, in the servile phrases of the Renaissance, offering to publish a retraction.⁵

That did not turn out to be necessary. Henry humiliated Luther again by having the epistle elaborately printed and circulated together with his own haughty acknowledgment "that you are sorry and ashamed of publishing so foolishly and rashly against us, not after your own mind but seduced by those unfavorably disposed against us . . . you know yourself to be quite guilty (as you say) of having so sorely injured us, that you were very hesitant to write."⁶

At Henry's behest Europe's most famous humanist, Desiderius Erasmus, at last took his anti-Luther stand. Their dispute on the subject of free will became a major chapter in the history of religion and philosophy, so that the emotional stress it placed on Luther may be all too easily forgotten. He had sincerely admired the distinguished older man and was pleased to regard his own reforms as in the Erasmian spirit.⁷ The dependence of his New Testament on the Greek (and Latin translation) by Erasmus was fresh in his awareness. Furthermore, the year of their falling-out had been a year of great turmoil for Luther, as can be measured by his strident condemnation of the peasants just at a time when (independently of him) they were being brutally put down. Lu-

ther's guardian, Elector Frederick, also died in 1525, and this was
the year the former monk exposed himself to European oppro-
brium by marrying Kate, his runaway nun. If aging is to be understood as our accumulation of injuries, then Martin Luther
aged considerably during the emotional traumas of the year
1525.

The relationship in which the increasing stresses of conflict became most apparent was probably his lengthy feud with Duke
George of Saxony. He was the most learned and sincere ruler of
that day, a reformer before Luther, friend of Erasmus, and one
of an older generation disinclined to put away the verities of
orthodoxy.[8] The quarrel with George may have gone back to
that prince's somewhat high-handed treatment of Luther when
he came to Leipzig to debate John Eck in 1519, and it always
had a highly personal flavor. By the time it reached its culmination in the middle 1530s it had revealed Luther as intemperate
and at times unfair. When George died in 1539, Doctor Luther
took the credit, claiming his prayers had been answered.

It has been argued that George, by his very opposition to Luther, was as much responsible for the development of protestantism as was Luther's benign protector in the early days,
George's cousin Frederick.[9] To understand this view, one must
know something of the Saxon situation. Their house had grown
powerful without the tradition of primogeniture, the various
sovereignties becoming so intertwined as to make Saxon territories mutually dependent. This sort of arrangement might work
out well—as was illustrated by the agreement between Luther's
own princes, Elector Frederick, who had forgone marriage to
devote life entirely to his subjects, and his brother John, responsible for making an advantageous matrimonial alliance and
providing legitimate succession. In the previous generation, the
Saxon inheritance had not worked out so felicitously. George's
father had insisted on division, so that in Luther's day Saxony
comprised a mosaic of districts, part ruled by his own elector,
the rest by Duke George.

George had been educated for the church, was much interested in theological questions, and held the most current scholarly views. Acutely aware of the abuses in the Renaissance
church, he had at first welcomed Luther's denunciation of the

papal indulgence sales. Like other rulers of his epoch, he held himself responsible for religious observance in his land, and had successfully reformed the churches in his parts of Saxony. In the course of time he became immensely frustrated by the more passive, *laissez-faire* policy of his cousin the elector.

When Henry VIII dispatched a very long letter to the Saxon princes, their replies to him pointed up their different attitudes. Henry demanded they put down the "rebellious, poisonous, criminal sect" of Lutherans before they, like the Hussites of recent memory, "rapidly grow from a little worm into a monstrous great dragon very hurtful to German lands."[10] Duke George immediately wrote how he had forbidden that Luther's tract against Henry be sold *or read*, and had imposed "a hard sentence on the bookdealer who first offered it for sale." Nor had he permitted subsequent publication of Luther's books to go unpunished, he said. He reminded Henry how he had ordered the king's tract translated out of the Latin into German and reissued at his own expense, for he regarded "all arrows of injustice hurled at a prince as not directed at the person of one prince alone, but against the estate of all princes—nay, against the entire nobility." He waxed prophetic in comparing Luther to Mohammed and predicting that, unless his teaching were rooted out, it would "introduce by rebellion, first among German peoples, then soon in all countries of the West, a new force which we shall no longer be able to dispel." Heartily agreeing with Henry on the virulence of Luther's New Testament, he told how he had bought up "all copies of this book, as many as were brought into this land and sold here." In conclusion, he explained why he regarded Luther's teachings as destructive of all social order, basing his views on standard theological tenets.[11] We may disagree with George's position, or with his squelching of the press, but we must admit this letter to King Henry was a thoughtful one, by a prince who held himself accountable for his subjects' religion.

His cousin Frederick was perhaps a simpler man. He certainly knew less theology, and he held to the old faith in papal indulgences. The purchase of sacred relics had been his only extravagance, and he had finally given that up. As Luther's prince, his reply to Henry was the more crucial one. It bore also the signature of his brother and successor, John. They expressed regret for any teachings, anywhere in the world, which were un-Christain or offensive to King Henry,

> wherefore we would not conceal from your royal majesty that we have never undertaken to represent Luther's doctrine, writings, or preachings, but have let them rest on their merits and his responsibility. This we have also told popes, the emperor, the imperial estates, etc. Nor have we ever involved ourselves in these matters, except that we gladly suffer the gospel, the divine word, doctrine, and truth to be preached and taught, and the honor of God and love of neighbor to be sincerely pursued.[12]

They drew Henry's attention to the recent call by the imperial estates for a church council to decide these matters. The letter was cordial and gracious. Both Frederick and John received Henry's courier personally, piously removing their berets in deference when addressing him.

In later years Luther looked back on Frederick's official policy of non-involvement in matters of the faith as the most effective way the elector could have found to protect him, an excommunicated and outlawed professor. This impression went back to a time in his life when he had felt endangered. Just how strongly the emotional strains may have affected his profound admiration of old Frederick, and the extent to which his protector's aloofness from church affairs—indeed from Luther himself— may have influenced Luther's conception of the ideal temporal ruler, is a matter for speculation. It seems likely that Frederick may deserve some credit for the modern doctrine of separation of church and state as it is usually traced back to Luther. But Duke George, for so firmly opposing Luther's political teachings, would then deserve some credit, too.

Luther preached an arresting sermon on the "two kingdoms," spiritual and temporal, with George's regulation of church affairs in mind, especially his suppression of evangelical preaching. Frederick and his brother, among the congregation, liked what they heard and urged Luther to write a treatise on the subject, which was then widely read. Luther's idea of a strict separation between church and state is surely best understood in this context of those interwoven Saxon regimes, where one ruler was observing a policy of non-interference in religion, while the other actively opposed Luther's teachings and persecuted his followers.

It is perhaps not remarkable that Luther referred to George disrespectfully in a personal letter to a third party, but he should have known better, because letters were sometimes widely circulated. In this case the recipient, without authority, published it. The word *Wasserblase* occurred in the epistle. It means "bubble," or "bladder," and was also the German translation of Latin *bulla*="papal bull." The context was, in Luther's words, "straw and paper tyranny." As "an egregious example," he cited "that *Wasserblase* Duke George, flaunting his high paunch before heaven and renouncing the gospel—thinks he'll devour Christ the way a wolf snaps up a fly."[13]

The duke, quite in character with "straw and paper tyranny," sent a carefully polite, legalistically worded request that Luther please acknowledge or disclaim authorship of this letter, "so that we may determine what measures our honor requires."[14] Luther's reply was equally in character. After a most frivolous salutation it began,

> Ungracious prince and lord,
> I have had Your Disgrace's letter read before me, together with the pamphlet or letter . . . which I am alleged to have written . . . Now, inasmuch as Y.D. doth desire to know "how I stand" to this, I answer in short that it is immaterial whether Y.D. take me standing, sitting, lying down, or running around. I stand on my right to act and speak, and I will defend my right, commending unto God any who would do violence.

In this tone the letter continued, without offering satisfaction one way or the other as to authorship of the earlier missive—although Luther does say he fears no *Wasserblase*.[15]

George forthwith lodged complaint with Frederick, who responded in his usual cordial, dilatory fashion, being just in these months more concerned with Luther's outrageous bullying of the cardinal of Mainz (of which more later). George promptly filed suit with the imperial government, where the matter was received as a family feud and George was advised to seek remedy from his cousin. Luther let show just a bit of arrogance when a friendly member of the nobility tried to intercede. He said he had not been nearly so hard on the duke as on the pope or the king of England. "I should have given him a better tousling." He allowed that people, although shocked by his writings at first, soon learned to see them differently. "It is about time to knock some of these grand heads that are unaccustomed to it."[16]

He was as good as his word. It is easy to see how his treatise *Concerning the Temporal Magistracy*, even though it had pleased both Frederick and John as a sermon, incensed George. The essay takes its point of departure from 1 Timothy 1:9: "The law is not made for a righteous man, but for the lawless and disobedient." A good man does what is right, Luther explains, by his very nature. What a foolish man that would be, who gave

> an apple tree a book full of rules and laws about how to grow apples and not thorns, when the tree naturally knows how to do that better than he with all his books can describe or command. In the same way, all Christians have it in their very nature to do good and right, more than all the laws can teach them.[17]

The temporal magistracy, quite necessary for the prevention of wickedness, must not meddle with the few, scattered Christians in the world, "You have to distinguish these two regimes very carefully and maintain both: one that makes people devout, and the other to maintain the public peace and prevent wicked deeds."[18] In his *Address to the Christian Nobility* Luther had sought to drive the church out of temporal affairs. Here he makes clear that temporal rulers have no dominion over the spirit:

> I don't care how great fools they are, they still have to admit they have no power over the soul. Nobody can kill a soul or bring one to life, lead it to heaven or to hell—if they don't want to believe me, then Christ says it clear enough.[19]

This is the point which Duke George could not accept, for it amounted to inciting his subjects to disobedience:

> If your prince or temporal lord commands you to hold with the pope, to believe one way or the other, or commands you

to put away books, then you must say, "It is not for Lucifer to sit beside God. Dear prince, I must obey you with body and property, what you command me in accordance with your authority on earth I will follow. But if you tell me what to believe, or what books to put away, I will not obey."[20]

In explaining why a temporal lord must not regulate spiritual allegiance, Luther cited lands where his Bible was being proscribed and mentioned George's territory (although he did not use George's name). Knowing his readership accustomed to revering their prince, he remarked, "What a rare bird an intelligent prince is, and how much rarer a devout one! They are usually the greatest fools or the worst knaves on earth." He would expect no good from them, "because they are God's pillory masters and hangmen . . . He's a mighty lord, God is, and so he needs noble, highborn, wealthy hangmen and beadles. He wants them to have plenty of riches, honor, and awe."[21]

But Luther seems to be at no pains to augment their prestige. With the psalmist, "He poureth contempt upon princes," and announces that a new era is at hand, when "the common man" is catching on to these fools and knaves and will suffer their tyranny no longer.

> Dear princes and lords, you must accommodate yourselves to that fact. God will endure it no longer. The world is no longer what it once was, when you chased people like so many animals. So forsake your vice and violence, look to it that you deal justly, and let God's word take its course.[22]

After dire predictions of rebellion (which he would shortly regret, for the peasants' uprisings of 1525 were just around the corner), Luther concluded by coming back to the question, "What if your prince were wrong? Is his people obliged to obey him? The answer is: No. Because no one is supposed to act against what is right."[23] Such talk, in Duke George's opinion, was sedition.

But the next round belonged to him. It was in that difficult year of 1525. Just shortly after Luther's apology to Henry VIII he sent also a conciliatory, if somewhat less servile letter to George. George promptly published it, together with a tedious stipulation of all the offenses Luther had given him. He may thus have set a model for Henry to follow (the king's public humiliation of Luther coming about a year later). Shaken by the peasants' uprisings, Luther was intimidated of sovereigns like George and Henry who had branded his teachings as subversive from the start. "When has there been more rebellion against authority," George demanded, "than from your gospel?"[24] The words burned deep, and it was not George's last triumph. His spies were able to procure sheets of a Luther pamphlet still in press. George used it to extract an agreement to quash publication. Now it was his turn to keep archly mum when asked how he had obtained Luther's unreleased work.[25]

He got hold of another of Luther's personal letters, this time to a friend in Nuremberg (in handwritten copy). It contained a reference to George which George took to mean, "May God damn this supreme fool." Luther said the original had not contained the optative *confundat*, but the future tense, *confundet*="God will confound this supreme fool." At any rate, the entire comedy commenced anew, George demanding that Luther admit or deny writing the letter, Luther refusing to be accountable and asking not to be bothered. Again George came fuming to Luther's prince, in the meantime sending agents to Nuremberg to procure the original (which the recipient had no doubt destroyed). A gifted writer himself, the duke appealed to the public, at his own expense printing up about ten times as many copies of his pamphlet as the printers were accustomed to running off for popular items. Now it was Luther who got one up. By somehow obtaining purloined printers' copy of the duke's *opus*, he dashed off a formidable response to it. Thus George's complaint reached the bookdealers no sooner than Luther's rebuttal. So the paper and ink flew for some years.

Duke George was not a vicious man. He did not dip his hands in blood (as Henry VIII so frequently did, martyring his noblest subjects). But he was quite determined that the ideas of this "false, perjured, renegade monk" be banished from his dominions.[26] It was no easy task. Since his subjects often lived but a stone's throw from a reformed church on his cousin's territory, he sometimes was forced to absurd lengths in enforcement of orthodoxy. He proclaimed that any who did not receive extreme unction from a Roman priest must be buried in the knacker's yard. Holy communion, however, was the prime, fantastically powerful symbol in this contest. In Roman practice, the laity took Christ's body, while the priest alone drank the precious blood as well, the wine. George vigorously exiled any layman who took both the bread and the wine, or who refused orthodox communion. He conceded that the laity might have the bread and *unconsecrated* wine, so long as the precious blood of Christ were reserved for the priest alone.[27] At Easter of 1533 he had badges issued by his Leipzig clergy to those who took orthodox communion (brass for the nobility, tin for commoners), and required the badge be displayed by all who wished to maintain their residence in his land.

Luther, asked for advice by a Leipzig pastor, wrote that one must act in accord with one's conscience. For any who truly believed communion must be taken in both kinds, no subterfuge could be recommended. George deserved to be deceived, Luther admitted, because he had no authority to inquire into private consciences,

> but we must not concern ourselves with what others do, even murderers and thieves, only with what we ourselves ought to do and suffer. So in this case it is probably best to look the murderer and thief in the eye and say, "I will not do that. If you want to deprive me of life and property, then it is another whom you persecute, not me."[28]

Since this letter had mentioned George by name, the old routine unfolded anew. This time the mayor of Leipzig was required to ask Luther if he would acknowledge the writing, and Luther defiantly asked who wanted to know. This spat eventually led to a formal compact between the Saxon princes that in future their theologians must refrain from naming Saxon heads of state in their writings. Luther abided by the agreement, and thus might have ended the quarrel with George.

But we all tend to feel our oats when our birthday is approaching, and so it was with Luther in 1534. Besides, for him All Saints' Day heralded that invigorating season when he had "begun to write against the pope." His sermon for All Saints' quite naturally admonished against the worship of saints, recommending instead that we thank God for these examples of true piety. As the preacher, just beginning his second half century, looked out over the congregation he beheld many a young face there who could scarcely appreciate what he was saying, because they had never really experienced the papacy, and he saw many not so young to whom the Roman excesses of the past were but memories now. He expressed his concern about a future in which that wickedness would be entirely forgotten. Was not Cardinal Albert (to whom he had turned just seventeen years ago, begging that the bishop tend his flock) unregenerate to this day, and still persecuting the faithful? He urged the congregation to pray against such princes.[29]

Little edified by the sermon and prayer was the cardinal's niece, daughter of the refugee Elizabeth of Brandenburg, whom she was visiting and who had brought her along to church, as well as to Luther's table afterward. This was the same young lady who had betrayed her mother to Joachim some years earlier. Never very kindly disposed toward Luther, now she was just scandalized by the perfectly horrible things he said about the crowned heads of Europe. She promptly told her father so. According to the report which reached him in Berlin, and was soon relayed to George's court in Dresden, Luther had conducted public prayer against both Albert and George.

Praying was a serious business, and Doctor Luther known far and wide for the efficacy of his prayer. To think of him and an entire congregation lifting voices to heaven, inveighing against you, was sobering. Protest was not long in coming to John Frederick. Again Luther found himself required to answer yea or nay to an allegation, but this time it was his own liege lord the elector of Saxony who was putting the question to him. Must George at last be given satisfaction?

We marvel less at the old fellow's rashness thus to pray against princes in the presence of their relatives, than we do at his eminently sane handling of the repercussions. Written communication to Luther from John Frederick was stern enough, and it was accompanied by a more detailed inquiry from his chancellor, Doctor Brück, giving instructions as to a form Luther's defense might take. A delegation from George was expected within ten days. In the meantime, Luther should prepare

a statement setting forth both the facts of the case and the cause
for his actions. The latter must be supported with Holy Scripture so as to show "that it was fitting for you before God, and
incumbent upon your conscience thus to pray against them in
Christian congregation, hence not actionable as libel. For if they
can convict your reverence, they will not fail to demand
punishment."[30] He closed with a few legal pointers and an offer
to help in combing through the opposition's publications for possible offenses on their side. Brück attached a less formal note
which deserves to be quoted in full:

> His grace also desires that you prepare separate defenses, so as
> to make one set of charges against the [arch]bishop (for if
> your reverence would like to pour it on the cleric that is all
> right), and another for Duke George. His grace would be
> pleased if you wished to tread a bit lightly in his case—if it
> causes no offense to the glory of God and his word.[31]

Any real punishment of Luther was probably beyond the imag-
inings of Brück and his young prince. They obviously expected
—and not without relish—another of those delightfully scurrilous, demolishing philippics. But they were disappointed. Doctor
Martinus set aside a day or two, then returned two letters to
John Frederick. One was a somewhat paternal note of thanks for
his trouble, reminding him not to take Duke George too
seriously. The other seems no less personal, although Luther
called it a letter which could be "published and read"—

> Where shall I turn, most gracious lord? I would wish the
> noble prince had called me to accounts by someone less highly
> placed than a prince elector. I regret seeing your grace cast as
> servant on such errands, and am no little aggrieved that such
> an exalted prince [as your cousin], on the basis of hearsay
> alone, without seal or witness, should so blatantly and crudely
> inform on a poor man like me—nay, lodge formal complaint
> against me before the lord of my land to whom I have sworn
> allegiance . . . So I most humbly beg your princely grace to
> spare me, nor to desire that I reply to such a charge—not for
> my sake, but for that of Duke George. For I might render too
> coarse an answer to his crude, awkward letter. Should your

grace desire it, however, I will do yeomanly work, and answer it well.[32]

Toward Christmas a delegation from Duke George discussed the issue with John Frederick. He reported to Luther that he was unable to determine for a fact that George's name had occurred in Luther's sermon, as had been alleged. He therefore asked Luther to forbear, insofar as his conscience would permit, "mentioning our cousin by name," so as to preserve at least the appearance of peace. "We wish to set no limits, however, to what you cannot omit in good conscience or in preserving your honor against Duke George's theologians, nor do we wish you to apprehend our intent as other than gracious."[33] That is to say, unable to verify hearsay evidence or to extract a confession from Luther, John Frederick proceeded on the assumption of his innocence. We are not likely to make a much wiser determination at our remove.

Indeed, our view is obscured by the intervening generations of busy detractors accusing Luther of the sin of anger, and of pious Lutherans boasting of it as righteous scorn.[34] An American enthusiast actually compares his champion with two renowned pugilists of the ring in point of "finesse" and "violence."[35] In the protracted feud with Duke George, Luther was at no time *angry* if that would imply he had ever lost his sense of humor or his characteristically ironic distance. George was one of those adversaries against whom he employed language as a sharp instrument —much as he used the printing press. He did not regard his own writings as lasting, the way he looked on Philip Melanchthon's work. He said of himself:

I was born to go to war and give battle to sects and devils. That is why my books are stormy and warlike. I have to root out the stumps and clumps, hack away the thorns and brambles. I am the great feller of forests, who must clear the land and level it. But Master Philip comes softly and neatly, tills and plants, sows and waters with pleasure, as God has abundantly given him the talents.[36]

Coarse work wants coarse implements, and Luther attributed his heavy-handed writing to his blunt purpose, not to his emotionality.

At the same time, he did admit to being a "wrathful man,"[37] and our appreciation of how his personality developed does require attention to his increasing irascibility, especially in the late writings. The trend may have begun in a quarrel quite unworthy of his participation.

"They tell of a virgin," Doctor Martinus leered one day at table, "Eve of Trott, with whom Duke Henry of Brunswick begat three children in her maidenhood and five after she died."[38] It was true that this Henry of Brunswick had celebrated a bogus funeral for a favorite mistress whom he then secreted away to a pleasure palace, where he kept her for years. It was but one of the more lurid scandals connected with a prince who was every bit as willful and frivolous as the Saxons were conscientious and dutiful. Hostilities between Henry and John Frederick took the form of extremely vitriolic publications in which the princes hurled vile epithets. Luther was not affected until Henry happened to write the words: "That Saxon prince whom his dear devout Martin Luther calls Hans Wurst"[39]—Hans Wurst being the German Harlequin. The allegation cut Luther so smartly that we may suspect some truth to it. Perhaps Henry, like George, had access to comings and goings at the Black Cloister and to certain of the voluble doctor's unguarded moments. Luther's best defense was an aggressive pamphlet of his own: *Against Hans Wurst*, where he turned the appellation back against Henry and indulged in name-calling quite in tone with the ongoing war of epithets. It marked the beginning of a new era in Luther's literary career.

The philippics of his old age forsake the subtler rhetorical finesse of his earlier work, to rely more heavily on mere wrangling and scurrilous invective. It is a late development, which came after a quarter century of conflicts, some of them fraught with danger, others with bitter disappointment, like the dispute with Erasmus or quarrels with former disciples. The turn to invective was not, however, the mere product of righteous anger, as the Luther legend would have us believe. In the corrected manuscript of *Against Hans Wurst*, for example, we find some of the worst invectives entered in cool deliberation as Luther reread his work.[40] He wrote wryly to Melanchthon he couldn't imagine what had happened to him, that I was so moderate. I guess it was the condition of my head, which did not suffer my heart to be seized by more sincere and powerful drives. Let him just try me again, the Lord be willing. Still, I am happy to have written a little on the subject of the church.[41]

He was referring to the detail in which the pamphlet argued the Romans had deviated from the church, not the protestants.[42] The tract also offered occasion to recall his initial (1517) differences with Roman authorities over the sales of papal indulgences.[43] Thus *Against Hans Wurst* is an important source document for those early events. It is better known, however, for its insolent "tousling" of another grand head of Renaissance Europe.

Luther's friends as well as his enemies, perhaps more in awe of royalty than he was, have apologized for his scathing attacks on those in high places, and have used his own candid self-criticism, his admissions of moodiness and irascibility to do so. We should not forget the quality of men he was dealing with. The duke of Brunswick, for example, was reported to have chained the ambassador from Goslar to a wall and fed him bread and water, finally then to have nailed the poor fellow there.[44] Luther spoke his mind to that same daughter of Elizabeth of Brandenburg when she made an importunate visit to her mother, being nursed by Kate. She insisted on speaking to Luther, but he excused himself, saying,

> Gracious lady, I have few good days in the year, but suffer alternate afflictions of body and spirit. You'd be surprised to find as many sores on my body as stars in the heavens. I just wish the archbishop and grand reprobate of Mainz had them.

She tried to escape hearing worse about her uncle, saying, "Herr Doctor, we cannot all be pious." But he persisted,

> You of the nobility and high estates should of necessity all be pious, for you are few. Yet you are debauched. It is no wonder that the great multitude of commoners is dissolute. From you, whom virtue should elevate, we have a right to expect an example of piety, integrity, and upright living.[45]

We shall have further opportunity to examine Luther's motives for vitriolic writing when we consider his dealings with the cardinal of Mainz, whom on this occasion his niece made no further attempt to shield.

At our remove, however, there is probably little point in defending his harsh methods. When we come to the stark writings of his last years, his denunciation of the pope and disparagement of the Jews, few would support them. But even then we must not patronize Luther by dismissing his writing as mere emotional outburst. Few authors have had as much experience with the pen as he, and rare is the human who has so carefully searched his own soul. Luther knew what he was doing.

Print and Reprint

Luther's boldness seems incredible. He beards the king of England from afar. Close by all the powerful princes cringe—Brandenburg, Brunswick, George of Saxony. We must yet describe his rigorous disciplining of Germany's most powerful sovereign, the cardinal of Mainz. Luther was the first writer able so freely to castigate abuse at its source, and perhaps the last.

The sixteenth century had witnessed the concentration of enormous wealth. In this sense, the most influential European was certainly Jacob Fugger, by whose immense capital Charles V had attained to his outward show of authority. But to these sources of power, economic and political, a third was added around 1520, which no one yet fully appreciated: the power lent by technology. The printing press, in use for about three generations, quite suddenly became one of the major forces to be reckoned with in Europe. Historians often say it made the protestant Reformation possible. They like to quote Francis Bacon's remark that the printing press (together with the compass and gunpowder) transformed the whole face of the world. Such statements, though true, are misleading. By attributing everything to mere physical tools, they distract us from the forces which inspired their design, use, and change. Printing is history's very best example of a tool which was transformed by its employment. In the first heat of religious pluralism in Germany (1517–23) something entirely new in human affairs sprang into existence: general literacy. Print was used to bring it about, and the printing establishment was itself transformed in the process.[1]

Reading had been spreading among Europeans for some centuries, though only an infinitesimal fraction of the populace was

involved. Growth had been gradual, accelerated little by technical advances, such as printing from wooden blocks. The really
decisive limit on book production in the early Middle Ages was
the high cost of the page. A hundred head of sheep went to produce a vellum book. The success of paper mills in the thirteenth
and fourteenth centuries permitted a rapid and steady decline in
cost of materials for about the next three hundred years (until
the runaway inflation of the Thirty Years' War). Still, the cost
of paper remained larger than all the other factors in the price of
a book. As people became more well-to-do, the expansion of
trade and commerce quickened the spread of reading, but the
most effective limit to book production was the relatively small
readership: still only a fraction of a per cent of Europe's largely
rural population.[2]

Else movable type would have been employed sooner than it
was. Printing had been going on in the Orient for some centuries. Printed playing cards had long been circulating in
Europe: there was a demand for them. The question posed by
many authors is: what can have so long *delayed* the use of print
for books? A "Moslem barrier" is sometimes cited, the Islamic
objection to printing holy writings.[3] A better explanation may
be that the printing of books was simply not perceived as eco-
nomical. The massive effort required to produce movable type
wanted a mass readership.

The "invention" attributed to Gutenberg was a marvel of
synthesizing genius. Many technical problems had to be solved in
such disparate fields as metallurgy, paper manufacture, and ink
preparation (old scribal materials were not suited to the new
process). An entirely new theory of mass production and the
idea of interchangeability of parts had to be imposed on conservative artisans. Existing technologies had to be adapted, like the
screw press from its use in laundry and vineyard. What can have
motivated such an energetic breakthrough, probably by several
collaborators? It is not at all to detract from the nobility of Gutenberg's vision to observe that the use of movable type to produce books could not itself *create* a mass audience, but was
rather predicated on one. Reciprocal interaction between available technology and social forces characterizes the history of the
book. Literacy rates of the Middle Ages are anybody's guess, but

by the year 1500 they had grown to perhaps 3 to 4 per cent in Germany. The printing press had brought no explosion in literacy during its first half century. It had permitted the long-increasing demand for books to continue its gradual growth.[4]

The explosion in German book production was simultaneous with Luther's sensational rejection of papal authority. He appealed over the heads of bureaucrats to the written word. He claimed that anyone could form his own judgment of the issues under contention. In 1500, the press had been turning out about 40 German titles a year. By 1517 (Luther questioned indulgence sales in the fall of that year), no great change was apparent. In 1518, 71 German titles came off the presses, of which Luther himself had written 20. That was the start. In 1519, there were 111 titles, of which he had written 51. In 1520 the figures were 208 and 133. By 1523, 498 German titles were being printed, 180 of these by Luther.[5] Of course, these "books" were not the ponderous tomes to which people had been accustomed, but relatively cheap, aesthetically most attractive pamphlets. It was a new literary form. Families and friends read them together, delighting in the sport of sounding out the unfamiliar symbols on the page, puzzling over the many difficulties, roaring at the puns, guffawing at hitherto sacrosanct personages.

Latin titles were proliferating, too—not until the eighteenth century would as many books be published in German as Latin. Erasmus became popular in new editions. But the market was dominated by German. During the boom years 1520–23 the ratio of Latin works to German declined from 20:1 to 3:1. Press runs of German pamphlets rose from a few hundred copies to about a thousand. Melchior Lotter ran off four thousand copies of Luther's *Address to the Christian Nobility* (1520) and was soon reissuing it to compete with reprints by other houses. His run of five thousand for the first edition of Luther's New Testament is often cited. That outraged pamphlet which Duke George subsidized against Luther, mentioned earlier, came out in eight thousand copies. Probably as many as 10 per cent of the German population were reading Luther, and in the cities several times that proportion.

Gutenberg had demonstrated that there existed a demand for reading materials beyond that being filled by the medieval scriptorium. It remained for Luther to show how the Gutenberg press could meet a far higher demand than any hitherto dreamed —but it could not do so as the industry was at that time organized. Placing the product in the hands of the new mass public forced fundamental adaptations on the still embryonic enterprise. These adjustments, for which Luther was himself largely responsible, determined the conditions under which authors worked and books were published for centuries to come.

Quantity of production alone had ceased to be a problem. Although the printing venture required capital, profits were quick and new enterprises sprang up until no city of any size was without its printer-bookseller. These businesses were geared to the local market. The problems the printing industry had to solve were ones of logistics and transportation. Roads in central Europe remained notoriously wheel-and-axle-breaking right into the nineteenth century. To pack up barrels of books and ship them across the country entailed such great trouble, expense, and risk that it was never undertaken on a large scale. Yet Luther's popularity was not a mere Saxon phenomenon. His pamphlets and those by cohorts and adversaries were the talk of every German town. How were these markets supplied?

Printers, like the medieval artisans and merchants, traditionally relied on periodic fairs. The Wittenberg bookman would transport to Leipzig a few of his own products in numerous copies. There he did not exchange them for cash money, but for a few copies of numerous titles from abroad. These now he could sell or barter at home. By this process only a few Wittenberg imprints came to Strasbourg. Items in greater demand were reprinted on the spot. Authors' "rights" were unknown. Nor did Luther, the first immensely popular and profitable author, do anything to assert them. Reprinting became, in the 1520s, characteristic of the German book industry. It remained so for nearly three hundred years, or during the classical age of German letters.

"Wildcat printing" might be a more accurate term. It was not unusual for a Luther sermon, transcribed by some member of the congregation, to be printed by an unauthorized press, reprinted in various towns, but never to be issued in Wittenberg. It was through wildcat printing that he became widely read throughout his own and foreign lands. Only one copy of a sermon or pamphlet, not a barrelful, need make the perilous and sodden journey across Europe. The book fair was short-circuited. Reprinters provided the important service of making new titles available quickly and in quantity, and keeping them on the market longer than the original issue. The reprint enterprise, developed under the pressures of increasing literacy, became the distributing and marketing arm of the book trade. With the outreach thus provided, print became for the first time a true mass medium.

The entrepreneurship of printers had scattered Luther's 95 Theses against indulgences far and wide in 1518 (where they were first printed is unknown). Whether we hold with the legend that he did in fact post them for debate, or whether we accept the view that he intended them only for the eyes of his bishops and a few colleagues, it was the printing establishment and not he who took them before the public. After they became a *cause célèbre* he repeatedly said he would be silent if his opponents would but cease to publish against him. When he boasted of the power of the word, his victories in print came to mind. Luther and the printing press had imparted each to the other a power new on the face of the earth—mass appeal. He sometimes abused this power. He often felt victimized by it.

Of his venerable university printer who had for years been turning out sheets to be used in the lecture hall, Luther wrote bitterly,

> It is wondrous how I rue and despise Grunenberg's work. Oh, that I had never published anything in German, so shabby, careless, and garbled is the typesetting, not even to mention the quality of type and paper![6]

His author-like concern about outward appearance, though frequently expressed, was the least of his worries. In 1519, he preached a sermon on matrimony which, to his surprise, came back to him in copies from Leipzig and faraway Breslau. Puzzled to behold his alleged words in print, he blamed neither the surreptitious note-takers nor the printers in trying to explain why he was issuing his own edition:

> A sermon on matrimony has been published in my name; I wish it had not happened. Although I do remember having

preached on the subject, I cannot believe it was correctly transcribed. Hence I have been moved to change that version and improve it as much as possible. I ask every pious man to permit the first published sermon to perish and be forgot. Also, let him who would commit my preaching to writing be not hasty. Allow me to be consulted on the publication of my own words. There is a big difference between the living voice and dead print.[7]

By 1523, the poor fellow was actually pleading from the pulpit, "For Christ's sake I beg all who are down there committing my sermons to paper or memory not to print them until they have my own draft, or until I have myself had them printed here in Wittenberg."[8] He honestly felt he was publishing in self-defense, it happened so frequently that his sermons were printed, as he said, "without my knowledge or desire, perhaps for profit or for spite . . . The printers add what they will, and so corrupt my sermons I cannot understand them myself, even though they bear my name."[9] The quick profits promised by anything bearing his name brought more serious consequences than mere garbling of the text. During the Diet of Augsburg in 1530, a Coburg printer managed to come by certain articles being discussed by the protestants. To assure good sales, he issued them over Luther's name. It appeared as if Luther had decided to have them presented at Augsburg, and the papal side responded to them thus, dealing the protestants a diplomatic setback.

But even thievery was not a new experience for him. In 1525 he had been moved to add a preface to a collection of his sermons financed by Lucas Cranach which I will quote at length. It tells an interesting story:

What are we to think, dear gentlemen of the press, when you so openly rob and steal each other's property and ruin one another? Have you added highway robbery to your trade, or do you think that God will bless and nourish you for such wicked tricks? I began my postils from Epiphany to Easter— and a rascal, the typesetter, who makes his own living from our efforts, comes along and steals my manuscript [from the Cranach shop] before I have it quite finished, takes it away and has it printed somewhere else [in Regensburg, although

Luther had not yet figured that out] causing us to lose our investment and effort . . . the damage could be endured if they
did not set up my writings so inaccurately and shamefully. But
they print them in such a rush that when I get them back I do
not know my own books. Here something is dropped, there
the type is wrong, here what I said is changed, elsewhere you
find typographical errors. They have also learned the trick of
printing "Wittenberg" on title pages that were neither made in
Wittenberg nor have ever passed through the city . . . It is
not right that we work and invest money, while others take
the profit and we the loss. So let all be warned . . . In proof-
reading I frequently make important emendations in my own
original, so that it is unreliable. Anyone who wants that version should carefully correct it in accordance with this one.[10]

If outside printers robbed him, local entrepreneurs gulled him.
Persuaded that the manuscript thief was a radical from Nuremberg, he wrote a long letter to the mayor and council of that
city asking them to take measures. It had clearly been dictated to
Luther by his good friend Cranach and his partner Christian
Döring, or other Wittenberg money interests, and is valuable to
us for its detailed treatment of the business problems caused by
reprinters. The letter stresses the great expense involved in
"large" books (as distinct from pamphlets). It asks at least "seven
or eight weeks'" interval for sales of an original imprint before
reprints are issued so close by. The lively reprinting business in
the Rhineland is acknowledged, but that is said to be a separate
market. In short, a sophisticated business voice is here blended
with that of the sincere evangelist, who even complains he has
been holding back his Bible translation, lest it be the "ruin" of
local business—presumably because of the large investment.
When we consider, on the one hand, the handsome profits the
Wittenberg printers drew from Luther's presence, and on the
other the rush of events during these hectic months of 1525, then
the enlistment of the distracted scholar by Wittenberg financial
interests seems poignant—but when have businessmen failed to
take themselves seriously?[11]

We owe to the sharp business eye of Cranach and his partner a
very early example of the use of a trademark to protect financial

interest in an intellectual's work. When they began issuing the Old Testament in 1524, a Cranach woodcut of Luther's coat of arms (a rose with a cross in it—the so-called "Luther rose") appeared above the words: "Let this sign bear witness that the book has passed through my hands, for unauthorized and incorrect printing has become widespread."[12] In the 1541 Bible, he went so far as to enter a two-page preface warning how the sin of greed has led printers "one on the heels of the other to print for their own profit, so as to rob our local citizens of their work and investment."[13] He admits his own objection is solely to poor workmanship—"They go at it hell for leather, money's the thing."[14] As for the finances, "I have no personal interest. Freely have I received, freely I give. I desire no payment for it. Christ my Lord has rewarded me a thousandfold."[15]

That Luther remained a patsy for printers who gained his ear is evidenced by the scores of prefaces the busy man wrote for books by others. Some of these include positive encouragement of reprinting, as in the Bapst Song Book, which contained songs by Luther as well as others who had in no way authorized their use. Obviously, we should not impute to Luther notions about property rights which were not evolved until later centuries. The business ethic, which attaches pecuniary equivalents to talent, was quite alien to him, and he was ambivalent about the merit of reprinters. On the one hand, he recognized that the Wittenbergers' investments in his books were somehow important to them. At the same time, he did hope his Bible would be as widely distributed as possible. "I am just worried that people are not continuing to read much in the Bible," he said. "They are becoming sated, for the reprinters are no longer active."[16]

Luther's own total unconcern about drawing any monetary advantage from his prolific writing abetted the reprinting business and set a pattern which contemporaries and successors followed. No author was expected to derive a living from the new technology, as the printers did. An author's efforts, just as in the centuries before printing, were gratis. The lavish profits of the new technology fell to the printers themselves, who, as the first capitalist entrepreneurs, were awed at the tremendous investment they had made in their plant. Any man able to write was assumed already to have his secure station in feudal society. Writ-

ing continued, just as in the days of the scriptorium, to be supported by a noble patron.

Luther confessed that when he had first taken his wife, he had
thought he might have to earn his living. The electors of Saxony,
however, were most solicitous of him, and his vigorous mate
proved a skillful manager of their largesse. He took not merely
an independent attitude toward the printers, but a contemptuous
one. He proudly said that his prince required no duties of him
whatever. When printers offered him a handsome retainer he
said the ungrateful wretches wished to bind him to their presses,
as obligated to them. He had been stung when Hans Lufft had
held back free copies of the Bible—"These ungrateful beasts
wouldn't even give me a copy for my co-workers. Phooey, isn't
that terrible?"[17] He explicitly preferred aristocratic patronage
over cash payment and did not apply one of his favorite proverbs, "I sing his song whose bread I eat," to the lord of his land.[18]
He took it for granted that all cultural responsibilities, like the
support of the church, devolved upon the prince. As a consequence, later generations of German writers found they had no
realistic alternative to accepting—more often seeking—patronage.
Not so Luther. He felt his had been a conscious and deliberate
choice. When offered four hundred gulden a year by a printers'
consortium, he proudly said he would not "sell his favor"—

> I have quite enough and more than enough, praise be to God,
> who gave me a wife and children (my greatest blessing) as
> well as an elector who of his own free will endowed me with
> 200 fl. a year. Else my marriage would have reduced me to lec-
> turing for pay. God having prevented this through the elector,
> I have never in my life sold printers' copy or lectured for pay,
> and this boast—God willing—I will take with me to the
> grave.[19]

Thus the dominant figure in the crucial development of print
spurned his printers. As a consequence printers paid inconse-
quential royalties, or none at all, to German authors until well
into the eighteenth century, when men like Klopstock and Lessing made pitiful efforts to draw printer and author together.
Klopstock, the most celebrated lyricist of his day, was dependent
on the patronage of the king of Denmark, and spent his produc-

tive years abroad. Lessing, after establishing himself as Germany's greatest critic, received unsatisfactory sinecures, his precarious finances figuring largely in his tragic career. The publishing scene was still dominated by printers and reprinters.

Wildcat printing was the delivery system which evolved in a new technology under pressure of an overwhelming demand for its product. Even though book burnings, sometimes in great quantity, still occurred, they had now become admittedly symbolic. The terrible new effectiveness of print was genuinely feared. A pasquil of 1546, *Neu Zeitung vom Teufel* ("News from the Devil"), depicted devil and pope in great trepidation over the reissue of an older work by Luther—

> *Pope:* I certainly fear we shan't succeed, even though I and all my cardinals, bishops, abbots, their canons, and all our clerics have had it purchased throughout Germany, and burned, in the hope that not one copy might remain by which printers' type could be set.[20]

However flippantly this might have been intended, it suggests that the purpose Luther declared upon his original issue of the work was being fulfilled: "To reach each man's conscience."[21]

"That Damned Cardinal"

A church council imminent, Luther's correspondence in the middle 1530s reveals him ever busier with church affairs, but he had numerous other concerns as well. The most sensational was the judicial murder of Hans Schönitz by Germany's most powerful prince, the cardinal of Mainz. It eventually led to one of Martin Luther's most significant legal papers, showing how his relatively simple theological tenets could have implications for the thinking of ordinary men about their laws and government. Luther's relationship with Cardinal Albert of Mainz gives important insight into his character and career. It began when Albert, then a frivolous young man in his twenties, almost single-handedly precipitated the Protestant Reformation.[1]

He was of the prominent Hohenzollern dynasty in Brandenburg, younger brother of that willful prince Joachim, but was always better disposed toward Luther than his older brother. Joachim had acquired the archbishopric of Magdeburg for Albert, as well as other offices, before the young man was of an age to receive the pope's final confirmation. While he was yet in his twenty-third year, Albert was also advanced as the archbishop of Mainz. This title brought with it immense power beyond the church, for two reasons. Mainz was not only one of the seven electors in the Holy Roman Empire (together with Trier, Cologne, Bohemia, the Palatinate, Saxony, and Brandenburg), it was also the first of these, carrying the dignity of the archchancellorship of the empire. All important documents required not only the seal of the emperor, but also countersignature by the archbishop of Mainz.

The papacy regularly exacted a fee for any bishop's pallium,

and the house of Brandenburg had in this case to pay not only
for Magdeburg and Mainz, but also for special dispensation: Albert's privilege of occupying two archbishoprics at the same
time. The enormous sum was advanced by the Augsburg finan-
cier Jacob Fugger, who is said to have contributed fifty thousand gulden in all.[2] The Roman curia itself offered Albert means
of repayment. He was granted, for the space of eight years, the
right to indulgence sales throughout Germany for the building
of Saint Peter's Cathedral, that glorious project begun by Pope
Julius II in Luther's youth. Half the proceeds from the sales
were to go to Rome. The other half might be used to repay to
the Fuggers money already received by Rome.

Luther had known nothing, of course, about these financial arrangements, but in 1516 he did begin to hear tales about excesses
in the huckstering of papal indulgences in neighboring territories.[3] He was inclined to believe the very worst, because he
had seen the lengthy instructions which had gone out over Albert's name.[4] They read like some horrible parody on bureaucratic attention to the pettiest detail, and purblindness for any
genuine human values. It is doubtful, of course, that the young
archbishop had ever read the instructions which bore his signature, much less had he composed them himself. He was, after all,
a Renaissance prince in the grand style, known for his sumptuous
taste in women and for his connoisseurship and munificent patronage of the arts.[5] The age did not wish its great lords, even
lords of the church, to forsake their representative life-style for
drudgery in administration. These tediously thorough instructions for the indulgence sales are clearly the work of professional
pedants in chancellery. They pay tribute to bureaucratic love of
precision.

They are timeless in the eloquent testimony they bear to the
nature of institutional corruption. The archbishop of Magdeburg
and Mainz, archchancellor of the Holy Roman Empire, was not
a wicked man, but a good-natured youth who, it was said, kept
the bones of a cherished mistress in his reliquary. His administration was not evil, but one of highly efficient functionaries,
certain in the correctness of their performance. It was characteristic of the thriving, advanced culture of Renaissance Europe,
a pinnacle of civilization, rightly confident of its arrangements

for refined living. Imagine the security at a Roman court able to confirm a lad in his early twenties, known only for his good family and frivolous ways, to the most powerful post in Germany. As a final touch of tragic irony, in 1518—after Albert's performance in office had precipitated the great reform of the church—the curia added a cardinalship to the stripling's other honorifics.

Albert's instructions in the sales of papal indulgences provoked not only Luther, but others as well. The authors of the instructions, in their fastidiousness about collections, were most encouraging about the deeds and omissions for which indulgences were touted as needful. Luther, perhaps supposing he might at the least call attention to what was going on, sent to bishops in his own and neighboring districts certain polite letters along with copies of a little treatise of his (probably from a sermon[6]) and, for good measure, a list of ninety-five theses for a hypothetical debate on the subject of papal indulgences. It was an attempt to formulate the issue in such a simple and provocative way that even a young fellow like Albert might grasp it. The theses eventually had a sensational effect precisely because Albert paid no attention. Others did.

The materials for Albert were sent to his palace in Halle at the end of October 1517, but since he was not in residence there at the moment they were routed on to his chancellery at Magdeburg, where they were marked received on 17 November. By the middle of the subsequent month, the archbishop had them, for he informed advisers in Magdeburg that there had been read to him a letter "with attached treatise and theses by an impertinent monk in Wittenberg touching the holy business of indulgences." He was forwarding the documents to his university for an opinion, as well as to Rome. In the meantime, he recommended steps be taken to prevent any further attacks on indulgence sales, be it in sermons, writings, or in the form of debates.[7] None were taken, however. Doctor Luther's little protest had become firmly bogged in the official machinery.

That lurid image of a resolute monk hammering his ninety-five theses onto the door of the castle church in Wittenberg, thus with his furious blows smiting Christendom asunder, has not stood up well under a cool examination of its sources.[8] That is fortunate, because it certainly led to a misapprehension of Luther's situation at the time. We who also live among mammoth, mindless institutions tended by correct functionaries recognize his predicament very well, and we sympathize with his quandary. He was no warrior, as the militant tradition soon began to depict him, but a timid professor not unhappy with his sequestered life. When no response came from the bishops, any hope of interfering with the flourishing indulgence trade faded. Yet, as academics will, Doctor Luther had brought the subject up for discussion among fellow intellectuals.

He knew that print, which he was accustomed to using for lecture-hall purposes, afforded little privacy. He therefore recopied the ninety-five theses by hand, making minor revisions as he went along. The way these articles were welcomed by the few recipients was an indication to him of how really widespread his own private concern had been. The theses were recopied by others, further circulated, and eventually printed—probably first in Nuremberg. By the time Luther himself placed such ideas directly before the public,[9] the Ninety-five Theses had become a sensation in Germany, and in Rome Sylvester Prierias was responding to them by invoking the absolute authority of the pope.

During the next two years the *causa Lutheri,* as it was called, took on importance for the entire European order of things—yet Luther's own writings strike a modern reader as very docile and orthodox. He thought so too, in retrospect. Early in 1520, he again addressed two nearby bishops, this time to express his concern about the way he was being condemned for no apparent reason. His tone in the letter to Albert—in the meantime Cardinal Albert—shows he honestly thought that dignitary might read it. For example:

> I am compelled to teach what I have learned and what I have read in sacred writings; and I am condemned for teaching what my accusers will not—or cannot—condemn. Oh, if you, most gracious lord, but had the leisure to read or hear my writings! I have no doubt that you, most reverend father, would by the grace of God recognize how alien to me the charges they heap upon me are.[10]

The reply sent out over Cardinal Albert's name would appear to have been composed by some wag bent on ridiculing great lords. After a pompous introduction, the letter says he

> cannot be displeased that you promise to hearken unto better ways, if instructed, and are prepared to give up your views. While we confess that this matter of Christian faith and piety mightily affects our heart in our official duty, we have not had the leisure for so much as a superficial look at your writings, which are circulating through everyone's hands. Wherefore we deign not to censure them, but rather leave it to the discretion of our betters, whom by law we revere and to whom in judgment we yield.

The letter went on to voice a kind of sublime disapproval of the disturbances caused by "frivolous opinions and quibblings, as for example, about whether the authority of the Roman pope derive from human or divine law, about the freedom of the will, and many other such trivialities which do not concern a true Christian." The letter closed in anticipation that these subjects may be discussed in the future by those authorized to do so, without troubling the "multitudes."[11] It must have been becoming obvious to Luther at last that, so far, he had never communicated with his excellency the cardinal archbishop at all.

But the pudgy prelate was beginning to be troubled by the "multitudes." The militant peasants' league, the Bundschuh, posted a threatening placard in support of Luther at the Diet of Worms in 1521. Few took it seriously, but Albert was shaken. His new, shrewd adviser Wolfgang Capito played on his trepidations in order to withhold Albert's all-important signature from the Edict of Worms (the imperial ban against Luther, issued after the diet), and to forestall its implementation in Germany. We have seen how Capito collaborated with Melanchthon and Spalatin in Wittenberg to temper the relations between the powerful, craven prince and the powerless, fiery professor. It was an early example of the importance of public opinion created by the press. Luther threatened, if Albert did not cease the sale of papal indulgences in nearby Halle, to publish a polemic against him. He promptly received a subservient, even sniveling agreement to comply. He suspected it had been composed by Capito, but Albert was at least sincere in a desire to preserve the peace. It may be that he attributed to Luther some influence with the rebellious peasants. The year of their uprising was also the year of Luther's marriage, and the cardinal sent an extravagant wedding gift of twenty gulden. Although Luther refused it, Kate made sure the money did not leave the house.[12]

In the later 1520s Luther actually began to entertain hope that Albert might join the reform of the church in German territories.[13] He overlooked evidence that the cardinal, far from turning conscientious, was guilty of criminal connivance, if not conspiracy, in the assassination of a reformed preacher, George Winkler.[14] And indeed, confrontation between Luther and his cardinal, when at last it came, was not in church matters at all, but pertained to a judicial murder. Luther did not act as promptly in the case as he might have, but in the end he did establish his thesis clearly and well. It was a point of special importance for his Renaissance public: equality must prevail before the law, even where a powerful prince may be implicated.

Any German prince, even Albert, required the approval of his estates for a new tax levy. His private purse was expected to cover expenses for his own lavish household. When he sought to levy a new tax in 1534, and was asked for an accounting of expenditures from the last levy, the cardinal quickly cast his chamberlain in charge of exchequer, Hans Schönitz, into the dungeon. Under torture Schönitz confessed to misappropriation of funds. Although the wealthy Schönitz family promptly put up surety in excess of the loss claimed by Albert, Schönitz was summarily hanged. He had revoked his confession. No visitors had been permitted him. No priest was allowed to accompany him to the gallows.

Luther became involved in the case when Albert accused one of the Black Cloister boarders who came from Halle of slandering him in connection with the Schönitz affair. Luther shot off a typically frank letter defending his table companion.

> You angry saints [it concluded] are not going to hang all your enemies (although you certainly might be able to hang all those who mean well with you and think highly of you). You

will just have to give the dear Lord his way, until at last a
hangman comes for you.[15]

His friend was troubled no further, and we might expect Luther's interest to have ended here.[16] What could he do to help
Schönitz or, for that matter, to bring the cardinal of Mainz to
justice?

That the issue continued to trouble him during that busy fall
and winter, 1535–36, indicates he still felt obligations in the matter. He recognized that his tremendous influence as a publicist
imposed duties on him which were as unique as they were
ineluctable. In early 1536 he wrote yet another letter to the cardinal, in language so strong that Melanchthon was embarrassed
by it. It announced flatly that he planned to lay the entire
Schönitz affair before the public.[17] The declaration brought a
deluge of appeals from the most powerful in Europe, members
and friends of the house of Hohenzollern, influential protestants
who saw the spread of church reform in Hohenzollern lands endangered, also Luther's own prince, of course, John Frederick.
Public opinion had become an important consideration in the
minds of people who had within recent memory spoken haughtily of "the multitude." *Against the Bishop of Magdeburg, Cardinal Albert* is an important milestone in the thinking of Germans about their rulers, and about the role of law among their
institutions.

Luther sets out to make clear that the nobility is not necessarily any nobler than the rest of humanity, and his charac-
terization of Albert is admittedly an apt one—"I know the pussy
well, craven yet vicious."[18] He tells how the Hohenzollern family has begged their tribe be spared, but says, "It is just one of
the misfortunes of this world that good parents beget whores
and scoundrels."[19] Then he goes on quite harshly,

> Listen, my dear princes and lords, you must not try to intimi-
> date us miserable preachers so. If you claim we are slandering
> your whole house when we say one of its members is a scamp,
> why then we would be forced to say you shouldn't use your
> august, honorable house as a screen behind which you nurture
> or defend vice and wickedness.[20]

He disclaims that he is presuming to pass judgment in the case it-self—"I am but a miserable member in the retinue of the true judge, in whose chancellery I have sat for thirty years (not far from the door) from time to time serving as courier and errand boy, so that I do have some idea what kind of decisions are handed down." He gives one such judgment he has heard, by quoting Job:

> If I did despise the cause of my manservant or of my maidser-vant, when they contended with me; what then shall I do when God riseth up? and when he visiteth, what shall I answer him? Did not he that made me in the womb make him? and did not one fashion us in the womb?

If Job granted equality to his Hebrew serfs, Luther wants to know, how much more must a German prince grant to his Chris-tian brethren? "That's the point!" he exclaims,

> Namely, that a master is obliged by the eternal wrath and dis-pleasure of God to defend the right of his servant, and to sub-ject himself to it . . . in which case servant and master are equals: one party against the other. The master can then no longer act as judge over his servant.[21]

This argument, that master and servant are equals before God, Luther calculated, had to be made before he could get his Renaissance audience to accept his fundamental thesis: that no man may act as judge in his own case.

He was probably right to present his case thus, and especially so where the master was, in one person, the highest spiritual *and* secular overlord in all Germany. His technique is one with which we have become familiar: ridicule and frontal attack. He draws out into the open that reservation which he knows his readers feel—must not Cardinal Albert, as an anointed priest, be believed?

> What nonsense does this miserable courier, Doctor Luther, speak! Should a Roman priest fear God? Can Luther's yarns be the truth? Why certainly not. What his Roman priestness thinks and says, *that* is the truth.[22]

Luther confesses himself to be but a goose compared with all the legal experts at Albert's command. Who, indeed, would dare dispute them? "Since the entire world is just a bunch of geese and ducks to the cardinal, they will have to accept his goose sermon as adequate, and believe that Hans Schönitz was legally hanged unheard, unconvicted, and on the testimony of one man, the holy Roman priest."[23] Like the "goose sermon," the phrase "one man" becomes a theme. The biblical admonition that no man may be put to death on the testimony of one man (Num. 35:30) serves as transition to the central argument, *audiatur altera pars*, "Let both sides be heard":

> All right, Hans Schönitz, you have heard how the cardinal accuses you of taking bribes. What do you say to that? The cardinal displays your letters. You are one of the parties to this case. The cardinal is the other party. Ye Gods! He's hanging on the gallows! He cannot speak! Who hanged him? The bishop. Why? The bishop wants to be the sole speaker. The other party must hold silent while he preaches to his geese.[24]

This essential point in due process is a major concern of Luther's tract.

He also relishes of course, and knows his audience does too, making a high-placed figure the butt of his jokes, but to regard the tract merely as invective against the cardinal of Mainz would be as mistaken as to read it solely in the context of church history (as is customary). Luther's purpose is to establish the legal precept of equality before the law—no matter how highly placed the one party might be. He accomplishes his end in some detail, indicting Albert on various counts. From the modern point of view, the most interesting may be his charge that torture was improperly applied to Schönitz. Luther does not condemn the use of torture outright, as we might wish to hear him do, but he does point to the dubiousness of information thus extracted. He relates several instances in which such testimony brought destruction to the innocent while setting the guilty free. He is eager to show the range of human dispositions, some unmovable by the most horrible torture, while others faint away at its mere mention. Resignedly, he quotes Augustine that judges must often perpetrate injustice, and admits that in this wicked world where "we live among the husks, we just have to take the chance that the swine may eat us."[25] After all, the propriety of torture to draw out evidence (and not merely from the suspected criminal) retained its well-codified place in criminal justice far into the eighteenth century. Luther is instructed on the subject and knows that torture is condoned only when information can be obtained in no other way. Schönitz begged for an open trial, the family made every effort to bring the case to court. Luther notes that the imperial court was made available, but the cardinal

> fled the light and skulked into the dungeon . . . He is rightly regarded as a desperate knave and murderer. No goose sermon will help him, no forced confessions. The judge on high has rendered his verdict.[26]

Albert used torture, Luther charges, for the purpose of avoiding due process.

The writing *Against . . . Cardinal Albert* did not occur until 1539, and it shows Luther growing a bit cranky. He says he cannot close without scolding the "gold and silver lawyers" who abet such chicanery—

> It is a brand-new world. The magistrates and the nobility cannot act as police lest they injure the mighty. The lawyers will not be our defenders lest they endanger the powerful. Theologians will not scold lest they offend someone.[27]

But Luther's later years had not become humorless. That satire *News from the Rhine* was directed against Albert in 1542. The richly living prelate, though seven years younger than Luther, preceded him in death. Luther, right up to the eve of his own death, continued to refer from his pulpit to "that damned cardinal."[28]

It *Is* the Devil

In February of 1536 Doctor Luther presided at the wedding of Duke Philip of Pomerania. At the crucial moment, the ring slipped from a nervous hand and went bounding across the floor, provoking from Luther a cool reprimand: "Listen here, devil, this doesn't concern you and you're not going to accomplish one thing."[1] It is a remark we might bear in mind whenever we consider the doctor in connection with worldy powers.

For in his view the devil was always around. It was not merely that the devil "is deeply concerned about us and sends his servants among us . . . comes walking right in without a 'by your leave.'"[2] Even to call the world full of devils would be an understatement: "The world is not just the devil's, it *is* the devil."[3] We are here as in some wicked hostelry where we must serve through the night.[4] "The devil is as big as the world, as wide as the world, and he extends from heaven down into hell."[5] This universe of ours, which is the devil himself, also teems with individual imps. Someone at Luther's table mentioned that an enlightened Nuremberg citizen (the editor of Copernicus's *De Revolutionibus*) did not believe in *Poltergeister*. Luther was patronizing—"Osiander always has to be different. I have experienced *Poltergeister* firsthand." He proceeded to enumerate their importunate visits and how he had confidently defied them, often by just pulling the covers up round his ears.[6]

During both his stays at remote mountain fortresses he had observed a devil descending over the vast, dark forests below.[7] When he first confronted religious fanatics, he was as sure he had been talking "with the devil himself as when I saw him physically at the Coburg in the form of a serpent and star."[8] A

vision of Christ with his five wounds had also appeared to Luther there, but he knew it for the devil, whose consummate ability to deceive man is, after all, his outstanding characteristic.[9]
How easy the devil must find it in these latter days, when mankind has grown so silly, and he has accumulated so much experience!

> Ah, we really can't be so smug. We have so many enemies,
> devils in infinite number—and they're not all little piddling
> devils, either, but territorial devils and devil-princes. Through
> very long experience, over five thousand years, he has grown
> skilled and very clever. Just think, even if the devil had been a
> simple fellow at the beginning of the world, he must have be-
> come pretty sly through the long practice of tempting Adam,
> Methuselah, Enoch, Noah, Abraham, David, Solomon, the
> prophets, Christ, and all the faithful. He's much too sophis-
> ticated for us in these latter days.[10]

It was revealing of his conception of the infernal powers that he
started out talking about devils, but shifted quite easily into the
singular.

He espied one principle of evil lurking in many costumes—the
pope and his saints, the multiplying religious sects, all kinds of
natural and social ills. Beneath all the colorful masks Satan
remained himself and had a distinctive personality. Of course he
was a *Poltergeist* "and a rowdy spirit—he just can't resist
hooliganism."[11] He liked the forms of exotic beasts—"I believe the
devil is in parrots, apes, and monkeys—the way they are able to
imitate humans."[12] "We must not think it is God fooling around
in these masks. He just permits his creatures to be what he
created them."[13] The devil loved the garb of insects, and one
June day, strolling in his garden, Luther remarked how the caterpillars moved in exactly the same sinuous folds as the devil, and
had similar coloring, too.[14] These destructive little vermin, he
believed, had been placed among his plants by the same devil
who had strewn sectarians to chew upon the church.[15]

Devils were in evidence everywhere. Luther's sermons and private remarks are brimful of tales about that grim, mocking
demon, a helpful but ever insolent servant. He was held responsible for pretty much every trivial inconvenience and monstrous

evil in the world, from the sulphur taste clinging to certain beers,[16] to the crazy carryings-on of the radical sects and the unspeakable perversions of the papacy. There is scarcely a motif in devil lore that does not turn up somewhere in Luther's sayings and writings. Among his associates it was a truism that the weakest of all this infernal host was stronger than ten thousand worlds.[17]

One whom they especially plagued was a melancholy Moravian named John Schlaginhauffen. Perhaps around forty when he came to Wittenberg, he was soon most devoted to Doctor Luther, in whom he found succor against the attacks. Schlaginhauffen's great admiration led to a wonderful accuracy of detail in notes he took while at the Black Cloister. He had a fine ear for the trivial yet characteristic remark. It did not take Luther long to see he was a troubled soul, in need of an encouraging word.[18] He quoted 2 Corinthians 12:9 to him, how Christ is "made perfect in weakness. . . . therefore will I rather glory in my infirmities." Also Isaiah 42:3, "A bruised reed shall he not break, and the smoking flax shall he not quench," as well as numerous psalms, for Luther was just in these days working on his final revision. "How do you like the Psalter?" he asked, when he met him with one in his hand. "Do you have a sense of joy when you read in it, or of sorrow?"

"Sometimes I find comfort in the psalms, but then Satan intrudes with his argument: 'These things that are written here, what are they to you?'"

Very solemnly Doctor Luther made the sign of the cross to banish the evil spirit and at the same time quoted Paul again, "Whatsoever things were written aforetime were written for our learning, that we through patience and comfort of the scriptures might have hope." Then he revealed his own view of the Old Testament: "Abraham, Isaac, Jacob, and sweet Joseph, Rebeccah, and Leah do not know a single word of the legends we read about them. David does not know his psalms are giving comfort in Germany now, as he took comfort from them. So long as the devil holds sway, you hold onto that Psalter and read in it. Trust God who helped David. He will help you too. 'For all the promises of God in him are yea, and in him Amen.'"

In a characteristically mercurial change of mood, he began to clown: "Ask him, 'Devil, in which commandment of God does it say that?' And if he cannot tell you, then say, 'Aroint thee, jackanapes! Spare me your hackneyed jokes.' If he still won't cease, why, excommunicate him in the name of our Lord Jesus Christ and say, 'Your coin is not acceptable here. It is neither of Bohemian, Hungarian, nor of Saxon mint, but was struck by the devil. We reject it in these parts.' "[19]

This conversation occurred right around Christmas of 1531, just shortly after Schlaginhauffen arrived in Wittenberg. Late on New Year's Eve he suffered a fainting spell in Luther's house. While they were bringing him to bed, Luther cleansed the air with a solemn deprecation, "May the Lord chide thee, O Satan, called to be an angel of life, but now become an angel of death. Thou attackst first with thy lies, now with blows."

As Schlaginhauffen began to recover consciousness, Luther told him he must become accustomed to these trials and "not be anxious, but treasure them. David knew them well, and I experience them often (though I must say that I had a fine day today —except for just my usual dizziness). Let the godless be anxious . . . This is a spiritual trial. It does not harm us, for we are servants of God. If *we* are not God's servants, well who might be?"

Amid such exhortations, Schlaginhauffen cried weakly, "Ah, my sins!" and just as automatically as one might offer a sip of water to a feverish child Luther held out the four signs which repel Satan (baptism, forgiveness, the Lord's Supper, and the catechism). Then his tone became sardonic.

"His trials hurt us a little, but do no damage. If we will but call upon the Lord God, he'll give us a bitter pill to swallow; pray to the saints, and the devil will soon help you."

Thus having elicited a smile from his patient, he asked him, "Why should you worry about sinning? If you had the sins of a Zwingli, Carlstadt, and Müntzer all rolled into one, faith in Christ would still defeat them all. Ah, we but lack faith. Do not argue with Satan about the law. Make him discuss grace. Why, that scoundrel knows how to make a camel out of a louse!"

As Luther continued to scoff at Satan, poor Schlaginhauffen sighed, "Ah, my dear Lord God, even the tiniest devil is more powerful than the whole world."

One angel, Luther countered quickly, is more powerful than all the devils put together. He reminded Schlaginhauffen how Peter calls the devil a roaring lion who attacks all of us, yet that Peter, fearing not, urges us to "resist steadfast in the faith, knowing that the same afflictions are accomplished in your brethren."

Thus he helped Schlaginhauffen up out of his bed with the words, "Let us call this bed: resurrection. Do not immerse yourself in deep thoughts. Get together with the church: 'Where two or three are gathered together in my name, there am I in the midst of them.' That means you can be sure whatever your fellow Christian says, God is saying to you." Thus bolstered, Schlaginhauffen went off home.[20]

When Luther discovered the morose fellow in one of his pensive spells, he might say, "A penny for your thoughts,"[21] or, "What are you sitting there pondering? Be joyful in the Lord!"

"Ah, dear Herr Doctor, I would truly like to," Schlaginhauffen would reply. "But many frightening trials prevent me."

"What kind of trials are you talking about?"

"Ah, I really cannot express how I feel."

Luther would not be put off. He laid out a scholarly analysis (based on the Creed) of all possible doubts which a Christian might have. His own greatest trial, he said, had to do with faith in the Holy Spirit, for he sometimes doubted his own calling.

"When I think about God," Schlaginhauffen insisted, "it comes into my mind: 'Thou art a sinner! God will not hear you. He is angry with you.'"

"If I am not to pray until I become devout," Luther snorted, "when shall I pray? If Satan recites to you, 'Now we know that God heareth not sinners,' you must turn it right around and say, 'I pray because I *am* a sinner, and I know that the prayers of the afflicted are heard by God.'"

"Oh, we are happy," Luther went on, using his sardonic approach, "if we can have peace of mind. But we want it on our own terms, not as a gift from God. Now, why would God want to be gracious and helpful to us if we feel no discomfort and acknowledge no sins? Only when we are genuinely entrammeled does God say, 'Now I can help you.'"

In conclusion, he returned to that verse from 2 Corinthians which he found so appropriate for Schlaginhauffen: "My strength is perfected in weakness."

But Schlaginhauffen would not be comforted. "Herr Doctor, I am not able to believe that all sorrow comes from the devil, because the fear in my heart is fear of the law. But the law of God is good. If it is the law of God that causes despair, then my sorrow is not from Satan."

Luther brushed aside the implication that this was some problem which troubled Schlaginhauffen alone. "On this point," he said, "I am helped by Paul: 'Wherefore then serveth the law? It was added because of transgressions . . .'" Luther went ahead to explain the passage, comparing God with the emperor and calling the devil his executioner, who was especially active in these latter days. "The devil senses the end of his kingdom at hand. That's why he is twitching and jerking about." The doctor was not above mocking the devil in grotesque pantomime.[22]

He was full of little encouragements like, "Schlaginhauffen, if you didn't have so much going for you with God the Father, you wouldn't suffer these trials,"[23] and he kept close watch over his protégé, refusing to let him wander off to himself in a despondent mood. One evening late, after Luther's conversations with Justus Jonas might have cast a listener into theological speculations, he took Schlaginhauffen by the arm.

He did not want him to leave with the others, "You just live next door. You needn't go so soon." Once they were alone, Luther continued, "I am displeased with myself that, in the bottom of my heart, I do not really believe our sins are forgiven." He confided that he shared such doubts with King David and others of olden times, then went ahead to describe his worries in a detail which he knew would strike a responsive chord in pensive Schlaginhauffen.[24]

As the months passed, the two became very close. Schlaginhauffen would be the first whom Kate called when her husband felt faint.[25] They spent a great deal of time together, the older man regularly comforting the younger. Walking in the cloister garden, they frightened two little birds out of the nest. "Herr Turbicide"—Luther liked the Latinization of Schlaginhauffen's name—"the little birds just need faith. They cannot believe they are most cordially welcome in my garden, and that I wish them no harm. And we won't believe God means well with us, from the bottom of his heart."[26]

By May, Luther was on a first-name basis with "Master John," and resorting ever more frequently to humor to divert him. In conversation with a visitor about the crazy carryings-on of sectarians, he had made a reference to the madness of old King Saul. He realized that Schlaginhauffen might take the allusion personally, so he turned to him and demanded gruffly, "Why are you looking so serious?"

"Oh, Herr Doctor, I was occupied with such serious thoughts, and can find no answer. I cannot distinguish between law and the gospel." This, of course, was the very crux of Lutheran doctrine.

"Well, dear Hans, when you are able to do that, you'll be a great doctor." Luther arose gravely from the table and with great ceremony removed his own distinctive beret, of the sort which a doctor of theology wore indoors and out. "So soon as you can do that, I will say to you: 'Dear Herr Doctor Johann, you are a learned man. Paul and I never did progress so far as you have.' Paul was told, when he wanted that thorn removed from his flesh: 'My grace is sufficient for thee.'"

This was a part of that same verse from 2 Corinthians, as Schlaginhauffen well knew, "My strength is perfected in weakness." He now listened gratefully as a child to the familiar assurance that a Christian must not be troubled in conscience. Then he asked, "Herr Doctor, are you saying it behooves me to remain a scoundrel and a sinner?"

"That thou mightest be justified when thou speakest," replied the doctor weightily in the words of Psalm 51, "and be clear when thou judgest." With that he was ready to move his long-faced friend to the laughter which meant all was well, so he reeled off some of his endless devil advice:

When the devil comes at night to worry me, this is what I say to him: "Devil, I have to sleep now. That is God's commandment, for us to work by day and sleep at night." If he keeps on nagging me and trots out my sins, then I answer: "Sweet devil, I know the whole list. Also write on it that I have shit in my breeches. Then hang that around your neck and wipe your mouth on it."

Then, if he won't cease to accuse me of sins, I say in contempt: "*Sancte Sathana, ora pro me*. Oh, *you* never did anything wrong. Thou art alone blest. Go now to God and find grace for yourself. If you want to perform your good offices on me, then I will say, 'Physician, heal thyself.' "

Here the ponderous Bugenhagen could not resist a lame attempt to emulate Luther's calculated coarseness. Luther, a little chagrined to hear his respected colleague use such foul language, admitted it was precisely the kind of comeback the devil cannot suffer, but he added, "I often call my wife to help me ward off vain thoughts."[27]

The devil of folklore and magic was one whom Luther could dismiss with contempt. At the mention of one "certain sorcerer by the name of Faustus," he observed matter-of-factly that the devil did not use such efforts against him, but used scripture instead. "I've been brought to the point where I didn't know whether I was dead or alive, and he has cast me into such despair that I didn't know if there was a God—quite gave up hope in God."[28] Not that the devil knew scripture better than Doctor Luther, though he did know it every bit as well. It was on the formal side of debate that the devil knew no equal. Hopeless to try to penetrate his rhetoric, much less excel him at it, he swaggered forth with a commanding presence and consummate skill. He studied his opponent and knew his weaknesses, so that Luther was ever ready to admit, "When I debate with the devil I am lost at the outset, and captive, because I am a sinner."[29] He liked to issue his challenge on a strictly theoretical subject, preferably the law, then subtly work around to Luther's past.

When you debate with the devil about the law [Luther warned], you are whipped—about the gospel, and you've won. So let nobody debate with him about the law or about sin. Just stop the disputation right there, because he has "the handwriting of ordinances that is against us." For example, when he says to me, "How many evils have arisen from your doctrine!" I answer, "So what? How many good things have come from it?" "Oh," he says, "those do not amount to anything." He is such a master of rhetoric that he can make a beam out of a mote and, conversely, he is marvelous at minimizing the comforts of our doctrine.[30]

Luther had long searched his heart in all points of doctrine and did his best to cling to his position—"nevertheless, [Satan] often starts a debate with me and makes me yield. He is full of rage. I know it and I feel it, because he sleeps with me more often than Kate does."³¹

His power of logic and polished rhetorical skill made theology the devil's *forte*, but his true focus was Luther's past deeds.

It is good for us to know the arts of the devil. He takes the most trivial sins and can exaggerate them until you don't know where you stand. He once tortured me with Paul to Timothy and just throttled me until my heart almost dissolved: "Thou wast the cause that so many monks left the monasteries!" . . . and he held the text up before my eyes [probably 1 Timothy 5:11], moved from the topic of grace into a debate about the law, and he had me.

About that time Pomeranus came, and I put the question to him. We walked up and down the corridor together. He, too, expressed some doubt, not knowing how vitally important it was to me—and now *that* really scared me. I had to suffer through the entire night with a tortured mind. The next day Pomeranus said to me, "I'm disappointed in you. I've finally read the text aright, and that was a ridiculous argument."

Well, of course. If I'd just been able to study the text alone. But he keeps you company. He is always lying in wait for you.³²

The emptying of the monasteries troubled Luther considerably. On the one hand, he was appalled at the greed with which church property was being gobbled up, and he despaired that so little of the wealth would ever find its way into education, or be used to assist destitute former monks and nuns. He told how the devil assailed him "with a voice like this: 'Who told you to teach against the monasteries? Where once there was the most serene peace, *you* disturbed it—at whose command?' "

Veit Dietrich interrupted with the assurance, "You commanded neither that they leave the monasteries nor that they disturb the peace. You only taught how it is vain to worship the doctrine of man. Then those things of which you speak followed of themselves, and out of the love of God."

"My dear friend," Luther replied, "in those struggles of mine, by the time I remember that fact I have already sweated a lot."[33]

When he learned that the pastor in Herford was attacking the pious life in a local cloister, Luther demanded he be restrained, "for innovations are dangerous, especially in religious matters. Without cause they disturb the heart and conscience, whose peace and calm take precedence over all else."[34]

Debate or no, the devil liked to visit at night, when worries of all sorts were effective—

> At my age I'm not bothered by people—don't have anything to do with them—but the devil disports himself in my bedroom. Why, I've got one or two devils who pay special attention to me, really pretty fellows. When they can't accomplish anything in my heart they grab my head and make it ache. When I can't take it any longer I'm going to stick them up my ass. That's where he belongs.[35]

Here again the devil was both singular and plural, for the mind in sleep blurs such distinctions. Luther was suspicious of dreams:

> The soul of man cannot rest, and Satan is in us when we are asleep. But angels are with us, too. The devil can make me so anxious that I sweat in my sleep. But I take no stock in dreams, or in signs.

He went on to say he would believe no angel that came to him in a dream, and he hoped one never would. He knew for certain that sad dreams came from the devil. "The worst struggles I've had with him were in my bed at Kate's side."[36]

For the sixteenth century, the devil was quite as palpable as the computer program is in the twentieth. It would be false to attach fear of him to Luther alone. On the contrary, we often hear him reassuring his congregation from the pulpit that the devil's powers are limited.[37]

> With God's permission, he would ruin all that is good. If he had his way, not a blade of grass, not a leaf would grow. Well, such may be in Satan's power, but he cannot see into our hearts, or conscience, or faith. He does have some similitude

with deity, but God reserves true divinity to himself. He can handle the devil.[38]

Like his contemporaries, Luther supposed idiots and the retarded to be possessed, but he by no means accepted the popular idea that they were therefore damned. This he left to God's ultimate authority.[39]

Would it be proper to explain Luther's "Satan" as a kind of metaphor for self-reproach and other psychological torments? Perhaps like our glib word "psychology" his devils constituted some explanation for many trials of the spirit. They offered a meaningful context in which to formulate one's understanding, and were a presumed grounding in reality for phenomena which otherwise eluded the grasp. Coarse language in treating of and with the devil was an appropriate way of showing contempt for doubt and despair. It also produced good humor, that most effective means for warding them off. He liked to tell of the lady in Magdeburg who, when approached by a ghoul, "let a fart out of her bed and said, 'There you have a staff. Use it for a pilgrimage to your idol in Rome.' "[40] He hastened to add that our show of contempt must occur not in self-confidence, but in the faith that God's strength will prevail. Famous because it eventually found its way into the Faust legend is a story which Luther told with all the sound effects necessary to evoke the vision of pigs grunting:

> Ssoh, ssoh, ssoh, hah, ho, hah! Thus the devil once interrupted the prayers of a pious old man. But he only laughed and told the pigs they had got what they deserved: "Since you did not wish to be an angel in heaven, you can remain a devil down here." Such a proud spirit cannot bear contempt.[41]

He also recommended song for driving the devils away. "I really like it when we sing loudly in church, 'And the word was made flesh.' The devil cannot bear to hear that. He has to get several miles away."[42]

He wrote numerous letters of comfort to those in distress. One to the sister of a former student treats the devil as theologian.

> Your dear brother Jerome Weller has told me how troubled you have been by the problem of eternal predestination. I

am truly sorry for you, and I hope Christ our Lord will save
you from it. Amen. I know the disease well, and have lain
deathly ill in that same hospital. So, besides praying for you, I
would like to advise and comfort you. I know that writing
about matters of this sort is poor help. But I do not want to
neglect it, so, with God's grace, I will tell you how he has
helped me in the past, together with what arts I continue to
employ every day.

In the first place, you have to resolve very firmly in your
heart that these thoughts are certainly insinuations and fiery
arrows of the abominable devil. Scripture says so [Luther at
this point gives plenty of examples]. So it is certain that your
thoughts do not come from God, but from the devil. He
plagues our hearts with them to make us hate God, and despair. God has forbidden that in the First Commandment, desiring us to trust, love, and praise him, for that is our life.

In the second place, when you have such thoughts, you
should remember to ask the question, "Pardon me, please, but
in which Commandment is it written that I should take any
thought of these things?" And if there is no such Commandment, then do not fail to say, "Begone, abominable devil! You
are trying to entice me to look out for myself, while on every
hand God is telling me I must let him take care of me."[43]

Except that the language is somewhat gentler, this is exactly the
same advice we hear poured forth for his colleagues and companions and students: unmask the abominable devil, and he is
defeated. The crux of the problem was recognizing the ultimate
source of our thoughts—no easy matter, for

No one is able to fasten in words just how variously that
damned majesty can transform himself. If we once recognize
Satan to be Satan, why, then it is easy enough to confound
his pride by saying, "Kiss my ass," or "Shit in your pants and
hang them around your neck."[44]

We know there is none to fear but the devil, and that the source
of our strength is greater. Hence let us be proud of our weakness, he wrote to the despondent young Prince Joachim of
Anhalt.

> Let the devil be pure strength and have no need of Christ's
> help and power. We ought to be weak and we want to be
> weak, just so Christ's strength can dwell within us, as Paul
> says, "Christ's strength is made perfect in my weakness."[45]

Recognizing our sorrow and uncertainty as coming from the
devil permits us to externalize them. Then we can draw on the
inner strength which comes from God. When seeking to comfort a fellow preacher Luther wrote with rhetorical flourish,
"What is the world? What is wrath? And who, indeed, is its
ruler? Is it not smoke, and a bubble upon the water, compared
with the Lord?" It was a Latin letter, but here he fell into German. "Ah, we live in the devil's realm only as the externals go.
So we ought neither to see any good nor to hear good about external things." Then back to Latin: "But internally we live in the
kingdom of Christ, where we see the riches of glory and
grace."[46]

He wrote a letter of comfort to a woman whose husband had
just committed suicide. Death had not been instantaneous, and
the victim had commended his soul to Christ before dying—

> That should be a consolation to you, for the difficult struggle
> in which your husband found himself was finally and conclu-
> sively won by Christ. Furthermore, your husband's final mo-
> ments were rational and in Christian acceptance of our Lord—
> I was happy beyond measure when I heard it. For thus did
> Christ, too, struggle in the garden, winning out in the end and
> arising from the dead. As for the fact that your husband
> inflicted injury upon himself, it may be that the devil has
> power over our members, and moved his hand forcefully,
> against your husband's will. For if he had done it willfully, he
> would not have come to himself again, you know, and been
> converted to his confession in Christ. How often does the
> devil break someone's arm, neck, back, and other members?
> He can certainly gain control over our limbs without our
> will.[47]

He was entirely sincere in suggesting that suicides are not necessarily damned. Like victims of a highwayman, he said, they may
very well have been seized against their will. Nonetheless, Luther

did hold to the folkway of denying the corpse of a suicide passage across the threshold, or rest in hallowed ground. He said it was God's purpose to terrify us with such examples.[48]

In this, he was not presuming to speak for God. Luther's remarkable diffidence and deferral of understanding permitted him to live with paradoxical views. Theoretical problems in the relationship of God to the devil did not concern him much. In his lectures on the Book of Genesis, he ironically faulted the "author" already on the second day of creation:

> Here Moses must have nodded, for he says nothing about the two most important things—namely the creation of the angels, and their fall. He goes right on into the creation of corporeal things.

Luther good-naturedly explained how the church fathers, lacking any scriptural statements on the subject, were constrained to invent all sorts of stories which, the professor said, he was willing to let stand on their merits. For all he knew there were good angels and bad, maybe there had indeed been a struggle between them. He said it stood to reason, but "Moses, writing for a crude and primitive people, restricted himself to those things which are necessary and useful to know, passing over other matters which are not necessary, as the nature of angels and such like." As to the speculations of the fathers, the students could take them or leave them, "So now let's return to Moses."[49] His quite unprofessorial attitude was that there are many things which simply cannot be known.

He understood, of course, that it would be heretical to call all the world evil, for it was God's creation, and Satan himself must be utterly subject to God.[50] Yet at the same time it would also be heresy to admit that God partakes of any evil.[51] One day John Schlaginhauffen asked whether the devil acted by the "permission or at the command of God."

> Oh, heavens, no! [Luther burst out] He does not act at God's command. Hell's bells, no! Our Lord God simply does not *prevent* the devil, but connives at his deeds, as when some great prince sees a shed torched, and just winks at it. That's the way God treats the devil.[52]

This view permitted his optimistic comparison of God to a gardener and the devil to his pruning hook.[53] It was the familiar notion of a negative force as necessary to work the good. Luther liked to remind people that smugness would have sent them all to hell were it not for the devil's onslaughts.[54] But did that not leave God looking pretty silly, if his "pruning hook" operated only at his connivance and not at his command?

One spring morning from the pulpit he was comparing God with a prince who so loved his people he had to say "yes" to all who came before him, yet who could not dispense with executioners, dungeons, and torture instruments. Somehow that seemed jarring on such a nice June day, when what he had really hoped to convey was the warmth of God's love. The bees buzzing at the flowers reminded him of those wonderful political arrangements in Kate's beehives:

> All the bees have a sting, we are told, save the king himself, who has none. He is a little beast utterly without wrath. But the other bees have a sting, so they can protect the king and the hive they live in. In this same way God is by his very nature and essence incapable of wrath. He is pure kindness and warmth. Fire, flood, thunder, lightning, rocks, stumps, bears, plague, fever, the devils in hell: these are stings. Sometimes he has to unleash them to defend his majesty. Why, anyone who does not see God is nothing but love, is blind![55]

The metaphor, though it tax the indulgence of feminists and apiculturists, reveals a mind pressing forward to accept reality, seeking analogies to help, but resigned to its own limited powers of comprehension—and the limits of others.

Luther stooped to general modes of thought when addressing his congregation and aimed at some benefit for day-to-day problems. In the lecture hall he could assume a fairly high level of sophistication among the students, and he was eager to prepare these future preachers for various eventualities, so here he faced up to the question squarely:

> Let us respond to the objection: why are those things attributed to God which are but the instruments he uses? It is the devil who kills, it is the law that indicts, yet scripture as-

cribes both to God. It is done that we may be made firm in our faith that there is but one God, and not create more than one God, as the Manichaeans did. They supposed two Principles, of which the one was Good, the other Bad. They ran off after the good God in good things, in bad ones after the bad God. But God wants us, in success as in adversity, to trust him alone. He does not want us to be among those of whom Isaiah says, "The people turneth not unto him that smiteth them." It is in our nature to turn away from the true God in sudden panic or danger, thinking him angry, like Job when he says, "Thou art become cruel to me." That is the same as to invent another God, and not hold to the simple faith that there is but one God. Nor is he cruel, but he is "the father of mercies." All he needs to do is suspend his help, and our hearts make a wrathful idol of the unchanging, constant God. The prophets would forbid that, saying with one voice: "I am the Lord God, who created good and evil" [the reference seems to be to Isaiah 45:7]. We must not imagine, when a cloud obscures the sun, that the sun has been totally removed from the universe or transformed from a glowing body into a dark, black one. The sun still shines, only the clouds keep us from seeing it. And God is good, just, and merciful even when he smites us. He who does not believe this has departed from the bond of faith that there is but one God, and has made himself a strange God, inconstant, now good and now bad. But to believe in the gracious and merciful God even while he is sending evil does take a special gift of the Holy Ghost.[56]

Joseph, alone and in a foreign land, cast into prison not as a consequence of the crime he was convicted of, but precisely for resisting it, gave the old professor an opportunity to clarify the matter in his best style. Our human notion, he said, that God is good and merciful and wise is "the merest theory." The students before him, when they went out into the real world, would find themselves precisely in Joseph's miserable condition.

Let us recognize, therefore, that God is hidden under the mask of the horrible devil. We have to learn that the goodness, mercy, and power of God are not capable of being comprehended theoretically, but only by experience.[57]

Joseph must accept his persecution as the goodness of God. Doctor Luther's future preachers were being told they need not "justify the ways of God to man," but rather teach a Joseph-like acceptance, and trust that wherever we encounter the devil God is near at hand.[58]

Luther's metaphors do not satisfy us. Biology knows the bees have a queen, not a king. Astronomy has broken through all the crystalline spheres that enclosed Luther's cozy medieval creation. But we have not penetrated the void beyond, where he placed his faith, nor filled the void within, where Doctor Luther gave answer to the abominable devil.

Paralipomena

What good comes of man? He eats and drinks only the best—bread, meat, wine, beer, precious spices too. He excretes nothing but corruption, snot, sputum, matter, sweat, sores, pox, scruff, slough, discharge, pus, dung, and urine. He clothes himself in satin and gold, spreads lice, nits, fleas, and other vermin.

Why, if he had to answer everybody's questions he would be a most wretched God. Let us look to the word of God and in it find refuge from the "Wherefore?" We ought to know his word, but should not inquire into his will, which is often hidden. That would be to measure wind and fire in our balance scales.

The people of Israel had no theoretical, abstract God, the way naive monks do, who rise up to heaven on their theories and speculate about God in absolute terms. Every man should flee that abstract God for dear life, because human nature and an abstract God are irreconcilable enemies . . . No one supposes David spoke to an abstract God, but he spoke with a God clad and covered by his word and his promises. David's name for God did not exclude Christ, concerning whom promise was made by God to Adam and to the patriarchs. We too must heed this God—not naked, but clothed and revealed in his word. Else we shall surely be crushed by despair.

As much as a cow understands about her own life, that's how much we know. What, then, are we able to understand about eternal life?

All men know, guided by nature alone and without any schooling or logic, that there is a God. That is divinely impressed on the minds of all men.

God walks about in a mask, as at Mardi Gras.

Let us not pluck [the pope] the way we did Duke George and the king of England, but go for the throat. We'll skewer the goose, for if you but pluck her she'll grow her feathers anew.

FOUR

SUFFERER

The Two Testaments
of Schmalkalden

Many conditions already present, and developments long under way, became manifest only about the time of the Wittenberg Concord and shortly thereafter. During those spring days which found Bucer and Capito ambling across the Golden Meadow, heads rolled in London, first of the men accused of adultery with Anne Boleyn—then, on Friday, her own. Just two days later, on that same Sunday morning in May when the Strasbourg divines called upon Doctor Luther, Henry VIII celebrated his marriage with yet another wife. The news came as a shock to those in Wittenberg who had been negotiating with Henry in good faith during the winter and spring, presuming he wished to legitimize a union he had now bloodily disposed of. And there were deaths more important before the year was out, for some of Europe's luminaries were growing old. Capito's first letter from the Rhineland after his return told of Erasmus' passing and of the death of his French counterpart, the eminent Bible scholar Lefèvre d'Étaples. By the end of the year Luther must also have heard that his most admirable English emulator, William Tyndale, long hounded through Europe by England's most brutish king, had finally been run to earth in Brussels. They strangled the gentle scholar there, and burned his corpse at the stake in October.

The stately language of William Tyndale survives in our Authorized Version of the Bible. Careful studies have shown how dependent his translation was on Wittenberg.[1] Historians generally agree that Tyndale had spent 1524–25 there under the pseudonym of Peter Daltic, while dodging Henry's agents.² His New Testament, printed immediately thereafter in Cologne and Worms, had to be smuggled into his homeland. By the time of his murder in 1536 parts of his Old Testament were circulating as well. There is no evidence but little doubt that Luther and Tyndale met. The great man's death touched Luther deeply in any case—and at a crucial moment in his own life.

A papal bull of 2 June at last issued a call for a council which had to be taken seriously. The date was to be Pentecost of the next year; the place, Mantua, just as Vergerio had forecast. It seemed as if Martin Luther had waited all his life for this forum. He still dared not hope it would materialize. Having grown up in a world which devoutly believed in authority, he had spent his youthful years in quest of certitude. Of all people then it had been he—led blindly (so he said)—who challenged, then finally even rejected the supreme authority of the medieval world, the pope. He accepted the early church position that final sanction must be sought from a general council. Many agreed with him, especially in Germany. Interim arrangements "pending the council" had succeeded one another for twenty years. It was difficult to believe that Rome really desired the council now, though called, and Luther feared that even if it did come about the German protestant estates might not attend. Did not the bull itself speak of "extirpating heresies and errors from the Lord's acre"?³ He read it and scoffed, "We are already damned."⁴ A bull of the previous year had referred explicitly to "the pestiferous Lutheran heresy."⁵ Nevertheless, when John Frederick proposed an anti-council to be called by Luther himself on German soil, Augsburg perhaps, Luther was among those who advised against such a "strong, frightening impression of a schism."⁶ The pope had the authority to call a council, he reasoned, therefore it was the duty of Christian princes to attend. However bleak the prospects, here was Luther's chance to be vindicated, if at all before his death.

His chronic colds and rheumatic ailments after the winter of 1535–36 had reminded his friends that they must prepare for a time when he would no longer be with them.⁷ John Frederick asked him to draw up his "testament" as concerned those points of doctrine which must not be relinquished in the negotiations at Mantua.[8] Luther responded immediately, was at work on it by September, and by December asked some of his closest associates to make a special trip to Wittenberg to approve what he would set down. Amsdorf came from Magdeburg, John Agricola from Eisleben. Although Luther had expected their discussions would proceed quickly, an attack of angina slowed him down and interrupted the sessions.

The document as completed in the early days of 1537 comprised twenty-two leaves in a German characteristically Luther's, even written in his own meticulous hand up to the point where his heart trouble required him to dictate.[9] It is a confession of faith most revealing of Luther's very simple theology. In his view it consisted in but one point, all the rest of his articles being an attempt at precise demarcation from the Roman position. The document was drawn up, of course, with an eye to negotiations at the council in Mantua, but it gradually acquired an independent status. John Frederick took it to the convention of the protestant estates held in Schmalkalden in February for their official sanction, and since that time it has been called the "Articles of Schmalkalden," eventually finding its place among the articles of faith in the Lutheran Church.

Luther began with the Creed, singling out faith in Christ as "the first and chief article": "We hold that man is justified, without the works of law, through faith . . . From this article no wavering is possible, even if heaven and earth pass away . . . Upon this article rests all that we teach and live against the pope, devil, and world."[10] Under subsequent headings he went on to reject the mass, religious orders, and the supremacy of the pope, specifying evils which had flowed from these institutions. He defined the authority of the church council and listed those points he would like to see settled there: the gospel, baptism, communion, confession, ordination, etc. He gave considerable attention to sin and penance. This is where his own hand breaks off. The subsequent topics, in the hand of a secretary, were treated more tersely.

Arguing the propriety of matrimony for priests led to the sharpest rejection of Rome:

> We do not concede that they are the church . . . For any
> child of seven years knows, praise be to God, what the church
> is—namely: the sainted faithful and the lambs who hear their
> shepherd's voice. Children pray, "I believe in one holy Chris-
> tian church." That holiness is not in surplices, tonsures, long
> gowns, and other ceremonies (all inventions which go beyond
> Holy Scripture), but in the word of God and in true faith.[11]

Final articles dismiss faith in good works, in religious vows, and
whatever other "human inventions" may augment church ceremony.

Recognizing that even his own attempt to strip away all but
the essential core of faith just might itself generate a kind of
orthodoxy, with new rules and disputes about them, Luther resumed his quill to set down just a few more lines for a cover
page:

> This is sufficient doctrine for the church. In the other spheres,
> government and the economy provide enough of law to vex us
> with. So there is no need to invent yet further burdens.
> Sufficient unto the day is the evil thereof.[12]

These final words bespoke his profound distrust of all codifica-
tions, not merely in church ritual, but even his own earnest
effort to dispense with it.

He was also anxious about the dangers which political involve-
ments might bring. He told John Frederick about reproaches he
had heard on this score when he forwarded his testament to him.
Four pages came back, painfully written and corrected in the
prince's awkward hand. At first neglecting to use the sovereign
"we," the prince had to go back and expunge each first person
singular pronoun. The letter began simply, "Herr Doctor," but
in his first sentence John Frederick lapsed back into the formu-
larisms of chancellery, "Worthy, learned, devout," because they
came natural to him. They ring down across the centuries as
uniquely sincere. Luther proudly brought the letter to table,
claiming he had a new interpretation for the adage of Frederick
the Wise, that "One must read a prince's letter thrice." Protesting near illegibility of the hand, he passed John Frederick's letter
around, crowing, "This one sure needs it."[13] John Frederick had

thanked Luther piously for the excellent articles of faith, then turned to those people who might regard such a clear declaration as dangerous: "One must conclude that they would care little if they lived under the papacy or the Turk, if they could but be at peace, have good, quiet, restful days with their Mammon, and plenty of time to grub for more lucre."[14] As for himself, he supposed the articles dealt with divine matters and not human ones. He said he had read them through twice. Although but a layman, he judged them in conformity with the Augsburg Confession, and was prepared so to acknowledge them before council and world. He regretted only that Melanchthon, in signing the articles, had affixed a reservation lenient toward the papacy.

This particular ripple betrayed but one of numerous rocks in the widening stream of protestantism, many more than met the eye. Each theologian had his own ideas. It seemed to Luther as if all except Philip were sticklers for precision in small points. A new scholasticism seemed to be developing, thin intellectual issues prevailing. Luther had expected some problems before the Wittenberg Concord was completely accepted, but now quite separate spats were arising. In the city of Nuremberg they wanted to know what, precisely, was required in the forgiveness of sins. Did the minister still have to speak special words of absolution to each individual as the priest had ever done, or was the general benediction enough? Ah, tiny indeed was the true flock for whom rules and regulations were unnecessary.

Old Conrad Cordatus, the first to preserve notes from Luther's table and eternally at outs with its no-nonsense mistress Kate until he took his own parsonage, had paid a call in late October, just when tensions were mounting on the issue of the council. He indicated the need for a confidential talk, and the doctor invited him to stay after dinner. At this time he solemnly charged Philip Melanchthon and young Caspar Cruciger, the major scholars of the university, with deviationism. The complaint, sad to say, was not new to Luther. The older colleagues were especially sensitive on doctrine, and there was also some professional jealousy of the bright younger chaps. His important old associate Nicholas von Amsdorf, pastor in Magdeburg, had let him know that some outside Wittenberg perceived a conflict in the preaching there. Luther had called even the babe in the womb blessed, it was reported, while Melanchthon favored good works.[15]

In his opposition to indulgence sales Luther had stated that man can *do* nothing whatsoever to be deserving, or to justify himself before God's law. Debate had hardened this position until it found classical form in his reply to Erasmus, denying free will. Melanchthon had understanding for liberal-minded souls who wanted to encourage people to do good, so he was constantly being charged with synergism—the doctrine that man can make some little contribution to his own salvation. Melanchthon in these days certainly was eager to effect conciliation in Europe, and Cruciger was similarly inclined. Now Cordatus wanted Cruciger called to order, for preaching good works in the castle church. He backed away from his charge against the facile Melanchthon, but his squabble dragged on.

Luther, although an incisive thinker who liked to reduce issues to clear-cut terms, had never been dogmatic. Melanchthon knew him best, and in his fondness for attaching classical Greek sobriquets called him "Arcesilas," that skeptical advocate of *epochein*, suspension or deferral of judgment.[16] Where rigorous logic could eventually lead Calvin to infer predestination, Luther quite flatly refused to probe into imponderables like that.[17] As an Arcesilas, he was able to accept what he thought was the clear word of scripture without following implications into areas where he lacked evidence. He could accept Paul's statement that man is saved by God's grace without concluding some are therefore predestined to be saved, the rest to be damned. Melanchthon appreciated Luther's Arcesilan willingness to suspend judgment in this way. Perhaps it even helped him in his diplomatic efforts. While Luther might poke fun at his friend's agreeability or voice suspicion of superficial accords, he was always confident of Melanchthon's soundness.

What was troubling him was pedanticism and legalism among his older disciples. Cordatus had opened a rift which he knew went right to the heart of his teachings, just at a time when harmony was important. Precisely this issue of good works was destined to drive a wedge into Lutheranism after his death, Melanchthon retaining the Wittenberg wing and Nicholas von Amsdorf becoming the bastion of self-styled orthodoxy. Luther was astute and sensitive enough to see this potential in pedantic dogmatism. Those last words he wrote across the cover of his testament struck a major theme of his career, especially in its last years (p. 210 above).

These were some of the anxieties that followed him to Schmalkalden. He set out in a coach with the jovial Bugenhagen and tender Philip (who called the big man "a gross Pomeranian"). Bugenhagen wanted to encourage Luther in precisely the firmness which caused Melanchthon to "shudder all over at the thought of the horrible disputes" which awaited them.[18] Justus Jonas, senior professor of theology, had started out with them but was constrained by an attack of the stone to turn back. Farther along, his place was taken by another old friend, that former adviser to Frederick the Wise and John, George Spalatin, and the trip rolled along in high spirits despite unusually wet weather. Luther sent verses to Jonas encouraging him to come ahead to the convention. He had heard tell there would be more learned theologians assembled here than at Mantua.[19] In all, they took seven stopovers on a stretch which, even allowing for the tortuous windings of a roadway growing ever more mountainous, was much less than two hundred miles. When they at last arrived among the few half-timbered houses of Schmalkalden the weather actually cleared up, so that Luther wrote of the bracing air and the great confluence of distinguished men. His old friend Eobanus Hessus was even here, writing enthusiastically that eight princes were personally in attendance, as well as legates from the king of Denmark, the emperor, and the pope. He estimated forty theologians.[20] Many were Luther's pupils, others had been friends and supporters for a generation. He was invited to dine with princes, and many an admirer slogged through the muddy streets to the Rentmeisters Haus, where he lodged.

Such a throng could be housed in the little Hessian town only with difficulty—the rulers' entourages alone were legion. No wonder that even Doctor Luther's accommodations left something to be desired. He complained of having to sleep on wet linens. This might help account for the physical weakness which he attributed solely to nagging anxieties. The rough trip through the mountains may have been the cause of a kidney stone drop-

ping into his bladder. Such a passage is commonly associated
with excruciating back pains, but this ailment was now so far
progressed in him that despite bleeding he noticed no pangs and
described the dark, coagulated urine with no awareness of how
ominous it was.[21]

The first business in Schmalkalden being of a political sort,
Luther felt useless and fell to brooding about Mantua. Although
confident he would be vindicated if the council were conducted
fairly and freely, he thought the curia would yet find some pre-
text for calling it off. He set down a ten-point argument urging
John Frederick not to be provoked into declining the invitation.
In the somber and poetic tone of one speaking from a great
remove, and for whom decisions of the moment are threads in a
grand fabric, he began,

> I see with foreboding that it will eventually come to a combat.
> We must not be afraid, for God instructs us, who is all-power-
> ful and who has before this disposed differently than we ex-
> pected.[22]

The stone continued to distress him. On his first Sunday in
Schmalkalden he satisfied those who desired to hear him preach
by conducting a sermon in his lodgings. The next Sunday, feeling well enough to venture out, he preached in the city church
and marveled at how small his voice sounded there. In the afternoon he was stricken with a most painful attack, by evening he
was quite unable to urinate. There were numerous physicians at
the convention, and Europe's best plied their skills on the distinguished patient. They attempted to catheterize a sufferer "almost
drowned in his own urine."[23] "They made me drink as if I were
a great ox," he complained, "treated my body the same way, and
all its members, abused my private parts."[24] They had a hearty
bedside manner: "You're a strong fellow, and we're going to use
strong medicine." They made him swallow a mixture of horse
dung and ground garlic. Finally he drove them away, declared
he'd rather die than live by their ministrations,[25] and persuaded
Melanchthon to summon his friend George Sturtz, whom he
knew from Erfurt. Sturtz arrived in the middle of the week with
drugs not available at Schmalkalden (including something to
strengthen the heart).[26] They may have provided some relief,

but Luther's anuric state was causing poisoning and a general edema. He was wracked by sleeplessness and vomiting. He wanted to go home, he said, and not give the Roman emissary the satisfaction of seeing him die in this "devil's belly." Melanchthon hesitated, of course. Luther claimed later it was because of his "incorrigible, crazy astrology," and biographers have solemnly accepted the gibe ever since (for Philip was an astrology buff, and Luther did love to twit him on the subject).

When Melanchthon arrived at Luther's bedside the next Sunday morning and beheld his friend's disgusting color and horribly swollen body, he broke down and cried right in Luther's presence. Luther, still able to summon humor, reminded Philip of a mutual friend

who always said there's no art to drinking good beer, but to be able to drink bad beer—now that's an art. You should remember this in my case now, and teach me how to practice that art, so I can retain a calm heart in the face of pain and in despair of my life.

He then embarked on a sermon to Melanchthon on the art of dying. He drew upon Job. He said his death was nothing compared to Christ's. He remembered the wonderful, sainted men who lay buried, and said he welcomed the prospect of lying down among them. Luther was but practicing what he had hundreds of times admonished others to do, and carrying forward a familiar tradition, well established since the early Middle Ages, "the Art"—to quote the title of numerous little handbooks—"of Dying Well."

He looked down on his swollen limbs and marveled at the change man can undergo here on earth. He quoted Virgil, *Quantum mutatus ab illo,* one of the most often adapted themes of world literature ("O Hamlet, what a falling-off was there"). The passage was that famous one in which the dead Hector appears in a dream to Aeneas. He knew Philip would savor the analogy, for these were the lines where Hector passed on his leadership to the younger man. Virgil brutally describes Hector's filthy body, feet all swollen after being dragged behind Achilles' chariot: "Now his beard was ragged and his hair clotted with blood, and all those wounds which he had sustained trying to de-

fend the walls of his homeland could still be seen." Hector tells
Aeneas that "if any strong arm could have defended our fortress,
surely mine would have defended it," and tells his old friend and
comrade now to go out beyond the horizon and "find a new
walled city for the sacred shrines of Troy." Melanchthon recognized that Luther, unlike Hector, must die far from home. "I
would have liked to entreat the Lord God, even at the risk of
complaining," Luther told him, "to let me die in the land of my
prince."[27] Melanchthon resolved to send him to Saxony the next
morning.

Dying was a familiar and important part of Renaissance life.
Family and friends gathered at one's bedside and the scene often
possessed a rare dignity. The dying endeavored to display ex-
emplary composure and to instill into survivors proper faith in
the life of the soul. One's last moments and sayings were noted
well and long remembered. The death of eminent personages
would be sharply observed and fully reported. Luther's father
had, of course, been asked if he affirmed his son's religion, and
had replied doughtily, "I'd be a scamp if I didn't!"

Friends in Schmalkalden began to assemble. The papal legate
came to pay last respects, but was brusquely turned away by
loyal, suspicious John Schlaginhauffen, who flung into his face
the words, "You'll not see Doctor Luther in eternity."[28] John
Frederick, whose visit had both personal and policy import,
came with a train of officers and nobility. "Our dear Lord God
will have mercy on us for his name's sake, and extend your life,
Herr Doctor," he began.

Luther urged all to pray, and he let it be known he was his old
self by tossing off a defiant word about the papacy. "Yes, it is
the apple of Adam that has got stuck inside me," he went on,
"and I just cannot digest it. But my Lord Christ digested it." He
thanked John Frederick for his willingness to suffer so much for
the gospel.

John Frederick had some important matters to clarify in the
presence of officers and theologians. "I am concerned, my dear
Herr Doctor, that if God takes you from us he may also take
away his word."

"Ah, my gracious lord, there are so many learned, loyal people
who are sincere and competent. I hope they will watch over it

and, with God's help, maintain it." He folded his hands piously and added, "Grant it, almighty God."

John Frederick turned to the theologians standing at the bedside and said, "My dear sirs, look ye to it that ye watch over the pure word of God, that we may remain in our dear Lord God." He demanded to know if all present had subscribed unanimously to Luther's articles.

This was a touchy point. He was referring of course to the "testament" which Melanchthon had signed with reservation, fearing trouble both here at Schmalkalden and later at Mantua. The question seemed to have been addressed to him, so he replied with the flexuousness which some were already beginning to hold against him. He said all had signed the Augsburg Confession and the Wittenberg Concord, and he mentioned at least one new signature recently acquired to those documents.

John Frederick finally spoke personally with Doctor Luther and, since it might be the last time he was to see him alive, he said before leaving, "You must not worry about your wife and children. For your wife shall be my wife and your children, my children."

When he was gone, Luther tried to brighten the gloomy assemblage by saying he had thought it was the atmosphere in Schmalkalden had caused his illness, "but it is the devil's fault, of course. He takes whatever he can find to pester me with. He stoned Stephen with stones; he stones me with the stone." In his wretched condition, that vast range of humors always characteristic of him became even more apparent. He prayed, succumbed to "many bitter tears, sighed deeply, and sobbed, folding his hands"—but ever and again he would crack a joke. He began to worry about his family, thinking of that arrogant and adulterous Hans Metzsch, who would surely use his power against them to avenge himself on Luther. He begged Chancellor Brück to protect his "innocent wife and child." Writhing in pain, he grimly jested that this must be that thorn in the flesh of which Paul speaks. He began to question his sanity, having thoughts of suicide. "Well, all right. If I go mad, God will remain sane and Christ my Lord will be my wisdom."[29]

The dying man's wish to be removed from this "devil's belly" in Hesse back across the Thuringian mountains to "my prince's land" was accomplished with great circumstance. John Frederick sent his own coach to bear the patient and his physician. Two strong men walked along beside it seizing the axles at bad spots along the rocky mountainside, while Luther within wished the Turk would come and slaughter him. The prince had a special copper basin forged in Schmalkalden to hold glowing coals. In a separate coach hot towels could continually be prepared for application to the sick man. Spalatin and Bugenhagen rode in their coach with John Schlaginhauffen and Frederick Myconius, the pastor from Gotha, that Saxon city which Doctor Martinus hoped to reach before he died. John Frederick had dispatched a courier to Wittenberg with instructions that Kate should meet her husband there.

Atop the first ridge lay the village of Tambach. Here, scarcely ten miles from Schmalkalden, the little caravan of seventeen pulled up before the inn. A tortured body, its swollen bladder protruding despite the man's corpulence, was carefully removed from an ornate coach. For the first time in over a week, Luther thought, as he was being carried inside, he might be able to urinate. He was given some red wine. The obstruction in his bladder or urethra must have been affected by the jolting ride or by the shifting of his body as he was lifted out of the coach. Shortly after midnight, he was able to write to Melanchthon:

> Praise be to God the father of our Lord Jesus Christ, Father of mercy and all comfort, who in this second hour of the night, dear Philip, has opened urethra and bladder quite unexpectedly. I got up, as you have seen me to do, to make a vain attempt. Scarcely a quarter hour passed, and I urinated eight times, each time more than a pint, so that I excreted over a gallon in all. Thus does joy make me measure this liquid, so vile to others and so precious to me.[30]

Urine continued to flow (about three more pints) after Schlaginhauffen had taken the letter, seized a horse, and gone galloping down to Schmalkalden. He burst into the sleeping town singing out "Lutherus vivit, Lutherus vivit!" calling especially loudly as he passed the papal legate's lodgings. As bearer of good tidings he received ten medallion coins from the elector, stamped with that prince's own countenance.[31]

It was the night of 26–27 February. Tambach was about half-way to Gotha. The road grew better the rest of the way, and Luther arrived in high spirits. He felt he now had a new under-standing of the 23rd Psalm, which he elucidated for Myconius.[32] His eased condition permitted him to contemplate how close to death he had been—and still was. By the next day he weakened again. Pathos at the thought of his own demise took the form of passionate lament over those he must leave behind. The gospel would be forgotten now, he said, and the church lapse into its old ways. "Didn't we intone, murmur, sing, and damn the Bible at church, at table, at mass, and in the canonical hours? Yet what did we comprehend? If it should come to that again, how pite-ous it would be! I hope the day of judgment will intervene." We are told he spoke *plenissimis affectibus*, "with abundant emo-tion."[33] He was sure he would not live through the night of the twenty-eighth, so John Bugenhagen took his confession.

Alone in the room with him, he also received Luther's last will and testament, and wrote it later from memory. Although it was no doubt spoken in German, Bugenhagen was accustomed to taking notes in Latin, except where a phrase seemed especially remarkable. For example, he retained the opening words exactly: "I know, praise be to God, that I did right to storm the papacy with the word of God, for it is an abomination unto God, Christ, and the gospel." Luther asked that his closest associates forgive him for offenses against them, and that they comfort Kate, "for she was happy with me for twelve years. She served me not only as a wife but as my assistant." He expressed thanks to many, including the citizens of Wittenberg, but the bulk of his testament consisted of encouragement to John Frederick and the Landgrave Philip of Hesse, leaders of the Schmalkaldic League. He would not have them heed the reproach that they were despoiling the church, "for I see that they are using this property to support those things which pertain to religion. Should something fall to them from such property—who is more entitled to it? . . . Command them in my name to be confident in God and to act as the Holy Ghost inspires them for the good of the gospel. I would not prescribe ways and means to them." In conclusion, he admitted he was ready to die now, "I'd just like to live until Pentecost [the opening of the council in Mantua] to publish before the world yet graver charges against that Roman beast."[34]

The next morning he expressed surprise to have awakened. "I lay down last night expecting to be a corpse today, but it didn't work out. All right, Father, thy will be done."[35] He still did not expect to recover, and wanted to arrange for a grave there in Gotha. Myconius protested he must be buried in the Wittenberg church where his gospel had originated. His bladder had again ceased to function, and he began the whole ordeal anew, hoping no doubt he would expire quickly this time. But this stoppage lasted only two days. Myconius recorded words which give voice to what many have felt in serious illness:

> Oh, dear Lord, how little we have to do with our own lives! We live by your will, and know not when our life begins. We die by your will and do not comprehend. Some people are in such good health, go tripping about thinking to live a long time—you come and take them suddenly away. Yet here lie I and others who want to die, and you will that we must live.[36]

Schlaginhauffen went back to Schmalkalden. Justus Jonas met the party and they journeyed on to Erfurt, then to Weimar for another short rest. John Frederick sent some game. Luther wrote a classical distich warning the whole world against the damp beds of Hesse. They were back in Wittenberg by the middle of March.

Medicine today recognizes a multiplicity of causes for kidney stones. One of the latest theories is based on the new concept of plate tectonics, and associates incidence of the disease with the continents of an earlier geological epoch. Certain established views, about which there is little disagreement, are that these calcifications are favored by stasis in the urinary tract, and that they are apt to form about any particles already present there. Thus, for example, a deficiency of vitamin A in the diet may cause flaking of epithelial layers in the tubes leading from the kidneys to the bladder, and result in the formation of stones. Similarly, tubes once damaged by the passage of stones are predisposed to the formation of others. This seems to have been a part of Luther's problem, who had long suffered with the complaint. Of more interest to a biographer than the cause of a disease, however, are its effects.

In all likelihood, Luther's kidneys never worked properly again. Retention of urine for such a protracted period does irreversible damage to the pelvis of one or both kidneys. His vomiting and sleeplessness indicated uremic poisoning at the time of the blockage, of course, and there is some evidence that uremia may have become chronic with him from this time on. The use of dialysis for kidney patients in recent years has facilitated research into the effects of renal disease on personality. Foremost among the recognized effects are an "undercurrent of irritability," "striking swings between states of confusion and mental lucidity,"[37] and "difficulty with thought, attention, concentration, and memory."[38] These effects differ greatly from patient to patient—"The precise form of a uremic psychosis is undoubtedly conditioned by previous personality, and every type from depression to a catatonic state may be seen."[39] Luther's behavior during his last nine years easily falls within this rather broad range. He also showed the well-known physical effects of uremia, a weakening of the heart and a predisposition to disease. His condition may account for Melanchthon's recollection that the older Luther's still flashing eyes were surrounded by yellow.[40]

Just as his misery had been approaching its height (on the Saturday before he left Schmalkalden), the League had formally rejected the council at Mantua. The papal legate had remonstrated, but received final rebuttal on the last day of February (the day Luther dictated his will to Bugenhagen in Gotha). As it turned out, a spat arose between the pope and the duke of Mantua as to necessity and propriety of security forces for the assemblage there, and the council had to be postponed. It was the last time a general council was contemplated or convoked.

For various reasons which need not be discussed here, historians have been accustomed to hold Luther responsible for protestant refusal to attend the council. As his nineteenth-century biographer Julius Köstlin explained, however, the rejection gave him cause for regret when he learned of it.[41]

Loss of a Friend

Schmalkalden marked the turning point and steepening decline, not only in Luther's physical powers, but also in his relationships with others. His quarrel with an old friend, John Agricola, showed the nervousness that came of his ill health, and his anxiety about the future of the church, once he was gone. The break itself was probably inevitable, determined by the structure of revolutionary intellectual movements like that which had bonded these two men together. Agricola incurred Luther's displeasure by advocating what he claimed had been the master's own preachments against law. That such a claim was possible points up a fundamental irony in Luther's life.

Next to Philip Melanchthon, Luther said, John Agricola had been his nearest friend.[1] Both were more than ten years his junior. He felt drawn to such brilliant young fellows (of whom the reform movement largely consisted) more even than to beloved associates nearer his own age, like Nicholas Hausmann and Amsdorf. The young Agricola had arrived in Wittenberg as a student just at that time when Luther was becoming prominent, first for his scholarly views, then as reformer. He fondly recalled how Luther had singled him out of the congregation by asking, "Aren't you from Eisleben?"

"Yes, my lord," the young man had replied.

"Well, then we'll have to get acquainted." Eisleben was Luther's own birthplace.[2]

But with this student the professor had yet more in common. Master Eisleben, as they called him, was open, affable, extremely self-conscious, very sensitive to his native tongue. Overzealous, he published one of Luther's sermons without authorization, a portentous act as it turned out. Tutor for a while at the university, he returned to his hometown, "fleeing public office and seeking obscurity," as he put it later, "creeping into a corner to eat bread and cheese with my wife and little children."[3] He continued to correspond and to collaborate with Luther, just a bit jealous of Melanchthon's rising star in Wittenberg. He let it be known he found his younger rival's reform measures unduly stern, for he remembered Luther's teachings as being full of comfort, stressing grace, and opposed to law. He tried to work in Luther's spirit, the Agricola collection of proverbs being the first such in the German language.[4] With Luther-like brashness he damned his local princes, and Luther defended him; when he was accused of preaching faith without works, Luther but chided him gently.[5] At the approach of the council in Mantua, the two made Latin and German editions of letters that Bohemian reformer Jan Hus had written from the dungeon where he awaited execution at the Council of Constance.[6]

Luther, who frustrated Kate with his profligate handling of expensive presents, once told Agricola he was sending him "that little vessel adorned with pewter, before it acquires another master—for Kate is set upon it." But he was too late. The letter bears a postscript saying that when he looked for the cup it was not to be found. He feared a conspiracy among Kate, Bugenhagen, and Justus Jonas, one of whom must have absconded with the treasure.[7] The ties between the households were close. When Agricola's wife Elsa fell into a depression, Luther took her into the Black Cloister for a few days' rest and advised his friend on the importance of bolstering woman's self-esteem.[8] Agricola was at odds with the count of Mansfeld, and Luther succeeded in arranging a professorship for him at Wittenberg. That conference called in December of 1536 presented an opportunity to provide him expenses for the trip. Agricola somewhat precipitously fired off a nasty letter to his count and pulled up stakes, bringing Elsa and their seven children plus two adopted daughters. They all moved into the Black Cloister, and when Luther went off to Schmalkalden he turned his pulpit over to the younger colleague. He had immediate cause for regret.

During those uncomfortable, anxious days in Schmalkalden a letter came from the count of Mansfeld accusing Agricola of an-

tinomian heresy—denial of the law—and warning that he was a
new Thomas Müntzer. It found Luther in a weakened state—and
the name of that revolutionary preacher was enough to strike
horror in him at any time. Müntzer (a figure from the peasants'
uprisings today revered by Marxists for preaching the social implications of the Reformation) had exploited the close connection in Renaissance minds between the theological concept of
law and the civil law. The Ten Commandments stood on one
continuum with municipal police regulations. A truism of the
day was that disrespect for any civil authority violated the Commandment to honor thy father. Law therefore cut a very broad
swath through a culture in which theologians were the prince's
first political advisers. Law had been one of Luther's central concerns throughout his career. The charge of antinomianism was a
serious one indeed.

While Luther's illness was progressing, Agricola's appointment
as court chaplain came through. The protégé thus naturally assumed a task—or, rather, the honor—of preaching before the assembled protestant princes just after the close of the Schmalkalden conference. He tried to show himself worthy of his recent
advancement by devising a new terminology for essential points
of doctrine, and avoided using the word "law" at all. Orthodox
Lutheranism contrasted Old Testament *law* with New Testament *gospel*. Agricola preached *gospel* only, calling it the "revelation of grace." Incidentally to the revelation of grace he recognized also the "revelation of wrath" (the old notion of *law*).
Luther when he heard it was full of scorn:

> It's the same as if I said one mustn't preach of death, but of
> "passing"—wouldn't that be silly? I entrusted him with so
> much, my doctrine, pulpit, church, wife, child, hearth, and
> confidence.[9]

Having plunged himself into Luther's disfavor, Agricola fell also
from grace with later Lutheran writers, who seldom even allow
for the possibility that his intentions were sincere. This is the
more understandable, since most of what can be learned about
the case comes from Luther's complaints in a despondent period
of his life.[10]

What Luther called invention of a "silly" new terminology

was but a well-known, recurrent phenomenon in the history of all the sciences. It is motivated in part, as Luther suspected and resented, by ambition. In order to attain recognition among one's professional associates, one displays a firmer, more effective grasp of problems they at the moment deem important. In theology the major tool *is* vocabulary. What could be more appropriate for the new court chaplain than promulgation of his own terminology for the most pressing issues? He had arrived in Wittenberg just at a time when the senior men, not only the squabbler Cordatus but respectable pillars like Bugenhagen, were at pains to assert the adequacy of God's grace. They feared their younger scholarly associates, Melanchthon and Cruciger, were backsliding into papish acceptance of good works. Agricola wished to make his agreement with the older men known. Had he not been in Wittenberg before any of them? Who could confirm Luther's position more reliably than he?

He remembered the early sermons full of comfort for those in despair of fulfilling the law. He knew an abundance of passages where Luther, with Paul, declared the law does not bind a Christian. Luther had blasted canon law,[11] and Agricola had been thrilled to see him burn it publicly before the city gates. But Luther's pronouncements of those days had been (as Luther recognized they always were) largely determined by his adversaries. When his elevation of scripture above canon law was taken quite literally by fundamentalists who wanted to live by the letter of the Mosaic code, he had vehemently rejected that, too. "The sectarians want to shove Moses down our throats with all his Commandments . . . We will accept Moses as teacher, but we will not accept him as lawgiver." On this occasion, Luther had added, "Unless he agrees with the New Testament and natural law,"[12] but such qualifiers were less memorable than rhetorical flourishes like, "So I'll help stone Moses. Let the stiff-necked and ruthless have him, not the meek and the faithful." "If Christ comes to you when you feel guilty and speaks with the voice of Moses, 'What hast thou done?'—then strike him dead! If he speaks to you as God and savior, then prick up your ears." "It is impossible for the gospel and the law to reside and rule together in one heart at the same time. Christ must necessarily yield to the law, or the law to Christ, just as Saint Paul says in Galatians 5, 'Who-soever of you are justified by the law are fallen from grace.'"[13]

Agricola had heard all this and more. He was confident he perceived the core of Luther's teaching in rejection of the law. He thought he had arrived in Wittenberg at a most opportune time, when his insight was needed to squelch Melanchthon's mistaken bent to compromise with the papists. He could scarcely have made a graver error.

When Luther considered that important sermon before all the princes, which he might have preached but for his health, he cried out, "Is that going to start now, while we are yet alive?" In characteristically accurate overstatement, he said Agricola's opin-ion had been dictated by "hatred and ambition. Ah, if we could but give Master Philip his due, who teaches the use of law with great clarity and eloquence . . . Count Albert's prophecy is being fulfilled, who wrote that he'll become a Müntzer yet. Whoever undermines civil law undermines the political and eco-nomic world."[14] Although it might take him a while to admit it, the irony of the situation was not lost on Luther: not only was Agricola drawing on his teacher's own utterances, but the very first objection which occurred to Luther was precisely the one raised twenty years earlier against his own doctrine, and by Duke George much more recently.

Far from awakening understanding in him, this recognition of his earlier teachings in Agricola's "new vocabulary" only made Luther the more vehement. The other Wittenberg theologians did nothing to calm his anxieties. Bugenhagen, summoned to Denmark in the summer, stipulated that Agricola must not preach in his church while he was gone. The chief agent of har-mony for the group, Philip Melanchthon, was in this instance understandably disinclined to intercede. In fact, his own inti-macy with Luther is a part of the background for poor Agri-cola's vain efforts to please the master.

Luther would creep up behind Philip to remove his pen from his hand, insisting that he conserve his strength. Agricola may have witnessed exchanges like the following—

Luther: "Wouldst thou obey God or man?"

Philip: "God, because it is written, 'Let me fall now into the hand of the Lord . . . but let me not fall into the hand of man.'"

Luther: "Wilt thou hear the word of God directly, or through man?"

Philip: "Through man."

Luther: "I command thee by authority divine that thou cease now from thy studies and labors until I command thee differently, for God wills that we observe the Sabbath."[15]

The close bond between Melanchthon and Cruciger was known far and wide. It was said that at the Worms conference of 1541 Cruciger not only maintained a running protocol for his colleague, but advised him at the same time on crucial points. They presented a paragon of German thoroughness. This was the famous occasion when Melanchthon, after hearing John Eck's presentation, said he would respond on the morrow.

"It brings little honor," bullied the redoubtable Eck, known for his debates with Luther, "when one cannot respond directly and *ex tempore.*"

"Herr Doctor, I seek no honor in these talks," was Melanchthon's gentle answer, "but rather the truth. Tomorrow, God be willing, you shall have my reply." Of such mettle were the men with whom Agricola had to compete for his teacher's favor.

His first overt offense was to give his *A Summary of the Gospels* to the printer. He had shown the work to Luther a few months earlier, and he flattered himself he had his approval. Either Agricola was wrong, or Doctor Martinus forgetful, who when he learned that printing was in progress had it stopped forthwith. Sheets already printed he ordered destroyed. He sincerely felt that Agricola was undermining him behind his back, and just waiting for his death.[16] Although Agricola had settled down in Wittenberg by now, the two were seeing each other only in church, and communicating by letter. This was not the Luther whom Agricola had known, and he was at a loss. Members of the inner circle were diligently recording, and no doubt repeating, Luther's grumblings, e.g.,

With a great sob [Luther] said, "Ah, how it hurts when one loses a good friend whom one has loved most dearly! I had this man at my table, he laughed with me, and now he attacks me behind my back. I cannot tolerate that. Nor can he defend it, for to reject the law is the crassest of errors."

He resolved to bring his enemy out into the open—

My closest friends would tread me underfoot and confuse the gospel, so I shall arrange debates for the purpose of calling them out. They will present themselves humbly, but I will not be content with their dissembling. I'll call them by name and make them take a public stand. This is no joking matter![17]

He had in hand a series of theses which he said had been circulating in town (Agricola denied them). Some were especially outrageous propositions which Luther admitted he had invented himself, just to show the logical consequences of the rest. The most notorious of these was,

If you are a whore, knave, adulterer, or any other sinner, yet have faith, you are on your way to blessedness.

But some were strikingly reminiscent of Luther's utterances in earlier years, e.g.,

All who rely on Moses will go to the devil—to the gallows with Moses![18]

The academic debate was held on 18 December 1537, Doctor Martin Luther presiding. Agricola was summoned and publicly invited to step forward, but was not in attendance. The debate proceeded without him, Luther himself representing one side, other members of the faculty taking turns at the other. The only participants whose names are in the record happen to be Justus Jonas and Conrad Cordatus. The audience was especially large.[19]

The real thunderbolt struck a dismayed Agricola in the form of a brief note from Luther just after New Year:

I have informed the [university], my Agricola, that the theology lectures which you undertook, at my request (lest you be an idle burden) and by my permission, be dropped at my request, and at the same time that you abstain from theology entirely. I apprise you of this in writing, so that you understand you would have to obtain permission elsewhere to lecture, as from the university senate. I will not prevent your speaking against us in private. But make it easy on yourself. May you prosper, and humble your mind under the mighty hand of God.[20]

The hand of God would in this instance cut off the livelihood of a family full of children. Melanchthon recognized it was time to intercede. He came by night to Agricola with counsel. He advised that Doctor Luther had recently been wondering why he had had no visit from Elsa. Through Elsa then, Master Eisleben obtained an audience. Doctor Martinus laid before him two requirements. In the first place, he was to cease using his strange new terminology. Secondly, he must participate in a public debate with Luther next Saturday.[21] By thus subjecting himself to instruction before students, faculty, and citizens, Agricola did manage to hang on, for a time. Restoration of the old warmth and friendship was out of the question.

In this year (1538) Luther lost the closest friend from his own generation, Nicholas Hausmann, who had received a call to the superintendency of the church and schools in his hometown of Freiberg. In October he said a last goodbye before departing for the new office, and Luther openly wept to see him go. While delivering the inaugural sermon in Freiberg, Hausmann suffered a stroke and died within days. The news came to John Frederick in Wittenberg, but he gave Luther only a "dark indication." Justus Jonas, Kate, and Melanchthon conferred as to what they should tell the doctor when asked, and decided that on the first day they would only indicate that Hausmann's illness was serious. Thus they disclosed the news to him gradually. When he learned the whole truth, on the third day, he rushed to his bedroom to weep, but soon was able to return with a composed countenance.[22]

Agricola remained suspect. Luther maligned him in private, knowing full well that it would soon be on the streets how he had called "Grickel" a motley salamander.[23] Precisely the poor fellow's apology, that he thought he was espousing Luther's teachings, was unspeakably galling. In one of the debates (which he continued to arrange) Luther faced up to this point, and admitted that "we did use the words the antinomians are using now." He called upon considerable eloquence to make his audience, most of them young but a few who had served in his cause since the beginning, comprehend how different the world had been in those days. He spoke of the "miserable, anxious, afflicted consciences," to whom it had been unnecessary to teach the law. The whole sense of his gospel had been to comfort them.

> Now, however, when times have changed and are different from those under the papacy, these antinomians of ours, sweet theologians, retain our words, our doctrine, that joyous promise of Christ. And what is worse, they don't want to teach anything else, heeding not that mankind is no longer the same, but different from what it was under that executioner the pope.

With his considerable oratorical gifts, he contrasted people nowadays, "smug and wicked, hardened, iniquitous predators and Epicureans who respect neither God nor man," with the timid souls of earlier: "we were frightened to death and trembled at the rustling of a leaf when it fell from a tree."[24]

Over the space of nearly three years, Agricola was required to demonstrate his orthodoxy in debate, in delivery of carefully attended sermons, and in written statements. Twice his salary was placed in jeopardy. His correspondence was intercepted and examined. At last, unable to come up with a statement of his faith which entirely satisfied his critics, he asked Luther to write one for him. "He has commended his retraction to me," Doctor Martinus confided at table, "perhaps in the hope I would treat him more gently, but I seek Christ's glory, not his, and I'll paint the cowardly, haughty, impious man with his own words."[25] The writing which resulted, *Against the Antinomians*, revealed Luther's distraught frame of mind. Agricola might have drawn enlightenment from it, but he found himself so defamed in the opening paragraphs that he lodged formal complaint with John Frederick. The prince turned the matter over to a council of his theologians, of course (Melanchthon, Jonas, Bugenhagen, and Amsdorf), who sustained Luther and explicitly wondered how Agricola could have failed to realize that Luther was "not a man like any other man."[26]

They were quite aware that Agricola was not without his own following. There was even a move afoot among the faculty to name him dean at the university—but Luther abruptly scotched that. While Agricola's litigation had been pending, the authorities exacted from him an oath that he would not leave the confines of Wittenberg, something normally required of people implicated in criminal proceedings. He thereupon tried to withdraw his complaint, requested permission to visit Brandenburg, received no reply, and—fearing he was about to be jailed—fled in a panic. His "perjury" sealed the break with Luther.[27] The margrave of Brandenburg (protestant son of that Joachim who had cuckolded Wolf Hornung) received Agricola cordially, retaining him as court chaplain despite the difficulties this entailed in relations with other protestant princes. Luther, in the last years of his life, once again refused to accept a visit from his former pupil, admitting only the daughters to his presence, whom he found "immodest and gossipy." He tried to damage Agricola's position in Berlin.[28]

The efforts to apologize for Luther's treatment of his pupil, or to justify it in terms of presumed wrongs done him, seldom further our understanding of his personality. Obviously, a number of factors were converging. Luther's frail condition, his anxiety about the church after his death, the professional jealousy and backbiting among the Wittenberg clique—these are all obvious enough from Luther's own utterances, and require no further discussion. The same is probably true of an older man's apprehension about vigorous youth pressing forward, but it should be noted that Agricola was not the only devout protestant who was at odds with Wittenberg. This is not the place to depart into the complex history of protestantism, but Luther's anxious feeling that sects were springing up all around him was probably justified. He would come to the table "sad and moody, in throes which he would not admit to," recorded the diary of a friend. "He pretended to be at outs with his wife, but I suspect the cause was Master John Agricola's impenitence and dissembling."[29] He would set out to pay a visit of reconciliation to his beloved pupil, then turn back murmuring, "No fanatic or papist ever troubled me so."[30] He felt so betrayed and persecuted that he was willing to jeopardize the younger man's family and career by writing acrid repudiations to the princes on whom he depended. "Nothing so riles me," he wrote to John Frederick, "as that he acted as our friend, laughed, ate, all the while so treacherously concealing his enmity toward us."[31]

Luther could not be cheered by his colleagues. When Jonas voiced a rosy outlook for a future served by the fine theologians they were training, he shook his head and said, "I have a foreboding that the best is past now, and the sects will follow after."[32] He had seen his own efforts go the way of other intellectual movements, and could not accept it with detachment. What had begun as one man's sincere response to an urgently felt need in the world had naturally acquired followers who recognized the urgency. They had been drawn together by common interest, so that Luther rightly spoke of their "cause." But each also brought his own special interests, of course, and his own peculiar understanding of the common cause. Discussions among the group therefore became essential, and soon occupied a great deal of their attention, at times taking priority over all else. Motivations revealed in such debates were different from the motives which had drawn them together—and seemed unrelated to Luther's own. Now they were espousing views and expressing them not in response to a need in the world, but in response to views within the group. Cliques had formed, jealousies could not be denied. Group status was to be won by the writing of a treatise, or the preaching of an original sermon. Success could be measured in terms of following. All this encouraged formulation of distinctive positions. Thus a sociologist might perceive the dynamics of any intellectual enterprise as favoring fragmentation, the formation of sects.

Worse than the sects themselves, in Luther's view, was the speculative writing and debate that accompanied them, or gave rise to them.[33] His favorite example was the learned Andreas Osiander of Nuremberg, whose "turgid, high-flown, remote" sermons he liked to contrast with those of his own pupil in Nuremberg, Veit Dietrich, "which the common people can carry home with them." He said he did not himself climb into the pulpit in order to instruct Philip Melanchthon,

> My God, girls of sixteen, housewives and old men, peasants come to church. They don't understand such lofty things. But if you can offer them apt and memorable analogies, that's what

they will comprehend and retain. He who teaches most simply, childishly, popularly, trivially, that's the best preacher. I
like it to be easy and earthy. But now if it is debate you are
looking for, come into my classroom! I'll give it to you plenty
sharp, and you'll get your answer, however fancy your questions. I'm going to have to write a book against these smart
preachers![34]

Here may lie a potent source of his irritation with Agricola. As
deep as Luther's rejection of the law lay his disillusionment with
scholasticism, "sophistry" as he called it: speculation which had
only academic reference and was not a response to the disturbed
souls who were, in Luther's view, the only justification for theology.

For him the motivations of Osiander, Agricola, and the other
sectarians were not explicable in terms of group sociology. He
judged them to be the creatures of ambition. In no way was ambition a commendable virtue in his mind, or even a tolerable
weakness. It was one of the seven deadly sins, called pride. It was
instilled by the devil.

He had come to look upon the sects as a part of the necessary
weave of history. The true church of Christ, and the infernal
forces masquerading in the pomp of piety, together constituted
the warp and woof of the world in time. The tract which he
wrote at poor Agricola's behest, *Against the Antinomians*, placed
Agricola's error in this larger historical frame and gave Luther's
view on the formation of sects in general—

It is their peculiar pride and license that they want to produce
something new and special themselves, so people will say,
"Well, I vow, that is a man. He is a second Paul! They in
Wittenberg are not the only smart fellows. I have a head on
my shoulders, too." . . . From all this we see, and could understand it if we just would, what the history of the church
has always been.

He called the faith a little candle, which the forces of evil had
been trying to blow out since the days of the apostles. "I guess I
have endured more than twenty blustering storms of sects myself, not even to mention those the fathers suffered." Not with-

out pathos, and against the full background of the history of the church, he detailed the various blasts the devil had whipped about him until he wished he might just die now. "And when we are dead, he'll remain the same as he has ever been, unable to cease his gusting. I see from afar how he puffs up his cheeks until he gets red in the face."[35] This concept of his own historical position continued to determine Luther's attitudes and the tone of his writings for the rest of his life.

The Agricola experience compelled him to take stock of himself and of his past pronouncements as never before. The debater's heritage disinclined him to abandon any position once asserted, and his advancing years reinforced tenacity with stubbornness. But since the world seemed to have become so much wickeder now, he supplemented earlier statements, even changed their emphasis. In *Against the Antinomians* he readjusted his views on the subject quite central to his life: the law.

The treatise argues in favor of the law on two points. Neither is new, but they were never so prominent in his writings before this. The first is a simple matter of logic, and is of significance for theology. God, Luther says, is hostile toward "secure spirits who do not fear him," who deny the law and, with it, sin.[36]

How are you going to know what Christ is, and what he has done for us, if we are not to know what the law is, which he fulfills for us, or what sin is, for which he made amends? Even if we did not need the law, and could rip it out of our hearts, although that is impossible, we would still have to preach it for Christ's sake.[37]

Thus he touches on the second point. It is of major importance in the tract, and in his future thinking. His idea that "the law is written into the bottom of our heart" was an ancient notion.[38] He had learned it from his studies of the classics. The Aristotelian distinction between natural law and positive (manmade) laws was taken over by the Romans, as Luther knew from his Cicero. Saint Paul reflected Roman influence when he explained (Rom. 2:14 f.) how both Jew and gentile "have the law written in their hearts." Luther used and thought about the expression often.

In Gratian (to whom the founding of canon law in the

twelfth century is attributed), he encountered the equation of Aristotelian natural law with the Ten Commandments of Moses and the Golden Rule of Christ. He wrote,

> God has his measures and rules, you know. The Ten Commandments are rooted in our flesh and blood. Do unto others as you would have them do unto you, and with what measure ye mete it shall be measured to you again. He plotted the entire world with that plumbline and compass. May they prosper who observe them! God will reward them, and a Turk or heathen can partake of the reward as well as a Christian. It has nothing to do with eternal life, of course.[39]

Modern times, let us say from Hugo Grotius in Luther's own century, but especially since Thomas Hobbes in the Enlightenment, came to equate natural law with rationality, or with enlightened self-interest. This view was fundamentally different from the two-thousand-year tradition Luther knew, which gave natural or divine law priority over human reason.

Toward the end of the twentieth century, natural law is again of some interest. Current preoccupation with the genetic code, for example, is but one impulse nudging thinkers in the direction of the older tradition. The modern biologist reminds us that man comes into the world bringing a complex network of preestablished tendencies, selected out and refined during vast numbers of ancestral generations. Human reason arises from a past which consciousness cannot itself overview. This thin rationality of the recently evolved brain tries to devise certain rules to live by. Such rules are bound to conflict at times with man's ancient, intuitive awareness of what must be best for himself and his environment. It is like Paul's law "written in the heart."

In medieval anatomy, the heart was the seat of understanding, so that we might best translate Luther's reading of Paul as: "ingrained in the mind." When a younger man, he had not yet considered that reason and natural law might conflict. Indeed, he equated the two, recommending reason as "the bourne of justice."[40] By the time he came to write that advice to his prince, the *Interpretation of Psalm 101*, he was ready to elaborate on Aristotle's distinction between natural and positive law: "I will call it healthy and sick law. For the force of nature prevails without any law, indeed penetrates all laws. But where nature is absent from laws, what remains is mere beggary and patchwork, as in natural sickness."[41] After the Agricola crisis, the problem of natural or divine law came to occupy his mind more and more. "Natural law is implanted in us like heat in fire," he was sure, "or like the spark in flint."[42]

The question as to how this revered inner spark might be reconciled with the hated, yet necessary day-to-day rules men must live by gradually approached resolution in Luther's last years. Indeed it was the major concern of his last days and hours. He came to look upon the problem of law as the theme of his life. But he admitted that he could understand his life, if at all, only in retrospect.

"Like a Horse
with Blinders On"

A dozen devoted Boswells hung upon every utterance by Doctor Luther, from about his fiftieth year forward recording his colorful pronouncements in an abundance and with a degree of fidelity never attained with any other man (nor should it be supposed that the magnetic tape recorder equals the Renaissance quill of a Veit Dietrich, a John Schlaginhauffen, or a George Rörer—to single out only a few names which occur elsewhere in these pages). This invaluable record has been abused over the centuries in at least two ways. The present chapter is the best place to acknowledge that my own use of the material is subject to the same errors.

I have, for example, tried to reproduce Luther's words in my own vernacular while making them as characteristic as I can. The first to attempt this was a Luther pupil, John Aurifaber, who was not above improving on his source. The *Table Talks* in Aurifaber's edition (1566) were for centuries among the best-loved books in the German household. They did not begin to become discredited as free adaptations until the nineteenth century, and by then they had found their place in the German mentality, as an indelible part of the national self-image.[1]

A more serious abuse of Luther's reminiscences also began with the colleagues who preserved them, but it did not assume damaging proportions until the self-assured researchers of the last century turned their analytic efforts upon the record. They ferreted coldly among the *Table Talks* for facts about the dra-

matic events which had transpired ten or fifteen years beforehand—or even to extrapolate speculations about the old man's
childhood. This academic peccadillo led quickly to major distor-
tions of Luther's personality. When a man in his fifties or sixties
muses about his past, he is telling us first of all about himself, of
course, about attitudes and concerns of the present. Secondarily,
he may be offering his interpretation of the past as he sees it—
but it is still likely to reveal more about his own personality now
than about those events, especially if they are but dimly recol-
lected. In any case, we would want to become well acquainted
with this old fellow before we began to apply his testimony to
reconstruct history.

I know I am vulnerable to both these errors. Aurifaber's
falsification of Luther occurred in a sincere effort to adapt his
beloved teacher's words to a later audience. All translation is precisely that: adaptation. The mistake, on the other hand, of using
Luther's own remarks out of context with his frame of reference
may be avoidable if I *and* my reader are willing to forgo our
own curiosity about the unknowable, not try to get at the
"facts," but merely accept his memories as he chose to relate
them.[2]

His recollections occur for the most part by way of illus-
trating particular arguments or situations in the 1530s and 1540s.
In almost every instance they are inseparable from the occasion
which prompted them. His major preoccupation was, as we
know, that great general council of the church (he regarded himself very much a part of that catholic church[3]). From the vantage of Wittenberg, one looked down on those corrupt con-
servatives in Rome, toward the ultra-rationalists of the
German-speaking southwest, and upon the great rabble of radical
sectarians who claimed (impudently) to be true followers of the
reformation. In alliance with these were—most horrible to relate
—some of Luther's own pupils, like John Agricola.

The older Luther's most frequent recorded allusions recalled
his own long experience as, not just a reprehensible monk, but a
very Saul, most rigorous of papists and persecutor of Christ.
Next in importance was his conflict with the Roman authorities
and how it had turned out to be, to his own chagrin, a conflict
with the papacy itself; how it had led to a slow development in

his own thinking and had at last put an end to his monastic period. He did not like to dwell on precise circumstances, not even on the intellectual paths he had followed—which in retrospect appeared pocked with errors—but wanted to impress his listeners with the great power of the subjective experience he had undergone. Ranking a distant third in quantity of biographical material are Luther's thoughts about his misspent youth, and what might have occasioned his entering the monastery in the first place. The notions entertained by the young man seemed to the older of little consequence, for God's purpose had been hidden from him. In short, Luther's "fifteen years under the papacy" dominate the older man's reflections on his past. Bearing that in mind, let us go ahead and review his career from his standpoint, although not in the order of importance to him, but—for our own convenience—chronologically.

We learn next to nothing from him about his childhood. On the rare occasions when he referred to it, he did not expect to be taken seriously. He might never have mentioned such things at all had he not had children of his own.

Luther treasured the experience of fatherhood, he named his first son Hans, after his own father, and dwelled on the importance of the father figure in a child's total world view.[4] He recalled how his father had once whipped him so hard,

> that I ran away from him and was afraid of him until he won me over again. I wouldn't like to spank my Hans very much, lest he get scared and hostile toward me. I cannot imagine anything worse than that. That's the way God does: "I will punish you, my children—but through another, through Satan and the world—and if you cry out and run to me, I will take you up and comfort you." For our Lord does not want us to be hostile to him.[5]

One might infer from this that Luther had been a sensitive child and had an affectionate father—or that he was an affectionate father sensitive to his children's feelings. In any case, he was acutely conscious of a father's importance. He frequently told how Paul's admonition to the Ephesians (6:21) impressed him: "Fathers, provoke not your children to wrath, lest they be discouraged." Luther thought this meant,

Whip them when they deserve it, but speak kindly to them at the same time, lest you make them fearsome, and they don't think you mean well with them. It is very bad when a son loves anything more than he does his father. The father needs somehow to show that he does not intend the utter destruction of his child. Law by itself is worthless—more than that, it is unbearable. Paul and Peter were experienced fellows. They must have had a wife and children.[6]

Hans was just six at the time of these musings, Magdalena nearly four, Martin going on two, and Paul at the breast. Their father recognized that in the eyes of these wee tots he was himself all they could know of God, so that his treatment of them was apt to determine their conception of deity, perhaps permanently. It was a subject much on his mind.

In the lectures on Genesis he explained to the students how God's discipline demonstrates paternal love. In the midst of his Latin delivery, he fell into German to assure them, "When you think our Lord God has rejected you, you must recognize that our Lord God has you in his arms and is hugging you."[7] Since the father is primary in the child's conception of God, he must be very circumspect.[8] "Extreme piety," for example, had in the past led to idolatry, as when good parents tried to impress their children with the omnipresence of God. A later generation adored the external, visible objects, forgot the original sense, "until now they are worshiping onions and shoats. Such is the forgetfulness of God in human flesh without the gospel."[9] It is the loose, colorful imagery of the post-Schmalkaldic Luther. In these same days, the spring of 1537, a troop of wandering gypsies came up for discussion at table, what incorrigible filchers they were. Luther was reminded of how children share that weakness, and he suggested they be disciplined for it, but in moderation—

When it is a matter of cherries or apples and the like, they are not to be punished severely, but when money, clothes, or valuables are involved, that is the time for correction. My parents disciplined me most harshly, to the point of breaking my spirit. My mother whipped me till the blood flowed for the sake of one little nut! It was such harsh discipline that finally drove me into the monastery! They meant well, but I became fainthearted.

He went ahead to stress that good judgment is required in dealing with little children after they start to school, too. "The apple must ever accompany the rod," he concluded with one of his favorite aphorisms, and added that was not the way it had been when he was in school.[10] It is doubtful that these remarks really tell us much about his own pre-school and early school days.

Although the classical dramatist Terence was sometimes regarded as wicked, Luther loved him. He once recalled the play *The Self-Tormentor*, how it begins with a lonely father regretting that he "in the common way of fathers, constantly reproached" his son for taking a mistress. Someone had asked Luther about that passage from Ephesians, "Provoke not your children," and he responded genially, "Haven't you read your Terence? 'The common way of fathers, constantly reproaching.'" He said Terence had intended that line as an adage, warning us against making our children too timid, and he thought of another Terence character who is too strict with his children. All punishment, he concluded as usual, must be judiciously balanced with reward. He admitted that Solomon advises, "Chasten thy son while there is hope." But even after giving up all hope he will ever learn, Luther added,

> You shouldn't beat him to death, but find something else for him. Some teachers are as cruel as hangmen. Why, I was once whipped fifteen times before lunch! I hadn't done anything wrong except that I failed to learn my declensions and conjugations.[11]

There is other evidence that the schools of Luther's day were harsh, balanced of course with indications of how conscientious the teachers were.[12]

If there was indeed some connection between his disciplining when a little child and his decision, at twenty-one, to become a monk, he never elaborated on it any further. There is little evidence that he was shy or timid—we know too little to comment.

The old man told us little. The early years he dismissed as "lost" because spent "under the papacy." His youth was a time of life he preferred not to remember: "For thirty-five years I was the son of Hagar. I sought salvation as a monk, through works."[13] He recoiled from his student days with distaste. Occasionally he would condemn the Erfurt university as he recalled it during his attendance, but we know little because he preferred not to think about it. Only from time to time did a telling phrase slip through, as in 1539, when he was explaining why he planned to excommunicate certain notorious sinners. He said otherwise he would have their transgressions on his head, and "I have sins enough of my own—my youth, which I lost, and then my monasticism."[14] At other times he might speak of a "misspent youth."[15]

Is it not common for men in their middle years, especially leaders who have acquired a strong sense of mission, to look back with disapproval on the self-centeredness of youth? The circumstances of Luther's development had been such as to intensify this normal maturation experience (something he had in common with Paul). "Under the papacy," the older man recalled, he had been able to think of nothing but his own salvation. "I kept on asking, 'When will you ever become good, and do the things you should in order to acquire a gracious God?'"[16] "I entered the monastery lest I be lost, and in order to have eternal life. I wanted to help myself by relying on my own wisdom. I relied on my own resources to help myself by donning the cowl."[17] Most men at sixty look back upon themselves in their twenties as brash youngsters; Luther attributed his own youthful arrogance to the papist error.

The best testimony we have to the young man's frame of mind at the time he entered the monastery may be what he said to his father in the dedication to *Concerning Monastic Vows* (1521), that pamphlet which contemporaries credited with "emptying the cloisters." These are admittedly words of the mature Luther, not set down until some fifteen years after his actual taking of the vows. He speaks of how his father, having planned a favorable marriage and profitable career for him, resisted the loss of his son to the monastery—

At length you gave up and yielded to God, but did not cease to worry about me. I remember as if it were yesterday, how gently you spoke to me, and how I claimed I was called by terrors from heaven, was not becoming a monk of my own free will, much less to gratify my belly, but surrounded by terror and in the agony of sudden death had vowed a forced and necessary vow. "Let us hope," you said, "it is not an illusion and apparition." That remark, as if it were God thundering through your mouth, penetrated my breast and remained there, but I closed my heart as best I could, to you and to your words.[18]

The great beauty of this passage arises from an irony of which its author is quite aware. God had been "thundering" to him both in the "gentle" voice of his tender father—and in his compulsion to enter monastic orders, an impious yet at the same time necessary stage in his mission.

Nearly twenty years later the old man couched that same irony in a sardonic and probably mildly obscene tale which a companion recorded as follows:

"Today is the anniversary of my entrance into the monastery at Erfurt"—and he began to tell the story of how he had vowed his vow. About two weeks earlier on his way through Stotternheim, not far from Erfurt, he had been so shaken by lightning that he had said in terror, "Help, Saint Anne, I promise to become a monk!"

"But God heard my vow in Hebrew," he went on, "where *anna* means *by grace* as opposed to *by law*."[19] The pun aside, Saint Anne was known as a sorceress who assured chastity by rendering babes and men impotent.[20] Since she was also the miners' patron saint, Luther (son of a miner) knew her powers well. Apparently his students did, too, because he characterized his years of monkish celibacy and doubt by quipping, "Saint Anne was my idol and Saint Thomas my disciple. Others ran to Saint James in the belief that works would achieve the object of their hopes."[21] (Thomas was the doubting disciple, the Epistle of James the book of the New Testament Luther most stoutly rejected on the grounds of its preachment of good works.) The

Stotternheim anecdote was not intended to relate any event, but to express the older Luther's hearty disapproval of monkery.[22]

It was the old man's favorite theme. "I did not become a monk to serve the devil, but in order to merit heaven by my poverty, chastity, and obedience: that is the same as raising up a golden calf and worshiping it."[23] What an excellent debater's position he assumed in this way—not a one of his opponents had ever been such a holy papist as he himself for fifteen years! "The more holy I became, the more uncertain I was. At this point I said: despair of all things, cast thyself upon Christ."[24]

Although he could rationalize those horrible monastery years as part of the divine plan, he still deplored them. His hostility toward the law and lawyers may be connected with his having scorned his father's guidance and forsaken that career. After he had finally (reluctantly) forsaken the monastery also, the devil could taunt him with self-doubt about having destroyed that serene life. Now the old man claimed he had experienced no good days during his many years as a faithful Augustinian. He spoke exclusively of bitter remorse at having wasted those years. He was accustomed to personifying all of papal history as "the pope," toward whom he expressed his animosity thus:

> He executed emperors like rogues and criminals—that may be barely tolerable. But that he consumed my sweet youth so miserably, and beyond that, so tortured and tormented my conscience that even today I find no peace—that is too much![25]

Whatever the deep-lying cause, Luther's conscious antipathy toward monasticism was quite sincere.

He abjectly feared its resurgence. On one of the many occasions when he was detailing the miseries of life in the convent he turned to a student and pleaded,

> Struggle with life and limb against reinstatement of the cloisters! It is hell. Let them bring back habits, fasting, and feast days—but let them not oppress the conscience! We will not support cloisters and celibacy! No one will believe today what misery was in the cloisters![26]

It was an emotional issue for him, which he was prompted to express in a multitude of ways. Monasticism transformed Christ from redeemer to cruel judge,[27] an enemy who had to be appeased.[28] The convent was a place of physical deprivation and emotional anguish.[29] The story of Luther's fasting, endless prayers, and self-castigation goes back, not to any remarks he made while in the cloister, but to his extensive recollections and bitter descriptions made many years later,[30] faithfully recorded by his disciples. The powerful emotionality of these depictions was now charged with that grand intellectual issue which the mature Luther saw as having dominated his entire life: the problem of the law.

Monasticism, like positive law, was a mere human device, yet it gave itself out as divine. When advising John Frederick against the clever machinations of his counselors, Luther cast about for a good example, but did not come up with some glaring political chicanery at all—he thought of monasticism.[31] He wanted John Frederick to appreciate the fact that "the law in the chancellor's books, or head, is not the only law, much less eternal law,"[32] but he knew no better illustration than the outrage of monasticism. He was willing to accept, provisionally, positive laws as a necessary evil, but not monasticism. It was both evil and unnecessary, he thought. Paul, in describing the "armor of God," uses the figure "feet shod with the . . . gospel." Luther remarked bitterly: "I became a shoemaker, cobbled my life into a pair of shoes, put them on, and thought, 'If I perform this or that work, then I am saved.' "[33] This, he said, was the supreme abomination. He concluded a long explanation with the lapidary utterance, "The justice of the law justifies no man. Prayer performed as a duty is naught."[34] His execration of monasticism as a self-seeking device was so fundamental to the older Luther's thinking that it manifested itself in all kinds of self-reproach. He accused himself of having been so arrogant as to deserve the terrible uncertainty, which he also dwelt on, and deplored his insincere, selfish show of scholarship.[35] He never tired of blaming himself for having "crucified Christ" during his fifteen years at the arcane magic of the mass.[36] But when he called himself a "murderer," he was referring to more than that sacrificial function. His inexorable logic had led him to the categorical conclusion that anyone who accepts and follows any human cause is by implication a murderer! He wrote quite coolly:

The servant of any tradition is an idolater or a liar. And all idolatry is murder. Because, even if one does not kill overtly, in one's heart one hates all earnest men who oppose one's religion, and one consents and welcomes their demise. This is what I would have done as a monk to any good people who opposed my stupid religion or tradition, however vain or idolatrous it was. For, as I was a wicked idolater, I would have been a cruel murderer if given the occasion. It cannot be any other way. Whoever thinks what he does is in the service of God has to be hostile to all who condemn that service.[37]

Luther's disillusionment with monasticism lent much of the force to his reprehension of good works. With his usual frankness, he said he would have thought it good to burn Jan Hus, would have carried the wood himself.[38] "I was the greatest of papists."[39]

His many boasts that he had himself been the very acme and epitome of monkishness were no doubt true.[40] Nonetheless, that claim was also closely related to exigencies of Luther's later life. God, he said, had no small purpose in causing him to become a monk, for it had enabled him to write against the papacy on the basis of firsthand experience—

Indeed, I was compelled against the will of my father to become a monk, and I worshiped the pope so reverently in my monkery that I can defy all papists there are, or ever have been. I took my vows and observed them most rigidly, not for the sake of my belly, but for salvation.

He had worn his religious habit until 1523, years after his colleagues had laid theirs aside, and he recalled giving it up at last with great sadness.[41]

The frequency and inner consistency of Luther's many outbursts against his time as a monk led his listeners to believe they must be learning a great deal about that period in his life. They tended to overlook one inconsistency: how had it been possible for that young man to remain in the convent so many years, to rise so rapidly in the Augustinian ranks, at last to district vicar, doctor, professor in the Bible, all the while burdened with doubt and self-loathing? As we try to resolve this problem we recognize that the picture painted by the older Luther of his monastic

experience, like that much meagerer and more offhand sketch of
his childhood, is quite inseparable from the circumstances and
purposes of the older man himself. The picture reveals more
about the painter than of the subject—or, rather, the painter *is*
the subject. If we look upon it as a self-portrait we can better
appreciate the occasional light of faith which does shine through
the dark ignorance of the cloister years. A pious brother reminds
him of God's command that man have hope.[42] His confessor tells
him, "God is not angry with you, but you with God."[43] Doctor
Staupitz, his prior and second father, is a personality we shall
never fully recover, so thoroughly have his ministrations become
merged with Luther's own comforting of his young protégés in
the 1530s against devil and despair. Or was it these young men
themselves who combined the two characters as they took and
assembled their notes? On one occasion we hear of the monk
Martin crying out John Schlaginhauffen's very words, "Oh my
sin, sin, sin!" and Staupitz telling him dryly he is going to have
to accumulate some genuine vices if Christ is to pay him any
heed: "You cannot make do with such flummery and fake sins,
calling every fart a sin."[44]

While the somber shades of the monastery in Luther's painting
may be largely impressionistic, the rays of sunlight he lets fall
through the leaves of the pear tree in the court of the Black
Cloister reveal a genuine scene, so terrifically important to him
that he preserved it quite accurately. Over the monk's objections
that it would kill him, Staupitz persuaded him to take a doctorate
and become a teacher, "for God needs some good theologians in
heaven, too."[45] The old Luther was at pains to make clear that
just as he had not entered the cloister of his own will, the doctorate in no way represented *his* decision. There was a higher ordering of things which he could not presume to comprehend.
This contention was supremely important when it came to the
doctorate; it constituted his vocation, his legitimation for teaching *what* he had, just *as* he had. Here we are not dependent on
memories of the older man—although he, too, made the point
often enough. We can also refer to frequent utterances from the
early years of conflict with the authorities.[46] Of course, it was
the mature Luther who hit upon the most succinct formulation:

I, Doctor Martinus, was called and compelled to become a doctor, against my wish, out of pure obedience. I had to accept the office of doctor and swear fealty to my most beloved Holy Scripture, to teach it faithfully and pure. The papacy got in the way of my teaching, and experienced the fate which all can see.[47]

His own consciousness of calling enabled him to say flatly to the sectarians that they should show their "command and calling to preach, or be silent." As an example to them of "command or calling," he went on to point out,

I would not take all the world for my doctorate. I would truly have given up in despair, such grand and weighty issues burden me, if I had undertaken them as an interloper without calling and command.[48]

He was quite sincere in urging his students to beware of following their own initiative at all. They should rather fold their hands in secret prayer and thrust any office entrusted to them back upon the Lord, just as he himself had done, "as the German proverb puts it, 'Cast the keys before his feet.'"[49]

By no means had his original conflict with the Roman curia come about through his volition, or even understanding:

I freely confess that I did not intentionally undertake this arduous affair—I was such a papist that I wrote against Erasmus for chiding the papacy. But God called me into this cause over a period of time and by successive occasions. I would have carried wood to burn such a heretic as I, who had attacked the mass and celibacy . . . the papists wrote remarkable things against me, and I had to defend myself. It all happened by a divine plan.[50]

As doctor and professor he had persisted in poring over the papist writings. Gabriel Biel had seemed to him to be the best of the scholiasts—

When I read him, my heart bled. The authority of the Bible was nothing compared with Gabriel. I still have the books that so tormented me . . . Well, God led us wondrously out of all that and, for twenty years now, has held my head above water without my understanding how.

Oh, how haltingly it began at first. It was in the year seventeen, after All Saints' Day, we were on an outing to Kemberg when I first proposed writing against the horrid errors of indulgence sales. Doctor Jerome Schurff objected: "You want to write against the pope? What are you thinking about? It will not be tolerated!" I said, "What if they had to tolerate it?" It was not long before Sylvester [Prierias] entered the lists, Master of the Sacred Palace, hurling at me the syllogism: "Whosoever doubts the words and deeds of the Roman Church is a heretic. Luther doubts the words and deeds of the Roman Church. Therefore"—and so on. That's where it began.[51]

As the mature Luther looked back upon his career, all fell into a quite clear pattern which had not at all been obvious to the participants. God had regularly led him into the most arduous trials in defiance both of his father's good counsel and his own better judgment, toward a distant purpose which he could not begin to comprehend.

This happened against my wishes and against the urgings of my friends not to offend the pope, upon whose merest whim my life depended. But when I was provoked I went ahead like a horse with blinders on. Tetzel [that Dominican charged with promoting indulgence sales] was just too brash with the indulgences, crying out brazenly: "Think of your mother, tormented by the flames of purgatory, suffering because of you, who might release her with one penny. Ah, woe unto you with your ingratitude! For such a small price to scorn the grace of God's blood shed for thee!" . . . He carried on with such insolence that none dared oppose him, so I was provoked into my [ninety-five] theses, of which the gist was: it is better to give to the poor than to buy indulgences. He was soon foaming at the mouth, and he preached in Berlin, "I'll have the heretic in the fire within three weeks! I'll send him to heaven in his underwear!"[52]

Luther could not, in retrospect, sufficiently stress his own incomprehension at the time, his ignorance of the course all was to take. He assumed God had not wanted him to understand, and he loved his metaphor, "He simply put blinders on me, the way they do a racehorse."[53]

Lutheran theologians have been moved to discover exactly when and even where the young man "discovered" his gospel of justification by faith. Where did the "breakthrough" occur? This is probably not the kind of fact one could draw from the old man's recollections. As a consequence, much effort has been expended during the present century on Luther's very early lectures to discover his theology when a monk. By and large, therefore, modern theologians give less credit to Luther's adversaries than he himself did. As early as 1525 he was writing to Duke George—defiantly, perhaps, but nonetheless sincerely—that vigorous opposition was the best thing that could happen to him. "I am not able sufficiently to stress how useful persecution has been to me up until now, so that I must in good conscience thank my enemies."[54] This then became another major theme among his recollections. His doctrine, so it seemed to him, had evolved gradually, in the heat of debate and through the research it prompted.

God, he imagined, had operated pretty much in the same way a professor at a medieval university did, using debate to establish the truth in the minds of participants. Hence Luther accepted all his adversaries as heaven-sent, gradually to lead him out of error. "Reading the Bible," this greatest devotee of the written word admitted, "never would have led me to that perception, if the issue raised by my adversaries had not instructed me."[55] Should he have been pressed to reveal the exact *locus* of his "discovery," he probably would have said it was the debater's platform.

At first he had not perceived, he said, "all the abominations of the pope, just his crass abuses."[56] And even these did not interfere with his accustomed reverence, so he recalled, during the first three years (1517–20) while he toiled quite alone against the indulgence sales.[57] His first glimpse of how the "crass abuses" might go straight to the heart of the papacy came, he said, amid the zest of the early fray—

> When Sylvester wrote against me under the title Master of the Sacred Palace, I thought, "'Sblood! Will it come to that? All

the way to the pope?" But our Lord God did me the favor of letting the sophomore write such stupid things that I had to laugh. I haven't been frightened since that time.[58]

So obviously God was at work. It was he allowing the papacy to destroy itself. "It was the opposition caused it all. If they had been moderate, gad, fa, re, mi, what might they not have accomplished?"[59] He had but acted the part of a docile monk, while his opponents drew their defeat from their own attacks upon him. Of the greatest debater on the Dominican side, Doctor John Eck, Luther said, "He evoked my first thoughts, at which I had else never arrived. So our adversaries are very helpful to us when they are trying to damage us."[60]

Luther's own early ignorance had been, so he thought in retrospect, an important part of God's plan. "I thought I was going to please the pope, but he condemned me. If I had been able to see as far in this affair as it soon led, then I would have kept my mouth shut."[61] So the Lord had simply put blinders on him and led him through the fire. To what, in the end? Whither was God leading his dumb horse, that would be worth all the anguish? Luther quite sincerely denied any knowledge of God's intent in worldly affairs (to these he attached little significance) and liked to observe diffidently that things usually ended up quite differently from what he had supposed they would.

Among the most skillfully (because frequently) narrated and most conscientiously recorded motifs from Luther's early adventures was that of the lone and uncomprehending monk on his perilous journey to face hostile worldly powers. First came the anxious trek to Augsburg in 1518, "in mortal fear, because I was alone."[62]

In Rome they had already burned me as a heretic [he would observe ruefully]. Good God, how can the Lord have put a wretched monk up against such powers? At that time I didn't own a penny. I had to borrow a cowl from Doctor Linck to walk to Augsburg in. The last three miles [=German miles, perhaps a day's journey], I climbed on the coach of a nobleman. I was in anguish the entire three miles, for the devil assailed me with many a worrisome thought. In Augsburg

Staupitz provided me with a horse from some prior, so I could ride out again with a companion, unarmed, unshod, unhosed, just in my cowl and a linen tunic—clad but in *pilleus* and *pallium*, I fled from Augsburg to Coburg.[63]

He explained what had caused him to depart in such a panic. On his way to Augsburg, he had been turning over in his mind how to defend his teachings before his father in the church, Cardinal Cajetan. But to the poor monk's dismay, the cardinal was willing to hear "only the six letters REVOCO"—*I recant*. Unable to speak that word, the naive professor had insisted on discussion, thus clearly arousing the powerful churchman. In fear that he was about to be dragged off to Rome in chains, he fled the city.

But where was he to turn, "bereft of all human protection, of emperor, pope, cardinal legate, my prince, Frederick duke of Saxony, my order, my closest friend, Staupitz . . . There was no hope in Germany. Papal threats also made France an unsafe refuge."[64] He let that "hard-trotting nag" from Augsburg jolt him on back to Wittenberg, where at one point Frederick actually commanded him to leave Saxon lands. Dramatic indeed was Luther's account of the farewell supper. "In this very meal a letter came from Spalatin [at that time confessor to Frederick] indicating how the prince was wondering why I had not yet gone." His extremity could not have been greater, but "not long afterward, during the same meal, another letter arrived in which Spalatin said if I had not left yet, I should remain."[65]

Fightings and fears within, but resolute without, this unswerving pilgrim no longer appears as "a horse with blinders on," for he is fully alert to the threats on every side. We visualize him as a figure quite in the frame of that most celebrated German work of art created in those years, Albrecht Dürer's *Knight, Death and the Devil*. Dürer allows no question to arise that his calm, armored hero, gaze fixed confidently ahead, is acutely aware of grim death lurking at the wayside, and of that hideous devil striving to distract him. Luther wrote,

I came to Augsburg to face my worst enemy, without safe-conduct. I stood at Worms before emperor and all the empire, although I knew beforehand that my safe-conduct had been rescinded, and that wanton, unprecedented malice and intrigue were being planned against me. As weak and helpless as I was at that time, my heart was such that, had I known as many devils were taking aim at me as tiles were on the rooftops in Worms, still I'd have ridden in. I was shunted from one corner to the next, to face first one and then another, as they chose. My poor, weak spirit stood as free as a wildflower, attuned to no melody or beat, to no time, place, or person. I gave ready answer to each and all, as Peter teaches us (1 Pet. 3:15).[66]

He marveled "with what wondrous stratagems and tricks they would have hindered my coming to Worms, so I might fail to appear before the emperor, and they could then vilify me for fleeing the light of day. First they rescinded my safe-conduct and burned my books, posted my condemnation on all the doors in Germany."[67] Even friends joined in the attempt to divert him in his passage across the land, Bucer being enlisted to persuade the traveler to turn aside and confer with the emperor's confessor at the renowned castle of Franz von Sickingen. But they could not distract him from his goal.

Even after he had almost reached Worms, his friend Spalatin sent out a warning to him to proceed no farther. It was in a note back to Spalatin that Luther first used the phrase so often to be quoted later—

But I responded, "If there were as many devils in Worms as tiles on the rooftops, still I'd come in." For I was undaunted. I was not afraid. God can make a man that foolhardy—I don't know if I'd be so foolhardy today.

I drove into Worms on an open wagon, in my monk's cowl. Everyone came out onto the streets to see the monk Martin Luther. [Albert of] Mainz didn't think I would come, and if I were so distinguished as he by cowardice, I wouldn't have.[68]

Of all the tales they loved to hear told and retold, this was the one Luther's pupils held most central to all else they had learned. Among the men who heard it were John Mathesius, Luther's first protestant biographer, John Aurifaber, the collector and first publisher of the *Table Talks*, and many another who passed it on to posterity. For historians and biographers in later centuries, it shone forth as their most stunning scene—they knew none to compare with it in modern history: a lone, committed monk defiant before the assembled might of the most comprehensive world empire since Caesar.

According to Luther, the emperor's advisers nearly came to blows with one another over whether the safe-conduct should be honored or Luther, like Jan Hus, disposed of. But on the morning after his arrival (17 April 1521), he stood there before the emperor and the imperial estates.

> Doctor Eck, the chancellor of the bishop of Trier [he recalled], spoke on behalf of the empire, saying, "Martin, dost thou confess these books to be thine?" My books lay on a window seat all together. I had no idea where they might have got them. I was about to say yes, but Doctor Jerome Schurff called out, "Let the titles of the books be read," and they read the books—they were all mine.
>
> Then I said, "Most gracious emperor and gracious princes and lords, it is a matter weighty and serious, which must not be answered rashly. I beg time, therefore, to consider it." This was granted, and the meeting adjourned.

He remembered how, in the interval, he had been approached by many who were anxious about his safety, and who wanted to assure him of armed support. Also the placards posted by the insurgent peasants' league, the Bundschuh, portended violence.

> When I was called back before the diet, there was a great multitude of men with their aides, all wanting to hear my answer. Many torches burned above me, for night had fallen. I was unaccustomed to such crowds and bustle, but when I was commanded to speak I raised my voice and said: "Most gracious emperor, gracious electors, princes, and lords, the books which have been laid before me, they are mine."

He divided them into three categories: exegetical writings which contained no wickedness; polemical pieces, whose harshness he declared himself willing to mitigate; lastly, disputations on scripture—"I'll stand by them, God send what he may."

> While I was speaking, they demanded I repeat it all in Latin, but I was perspiring heavily and was very warm, crowded

thus in the midst of the princes. Lord Frederick von Thun said to me, if I could not do so, then "that would be all right, Herr Doctor." But I repeated my every word in Latin, wherewith my prince elector, Duke Frederick, was well pleased.

When I was finished, they let me go, assigning two men to lead and acompany me. That occasioned an uproar among the nobility, who demanded to know if I were being constrained. But I said, "They are only conducting me." So I came back to my lodgings and did not appear again before the diet.

The curtain had rung down on the high, the public drama. Now the real trials began, behind the scenes, where true heroism was required.

Luther's narrative depicted the grand lords, George of Saxony, Joachim of Brandenburg, how they and their learned advisers persisted in the plea that Luther be sensible and place his cause at the discretion of the emperor. "But I said I would gladly suffer the emperor's power, though I could not depart from scripture. When they continued to press me, I said that this was the long and the short of it: before I would place my cause at the emperor's discretion, I would renounce his safe-conduct." Not long after that, the archbishop of Trier summoned Luther to a private meeting, where he congratulated him.

"My dear Herr Doctor, my doctors tell me that you are now content to abide by whatever the emperor decides in the matter." When Luther tried to disabuse the archbishop, this great lord claimed he could not believe his learned advisers would willfully have deceived him.

The rapt listeners at Luther's table loved to hear the individual incidents retold, to envisage those grand personages who figured in the drama, and to think what had become of them since. "That's the way it all began," their teacher would remind them, "without my intention. It is not my fault, but theirs. They wanted to drive through with their heads, and thought they could not go wrong. And the devil has defended it well, that papal regime—continues to uphold it. But Christ did poke a hole in it."[69] Just as all these things had transpired without his will or understanding, the present teller of the tale professed to remain ignorant still, though perhaps not in the same ways as before.

His confidence, for example, in the law of the heart had been strengthened since his days in the monastery; the contempt for human reason which had brought him there, his scorn for rules and regulations had all been reinforced along the way. For as an instrument in God's hand he had to admit he enjoyed certain incidental recognitions. One of these was that man alive must use his life to rise above the law. This meant that the law could not simply be cast aside, as John Agricola and his followers wished. They had forfeited the whole sense of Christ's coming, which was to fulfill the law. Of course the laws were not to be suffered as man's masters, as papists, Jews, and lawyers would have us believe. Doctor Luther's mission, as he came to see it before he died, had been as an instrument of reform, whereby the original Christian sublimation of law was to be recovered, for his time.

"No Sweeter Thing Than Love of Woman— May a Man Be So Fortunate"

Martin Luther stands above an age known for its misogyny as an almost courtly figure in his homage to woman. When putting glosses to his first complete Bible edition, he came to the famous encomium on the virtuous woman at the end of the Book of Proverbs (31:10 ff.) and set beside it those words I quoted above in the chapter title. They had been spoken to him by his landlady in Eisenach, when he had been a schoolboy there nearly forty years earlier. His retaining them for so long bespeaks an important side of the man's character.[1]

His treatise *On Monastic Vows* (1520), rejecting monasticism as just another misguided effort to please God with human notions, had justified many in leaving their convents, and marrying. But Luther himself continued his life as a monk for another five years. Most of the sincere reform pastors had been preaching in street clothes for some time, his old friends (Justus Jonas, John Bugenhagen) were married. There was some pressure on Luther himself to practice what he preached, and take a wife, but the suggestion struck his deeply conservative nature as an adventurous one. His position was precarious enough, he felt. Events on every hand showed how the reform was easily imperiled if carried too far. There was no question in his mind, however, that monasticism required reform.

In April of 1523, he had issued a slender pamphlet, *Basis and Rationale for Permitting Young Women to Leave the Convent.* It was dedicated to one Leonhard Koppe, who had earlier in the same month led a little party to help twelve nuns slip away from a cloister near Grimma. Luther wrote that he was proclaiming the deed for honest reasons. "In the first place," he set down impishly, "I did not instigate it for the purpose of keeping it secret."[2] Furthermore, he was interested in the reputations of those involved. They shoud be taken as courageous examples for others to emulate. Therefore he concluded with a list of the young women, one of whom was Catherine von Bora.[3]

The pamphlet's central argument was that, while monastic life itself was at best vain, to place young women into convents against their will was a serious offense. He was not categorically against nunneries. He thought they might fulfill a useful teaching function.[4] When he heard of one that had been converted into a school, he approved, and hoped the girls, "thrust into convents" because their aristocratic families had been able to make no suitable match for them, would be permitted to marry.[5] He wrote that one of his major considerations in supporting Koppe had been

> that it is impossible for the gift of chastity to be as widespread as the convents are. A woman is not made to remain a virgin, but to bear children. In Genesis God was not speaking to Adam alone when he commanded, "Be fruitful and multiply," but to Eve as well—as the physical structure of the female body, so disposed by God, proves.[6]

Koppe had brought his wagonload of girls to the Black Cloister, at that time a great empty dormitory used as a kind of halfway house for the refugees from religious orders. Luther and his associates gradually obtained good husbands or livings for all save one, Kate of Bora. She came from an impoverished background ("of the nobility" meant little more than "landowning"—or, in her case, "having landowning ancestry"), but she was on that very account perhaps more assertive of her aristocratic status.

Luther made a match for her with a promising young Nuremberg burgher, but it fell through. When another, less acceptable
groom was in the offing, Kate approached Luther's dear friend
Nicholas von Amsdorf, a bachelor and of the nobility, begging
him to intercede. She said she would marry only Amsdorf himself, or Doctor Luther.[7]

Scarcely would she have been so bold had she not sensed that
there was some possibility here. Luther, in his early forties, had
become an outspoken advocate of the married condition, occasionally publishing his private advice on the subject. One such
open letter read, in part:

> Let him who would live alone cast aside the name "man" and
> prove that he is an angelic spirit—or let him become such. For
> God does not give it to man, or in any way permit him to live
> alone. So we quite correctly sing of holy virgins that they did
> not live a human life, but an angelic one, living in the flesh
> without the flesh, by the sublime grace of God. Our body is
> largely the flesh of woman, wherein it was conceived, grew,
> was born, suckled, and nourished, so that it is downright im-
> possible to separate ourselves from it and renounce it . . .
> That is why even those who are impotent toward women are
> filled with the natural inclination. Indeed, the more impotent
> they are, the more they desire the company of women.[8]

In these same months, he and his old fellow Augustinian George
Spalatin were coyly urging one another to marry. In one such
letter in the Hudibrastic self-consciousness to which Renaissance
Latin so lent itself, Luther refers to himself as a "famous lover,"
successful now in marrying a house full of nuns. He accuses
Spalatin of being a "lethargic lover" by comparison, and tells
him to "watch out lest I, the least disposed to matrimony,
precede you eager suitors (God being accustomed to perform
the unexpected)."[9]

Kate's biographer, a pious Lutheran, says she profited much
more than he from their marriage.[10] On more than one occasion,
it is true, he stated he had felt no erotic inclination toward her,[11]
and we certainly cannot attribute the denials to any false modesty in a man who proposed to his newly wed brother Spalatin

that on an appointed night they make love to their wives, and think of one another.[12] Eroticism aside, among the many testimonies of his love for Kate, the most eloquent was surely Luther's attempt to express how much Paul's Epistle to the Galatians meant to him: "It is my Kate of Bora."[13] When he called her "the morning star of Wittenberg" he probably had a twinkle in his eye,[14] and his compliments were, of course, seldom without irony, e.g.,

I would not swap my Kate for France with Venice thrown in. Now in the first place, God gave her to me and me to her. In the second place, I often notice that there are more faults in other women than in my Kate—although she has some all right, she has much greater virtues to balance them. In the third place, she is faithful to me.[15]

He might tease her, but he recognized in her his principal support in this world during the difficult epoch which had already begun at the time of their wedding (13 June 1525). Furthermore, his marriage with her was the single greatest new influence on his life and thinking after the monastery.

The central thought of Luther's mature life was that God reveals himself to us through our experiences in this world. His marriage was invaluable to him as firsthand acquaintance with the very node of creation. He never tired of observing that the weakness of the scholastics went back to their celibacy, or that the apostles must have been married men, else their judgment could not have been so sound. The experience of awakening to find two pigtails on his pillow was indispensable to the theologian; the excitement of fatherhood was the supreme earthly joy. The two together caused him to bubble over with deprecations of the papacy, both of whose pillars, the sacrificial mass and celibacy, he, Samson, was now jubilantly pulling down.[16]

The former nun was an enthusiastic manager of her enormous new household. As they walked through their garden one fall day, she boasted of her pond and its stock of table fish. "Kate," Luther chuckled, "you take greater pleasure in these few fish than many a nobleman with several big ponds and hundreds of fish." He went on to sermonize the "amenity" of God's creative urge.

Behold how delightfully the little fishes spawn, one producing thousands. The male spurts his sperm into the water from his tail, and that's the way the female conceives. Just think about the fowl, how very chastely their reproduction is accomplished! The cock pecks the head of the hen, she lays her little eggs in the nest, sets upon them till the little beasties pip. Then behold the chick! How in the world can anything like that be in an egg? If we had never seen an egg, and one were brought out of Calcutta, we would all be shocked to death. All the philosophers cannot explain such creatures. It is only Moses who offers any sense: "And God said . . . And there was." "God commanded, 'Be fruitful and multiply.'" And so it continues.[17]

He was voluble on the miracle of childbirth, "most difficult, for the fetus is forced to exit through the pelvis where an apple would not appear to get through. It is a great and immense miracle of God."[18] He looked on with satisfaction while Kate, pregnant with Paul, nursed the second son, Martin. "It is difficult to feed two guests," he said gravely, "one in the house and the other at the door."[19] Among the Lutheran pastors, all so recently in religious orders, women's breasts became the subject of wise deliberations, the quality of mother's milk, the advisability of wet nurses. Luther for his part gave preference to firm-bosomed women as able to nourish children best. Large breasts, he said, "promise much and deliver little."[20]

"The sweetest pledge of matrimony, the best wool from the sheep," were the children.[21] Hans, Paul, and Martin all grew up to be respected men; only the youngest daughter, Margaret, reached womanhood. The first daughter died in infancy, and Luther had yet to experience the death of his second, Magdalene. He felt powerful attachment to them all and, wanting an adequate word in German, turned to the Greek *storge* to express the feelings that often overwhelmed him. This emotional parental bond *storge* was connected in his mind with death, for he had felt it most strongly in Schmalkalden, when he had thought he would not see them again.[22] Also when smitten by the innocence and perfect faith of the little ones, he might exclaim, "How happy are those who die at this age! It would be the greatest grief for me, because a part of my own body would die, and a part of their mother's viscera. *Storge* is unceasing in honest people."[23]

Luther was nearly forty-three at the birth of his eldest, and fifty-two when Margaret was born. While he took great delight in the infants, he was growing cranky by the time they were old enough to remember him. A stern father, on one occasion he denied Hans his presence for three days. His were not the only children at the Black Cloister, relatives from both sides of the family lodging with them for shorter and longer intervals, so that he found himself the court of last appeal in a sometimes rowdy household. And it was a glass house, held up as a model by admirers, as an abomination by Romanists, and closely observed by all. Luther became a severe and self-conscious disciplinarian.

Touchingly determined to experience all aspects of family affairs, he was supremely inept at household finance. In the early days he resolved to learn a trade, but that came to nothing. He was a devoted gardener, and did not think himself above even petty tasks. Kate once came upon him patiently cutting out leather to patch a pair of old breeches. His material was, to her horror, a new pair belonging to one of the boys. "A grand patcher," he explained splendidly, "needs a lot of patching material. I seldom get a pair of breeches, so I have to take good care of them."[24] One of the important benefits of matrimony for the single-minded churchman was Kate's competent management of the Black Cloister, both his own base of operations and a model for the Lutheran household in centuries to come. We must not pity him there, having to patch his own breeches or eke out a living at a woodturner's lathe, toiling over his accounts until they trail off into remorseful doggerel. Far from it. These were all aspects of life which he longed to experience, however awkwardly. When he first married, he did have some qualms about how he would feed his family, but thanks to his prince and to Kate he was as free as a monk of all care about money. "I am rich," he admitted. "My God has given me a nun and three little children besides [it was before Paul and Margaret were born]. I don't worry about what I owe, because when Kate pays that, there will be something else [to pay]."[25]

Her indebtedness was a part of her vigorous management. In Luther's will of 1542, he estimated his debts at 450 fl. (one might multiply gulden by 10^2 to get a rough equivalent to dollars in 1980). In readily convertible valuables, such as gold and silver goblets, he could have raised that amount twice over, and Kate had acquired real estate worth easily ten times as much. The Renaissance did not have a cash economy, of course, but that will not explain the doctor's eagerness to give away whatever was on hand. He was childishly profligate, and Kate correspondingly stern. Here is a typical request which he sent to her while away from home when an assistant was about to move on to another post.

> I know there is not much on hand, but I would like to give him 10 fl. if I had them. But you mustn't give him less than 5 fl., because we are not giving him a new suit of clothes. Whatever you can give beyond that, do so. I am asking you to. It may be that the community chest would give one of my servants something in my honor, since I do have to maintain my servants at my expense for their church services—but as they wish. Do you not be remiss so long as one goblet is around. See where you can get it. God will repay us. I am sure of that.[26]

He believed Luke's admonition (6:38), "Give and it shall be given unto you," quite literally: "That is a reliable saying, which makes all the world rich or poor . . . It maintains my house." Kate might not have agreed with him there, and Chancellor Brück quipped that if Luther had the income of a nobleman, several thousand a year, it would not support his openhandedness. But Luther was firm in his opinion that what he gave had God's blessing and would be returned. "Dear Kate, if we are out of money the goblets will just have to go. You have to give if you ever want to have anything."[27]

She thought you have to receive, and was sometimes impatient with him about his unconcern.[28] His friends can scarcely be blamed for resenting her firm hand. In a culture where wives were presumed subject to their masters, here was their great good doctor meekly yielding to a virago who pursued financial interests with more than masculine prowess. They suspected her of being the power behind the throne in other matters as well, and Luther freely admitted he was but an Aaron to her Moses.[29] He gladly cast himself into the role of henpecked husband (a matter most painful for his German biographers), regularly referred to Kate as *dominus meus* or, punning on her name, *mea catena* ("my chain"). An indignant Cordatus could not remain silent as Luther explained to Nicholas Hausmann how he sincerely looked upon all his possessions as truly belonging to the poor. Kate's recent purchase of a nearby piece of land, he vowed, had really occurred against his will.

"Well, why did you let her do it, if it was not your will?" Cordatus wanted to know.

"I can hold my own neither against her requests nor against her tears," Luther lamented.[30]

He liked to depict his wife as a self-willed woman. He had suspected her from the outset of being proud, he said, "and she is."[31] Ah, if he had to go a-courting again, he would just hew himself a compliant spouse out of stone, "else I have given up on obedient women."[32] He claimed she was domineering, talkative, and scatterbrained, but his very banter revealed his respect for her.[33] Rare is the serious remark, such as the close of a letter to Justus Jonas where, in lieu of greetings from Kate, he tells how she is traveling around, overseeing her farms, buying cattle and grazing them, brewing beer, etc. while trying to read the Bible between tasks. He said he had promised her 50 fl. if she read it through before Easter.[34] We cannot help wondering where he thought he was going to get fifty gulden.

When Robert Barnes was in Wittenberg for the last time before Henry VIII martyred him, too, he was still having difficulty with the German language. Luther told him Kate would be a good teacher. "She is most voluble. Her fluency exceeds mine by far." He went on to make it plain that such eloquence was not seemly in a woman and that his preference was "murmuring and stammering."[35] Such remarks, made so clearly with an eye rolled in her direction, establish Kate's comprehension of Latin. One day she broke into a learned discussion with a bit of wisdom she had picked up from a schoolbook, and Luther shifted wickedly from Latin into Greek. "Ye gods," she cried out in mock dismay, "who would say a thing like that?"[36]

But her good nature had its limits, as when Luther predicted gravely that he could see the day coming when men would take more than one wife. She said that was something the devil could believe.

"Now the reason, Kate," Luther informed her, "is that a woman can bear but one child in a year, but"—he shifted into Latin—"her husband knows how to beget several."

She not only gave him his Latin back, but did so with a Bible text. "Paul says, 'Let every man have his own wife.'"

"'His own,' but not just one—that's not in Paul."

The debate continued, Kate failing to see any humor in it and finally declaring that before she would put up with anything of the sort she would go back to her convent, "and leave you with all the children."[87]

As was usually the case when Doctor Martinus joked, there was a serious core. He and his colleagues had been considering bigamy as the best alternative in that quandary posed by Henry VIII in his desire for an heir—it was one of the rare issues on which Luther and the pope had come to the same conclusion. To appreciate his views on matrimony, we must place them in the context of the other institutions whereby man's life in his world was normalized. Matrimony was much more central there than it is in our society.

He saw the entirety of human life on earth as comprised within three realms under God. In his terminology, they were the ecclesiastical, the political, and the economic. Each extended from roots in the family, hierarchically upward to God. We have seen how it was in this sense only that he introduced the idea of separation of church and state, each independently serving one divine will. He did not reject a church hierarchy, but only tried to purify it of any political or economic interests. The political governance of the world was exemplified in the family's obedience to their father, the subjects' obedience to their prince, and mankind's obedience to God. Similarly, the nourishment of the world began in the household (*oeconomia* in Latin, *Wirtschaft* in German), which drew on the *Landwirtschaft*, "agriculture," and was ultimately assured by God's miraculous provision —Luther frequently observed that the miracle of the loaves and fishes was being repeated daily, for much more was consumed on earth than could possibly be produced.[38] These three hierarchies, the ecclesiastical, political, and economic, constituted the symmetrical and permanent arrangement of worldly affairs in Luther's quite medieval conception.

Just as governance began with the father of the household and was exemplified in his rule, the economy was woman's God-given realm. His own household confirmed that doctrine. "I freely concede the total dominion of the household [*dominium oeconomiae*] to her,"[39] he declared, much to the discomfort of his German biographers, who invariably stress his next sentence, that he will not be dictated to in his own sphere. He was giving voice to the ideal separation of the two hierarchies that begin in the home: all economics rests ultimately on the woman of the house, just as all temporal authority begins with the father. The two were of course under God, but Luther saw both temporal realms as essentially independent of the church. "No one can deny that matrimony is an external issue, pertaining to the world and its magistracy, like food and clothing, home and hearth . . . I find no instance in the New Testament where Christ or his apostles concerned themselves with it except where it affected the conscience."[40]

This view permitted that relativism which Luther was using to rile Kate. While he did uphold the pure doctrine of the church as changeless, political and economic institutions obviously varied with time and place. He explained polygamy and other Old Testament marriage customs in terms of ancient Hebrew society and its needs.[41] He also appreciated polygamy as a solution to royal problems of succession, such as those experienced by Henry VIII, who had given up hope of an heir by his first wife, Catherine. To pretend the marriage invalid, as Henry wished, seemed to Luther pure humbug and cruel besides, both to Catherine and to her daughter, Mary. As to divorce, the Bible was quite unambiguous in prohibiting that. On more than one occasion, therefore, he recommended the ample biblical precedent for taking a second wife, without putting away the first.[42]

The marital bond was divinely instituted, it was true, but Luther held that in our imperfect world all absolute rules had to suffer exceptions. He recommended the Aristotelian concept of epikeia, or the use of discretionary judgment to achieve equitable

accommodation to varying circumstance. His concept of matrimony as an essentially economic arrangement (for the peasantry
and the middle class) or a dynastic concern (for the nobility)
was distinctly medieval. In the Middle Ages, however, a substantial number of marriageable youth had entered monastic life. Luther's own strident writings had abridged this alternative to matrimony, so he and his clergy now had to grapple with the
consequences. They felt themselves plagued with marital problems. Was a spouse permitted to deny marital rights? Luther
didn't think so.[43] Should troth plighted in secret be honored (this
was a frequent resort among students when parental consent was
withheld)? He advised pastors to shun these thorny thickets
whenever possible.

When a woman recently widowed came to him for help in
finding a replacement, he snapped, "Write that down, Schlaginhauffen, write that down!" Let posterity know and consider
what demands were made of him. "Matrimony is outside church
business," he opined, "being a governmental concern, hence up
to the magistracy." He went ahead to lament that "these cases
are without number, extremely high, wide, and deep. A lot of
them cause embarrassment and tend toward the dishonor of our
gospel."[44] This remark, made in the summer of 1539, soon
proved prophetic.

Kate's influence on her husband is probably most obvious in
his unusually high opinion of womankind, which contrasts
strongly with the misogyny so widespread especially in the medieval and Renaissance church. A painting of Kate by Lucas
Cranach (although not a very flattering portrait) evoked an enthusiastic outburst from her husband. He said he thought he
would just have a spouse painted beside her and send the picture
off to the Italian delegation asking "if they don't really prefer
matrimony." Then he began to extol the married condition, that

> divine institution whence all else flows and without which the
> whole world would remain desolate . . . Without Eve and her
> breasts no other institution would have come to be. That is
> why Adam, inspired by the Holy Ghost, called his wife Eve—
> that is: "Mother." He didn't say "Woman," but "Mother,"
> and added, "of every living thing." This is the ornament of

woman, that she is the fount of all living humanity. Adam's words were few, but neither Demosthenes nor Cicero ever composed such a speech. The eloquence of the Holy Ghost was worthy of our first parent. Let us heed Adam, for if he found such a name and such praise for woman, we can well shield whatever frailties she may have.[45]

To his way of thinking, there was no better evidence of God's hostility to the papacy than that he had denied it "the fruit of the womb. We would not have captured that blessing of the womb had not God implanted the desire in us, which produces children." Science from Aristotle to modern times held that the father supplied the formative germ, and that the woman was merely his nutritive vessel—not so Luther: "I say, pregnancy is not being a pipe, as through which water flows . . . but flesh and blood of the mother."[46]

He was a stout defender of womankind in a world where slighting remarks were in vogue.[47] Women did not escape his all-encompassing humor, of course, but one who seeks misogynist jokes from him finds none which does not poke fun at men as well. For example, he was inclined to make light of long-winded preachers by comparing them with girls chattering on their way to market. John Bugenhagen was notoriously longiloquent, and Luther once reported how a housewife had apologized for an underdone Sunday dinner—"Oh, I thought Pomeranus was preaching today."[48] Luther shared the medieval Christian's perception of women as temptresses. "We are conquered by fragile —ah, the indignity of it—girls."[49] He rued how David "tripped over a pair of pigtails," and opined that there never was nor would be a ruler "undeceived by pretty girls."[50] In such a vein he called attention to Cyprian's warning that we must flee the voice of woman as we flee the hissing of a snake, and he added with relish, "So it goes. Out of the fear of a whore they slide into the sin of sodomy."[51] He admitted before his students that since the time of Eve all great downfalls had been occasioned by women, "But this should not redound to the contumely of the sex. We have the Commandment, 'Honor thy father and thy mother,' and 'Husbands, love your wives.'" Eve had been the one to pluck the apple, to be sure, but only after she *and* Adam had fallen away from faith. "The guilt therefore lies not in the sex, but in a fault common to man and woman alike."[52]

Luther grew particularly scornful of the shabby treatment women received before the law. The Saxon legal code did not grant a wife clear right of inheritance. A man who wished to leave his wife an income was obliged to appoint guardians for her, a provision particularly galling, for Luther knew Kate would survive him. He gave his own opinion of the only reasonable way to interpret the absurd Saxon provision:

> After the death of her husband, a matron is to receive "a chair and a distaff." Many a woman has worked for thirty or forty years in her home—and is that all she is to receive according to the letter of the law? Why, any delivery boy is better rewarded, even a strange beggar at the door gets that much! This word "chair" is to be interpreted as "home, house, and hearth." The distaff means nourishment and what it takes to earn it at her age. This is the proper meaning of that law, yet here and elsewhere there are those who go according to the strict letter of the law and thrust the poor women out like dogs.[53]

It was a fine example, he thought, of how extreme justice wreaks the supreme injustice.

In 1542 Luther set up a will without benefit of legal counsel and in plain language, defying the law by leaving everything to Kate—no guardians. It states outright that he does not want her to depend on the children but prefers that they look to her, "for I hold that mothers are the best guardians of their own children."[54] It recognizes that there will be those who try to make things difficult for Kate, but he begs support from his friends.

Perhaps the greatest debt Luther as thinker owed to Kate was his open, happy espousal of play. He seriously recommended sexual fantasies as a good way to overcome depression, and mentioned the joys Kate afforded him as being among his defenses against the devil—even if they did not always work.[55] We must use our own fantasy to fill in this part of the Luther household, but Luther's wisdom in these matters points to a most sound and lovable side of Kate's personality. The dour further development of protestantism makes Luther's attitude the more noteworthy—

Dear lad, be not ashamed that you desire a girl; nor you my
maid, the boy. Just let it lead you into matrimony and not into
promiscuity, and it is no more cause for shame than eating and
drinking . . . God never let many virgins live very long, but
took them out of this world . . . He knows very well how
difficult it is to keep that noble treasure.[56]

Luther was confident God takes delight in the sex act,[57] and he
denied that the circumstances of original sin affected the essential
goodness of creation: "That sin might just as well have attached
to any other human activity."[58] He jeered at the papists' fixation:
"Those inept asses write about no other temptation than libid-
inous ones."[59] Jerome was one of his favorite examples of a
church father whom celibacy had caused to magnify temptations
of the flesh. "Ah, it is a petty matter! A little wife could have
mitigated this evil."[60] Luther often, sometimes vehemently,
rebuffed the pastoral advice given in his day that children were
the sole purpose of making love.[61]

Perhaps some of his enthusiasm about sensual experience may
be attributed to the late stage in his life (he was forty-two)
when Kate instructed him. He seems to have maintained a mature perspective from the outset, appreciating the many ways in
which woman uplifts the spirit of man, "for she is a born
minister unto others."[62] As our own culture has had to learn,
suppression of desires does not occur without some hypocrisy, a
trait quite alien to Luther's personality. He admitted from the
pulpit, shortly before his sixty-second birthday, that he was still
being plagued by the old Adam,[63] and privately confessed he had
not lacked "the right good will" to adultery.[64] Why should he
not be open? He could with equal candor boast of how marriage,
family, and public morality were upheld in protestant lands, yet
depraved where sexuality was denied.[65] He was justly proud of
the saner perspective he had attained. As he could urge young
people not to be ashamed of their passions, he could also warn
them how passions cool with alarming rapidity, so that a satisfactory match requires "a situation in which propriety and passion converge—sex just isn't enough."[66]

The numerous occasions on which he gave marital counsel
range from telling the abbot of Fulda, who wished to regularize

his relations without jeopardizing his position, that a secret wedding would be preferable to knavery[67]; to conciliation of parents whose son had taken secret marriage vows with a Wittenberg girl. Here is a typical bit of advice in one such case:

> You did not slip into her window by night for the purpose of praying with her. Now it may be that you did her no harm, but you harmed her reputation, so that now her wreath is withered. If you do not marry her, you will suffer from bad conscience and many torments. Beware, my dear fellow, of bad conscience. You know not what a worm it is. It will gnaw you even if you marry some other very honest girl.[68]

Had Luther not felt that the young man's conscience would forever trouble him, he would have been much less insistent that vows, in this case consummated, also be formalized. On other occasions, where a couple had been intimate without the intention of marriage, he saw no reason for forcing them to marry, or for betraying their secret. "If it has happened, then let it be. The conscience must be protected."[69] Luther was little influenced by traditional morality and would uphold propriety only insofar as it seemed desirable to set a good example. So far as he was concerned, the conscience was all that really mattered.

Correct as this view might have been strictly within the purview of pastoral counsel, it led to politically disastrous consequences in the notorious case of the bigamy committed by Philip, landgrave of Hesse, in 1540. He was the most powerful and energetic of the protestant princes. By taking a second wife he committed a capital offense under imperial law, thus placing himself entirely at the emperor's mercy. He was therefore motivated to enter into a treaty with Charles in 1541 which was quite debilitating to the Protestant League of Schmalkalden. The event marked the end of protestant ascendancy in Europe, as was probably clear to Luther before he died. Considering Philip's power and impetuosity, it may be that nothing could have been done. Luther could not blame himself with any positive action to encourage the outrageous breach of propriety, but he could reproach himself with having encouraged Philip's non-conformism at an earlier stage, and with failure to *prevent* the scandal.

He had not been able to withhold a kind of admiration for this "warrior, a true Arminius, small in person yet puissant in counsel and fortune."[70] At five years of age, Philip had lost his father and succeeded to the rule of Hesse, remaining under the regency of his mother only until he was fourteen. Before turning twenty he had waged war against the redoubtable Franz von Sickingen and defeated him. When the three most powerful princes in Germany, George of Saxony, Albert of Mainz, and Joachim of Brandenburg held that the peasants' uprisings had been sparked by the Lutheran heresy, so formed an alliance to put it down, Philip had been the one promptly to organize a counterforce. By 1531 he had brought the powerful League of Schmalkalden into existence. For ten years, until that unhappy treaty of 1541, the League was able to shield protestant advances by skillful alliances with France and England against the emperor. Philip was a rash, warlike fellow who took pleasure in magnifying his influence far beyond the real power of his little land. He was clever enough to perceive a certain non-conformist potential in Luther's reform as early as 1521, when he inquired of Luther at their very first meeting (at Worms) what his teaching would be with regard to bigamy.[71] Such a defiant and ambitious wight quickly perceived the political implications of protestantism.

He was married to the daughter of that implacable enemy of Luther's, Duke George. Although he got several children by her, he complained bitterly he had never been able to stomach the poor woman. She was ugly and smelled bad, he told everyone, and said he had resorted to prostitutes since the early days of marriage. Nay worse, he claimed to have committed sodomy (by which he may have meant most any kind of sexual activity which he thought was prohibited). In a day when princes were assumed to have as many mistresses as they pleased, his problem may have struck some as exaggerated, but perhaps his close association with the protestant leaders Zwingli and Bucer had made him more conscientious than they knew. However that may be, he had taken it into his head to marry another wife. Recognizing it would be no small scandal, he sought the support of his allies in advance, using protestantism (according to previous practice) as a diplomatic instrument. He persuaded Martin Bucer to act as go-between with Melanchthon and Luther, the idea being that

the learned men would write something on the subject of bigamy, if possible also preach in his favor. It was an era when politics were inseparable from the sovereigns' private lives, and policy justified by religious doctrine. No more impious than other
Renaissance princes, Philip was well aware of his strategic value
to the theologians. He let it be known he did not think the pope
would say him nay.

His confession of horrible sexual excesses did then elicit a letter signed by nine protestant divines (including Luther,
Melanchthon, and Bucer) which, while it stopped short of sanc-
tioning bigamy and was clearly intended as a pastoral letter of
comfort for a troubled conscience, did also include the following
paragraphs:

> Since the beginning of the world it has been proper for a man
> to have only one wife. This is an admirable law, accepted in
> the church, and no other law should be instituted against it
> . . . The precedent, however, in which dispensation has been
> used for those held captive in a foreign land, who took a wife
> there and, freeing themselves, brought her home with them; or
> for those who have on account of long-standing illness—as has
> sometimes happened in cases of leprosy—taken another wife
> on advice of their pastor, not thus establishing a law, but
> relieving a unique need: such a precedent we would not con-
> demn. Since it is one thing to establish a law, and another
> thing to use a dispensation, we most humbly beg your grace to
> remember:
>
> First of all, that every precaution should be taken to prevent
> this matter from becoming public, as a law which others
> would have the right to follow . . .

Now came a long list of reasons for Philip to desist from his
bigamous purpose, but at last the letter continued,

> Should your grace finally decide to take another wife in mar-
> riage, then we caution you to keep it secret . . . from all but
> your grace himself, the intended, and those few who know the
> heart and conscience of your grace through confession.
>
> Then there will be no great gossip or scandal, for it is not
> unusual for princes to keep concubines, and although the pub-

lic need not know what the arrangements are, thoughtful people would reflect, and prefer such a quiet solution over adultery and other wanton, licentious carryings-on.[72]

Luther had permitted himself to believe Philip merely wished to regularize an existing relationship. He probably imagined something like that between Frederick the Wise, whom he much revered, and a commoner whom Frederick had wedded secretly and with whom he had sired two sons. She was not permitted at court, and when she visited him she was slipped in by night in a coach lined with felt curtains.[73] In Philip's case too, Luther thought, the vows were being taken for the sake of conscience, and the bizarre ceremony would surely give this noble prince but more cause to be discreet.

Far from it. Philip had suffered no unrequited sexual desires. He was driven by some powerful psychological need to perform the extraordinary. Discretion appealed neither to him nor to his proposed bride, who was no simple commoner at all, but—as Luther discovered to his horror—a member of the high nobility! He said he guessed Philip had gone crazy, like his father.[74] The wedding took place in March of 1540, Melanchthon and Bucer among the witnesses. By June it was the talk of Germany. Friends urged Luther to dissociate himself by publishing a tract against bigamy and citing the urgent causes Philip had alleged in order to obtain his "dispensation." That, of course, was impossible, for the landgrave's confession was privileged communication. "It is better for people to say Doctor Martinus made a fool of himself when he gave in to the landgrave," he said. "Greater men than I have made fools of themselves, and continue to do so. They say a wise man commits no small folly."[75]

Although he admitted to John Frederick that no angel could have persuaded him to permit the marriage had he known all the facts,[76] he made a show of taking the matter, once accomplished, lightly. Others were outraged—and still are: a thousand times more apologies have been made by Lutheran writers for this slip than for all Luther's horrible attacks on Jewry. John Frederick called a conference in Eisenach to try to decide what could be done, especially when Hesse had to face the emperor. This was the occasion when Doctor Luther gave his notorious advice, "What would be the harm, if it would help and were in the interest of the Christian church, of telling a good, strong lie?" Why indeed, one might ask, if bigamy is no sin in God's eyes, would a lie be necessary, anyhow? Luther gave a characteristic answer to this: "The proposition that whatever is right before God ought to be confessed publicly, is not acceptable. It is not a universal proposition. There are a lot of things right before God which have to be suppressed before the world."[77]

Melanchthon took the whole thing very much to heart. Such was his natural disposition, but he was also closer to Bucer, who had instigated it all—and he had actually functioned with Bucer as witness, giving the union his blessing, so to speak. On his way into south Germany in June, the frail fellow came down with what was probably a severe influenza making its rounds with fevers and chills, but he wrote to Luther that his physical condition was declining "because every day I hear something worse about the Macedonian."[78] He had dubbed the warlike landgrave after Alexander the Great.

Luther worried. "I am a tough Saxon, a peasant," he growled. "I've grown a thick skin for this kind of ***"—he spoke a word too strong even for his admiring listeners to record—"I feel as if I am being called to Philip."[79] He wrote to his friend reminding him of the wild tales the landgrave had told them, and assuring Melanchthon he could be charged with no wrongdoing, only "mercy and humane helpfulness."[80] Toward the end of the month, he heeded the call he had felt, and traveled posthaste to Weimar in the company of Jonas and one of Melanchthon's sons.

They walked in to find their old colleague just at death's doorstep. He lay insensate, able neither to speak nor to hear. Of course he recognized none of them. This slight man, who appeared emaciated even in the best of health, must have been a frightening sight after having gone for some time without food or drink. Luther was shocked. He turned to Justus Jonas and used a Greek word, as was Melanchthon's habit: *organon*, which means "instrumentality for the acquisition of knowledge." He said, "God forbid, how has the devil violated this *organon* of mine!" Thereupon he turned his back on those in the room and strode to a window, that he might be the more clearly audible to God. He prayed long and fervently.

Luther prayed in German, for "the mother tongue is more effective."[81] He prayed frequently, routinely, every night falling to sleep in prayer. He believed prayer to be "an almighty great thing . . . an intolerable outcry in the ears of God. He has to hear it."[82] As we know, he had been guilty of abusing his tremendous power of prayer, not being above praying an enemy dead, for example.[83] At times he had felt the potency of his prayers flagging,[84] but when he set about earnestly to pray from the bottom of his heart he could move heaven. Whoever chanced to be nearby was transfixed. Veit Dietrich once overheard him while the two were at the Coburg, and he attempted to describe the effect on a listener. He said Luther spoke with respect, yet in the tone of confidence we use with a close friend. Dietrich could scarcely believe the imperiousness with which Luther laid God's own best interests before the heavenly throne. "My heart was inflamed to hear him speak so intimately, so earnestly, so respectfully . . . sure that all would come to pass as he asked."[85] Luther was indeed supremely confident in prayers, frequently responding to others' troubles by shaking his head and saying, "They don't pray enough." Prayer alone, he thought, had saved the church thus far, what there was of it—

> That's why Christ told us to "ask . . . seek . . . knock" [he once explained in an extempore exegesis of Matthew 7:7]. First we are to *ask*. When we begin to ask, he slinks off somewhere and doesn't want to listen, or to be found. So you have to *seek* him out—that is: keep on praying. Now when you seek him, he shuts himself up in a closet. If you want to get in, you have to *knock*. When the knocking becomes excessive he'll open up and say, "Well, what do you want?" Lord, I want this, or I want that. "Well, go ahead and have it!" . . . The verse, "Ask and ye shall receive," means nothing else than, "Ask, call out, yell, seek, knock, thunder!" You have to keep on and on at it, without respite.[86]

That is precisely what the old doctor was doing just now. He laid the entire predicament before the Lord, telling him in no uncertain terms that this was his concern just as much as it was Luther's. He "rubbed his ears" with all the Bible's promises that prayers will be heard, and reminded God that there was no avoiding hearing this one, either, if all those promises were to be believed at all. The exhortation took time, and when it was over the listeners in the room were hot with Luther's faith. Even the insensible patient stirred.

Luther crossed over to him and took him by the hand, speaking at first very gently. "Be of good cheer, Philippe, you'll not die. God may well have cause to kill us, but he desireth not the death of the sinner, but that he turn from his way and live. God takes his pleasure in life, not in death."

He reminded him of the sinners in the Bible whom God had kept alive, and insisted that it was not God's will for Melanchthon to pass away in his sinful and despondent condition. Therefore he conjured him to resist the "spirit of dreams," who would like to make him his own murderer, and "to trust instead in the Lord, who can both kill and revive."

Observers were sure that they saw Philip's life timidly returning, that they beheld him breathe again. He seemed to be trying to speak, but could not. At last he was able to focus his gaze on Luther, and he succeeded in asking to be left alone. He did not wish to be detained any longer, he said. He was on his way, and Luther should but let him go. Nothing, he was sure, could be better for him.

"By no means!" Luther answered. "Philippe, you must yet serve the Lord."

The patient, weak and unable to disengage himself from this insistent colleague, continued to become more aware of his surroundings. Luther demanded that food be prepared. He brought soup to the bedside and constrained Philip to eat, answering protests with a threat of excommunication (which the haggard man took seriously—and it was perhaps intended so). He did not swallow much food, but the crisis had been overcome.[87]

A few days later, Luther was able to write a letter home. It began:

My dearly beloved Kate, Madam Doctor Luther, Mistress of the New Sow Market [where she had recently purchased a plot of land],

Grace and peace, dear Maiden Kate, Gracious Lady of Züls-dorf [her recently repurchased family estate], and whatever other titles may apply,

· I must submissively bring to the attention of your grace that I am doing well here. I am gorging like a Bohemian and swilling like a German, thanks be to God, Amen. The reason is that Master Philip was truly dead, and has arisen from death just like Lazarus.[88]

He was exceptionally well pleased with this demonstration of the power of prayer, often referring to it in later years.[89] Philip, too, recalled it as one of the major experiences in his life, "when I saw written upon the wall that verse, 'I shall not die, but live and declare the works of the Lord.'"

Shall We Receive Good at the Hand of God and Shall We Not Receive Evil?

Despite waning health and waxing moodiness Martin Luther remained Germany's most prolific author throughout the 1530s, and even in the era of bluff and bluster, her most outspoken one. He preached his sermons and kept up university duties. So as to keep busy and to die in the work of the Lord, he had begun the lectures on Genesis which were to continue through the last ten years of his life.

The problem of keeping Old Testament chronology straight consumed many an hour. A manuscript of eighty pages with double columns survives, where ink of different colors and all kinds of devices to facilitate reference, as well as many corrections, show his attempt to keep present in mind the overlapping lives of patriarchs, judges, kings, and prophets, the rise and fall of kingdoms.

Noah lived many a year with Methuselah, and died when Abraham was fifty-eight [he reckoned]. No doubt they comforted one another, preserving their church despite sects and heresy. Our world has not been long in existence. Six generations achieving Adam's longevity would reach down to us. That is for God an even shorter time, "for a thousand years in thy sight are but as yesterday." I divide the world into six ages: the Ages of Adam, Noah, Abraham, David, Christ, and the Pope. Each of the [first] five, counting its posterity, attained to about a thousand years. The Age of the Pope began at about five thousand years after creation, that is, at about the time when Hildebrand forbade matrimony with women [Luther seldom let the chance pass for an obscene dig at "Italian nuptials"]. I don't think the Age of the Pope will finish its thousand years.[1]

The conception he outlined here was in line with the medieval assumption that the world was to last six thousand years in all, four thousand until the coming of Christ and two thousand afterward. Since the three days from the crucifixion to Easter had not been fully completed, however, Luther and others drew the analogy that God would not permit the last wretched throes before judgment day to run full course, either. According to Matthew 24:22, "those days shall be shortened," so Luther devoutly expected this last epoch to be brief.

His pupils found the *Calculation of the Years of the World* immensely useful, and had it published. It appeared in two editions and was widely circulated. A century later, Bishop James Ussher probably drew upon Luther for his own computation, which then found its way into many English Bibles. His format for the *Annals of the Old and New Testaments* (1650–54) is reminiscent of Luther's but he might have taken the scheme from any of several medieval sources. Luther himself found help in work by Philip Melanchthon and John Carion, the court astronomer of Joachim of Brandenburg. With Wolf and Catherine Hornung, Carion found his way into modern novels on account of a sensational event.

On 17 July 1525, so Carion predicted, the ominous relationship of the heavenly bodies to Aquarius would make watery disaster all but certain. Joachim wisely retreated with his family to the heights of Tempelhof, there to overview the inundation of low-lying Berlin. The heavens were stormy, as predicted, but the pious Elizabeth was opposed to her husband's undignified withdrawal. She urged him to return to his city and face its perils along with his subjects. As the coach drove into his courtyard late that afternoon, the team was struck by lightning and killed, together with the coachman. The incident was dramatic, but the attitudes it illuminated were in no way unusual.

Halley's comet returned in 1531, in Luther's view a sure sign of evil.[2] On 19 October 1533, the learned pastor Caspar Stieler assembled his congregation to meet doomsday precisely at 8 A.M. He was joined by hundreds, for although some might quibble with his precise calculations, it was general knowledge that the end was at hand. Luther dreamed of judgment day, knowing that "the present age compared with the past is scarcely a hand's breadth, just one last apple hanging in the tree."[3]

He rejected the superstitious predictions of Carion and Stieler, denying that events can be read in the stars—our servants, he insisted, not our masters—but he noted with gratification the many signs of approaching cataclysm. These were not merely meteorological (although even old people remembered no such extremes in weather[4]). The advance of the Turks, especially the terrible imperial defeat of 1537, was a distinct omen. Both the spread of the gospel and the spread of iniquity in the world could be interpreted according to the Book of Revelation as auguring the end. The Old Testament spoke of these matters, too, and not merely in the apocalyptic Book of Daniel. In Isaiah, for example, the Lord vows to break down the wall of his vineyard, "and it shall be eaten up . . . and trodden down."

> O Lord God [Luther responded to that verse], all too eaten up, all too trodden down, all too desolate and forsaken are we wretched men in these last days of wrath. Our shepherds are wolves, our police but fleece us, our guardians despise us, our kinsmen murder us, and our teachers seduce us. When, when will thy harsh wrath abate?[5]

In a letter to a friend he quoted Psalm 71. "'Cast me not off in the time of old age; forsake me not when my strength faileth.' I think these latter days are the old age of Christ," he commented, "and the decline of his strength, the extreme peak of the devil's attack."[6] Again, he admitted this was just a pretense on Christ's part, but "we are the last and weakest troop."[7] When lecturing on the wickedness of the world in Noah's day, he begged his students to bear in mind that Noah had lived "in the youth of the world, and the best part of it, when everywhere the best minds were flourishing, informed by the experience of great longevity. What is to become of us in the delirium, as it were, of a senescent world?"[8] He marveled at the powers which mankind must have enjoyed in pristine creation, and was convinced of our increasing degeneracy with each subsequent age of the world. The older and weaker he himself became, the more acutely he could perceive the decline of all about him. He fervently longed for the end—

> O dear Lord, come ahead! I await the day. It will be a morning, near the beginning of spring. (Ah, these are but my daydreams. Dare I mention them in a sermon? No.) All will be most beautiful. Then, suddenly, out of the sunrise a heavy, dark cloud, two or three lightning flashes, then a crash of thunder, and all heaven and earth will be destroyed.[9]

Until that glorious dawn, there was nothing for it but to scold the world for its increasing depravity. Every estate of the German nation came in for its share. Luther was perhaps justifiably harsher with the arrogant nobility than with the middle class, whose greatest failing was damnable greed, but he reserved his strongest contumely for the peasants. They had caused him such anguish by their rebellion in 1525, and they provided the mass membership for what he called the fanatical sects. Despite his famous claim that he was himself of peasant stock, he had grown up as a middle-class youth and spent his entire life within city walls. He looked out on the countryside as a pastoral Eden, which he regarded with typical city-dwellers' envy. "If the peasants only appreciated their condition," he grumbled, "they would be in paradise where they are."[10] He instantly attributed any shortage of food in town to a conspiracy between the two landed estates, nobility and peasantry, to drive up prices. They lived off the fat of the land, he thought, unappreciative of their blessings; he was himself "more grateful for a tree and a bush than they for all their lands and forests."

"Herr Doctor," Philip broke in at last, "you do except certain farmers—Adam, Noah, Abraham, Isaac?"

"They were not just peasants and farmers, but theologians as well, for scripture says, 'Isaac went out to meditate in the field.' That means, to behold God's gifts and creations there."[11]

Here was a prejudice mitigated by his ability to joke about it. He did not regard the peasants or the nobility as a true source of evil. The real wickedness of the world seemed concentrated in three global intrigues: the lawyers, the Jews, and the papacy. Each plotted in its own way to save itself by laws and hateful ceremony. None would admit their rules to be but despicable human invention, long since superseded by Christ. These worshipers of the law he held ultimately responsible also for the defection of his own into antinomianism.

During the same years when he was defending Old Testament law against Agricola and other "false brethren," Luther fell out with his faithful friend Jerome Schurff, the lawyer who had stood beside him before Cajetan at Augsburg and before the emperor at Worms—and one of the few lawyers who was probably in fundamental agreement with him on the administration of law. Schurff did insist, however, on teaching canon law at the university, and he even appealed to it in certain cases, as when defending the right of young people to marry without parental consent. This appears to have been the issue which brought Luther to preach a powerful sermon against lawyers in 1539, but the immediate occasion may have been no more than the usual rivalry between the colleges of law and theology. Some law professor or student had referred to theology as "sophomoric," or even "schoolboyish," and that was no joking matter for Luther.[12] He preached a sermon urging the students never to become good lawyers, for that was the same as bad Christians. His vehemence on this Sunday can be understood only as giving vent not merely to the moment's irritations, but to frustrations of a lifetime.

As a boy he had purchased his law books and even begun his formal study of law when, for reasons at which we can only guess, he threw it over and entered the monastery instead. He often spoke of his regret at having become a monk, and it probably helped if he reminded himself that the alternative at the time had been a "sordid and acquisitive" legal career, "whose ultimate end is money, not appreciation or knowledge."[13] That disagreement with the Roman Church which then occupied so much of his life rested upon a dichotomy which he made formulaic:

grace *v.* law. In an early lecture the young professor had made the following aside:

> Well that is why, if you will permit me a personal remark, it nauseates me to hear that word "justice" . . . which the lawyers always mouth. There is not a tribe in the world more unlearned on this subject than lawyers and the do-gooders or intellectuals. In my own life I have experienced, as have many others, that when we are "just," God is laughing at our "justice" . . . Man's only comprehensive justice is: humility.[14]

Shortly after that lecture he become embroiled in practical affairs. His work as church organizer and political adviser brought law and the legal profession into an ever more prominent place in his writings. He insisted that law is a study inferior to theology, and he was by no means above luring promising law students over into his own field. He never tired of baiting the "skinners, not of dead dogs, but of living humans," the "dirty mercenary shysters, unconcerned about agreement." "A lawyer," he chuckled at table, "wants a steel head, a silver purse, and an ass made out of lead."[15]

The scores of aspersions like these in Luther's works constitute for some a painful aspect of the great man's writings and sayings. One scholar argued that as a one-sided genius Luther simply lacked juridical understanding for "formalism, with which the jurist cannot dispense because, in the juridical view, he must not."[16] It is certainly true that Luther scorned codified rules. But he did have an imposing command of Mosaic law, canon law, Germanic common law, and the Saxon legal code, including an impressive technical vocabulary. He wrote on various legal and political issues, like civil disobedience, the legality of interest, etc. He frequently gave legal advice (solicited as well as unsolicited). A survey of cases in which he intervened or on which he was consulted offers a pretty fair introduction to Renaissance legal practice. On the eve of his death, having been drawn by some inner urge to the town of his birth to settle a dispute there, he again found himself across the bargaining table from lawyers. During these last few days he expounded a higher conception of the law, one at which he had been working since his youth. We shall consider it when we come to the end.

The excoriation of lawyers from his pulpit in 1539 constituted a crisis in Luther's lifelong preoccupation with the law. The language he used taxed even the loose standards of the Renaissance. But yet more striking than the coarseness was his strange pugnacity—

I'll tell you where your rolls of damask and satin, where your silver talers come from! And if you want to fight, I challenge you to do battle with me! Do you think I don't know what lawyers are capable of? I'll tell you, all right. If you're game, I'm not afraid of any lawyer, praise be to God, however clever and learned he may be. Put on your horns! If you're game, I'll put on mine and I'll gore you till it cracks your back. If you don't believe me, just try me. I'd be a poor doctor of theology if I feared a lawyer, or had anything to learn from one. I know better than you ever will what canon law is: donkey farts! If you want me to, I'll give you some to eat.[17]

These words from the pulpit typify that especially strident epoch in Luther's life which had begun with the Schmalkalden illness. It is true that the sixteenth century permitted more abusive language than the twentieth, and that pastors felt it their duty to scold—Luther encouraged it explicitly—but the use of such foul expressions by the preacher in church was nonetheless embarrassing. We have had ample evidence of the vigor of Luther's language and pen. Before Schmalkalden it had been, at worst, cruelly cutting, but often winged with humor. Now it had become gross and excessive. As a younger man he had regularly withdrawn from polemic exchanges, not deigning to reply to mere abusiveness. The terrible writings of his later period cling to a strife obsessively.

In twentieth-century eyes, the most shameful of such products are the outpourings against the Jews of 1543, three lengthy tracts in one year—Luther's sixtieth. He had never attained a balanced view of European Jewry even in his best, optimistic time. While freely praising the patriarchs as greater than any moderns (save perhaps Augustine[18]), he made a strict distinction between that great people Moses had led out of Egypt and "Caesar's Jews," who of their own free will cried out to Pilate, "We have no king but Caesar."[19] The pioneering Hebrew scholarship of the great humanist John Reuchlin (Melanchthon's uncle, who had sent him to Wittenberg) had nurtured a more benevolent attitude among some scholars toward their Jewish contemporaries. This was not the case with the devout young Luther. While welcoming and using Reuchlin's work, he still despaired of ever converting the "hardened" Jews.[20] It is true that he became more sanguine about proselytizing in the early 1520s, hoping his reforms might appeal to individual Jews, but by his fifties he had recovered his medieval pessimism on the subject.[21] Tolerance for unregenerate Jewry never occurred to him. If Luther could hear Christ calling out clearly in the songs he attributed to King David, if he recognized the patriarchs and prophets as leaders in his church, surely their own descendants could perceive these manifest truths! According to his holistic reading of the Bible, one Spirit had produced both Old and New Testaments through the agency of the Jews. How could a reprobate offspring so perversely deny its own glorious heritage?[22]

This medieval view was still almost universally accepted during Luther's lifetime, so that his haughty rebuff of the great leader and defender of European Jewry, the distinguished Alsatian Josel of Rosheim, was in no way unusual. John Frederick had issued a harsh edict in 1536, expelling Jews from all his territories, and Josel was undertaking one of his numerous (remarkably successful) trips in behalf of his persecuted co-religionists. He asked Luther to use his good offices to help him obtain an audience. At first Luther ignored Josel's letters, then at last sent a reproachful reply, refusing to receive a visit.[23] About this time he conceived a polemic against the Jews. Perhaps the word "polemic" is too mild, because what Luther had in mind was not an argumentative treatise directed against an adversary. He planned an appeal to Christians against Jews, and that is something quite different. Irrationality bordering on paranoia seems more apparent here than in the unfortunate quarrel with Agricola.

Like the harassment of his friend, Luther's first anti-Semitic tract was inspired by gossip. Rumor had it that in Moravia they were "circumcising many Christians and calling them by a new name, 'Sabbatarians.' "[24] If the fabric contained a shred of truth, it may have been the Old Testament fundamentalism of certain sects. Surely Luther knew harried and downtrodden European

Jewry was in no condition to "compel" Christians to do anything, but in his present frame of mind such knowledge may have lain beneath the surface of consciousness. His vehemence may even have arisen from some monstrous vision that these supposed "Jews" were in reality but another protestant sect, for which the ultimate responsibility would go back to him. Certainly some such explanation is eventually needed for the incredible violence and sly wickedness to which his writings against the Jews ascended. It is not enough simply to recognize that his mind was not as good as it had been, or that his illness subjected him to periods of great irritability. His response on hearing of circumcised Christians had never been that of a skeptical Arcesilas, but a rhetorical, "That's the way it goes in regions which expel evangelical preachers. They must put up with the Jews!"[25] After Schmalkalden such slogans yielded to wild fantasy: "They'll never force us to do that. I don't think I'll ever be so silly as to submit to circumcision—Kate and other women would sooner have to cut off their left breast."[26]

When that pamphlet *Against the Sabbatarians* evoked a rabbinical defense, Luther resolved to take up his pen again. "I hear some of our rulers are favoring them. I am going to advise that they drive them from their presence, and expel them."[27] Someone at table dared to mention the large numbers of Jews in Frankfurt, saying there they were not regarded as harmful at all. "They get money from them in Frankfurt," Luther explained. "How wise that may be is their problem. The Jews dishonor their own flesh and blood when they dishonor Christ. They hate us because we believe in him who is born of them."[28]

This exchange occurred in the winter of 1542. Early the next year the first sheets of his tract *Against the Jews and Their Lies* came off the press while he was still at work on the manuscript. It is the most vicious work from Luther's hand. Just as he had not hesitated to use vile language from the pulpit against lawyers, the medium of print here broadcasts the most revolting trash. In recent years Luther had permitted himself an increasing coarseness in oral utterance. Now there remained little difference between his private remarks and his authorized publications. On the heels of the first anti-Semitic blast came *The Shem-Hamphoras*, exposing the cabbala, and *David's Last Words*, demonstrating that the Christian doctrine of the Trinity is grounded in the Old Testament. All three works shared one central, anti-Semitic purpose, although the last two did not equal the first in sheer intensity of invective, baseness of language, or shamefulness of recommendations.

Luther dragged up all the ancient superstitions about Jews, dignifying them with his sanction. They poison wells, steal Christian children, whom they torture to obtain their blood.[29] And then they call themselves prisoners among the gentiles! "Indeed, we have taken and hold them prisoner just as I have 'imprisoned' my stone, high blood pressure and all my other sickness and misery which I'd so gladly send to Jerusalem together with the Jews."[30] He had specific measures to recommend. In the first place, burn their synagogues. If Moses lived, he'd be the first to torch them. In the second place, tear down their houses, lest they teach at home. Also, take their books, forbid their rabbis to teach, deny them access to public highways. He sternly enjoined Germany's rulers to heed him: "You shall not and cannot protect them unless you wish to partake of their abominations before God." Let the princes just consider the consequences of that.[31] With his royal audience in mind, he made one last, cunning suggestion—

> that their usury be forbid them and all their gold and silver specie and treasure be seized and set aside. This being the cause: whatever they have is, as stated above, stolen and robbed from us by usury, for they have no other living.[32]

Later on in the rambling work, he repeated the same advice, assuring the princes that their greatest rigor was kindest mercy. If these measures did not effect conversion of the Jews,

> then we must drive them out like mad dogs, lest we partake in their abominable blasphemy and vices, deserving God's wrath and being damned along with them. I have done my part. Let every man look to doing his. My hands are clean.[33]

The Jews obsessed him. He became a repository for the most farfetched tales. He reacted with vivid excitement—"I'd tear their tongues out of their throats. The Jews, in a word, should not be tolerated. One should neither eat nor drink with them."

"Herr Doctor," interposed a companion, daring to drip balm on the inflamed sore. "It is written that the Jews will be converted before the last day."

Luther challenged this with his slogan, "Where stands that written? I know no unambiguous text for it. Romans 9 has one verse they cite, but they cannot prove it there."

No colleague dared quibble, though all knew that not only Romans 9, but also Romans 11: 25–26 were very clear on Paul's sympathies with his brethren and hopes for converting them. Kate broke the silence with that brashness which the men held against her. "It stands written," she announced in Latin, lest she be held inexpert, "there shall be one fold, and one shepherd."

Luther showed patience. "Yes, dear Kate. That was when the gospel was being spread among the gentiles."

The irenic tone encouraged someone to express regret about Jews who had been killed or maimed. Luther actually conceded this to be wrong in cases where they had the protection of a prince's safe-conduct, but he went ahead to quote Isaiah on the obstinacy of the tribe: "Thy neck is an iron sinew, and thy brow brass."[34]

Melanchthon forwarded *Against the Jews and Their Lies* to Philip of Hesse, recommending it. He later sent the *Shem-Hamphoras*, but only "so you may see what he is doing."[35] Protestants in southwest Germany openly disapproved, Josel of Rosheim even obtained suppression of *Against the Jews and Their Lies* in Strasbourg, but it was not without influence in central Germany. John Frederick, although Josel had persuaded him to mitigate that edict of 1536, was now moved to renew it. Hesse took measures against the Jews.[36] They continued to find refuge in Brandenburg, much to Luther's discomfort. They were even shielded in his own native Eisleben. His trip there in February of 1546 scraped the old ulcer open and he devoted an entire sermon to the subject. It concluded in reference to Christ:

He is my shield as far as heaven and earth extend, my mother hen, under whose wing I escape God's wrath. That is why I can have no fellowship or patience with them. As your compatriot, I wanted to leave you with this warning at the end, lest you partake of others' sins. For I mean well and loyally by both princes and subjects. If the Jews want to be converted from their blasphemy and other offenses against us, then we will gladly forgive them. If not, then we should neither tolerate nor suffer them here.[37]

These were the last words Doctor Martin Luther delivered in public. Although we have them only in an imprint which appeared after his death, the language is characteristic, and there is little reason to question their authenticity. Even the expression "I wanted to leave you with this warning at the end" is not unlikely, because he knew he was near death, and departing Eisleben in any case.

Of *Against the Jews and Their Lies* Luther's greatest modern admirer, Roland Bainton, said, "One might wish that he had died before ever he wrote it." I certainly sympathize with Bainton's feelings, even though I am unable as biographer to accept his view. Bainton's great Reformer had weakened, his mind was impaired, depths of the personality were revealed painful to contemplate. But contemplate them the biographer must, for whatever understanding of humanity we can draw from the usually hidden recesses. If we are so pious as to avert our eyes from powers in the personality which we call evil, then we forgo, of course, true appreciation of the good.

The very intensity of the anti-Semitic writings guarantees their authenticity as outpourings of Luther's innermost being. We dare not dismiss them as mere products of a sick mind or of an injured brain—although they are that, of course. Especially the scatological vigor of all the late writings is reminiscent of the embarrassing language heard from neurological patients, often for the first time and to great consternation of friends and relatives. But the brain damage has not *produced* the language, or taught it, but only weakened accustomed repressive mechanisms. We shall have to look beyond the physical disease in order to glimpse the wellsprings of those terrible emotions which erupted in Luther's anti-Semitic writings. I have already suggested that the outbreaks are related to his antipathy against legalism.

Sometimes he brought his reference works to table, where he and his companions would inform themselves on Jewish usage. On one such occasion he noted how papistry and Jewry were alike founded on the concept of good works. The scholastic doctrine of *opus operatum* corresponded, he said, with the Jewish desire to perform certain acts pleasing to God. This, he protested, was simple idolatry—

> He who wished salvation had to do thus and so, put on a cap, clip his hair. He who did not do or practice thus was damned. And even if you did it, you could not be sure you were saved thereby. Fie upon thee, devil! What a doctrine that is! If you don't follow it, you are damned. If you do follow it, you don't know whether it pleases God or not. That is the error we poor wretches were stuck with.

One at table spoke up brightly, "If the world lasts but fifty years longer, there'll be some changes made."

"Oh, God forbid," the old man cried, "It would just get worse than it has ever been, for all kinds of sects would arise that have as yet lain hidden in the heart of man and we have never suspected were in there. So come, dear Lord, come, and let thy day of judgment break, for no longer can any improvement be expected."[38]

Not only was he inclined to see pope and Jew as but two visages of the same infernal error, two rituals in the same arrogant effort to gain merit with God. They symbolized his own personal disappointment, the vanity of his life's work, his final defeat in a long combat with the fundamental error. World and devil had proved too much for him: even his well-intended reforms had led only to splintering the church. The course of history appeared to vindicate those early voices crying out that he was a schismatic.

> Let me just begin at the beginning, with the horrid, wicked sects and heresy like Müntzer, the Zwinglians, the Anabaptists, and many more, in the name and guise of the gospel—because it is the gospel that freed them from the pope's power and tyranny, safely to teach and do as they please.

He went ahead to detail how all other evils, from arrogance to lazy, insolent servants, went right back to the liberties he had mistakenly provided.[39] No wonder he regretted having revealed the gospel to the crowd at all. If he had it to do over again, he would reserve it for the troubled in heart, that tiny group which, through the ages, constituted the church. "I'd leave the masses under the papacy."[40]

His despair tended to be self-fulfilling. Frantic preachings against the lawyers scarcely improved their behavior. He converted no Jews. His repeated excommunication of philandering Hans Metzsch merely gave the old roué a reputation to uphold. When he scolded another nobleman to his face publicly for lending money at 30 per cent, he received before onlookers the blatant retort: "If a man is able to sire forty-three children in one year, he ought to be granted forty gulden on the hundred."[41]

He involved himself in contradictions. Hungarian students in Wittenberg were denied mass in a language they could understand, for that was Latin.[42] His harshness with the Anabaptists— "Off with the heads of the Anabaptists! They are revolutionaries and will not give up their errors"[43]—must have oppressed him. He found himself almost in the same breath condemning those who had failed to recognize Jan Hus's piety, and warning against being misled by the "apparent, hypocritical holiness or patience" of the Anabaptists, whose persecution he was recommending.[44] It seemed all to go back to a basic contradiction in his own teachings and in his own ranks, one pertaining to the law. While complaining about the fortifications John Frederick was putting up, he had used a word so wicked that even Kate would not abide it. One of those preachers who denied the law, claiming his was Luther's own doctrine, tried to reach him by letter—it evoked that word again.

"Ay, my dear lord, that is too coarse!" Kate begged.

"They learn me to be coarse," he murmured, sent the messenger back with the unopened letter, and fell to railing that "The mindless, foolish, devil's thane understands not, knows not what he blabbers." Again the unacceptable word leapt forth, but, remembering Kate's presence, he continued to berate the antinomian in Latin.[45]

He felt increasingly isolated, deserted by those who owed him support.[46] He said he sang his mother's song: "Nobody likes you and me, the two of us are to blame for that."[47] But the blame went eventually, he knew, back to that unspeakably corrupt institution whose horrors, precisely because he had himself reformed them, were now in danger of being forgot.

> I am going to go ahead [he resolved], by way of a warning for posterity, and lay the monstrosities of scholastic theology before the eyes of the public, because there are adults among us who, not having witnessed the papal Lernas, are greatly astonished that there could have been people in any part of the world who ever believed the things we reprimanded the papists for having taught. They say no mule or horse would have believed what we are said to have taught and believed under the papacy.[48]

Thus the most immoderate of Doctor Luther's writings was reserved for the last, and for the pope. *Against the Papacy, Founded by the Devil* (1545) exceeded even the anti-Semitic writings of 1543 in coarseness—and in order to appreciate its impact on contemporaries we must bear in mind the reverence with which Europe was still accustomed to speak of the pope. Perhaps Luther himself was unable to gauge that, encouraged as he had been by those in his immediate circle. Were John Frederick not Luther's own product, we might place the blame on him, for he had political ends in view.

The emperor had at last been coming round to the idea that the German situation might best be settled by the Germans themselves, and at the Diet of Speier he made important concessions to the Protestant League of Schmalkalden, independently of Rome. In the same year, 1544, Pope Paul again convoked a council (this one at last to materialize), and the Wittenberg theologians were once more called on to draw up their position. They did so in an especially mild "gentle reformation," as Chancellor Brück called it in forwarding their memorandum to John Frederick, "wherein the rumbling spirit of Doctor Martinus is not heard."[49] John Frederick had in hand a papal breve in which Paul reproved the emperor for his conciliatory line. Somehow he had also obtained an earlier draft of it, more firmly worded than that actually delivered to the emperor. This John Frederick passed to Brück with the thought that "Martinus make something out of the pope's breve . . . for we do not doubt that he will know how to handle it. We could then have [his work] printed and circulated. It would attract the attention of many in the German nation."[50] Brück deemed it as yet too early for Luther to "come down with his poleax, which by the grace of God he wields with a higher spirit than other men."[51] He asked written confirmation of John Frederick's request, but Luther had already gone to work.

The purpose of this polemic was really no different from that of other, more reasoned arguments of twenty-five years earlier: to deny the supreme, divine authority of the pope, but its scurrility had not been equaled before—nor has been since. It launches right out into mockery—the pope may say to Luther,

> "Silence, heretic! What comes out of our mouth must be obeyed." I hear you. Which mouth do you mean? The one that emits farts? You can obey them yourself. Or the one you pour good Corso into? May dogs shit in it. "Oh, you shameful Luther. Can you speak thus to the pope?" Well, phooey on you, you licentious, horrid knaves and crass donkeys! Can *you* speak thus to emperor and empire?[52]

Such language caused some to feel Luther had more damaged himself than he had his opponent. His major effect was achieved by such endless repetition that we are scarcely able to read the work today. We are surprised to learn that the emperor's brother, King Ferdinand, read it through and approved of the content, if not of the scatology.[53]

Luther went further. He sketched out a number of revolting pictures which his old crony Lucas Cranach then perfected and published. Perhaps the most infamous was one with mercenary soldiers (the despised *Landsknechte*) defecating by turns into the papal tiara. Luther told Nicholas von Amsdorf his purpose had been to communicate with those who had to rely on Latin (*Against the Papacy* had been in German), but his main accomplishment had been to reach the illiterate.[54] One contemporary called them "fantasies of an impetuous old fool."[55]

That was not entirely correct. Luther can at no time in his life be dismissed as senescent or unaccountable. I have offered my opinion that uremia led to neurological complications after Schmalkalden, so that many of his utterances reveal an underlying irritability. Yet we have to admit that his periodic outbursts are not uncharacteristic of him. In general, Luther's mind remained sound. In the years 1538–39 he produced one of his most thoroughly researched scholarly papers, *Concerning Councils and the Church*, in which he drew on immense historical documentation for the purpose of delimiting the authority of the church council and giving a final, scholarly statement of the exclusively spiritual nature of the church. Perhaps the best evidence of the clarity of his mind was his continued ability to make fun of himself—even of his irascibility. In mock concern, he deplored Melanchthon's mildness toward Rome—

> He is moderate, and he acts with moderation. Nevertheless, he just might do some good. He hopes so. As for me, I kick over the traces, then I shatter the wagon. Philip, ah, in the beginning he was very moderate. In twenty years he has improved a lot.[56]

Luther's condition in advanced years was a product of his temperament and of the traumas by which his aging had occurred.

The major figure in German letters after Luther, Wolfgang Goethe, lived a long, admirable life. He took pride in having profited from numerous emotional and physical crises, drawing strength from them to emerge healthier than before. In his early twenties, on a geological excursion, Goethe alarmed his companion by dangerous flying leaps from one rocky crag to another. When warned, he only called back, "We have yet to become famous before we die!" More than a half century later, as an old man looking back over quite an astonishing career, he issued a wry challenge. Except for the imagery, there was no connection whatever with that earlier boast, so far back in time—but for me the two symbolize the precariousness of every significant career: "Follow me whoever dares, without breaking your neck."

In Luther's earliest conflicts with authority he had become accustomed to anxious warnings from his friends. He had been forced to rely solely on his own sure sense of the right. He loved the many biblical admonitions which alone confirmed him in his scorn of the world, telling him to be confident when all men revile you.[57] As his efforts bore fruit, he boasted, "Who has not been offended by Luther's madness?"[58] Theological writers correctly attribute his supreme self-confidence and fear of general approval to religious faith. Even so, on this earth the bold leaper had come to rely on his own surefootedness as well. At last he lived over into a time when his nerves were impaired, his responses jerky, his judgment no longer totally reliable. There were those who would take advantage of his irascibility, but there was none whose warnings he would heed.

Tentatio Tristitiae
The Sense of Theology

"In this act, all modesty is forfeit"—thus Luther on the indignity of an enema as remedy for dysentery.[1] It was but the first of his many illnesses after the Schmalkalden attack, this present infection being complicated by arthritic pains, excruciating sciatica, and intermittent recurrences of the stone. His pulse was irregular. From time to time he ran a high fever. He fell to speculating on the multitude of our tribulations, doubting that there could be any punishment in the hereafter to exceed them—

> Let us not talk of such things. I was merely thinking. God forfend we should ever experience it. In this life, let us be of that number of whom it is said, "Blessed are they that mourn." Here on earth the trials differ from one individual to the next . . . It is enough for us to know that sorrow is our immediate, momentary acquaintance with death.[2]

As he got better, he ventured out for a ride through the nearby Specke Forest. To the delight of those in the coach he broke out into song, exulting over the anguish it caused the devil, "who enjoys our fretting and groaning." He is the prince of this world, Luther added, matter-of-factly, so

> when we traverse his territory he naturally levies customs duties upon our bodies with various diseases. Doctors see only the natural causes of disease, and they do well to try to correct

them. They do not recognize how Satan lurks behind the natural causes of an illness, facilely manipulating the elements . . .
That is why we must have a higher medicine: faith and
prayer.

He said he had found such help in Psalm 31, but admitted he had
never really understood "My times are in thy hand" until his
present sickness. He planned to emend his translation accordingly. He never got around to it, but the modern Anchor Bible,
independently of Luther, now offers quite in his spirit, "The
stages of my life"—Luther: "That is, my whole life, each day,
hour, moment—which is the same as to say, 'My health, sickness,
misfortune, happiness, life, death, joy, and sorrow are in thy
hand.' "³
The dysentery spread among the dwellers in the Black Cloister, affecting Jerome Weller, ever a bit delicate, just at the time
when he was supposed to depart for an important new post. Luther by no means attributed the disease to contagion, but told
him firmly,

> Thinking can cause the flux. A heart full of thoughts inter-
> feres with sleep, with meals and digestion. When the heart is
> distracted, the entire body suffers . . . So you must offer your
> thoughts as much resistance as you can.⁴

Such plenteous advice to others was based on an abundance of
personal experience. It was not too much work, he was sure, that
caused his own headaches, but those trials that come out of
thinking. Just as with David, who

> could not be aroused by that young girl because the old man
> was just too exhausted by the trials of thinking. I know that
> for a fact. It was thoughts that broke him down. He had to
> stomach many a powerful trial. So you young fellows must
> guard against sorrow, I tell you. It is forbidden. It damages the
> body. Our Lord God commanded us to be merry.

He allowed that most people are stricken with care when
worldly aspirations go awry. His own sorrow derived from
thinking about God. The idea that God might not be benevolent,

he said, was more crushing than the fear of having taught false doctrine—and that had been enough to slay Zwingli and Oecolampadius—

> So you young fellows go ahead and suffer every physical ailment, but just shun that eternal anguish of heart and mind. Avoid sorrow however you can. Except for manifest sins, I hereby absolve you of all merriments wherein you may seek comfort, be it eating, drinking, dancing, gaming, whatever.[5]

Sorrow had been his own familiar companion since boyhood.[6] The man did not distinguish his acute spell of depression in 1527 (often diagnosed as his first heart attack) as being different in kind from earlier attacks of anxiety,[7] but his extreme moodiness had become more pronounced afterward. As early as 1530, he announced to his congregation he would never preach to them again, and did spurn his church for several Sundays.[8] Such spells became more frequent as the years passed. One bout, he said, followed another without teaching a thing.[9] Looking back over his long Wittenberg career, he sighed,

> I have preached here for twenty-four years, walking the street to church so often it would be no wonder if I had worn out the soles of my feet as well as my shoes on its cobblestones. I have done what I was able—and I am satisfied. The letters I have sent would alone build a house, had I but saved them. They bear witness to my labors. Yet nothing has so exhausted me as sorrow, especially at night.[10]

Luther's biographers have placed their various interpretations on his fits of depression, but generally agreed that the experiences were singular, if not unique.[11] Luther thought so too, when a young man.[12]

But he soon learned better. The mature Luther, concerned with the well-being of others and constantly called on for counsel by the afflicted, found sorrow to be the essence of human existence.[13] He recognized one of its great dangers to be the self-centered belief that "No one is suffering like me."[14] He hit upon an especially sententious formulation, "Sorrow is inborn in man," noted that several were recording the words, and added,

"Then along comes his nibs the devil, to add his bit. But the Lord God sustains us."[15] Sorrow as the characteristic lot of man became more and more explicitly central to his theology.

Far from the systematic apologetics of modern theology, Luther's religious thinking was never of a speculative sort at all. For medieval scholastics, as for moderns, "theology" meant inquiry about God. Luther had become convinced that delving into such questions *obstructs* the true purpose of a sincere theologian. His is a quite practical calling: ministry to the soul in distress. The test of theology is the comfort it brings. Nothing had been, in his experience, quite so dismaying as probing into God's unfathomable mysteries. He concluded that this was the sense of Christ's becoming man: to comfort souls else distant from the incomprehensible God.

He did not assume that all anxiety in others also arose from theological speculation, but he did say it came from too much thinking. That was why solitude was to be feared. "I'd sooner seek out John my swineherd than be alone," he admonished Weller, "or even the swine."[16] "I've had help from people who didn't have as much theology in their whole body as I do in one finger."[17] "The most ignorant servant girl can console me," he declared, "so incompetent is a man in sorrow and alone—even though he be well armed with scripture." He referred to monastic life to show how man is created to take part in economic, political, or ecclesiastic activity. "Outside these contexts, he is not a man—unless somehow miraculously exempt."[18] He loved to stress the promise that where two or three are gathered together Christ will be with them, and he usually added that we must accept encouragement from our brother as the direct word from God. Riding, hunting, eat, drink, and sex were his further, frequent recommendations.[19] Low spirits were to be avoided at all costs.

Of course, "the best thing for us is to double up our fists and pray,"[20] but he knew that is not always easy. He recommended music as an effective way to "banish trials and thoughts,"[21] since the devil hates it so. To express your grief also helps. "Repressed grief and despondency sap the body's strength and vigor—out with it! The way I do sometimes."[22] His associates were eager to copy down his advice, so that various schematic sets of instructions survive, on how to counsel the depressed.[23] When the prefect of Nordhausen became despondent and suicidal, Luther wrote him a letter of encouragement and witticisms, but also dashed off a few lines to the man's wife:

> Make sure you do not leave your husband by himself for an instant, or anything within his reach with which he could injure himself. Solitude is pure poison for him, and that is why the devil drives him to seek it. If you can tell him a lot of stories, read news and tall tales to him—it won't hurt if they are silly, false blather—yarns about the Turks and Tartars, things like that. Just see if you can make him laugh or want to join in. If he does, then be right there with comforting words from the Bible. Whatever you do, do not let the room grow lonely or still around him, lest he sink into thought. It won't hurt if you make him mad. Act as if you are sorry for it, and make a fuss, but go right ahead anyway.[24]

This advice came from a man who had himself toyed with the thought of suicide.[25]

Luther's theology of practical compassion came clearest when he was himself applying it, as at the deathbed of a Wittenberg teacher. It was clear the man had not long to live, and Luther told him to pray and be confident his prayers would be answered. He cautioned not to dictate time, place, or circumstance to God, these being—he explained in medieval terminology—but the *accidentia* of an individual existence. Only the *substantia*, the life of the soul which transcends time and place, can be of any concern to God.

> God will not forsake you. He is not the tyrant to hold a good, crass blunder against you, either, not even blasphemy in distress or denial of God, such as Peter committed—Paul, too. Don't be troubled by those to whom Christ is but a joke and a laughingstock, like Erasmus and his ilk. Let them live in their certitude, untroubled by the devil. Why should he bother them—they are his already. It is you and me he'd like to get hold of. Just how would he do that? He will keep on assault-

ing you with *accidentia* until he gets the *substantia*. But resist him. He who is within us is greater than he who is in the world.[26]

If the whole purpose of theology was to comfort the troubled in heart, "to raise one conscience up out of despair," then the taste of sorrow was the indispensable qualification for a sincere theologian. Here Luther agrees with his biographers insofar as he does feel himself eminently well qualified by the many sharp assaults the devil has directed against him. Theologians, he taught, draw both training and practice from human suffering. Unlike the physician, the theologian must *undergo* an affliction before he can comfort it. But how was that possible? Were not the trials of conscience manifold, different in every individual? Luther agreed that they were, but he felt they all stem eventually from doubt. Hence a sincere theologian must be, before all else, a doubter.

He recognized two attitudes toward religion. On the one hand, there are the simple folk who seldom scorn it. But the learned are above religion, he said, and disdain it. They do give thought to religious questions, judging them rationally "like Erasmus," but religion is not sensible and will not be accountable to their understanding. Which of these attitudes was Luther's?

He could not count himself one of the simple folk able to accept God unquestioningly. "I did not come to my theology of a sudden, but had to brood ever more deeply. My trials brought me to it, for we do not learn anything except by experience." Do not all professions require experience, he wanted to know. Surely this was no less true of theology than of law or medicine. The professional man must be able to say confidently of his text: "That's right. I know it to be true." Experience cannot be had from sermons, either, for it is not an intellectual matter.

As for me, I haven't even mastered the Lord's Prayer. Nobody becomes learned except by experience. That peasant spoke well who said, "It's a good suit of armor if you just know how to put it on." Holy Scripture is also sound, but God help me to get at the right text. In a debate with Satan I dare not cite, "They who love the Lord will inherit the kingdom," because

he will rejoin: "Thou hast not loved God." Nor can I claim I
have been a good teacher or preacher. You have to find a better nail for your horseshoe than that. I have to tell him: Jesus
Christ died for me.[27]

When his old friend Justus Jonas held Paul up as a paragon of
faith in precisely this point, Luther interrupted him. "I don't
think he believed as firmly as he talks. I cannot believe as firmly
either, as I can talk and write about it."[28] When he alleged
learned men disdain religion, he was able to speak from experience.

His was a theology which used the Bible less as doctrinal guide
than as a literary masterpiece wherein great spiritual trials were
so depicted as to offer solace to the heartsick. He said the church
fathers—Jerome and Ambrose were his favorite examples—had
not appreciated the Bible because they lacked the experience in
personal suffering to be able to say, "That's right. I know it to be
true." Not so Luther—"If I just live long enough, I'd like to
write a book on trials, because without them man can neither
know scripture and faith, nor can he fear and love God. If he
has never suffered, he cannot understand what hope is."[29] Not
through the intellect, but out of personal sufferings alone can
one grasp the ancient writings or accept the higher purpose in
the present sordid world.

If all went according to the wisdom of mankind, Luther
scoffed, the world might well be different. It would hold no
trials and tribulations. In our limited view, are they not quite
pointless?

We do not know how God is constructing his edifice, or what
is to come of all this. That is why we disdain God's intention.
But in a life to come we shall overview the design of his structure and be happy to have endured the trials here.[30]

Such thinking is, of course, by no means unique with Luther.
(All evolutionary schemes in the modern mind, be they biological or social, are predicated on the immeasurable sufferings of individual non-survivors.) Luther had grown up in the medieval
Christian teaching that sorrow is the warp and woof of creation.

The first of the 95 Theses in 1517, on which all the others had rested, was that Christ told us we are here to suffer. At the center of Christian theology stood the Man of Sorrows.

Racked by severe arthritic pains, Luther groaned with Job, "Blessed be the name of the Lord."

> We are able to say that so long as a penny is all that's at stake, or a coat, or our hide. But when spiritual onslaughts come, then we cry out, "Let the day perish wherein I was born, and the night in which it was said, There is a man-child conceived." Oh, then the going gets rough. This is the kind of trial which caused Christ in the garden to say, "O Father, if it be possible let this cup pass from me" . . . That is why the Christ tempted in our flesh is the best intercessor before the Father, when we, too, are being tried.[31]

He loved to parse Christ the prototype for suffering, the way a medieval exegete might.[32] In his sense of a comfort against sorrow—but in this sense only—Luther saw theology as the one truly significant force in the world, despite what the powerful might think, and even if the doctors in theology did not know this to be the case. "To raise one conscience up out of despair is more than many kingdoms."[33]

The one to whom he turned most frequently in his own prayers was an old friend, Nicholas Hausmann, a theologian not at all distinguished by his writings. Over the years Hausmann had shown consideration for tradition as he reformed the city of Zwickau with its refractory congregation, had resisted Thomas Müntzer and the rebellious peasants there, yet raised one of the few voices of restraint when they were defeated. Luther found in Hausmann his chief comforter in distress until that day when Kate and his friends so anxiously and cautiously disclosed Hausmann's death. He had believed in the power of the friend's prayer, and his frequent letters to him ever ended in a passionate plea to pray for him lest his faith fail and he become Christ's enemy—"unless I cling to the words of someone else my own knowledge is not sufficient."[34]

Luther suffered quite palpable visions of an almost stroboscopic oscillation between Christ and the devil.[35] His descriptions are often of the vivid sort which a psychiatrist might call hallucinations, but they arose from the earnest intellectual struggle for which Luther used the term *fidei tentatio:* despair of God's grace. He consoled himself that he shared this most difficult trial with Paul:

> Paul's "thorn in the flesh" means *fidei tentatio,* the tempting of our faith. He saw it as a big skewer to impale our soul and flesh. It was not sexual temptation, as the papists suppose—knowing no other temptations than sexual ones and never having experienced great wrestlings of faith.[36]

We have seen that Luther most frequently wrestled alone with this problem of the ultimate good or evil of creation, but one time the young John Mathesius, who was to become Luther's first protestant biographer, came upon him pondering. He said men do not even regret doing wrong, and have no compassion for the misfortunes of others.

"Whence comes such malevolence?" asked Mathesius, already accumulating notes. But his subject had fallen silent, did not even heed him, sat lost in thought.

At length he murmured, as if to himself, "And he must pay for it in eternity."

A distinguished guest from the Danube broke in on the reverie to observe that this aspect of God was indeed difficult. "We have a friend who finds no other article of faith so offensive as that God wills eternal punishment for devils and wicked men."

"That is true, dear Doctor Severus," Luther replied. "It is a supreme trial, to imagine the eternal wrath of God. There was a time when I thought about it a lot. God help me never to think about it again, but only of Jesus Christ, in whom we see the mercy of the Father."[37]

This was the solution, of course, which had long since led to the other great wrestling, that with self-doubt. As he recalled, it was when first studying the Bible in his university days, and coming face to face with discrepancies between its teachings and those of the fathers, that he heard the question which would ring in his head for the rest of his life: "Shalt thou alone be wise?"[38] Years later, the reform well under way, he wrote of the effort it had cost him to oppose the pope,

to deem him the Antichrist, the bishops his apostles, the
universities his brothels. How often my, heart fluttered,
scolded me, and hurled its strongest argument against me:
"Thou alone art wise? Shall all the rest have been in error, and
for so long? Suppose *you* are in error, and have seduced so
many others into error, to be damned in eternity?"[39]

That in 1521. Again years passed, but in his heart he still feared:

Shall you, an individual and insignificant man, dare such momentous undertakings? What if you are the sole sinner? If
God permits so many great ones to err, might he not permit
one individual to do so? Then come the arguments: church,
church, fathers, fathers, councils, custom, numbers, authority,
wisdom of men. Who would not be moved by such mountains
of arguments, such clouds and oceans of precedent?[40]

He sincerely felt that precisely this charge had killed less steadfast souls.[41] The years had passed, and the emptying of the cloisters, civil turmoil, the peasants' uprisings, the false doctrines of
the sacramentarians, the excesses of the sectarian rabble were all
laid to his account before the bar of his own heart.[42] There the
devil even impugned the legitimacy of his vocation as a doctor
of theology.[43] What wonder if the mature man was able when
lecturing on Genesis to paint the exiled Jacob's sorrow vividly?

In the infirmity of his faith he could not grasp the promise,
but wavered in his flesh and doubted the will of God—as is
the way of the flesh. There appeared unto him the very face
of God, so full of sorrow and reproach that he nearly died.
This is exactly what happens to each of us in our trials, when
we fail to rejoice in the clear goodness of God, but cringe and
dread a wrathful God. Then everything portends our imminent death, all is dark, overclouded, sorrowful, wretched, and
mournful throughout heaven and earth. Neither sun nor moon
shines. Our oppressed heart dies within us, and once it is dead
all else perishes.[44]

We know only through our minds, and sorrow is a condition of
mind. What more, Luther therefore asked, would death be, if
not our own abject fears and anxieties? These were occasioned,

in the sixteenth century, by dread "of sins, divine wrath, and judgment. Such dread is properly called death," he said. "Deprived of the dread, death would no longer be death, but merely an image of itself."[45] "That sickness of heart which they call sorrow," he recognized toward the end of his life, "is a sister of death. They grew up together."[46]

Paralipomena

All the sufferings of Christians are the sufferings of Christ. Whatever a member suffers is suffered by the whole body.

A short rule for preaching:
First, you must learn to ascend to the rostrum; second, you must know how to endure there for a while; third, learn to come back down to earth.

A sincere preacher must look to the children and to the servant men and women who crave instruction. He must give to them as a nursing mother to her babe—from the breast. They need no wine nor malmsey.

That must be a skilled master who constructed a vault like that without any pillars [the heavens by night].

Behold, how beautiful the trees are, all the lovely green. What a precious May! I remember none like it. If it goes on like this we'll have a most bounteous year, and the world is already replete. Ah, could we but trust in God! How will it be in that life, if God can reveal such joy to us on this pilgrimage?

The craftsmanship of God is great in his creations. That the whole tree will grow in accordance with this bud [he was grafting his orchard]! It would be more reasonable for the graft to accommodate itself to the tree.

With a wondrous gesturing of his fingers he tried to make the sign of the cross after the traditional fashion, but could not get it right, and said: Mary, Mother of God, weren't we plagued with the mass, and especially with crossing ourselves!

FIVE

EISLEBEN

Exspatiatur Animi Causa

Save for a baby girl which did not survive the first year, Kate succeeded in nursing her six children through all those diseases which modern medicine permits our generation to forget, but which until very recently laid the tiny low. In May of 1542, Magdalene entered her fourteenth year, time for a Renaissance father to be casting about for her earthly bridegroom. Summer's heat nurtured a virulent infection, which brought the maiden to bed.

A strong girl, she lay in her agony for many days, until both parents were crushed. Whatever formulaic moorings of faith had not been severed by Luther's intellect were strained and frayed as he rocked in this emotional tempest. The mother lay exhausted from weeping. He began to comfort her with assurances of the heavenly home, but soon trailed away into private musings about how schoolboys believe such things implicitly and die more easily on that account. He wheeled on a young student in the room and demanded, "Sir *Magister*, where were you sixty years ago? Where was I? Where did I come from? I do not presume we created ourselves, when we were nothing? There has to be someone who made us!"[1]

Having persuaded himself that he was able to forfeit his daughter if it be God's will, he leaned over Magdalene's bed and asked her, "Lenniken, little daughter, you'd like to stay here with me, with your father, but you are also willing to go to that other father, are you not?"

"Yes, darling father, whatever God wants."

"You dear little daughter!" He murmured in Latin, "The spirit indeed is willing, but the flesh is weak. Oh, I love her! If this flesh hath such great power, what then must the strength of the spirit be?"[2]

Kate collapsed before the death throes were finished. Doctor Luther was brought to his knees at Magdalene's bedside, weeping and begging God to free her. At last, on a morning toward the end of September, she "breathed out her soul into her father's hands." Luther spoke his farewell: "Sweet Lenniken, how fortunate you are." A child's coffin was brought.

As the adolescent corpse was arranged into it, he said, "The bed is not big enough for her."

Bursting into tears, so that "his very viscera shook with sobs," he rushed from the room. Businesslike carpenters proceeded to nail down the lid. The father, unable to escape the pounding, abandoned himself to grief. "Hammer away!" he bellowed out. "On doomsday she'll rise again."[3]

In the 1540s both colleagues and ancient enemies were passing from the scene. They burned Robert Barnes and other Lutherans in England. Duke George had passed away. Luther's old friend Spalatin died in 1545. His own condition was worsening, the left leg so bad that for a time he had to be drawn to church in a little cart.[4] There were intermittent spells of uremia, regular bouts with the stone, his heart was becoming frightfully weak. He beheld the world growing wickeder by the hour. The students knew no moderation in sumptuous clothing, they went a-whoring and carousing. All Wittenberg was given to luxury and immorality. Its government irritated him constantly with futile fortifications which kept his entire end of town in disarray. This second Jerusalem where he had imperiled his soul and safety to recover the gospel for a dying world, this very Wittenberg could so easily be returned to the papacy with but a few sermons —and he had a mind to prove it.[5] The people's coldness was apparent to him in their surly conduct at church. One June day in 1545 he finally had enough, and lashed out from the pulpit, "If you would but mumble and grumble, then go join the cattle and swine! You can converse with them and leave the church in peace." The next Sunday he simply walked out in the midst of the service.[6]

In July he made an excursion, *exspatiatur animi causa*, as Melanchthon wrote to a friend, using a classical idiom for taking a pleasure trip. The literal meaning, "He goes a-roving by cause of temperament," will not have escaped Philip, who found repeated occasion to use the phrase during coming weeks—and months.[7] An ordination and a wedding of state were scheduled in Merseburg. Luther and Caspar Cruciger took the opportunity to visit their old friend Nicholas von Amsdorf, now bishop in nearby Zeitz. Luther's oldest son, Hans, and a friend boarding at the Black Cloister went along. There was room in the coach, and the boys could watch over the somewhat frail doctor.

Around the first of August, Kate received a letter from her husband which began with a routine account of itinerary, then went on quite coolly:

> I would like to arrange things so I don't have to return to Wittenberg. My heart has grown cold, and I don't like it there any more. I also wish you would sell your garden and land, house and all, and I would give the big house back to his grace. You would do well to move out to Zülsdorf for as long as I live. With my salary, I could help you improve the little property—I expect my gracious lord will continue my salary at least for this last year of my life.

Actually, he did not have quite a year to live.

He said he did not think Kate would be treated well in Wittenberg after he died, so she might as well leave right now. "Just away, out of this Sodom!" He gave no reason for his decision beyond an allusion to the way the girls were wearing their blouses cut so low and twirling their skirts at the dances—and a somewhat cryptic remark: "I have found out more in the countryside than I am told in Wittenberg, so I am tired of the town and don't want to come back, God willing."[8]

Kate forwarded the letter to the university. The faculty deemed the situation grave. Melanchthon was sent to Chancellor Brück with the letter, John Frederick being at his summer residence in Torgau. It was Melanchthon's interpretation that Luther was troubled not so much by the behavior of the citizenry as by disagreement with Wittenberg officialdom. He thought the decision had come to him of a sudden on the road, but was not to be taken lightly, as Luther had been threatening something like this for years.

Even in a more optimistic condition he had been known to declare there was no one save John Frederick in official Wittenberg he could trust,[9] and that he thought he would "go into exile." He regretted the "swampy, dank and catarrhal regions," where "neither food nor drink is healthful . . . How long any of us shall hold out in Wittenberg with its strange, coarse food and drink, who knows?"[10] The perennial rift between town and gown was a part of his dissatisfaction.[11] His feud with the law faculty had caused him to threaten from his pulpit to "go somewhere else, where I can be content." He had considered one of John Frederick's remoter castles, as well as refuge with Nicholas von Amsdorf in Zeitz.[12] Frustration with the law faculty had driven him to actual preparations for departure just last year, and he had been restrained only by the profuse tears of John Bugenhagen.[13]

Hence Melanchthon advised Brück that the present threat was to be taken seriously indeed. He knew how the old man had been laboring under a feeling of confinement, and he probably recognized—as did Luther himself—that the walls of Wittenberg were but symbolic for the confines of the flesh and the abominable world. "I did not willingly become a monk," he had heard him say, "but now the world takes on such an aspect that I would almost willingly become one again."[14] Much as he despised the monasteries, there was no rest for a Christian outside them. "Tyrants have the power, usurers the money, peasants have the cheese, eggs, butter, wheat, barley, apples, and pears. The Christians are confined to the tower, where neither sun nor moon shines in."[15] His sense of confinement had grown more oppressive with the years, and now he had escaped, "gone a-roving for the sake of his disposition."

And he enjoyed himself. Old friends received him in a most honorific fashion. They indulged him as he was not accustomed at home. His was the central role in the festivities just under way. In Wittenberg in the meantime, Philip poured his pessimism out before Brück. The chancellor considered the consequences of this avolation and wrote to John Frederick,

If Martinus remains hardheaded in this, I can see that Philippus will not stay, either. He said the doctor had initiated their

cause; he, the least important member, had but joined it. If the
doctor was now willing to create such a scandal for the cause,
then he would have to withdraw. He could not support it,
etc.[16]

John Frederick approached his problem with princely cir-
cumspection. He penned a gentle letter to Luther expressing
royal regret that he had not been permitted to supply his beloved
doctor with a convoy of riders, with provisions, and appropriate
lodgings for the excursion. By no means did John Frederick risk
dispatching his message directly (for Luther might well take
umbrage to learn his correspondence with his wife had been intercepted by the highest instance). He placed it into the hands of
the diplomatic physician Matthew Ratzeberger, reputed to be on
especially jovial terms with Luther. Ratzeberger was told to go
by way of Wittenberg, there to take counsel with Melanchthon.
"Since Master Philippus knows the doctor better than others and
understands his disposition and ways, we have commanded Dr.
Matthew [Ratzeberger] to let him read a copy of our letter."
Philip was to make sure neither the written message nor Ratzeberger's own presentation would contain anything "which
might move the doctor to further displeasure or concern, so that
he may strike it out, or tell Dr. Matthew not to mention it."
Melanchthon and Bugenhagen must go along to Zeitz, but by no
means as a formal delegation. The only immediate purpose
should be to persuade Luther to come to Torgau for a talk with
John Frederick, who said he had "no doubt that we can satisfy
him." The ambassadors were warned not to depart Zeitz in a
body. Melanchthon was to hasten straight back to John Frederick in Torgau, so the prince might have the benefit of his advice before Luther arrived, "but not to let Doctor Martinus
know that."[17]

Such extravagant precautions reveal the extent of Doctor Luther's eccentricity as well as the great love and respect with
which John Frederick and others were accustomed to treating
him, Chancellor Brück albeit grudgingly and Philip with a mien
of self-pity. But by the time all these arrangements and confidential briefings had been accomplished, the object of their concern was in fine fettle. His journey had brought him near his old

stamping grounds, not too far from his birthplace (which he may have taken the opportunity to visit[18]). Luther himself ordained Prince George of Anhalt as bishop of Merseburg. Two days later he and his new bishop led the dean of the cathedral, Sigismund von Lindenau, down the aisle in matrimony with a mistress of seven years' standing. Luther was by no means in good health. He suffered a stone colic at the ordination and had to be supported as he left the cathedral in pain, but the exceptional clarity of his mind came through in his sermons.

After presiding at Lindenau's wedding he preached with relish on the glorious state of matrimony. We are God's creatures, he began, and this is his way of creating us. "All humans must be created thus by God in their mother's womb, maintained there, and afterward with God's help be born into the world."[19] Therefore monkish vows were to be condemned. "There is one thing I dare vow, a vow I can keep: that I will not bite off my own nose."[20] If God should discover us on judgment day lying in the marital embrace—why, then he will find us in precisely that institution he intended for us.[21] "In God's eyes, the marital bed is pure."[22]

It was as if these pulpits must afford him one last opportunity to epitomize. In Halle he took up John 5:39: "Search the scriptures . . . they are they which testify of me." It had been the motto of his life. Like Christ, he had spent his years among the Pharisees, so smug and insincere in their learning. Next day he was back in Merseburg to preach on Psalm 8:2, "Out of the mouths of babes and sucklings." His doctrine, condemned as heresy, was so simple and obvious that Christ had chosen beggars and fishermen to spread it. "What am I to do?" he asked. "The words and teachings are not mine . . . If they were my words, then they should be condemned and cursed as the words and teachings of a man. It is not my words, so it is not I, but the word of God through the mouth of sucklings and children."[23]

In Leipzig he preached on Christ's compassion with the obduracy of Jerusalem as he entered that city, where so soon not one stone would lie upon another. The parallel seemed so clear,

That is the way many learned and intelligent people are now, doctors, lawyers, etc. When Christ comes knocking gently and

sweetly at their door and causing his word to be preached to
them, promising forgiveness of sins and eternal life, they not
only refuse to heed him, but cry out: "Away with these
teachers, execute them!"[24]

Silly Jerusalem, vainly holding to a notion of the good old ways,
lay, no different from his own Germany, under the shadow of
imminent destruction. Christ had been preaching the ancient
faith of Abraham, nothing new at all. So the notion of the "good
old ways" was false. Right here in Leipzig were still Romanists
holding to "their human baubles, 'the old faith'—how old is it
then? Maybe two hundred years?"[25]

He remained in the area for about a fortnight, traveling then
dutifully to Torgau in the middle of August. John Frederick had
been indulging in pleasures of the chase with his cousin Maurice,
old Duke George's successor, for the moment friendly toward
protestantism. Almost immediately after Luther's death Maurice
would, in alliance with the emperor, wage a successful campaign
against John Frederick. Unaided by Philip of Hesse, Luther's
defeated prince would be sent off to prison, leaving his electoral
crown to Maurice and his heirs. Luther was to be spared this indignity. On his last visit to Torgau his prince must have made
good the boast to satisfy him, because Melanchthon brought him
back home. He had been absent just less than a month.

His lectures had at last reached those curious and wandering
prophecies by the ancient Jacob at the end of Genesis. Luther's
words from the lectern were mystical:

More closely, therefore, are death and life joined than we are
able to comprehend. Jacob dies, it is true, yet his death is tantamount to life—indeed, it is the closest thing to life.

What we are accustomed to calling life, he went on, is in fact
death. "We are ourselves dying and giving up the ghost, our
body putrefying and eaten by worms." No wonder Jacob died
so willingly—Luther could speak for him in the first person—

I am dying and shall lie in the sepulcher, but God lives. He
who has promised the land into which he will lead you will
also set me over into another, far better land. For it is his
promise.[26]

Here at the end of the chapter he was confiding thoughts which
had been occupying him all his life.

He confessed to the students that he thought about death a lot,
and said it was futile to do so.[27] If the child knows nothing of its
months *in utero*, indeed of its early years, what can we expect to
learn of existence beyond death? We know only that we are
safe.

> God will see to it that you are among the people of the elect,
> he who kept you alive and well in the womb, in the cradle,
> and while you slept . . . The human soul sleeps with all its
> senses buried. Our bed is as a tomb, where there is neither
> harm nor sadness. Nor has the place of the dead any torments,
> but they rest, as the saying goes, in peace.[28]

Comparisons between death and various unconscious or precon-
scious states had become frequent with him. He saw our conscious existence as very limited, both in time and in its powers of
comprehension, but not as separate from the totality wherein we
unconsciously rest.[29]

This seemed to him such a simple and universally known fact
that he took great delight in its terse biblical expression, as in the
final words of Genesis 49, where Jacob "gathered up his feet into
the bed, and yielded up the ghost, and was gathered unto his
people." How alien to biblical simplicity were the tortured con-
trivances of the Roman Church, with its four major categories,
so Luther claimed, to divide the dead—

> These are the merest dreams and human inventions! . . . It is
> enough for us to know scripture testifies that from the begin-
> ning of the world they who believed in the seed of woman did
> not die, nor were they consigned to forgetfulness, but were
> gathered unto their people. What kind of a place that is, no
> one can say.

He could only refer back to his own "crude similitudes" of the
fetus *in utero* or the soul asleep. "How great is then our folly,
and with what temerity do we constrain divine wisdom within
the confines of human reason!" Though it is not given to us to
know where we shall be, "it is certain that it is not bad, and there
is no torment or pain—only rest in the grace of God, just as we

sleep sweetly in this life, under the protection of God and the angels, fearing no danger even though surrounded by devils."[30] Toward the close of his lecture he became quite personal on the subject of his own growing curiosity about the threshold between consciousness and unconsciousness:

> I have often tried to catch just that moment at which I either fall asleep, or at which I awaken. But I have never been able to apprehend it, or to prevent sleep overcoming me unawares. This is the way it will be with our death and resurrection. We shall go thence, and at the day of judgment come again, without knowing it—nor shall we know how long we have been gone.[31]

The lectures on Genesis were subject to one last interruption. A kinsman from Eisleben paid a visit and expressed the hope cousin Martin might put in a good word for the family smelting enterprise. Luther's native county of Mansfeld was one of those typical Saxon districts which fragmented inheritance had brought under the governance of two counts. Expansion of mining operations and the growth of the city of Eisleben had led to a thicket of litigation; ill feelings were reported between the counts—in short, Luther saw at a glance that his good offices were needed. He must bring his sage judgment to restore peace in his homeland before he died. Away he flew, uninvited, with an anxious Justus Jonas and a protesting Philip Melanchthon in train. The feelings of the latter, a prolific correspondent, were made known to friends. As in the summer, the word he used was *exspatiatus*, "gone a-roving." It no doubt accurately catches Philip's impression of the old man's state of mind in these last few months. He perceived a distracted King Lear, prone to wander about the countryside.[32]

Mansfeld was the town where Luther had spent his boyhood. Here lay his earliest memories and, back beyond them, that infant existence of which there was no remembrance, only knowledge of its security at his mother's breast. He tarried in Mansfeld for about four days in all (not counting the same number spent traveling). October was a colorful time of year in the foothills of the Thuringian Forest, the air was crisp, and Luther thought the many smelting ovens further purified it.[33] This was to be his last outing in good weather. As for his ostensible purpose here, the counts were off to Brunswick, so the old peacemaker contented himself by leaving a long letter to them with their mother, conjuring good will toward one another and assuring them of his interest.

He lectured now for a few more weeks on the burial of Jacob, and on Joseph's death and burial. It was a subject to which he said he would like to devote more time, especially Joseph's request his bones be returned to the land of Canaan, for "here Joseph declared his faith, when he desired to be in that number who were to be raised with Christ." Luther powerfully argued one central message throughout the Old Testament and New. Here was a fine opportunity to demonstrate it to his students once more, but he was not sure just how long he could hold out. It was important to him to finish this series of lectures begun ten years earlier (shortly before that visit of the papal nuncio Pietro Paolo Vergerio). After affirming that Joseph, "as a testimony to his faith in Christ, commands that his bones be carried to the land of Canaan . . . as a monument before the eyes of all posterity . . . that they may persevere in the same faith and promise in which he had gone to sleep with his fathers," Doctor Luther closed his notes. It was a Tuesday, 17 November 1545.

> And that is the sweet Book of Genesis. May our Lord God give it to others to do a better job after me. I can do no more. I am weak. Pray God for me, that he may give me a blissful end.[34]

The wish for *ein seliges Stündlein*, the "blissful moment" of passing, seems almost fatuously frequent in Luther's last years, even though we make allowance for the Renaissance preoccupation with death and Luther's constant confrontation with the dying. It points up a painful ambivalence in his feelings on the subject. His disdain of the world and longing to leave it were entirely sincere. Yet he profoundly dreaded the death struggle.

He would reassure himself, "The fear of death is all death really is. He who has cast the thought of death out of his heart experiences no death, tastes no death."

One of his companions somewhat insensitively wondered if there were not pains connected with dying. "Ask my wife if she felt anything," Luther said. "She was near death." His reference was to Kate's severe illness in 1540.

"Nothing at all, Herr Doctor," she confirmed dutifully.

"That is why the fear of death is the greatest part of death," he went on. "In Hebrews we read how he tasted death for us. We are fortunate people, who do not have to taste death. It is very bitter and sharp."

He described Christ's passion in gripping terms, making one of his frequent references to the medieval view: "No angel knows what it was when blood flowed through his pores. That is the taste and the terror of death."[35]

He and his circle frequently reminded one another that the hour of death was a gift from heaven, and they regularly prayed God to keep his promise of John 8:51, whereby the faithful "shall never see death." Doctor Luther's attendance at the peaceful death of old Aunt Lene, Kate's relative who lived with them, was typical.

"Aunt Lene, do you know me?" he asked. "Can you hear me?"

When he saw that she recognized him, he said, "Your faith rests upon sweet Lord Jesus. He is the resurrection and the life. Thou shalt not want. Thou shalt not die, but fall asleep as in the cradle, and at dawn you will rise into eternal life."

She sighed, "Oh, yes."

"Do you have no cares?" She felt some pain, she indicated, around her heart.

"God will soon free you of all pain. Thou shalt not die."

To those at her bedside, he said, "She is fortunate, for this is not death. It is but a sleep." Then he walked over to the window, where he preferred to stand when praying.[36]

While Luther admitted that devils and the unrepentant are out of grace, he flatly refused to entertain the notion of hell as a place of torment.[37] He also made fun of the popular conception of heaven as fulfillment of earthly wishes.[38] Seldom would he indulge his colleagues' curiosity about the sojourn of the soul in that interim between death and resurrection, but they did once catch him musing on the various names for it in the Bible. He wondered if it might not be compared with the trance of ecstatics. Here he caught himself up and warned that nothing of the sort must be preached publicly. As for what to tell the congregation, Christ set the example:

> "In my father's house are many mansions"—that is pure allegory. Ah, dear Lord, thy words are not so cold and empty as our human words, but are beyond all human thought and wisdom.

Thus he returned to analogies he himself loved, like that of the babe in the womb. But now that he was in a speculative mood, he discussed Plato's concept of the soul, Aristotle's argument that the soul and body are one substance, and the positions of the church fathers. All these sages, he thought, might have shown somewhat more humility on a subject they so little understood. As for himself, he drew a clear distinction between body and soul. "But yet there is a great bond between them. They cling to one another, for the soul takes great delight in the body. They do not willingly part from one another." He concluded in praise of his favorite classical author, Cicero, for recognizing the immortality of the soul:

> He was a dear man, who read a lot, reflected a lot, and then was able to say a lot. He wrote with great sincerity, did not tease or play the Greek, as Plato and Aristotle do. I hope God will help Cicero and such men as he to the remission of their sins—and if he must remain out of grace, then he will at least be some levels higher than our cardinals, and the bishop of Mainz.[39]

On another occasion, Luther went so far as to consign Cicero to his place in paradise (shades of Zwingli!).[40]

Of course, there was another kind of life after death which much concerned Doctor Luther, and that was the continuance of his own earthly mission. In the early 1530s, when a learned physician had, upon inspecting a urine specimen, gravely declared Luther in imminent danger of a stroke, his patient informed him he would live for some time yet. God had no intention of permitting the papacy further triumphs so soon after the deaths of Zwingli and Oecolampadius. Gradually, however, he had come to recognize that his own life constituted a kind of final link between the papacy and the true church. As he became more of a historical figure in his own eyes, he referred to himself as a successor of Jan Hus, whose martyrdom had begun the papacy's destruction. Once he had to accept his own efforts toward a general council as doomed, he gained a new perspective on the thriving, healthy movement he was leaving behind. He could view even the Anabaptists, the antinomians, and other ultra-rationalists in a certain mischievous irony. Let the papacy try to stave off such radicals once the staunchly conservative Doctor Martinus no longer served as a buffer. The motto he coined as hope for a council faded was often repeated until his death:

Pestis eram vivens, moriens ero mors tua papa,
A plague I was while living, dying I shall be death, unto you, O pope.[41]

So his mission detained him on earth no longer—quite the contrary. About the time of Magdalene's death he was asked to inscribe a Bible. It was not an unusual request, but this inscription fell out more mystical than usual. After the words of the 23rd Psalm, "Yea though I walk through the valley of the shadow of death, I shall fear no evil, for thou art with me," he added:

God's word is a light that shines in the darkness and beckons, brighter than day. For in death not only does the light of the sun go out, but also the light of reason with all its knowledge. Then the word of God shines loyally as an eternal sun which faith alone may see and follow, into the clarity of eternal life.[42]

The Legacy

Martin Luther's influence has been so very diffuse as to be regarded differently by almost every judge. He is depicted by turns as a revolutionary, as a reformer, as champion of freedom of thought, profound religious thinker, archconservative, and reactionary. My final chapter will return to his own assessment and to that of his associates. Yet whoever may have spoken about his contribution, all have agreed that his Bible translation was at the very least his most effective vehicle for bringing his mission home to contemporaries and to posterity.

The Luther Bible became the major classic of the German language. Its example led directly to the Tyndale Bible and thence to the magnificent English Bible tradition immediately after Tyndale's murder. As the Bible became popular reading throughout northern Europe, a new age of literacy, even of poetry, began to disperse the dank fogs of barbarism. Thus Luther's Bible became not just a legacy, but an important stage in the still gradually awakening consciousness of man.

Yet there is no particular spot in a biography to discuss his Bible, for it was as central to all his accomplishments as it was to his personality. Nor was there any time in his mature life when he was not preoccupied with it. We observed him at the conference table for revision of Psalms pending the first publication of his full Bible in 1534. The last revisions in which he was able to take part during the 1540s led to editions in the last year of his life, 1545, and in the year of his death, 1546. Much scholarly effort has gone into the question of just how great a role he played in these, as distinct from the work of that tireless secretary of his, George Rörer. As we have seen, however, the Luther

Bible had been a cooperative effort from the start. The collaborative revision of Psalms had been but typical of the Wittenberg Bible since the early 1520s. Only Luther's initial work on the New Testament while he was isolated at the Wartburg in 1522, the "September Bible" of that year, might reasonably be called a one-man effort. But even that is a misleading dramatization.

That ancient metaphor of the scholar standing "on the shoulders of giants" has been appropriate for Bible studies since time out of mind. Luther said the Lord had called him to translate the Bible "lest I think myself a scholar."[1] His translation became possible when it did only as a result of massive humanistic labors by his own generation and that directly before him, Reuchlin, d'Étaples, Erasmus—this is generally recognized. It became possible *where* it did because of a long and lively German tradition. Hundreds of Bible translations had been made into German before Luther's. No less than fourteen were circulating in print before his. Earnest efforts to transfer the sublime message into this primitive, childlike language had reached their pinnacle around 1300 with the great German mystics, whom Luther consciously emulated. We must compare the German experience with the English if we would appreciate what the Luther Bible owed to a national tradition. When German poetry of the Middle Ages was enjoying a first flower, the English language was still laboring to digest the mass of French it had swallowed during the Norman conquest. As late as 1400 John Wycliffe's timidly literal rendition of the New Testament was regarded as radical, and we have heard how still in Luther's era an English king could with a straight face defer a Bible translation until such time as it should please him to command such be executed. Just as the church reformation took its start under particular political circumstances in Saxony, so Luther's translation owed much to a long tradition of Bible scholarship.

He brought to the tradition his own fervent love of literature and an ability to respond to the written word with rare passion. We saw how readily he related his condition on the sickbed in Schmalkalden to that of a literary figure (Virgil's Hector). How much more powerful was his identification with the ancient Hebrews! Had he not gazed into the belly of the whale with Jonah? Had he not governed the church with Noah?[2]

Luther gave much thought to what that literary quality might be, which let readers find their own deepest needs mirrored in a text. He concluded that the supreme literary merit is brevity. Holy Scripture he found distinguished by its ability

> to pour everything into one word. What Virgil says of Dido's love in many words, the Hebrew says most tersely: "Amnon loved Thamar." The words are few, but the import is great . . . That means we have to imagine David's thoughts when he slew the lion, or when he had to fight Goliath: "What if I shall be killed? But it shall not be so. My right hand is the hand of God." That's what you call rhetoric![3]

By "rhetoric," the old debater meant not so much the art of conveying powerful feelings, as success in engaging the audience, so that the emotions arise from within their own breasts. "Mere reasoning is like an empty pair of breeches, but rhetoric or eloquence blows up that hogsbladder, and lets you know how all sides felt about the business."[4] The most effective rhetorician was Christ, as is apparent from his economy of words: "He combines heaven and earth into one morsel, when he speaks."[5]

This highest literary virtue, pregnancy of expression, arises from richness of human experience, so Luther felt. His great classics were therefore those which distill great suffering. While he called neglect of classical studies "the last sin I would commit against youth,"[6] he was nevertheless fond of twitting his favorite Romans, Terence and Virgil, for imagining that temptation was merely something to do with pretty girls. The prophets, on the other hand, speak with that "unerring sense" which only the great temptations of Satan can produce. One word suffices them to convey their understanding to any able to comprehend.[7]

Luther's awe of the Bible as great literature did not exempt it from the vicissitudes to which he recognized the written word is subject. He deplored the palpable loss of so many of the writings treating the patriarchs, and he longed to know more, especially about Abraham.[8] He entertained his doubts about Moses's authorship of the Pentateuch, found the prophetic writings fragmentary, and attributed this both to the passionate nature of the writers themselves and to the vagaries of transmission.[9] As professor he repeatedly cautioned his students about the anthropomorphism of the authors of Genesis. The tendency of good men to impute their own passions to God was, he said, "a common practice in Holy Scripture."[10]

Not only were apocrypha like the Book of Judith "theological poems" comparable to the saints' legends. Such a book as Job, too, offered a kind of fiction:

> Job did not talk the way it is written here, but he had thoughts like these. You don't talk that way when you are being tempted. The event really occurred, and it is like the plot of a story which the author took up as Terence might have, adding characters and their emotions.[11]

Perhaps it was composed around the time of Solomon—"It is possible that Solomon himself wrote it"[12]—but the details in any case were inventions. While Luther took the human, hence fallible authorship and transmission of the Old Testament for granted, that in no way detracted from his esteem for the grand tales.[13] His verdict on the Book of Jonah was typical:

> This history is most comforting to us and a most certain sign of the resurrection. It is a pretty tall tale, and I wouldn't believe it if it weren't included in Holy Scripture. [The experience in the belly of the whale] is exactly the way God usually humbles his servants. Jonah gets a lot worse later on, and wants to tell God how to do things. He even becomes a murderer, wishing utterly to destroy such a populous city. Now there's a prophet for you![14]

Luther was intimately familiar with the thousand years of Bible interpretation which had gone before him.[15] Yet he removed himself as decisively as he could from that tradition insofar as it was "distinguished in matters of the intellect, yet wanting in warmth of feeling."[16] He admitted that he too, when a monk, had found abstract meanings everywhere in the Bible—but not after the history itself sank in, e.g., "how difficult it was for [Gideon] to fight the enemy at those odds. If I had been there, I'd have shit in my breeches for fright."[17] He taught that precisely this kind of imaginative participation was essential to the reading of any great literature, but especially of the Bible, for its profound authors had deliberately left their work unencumbered with detail. David knew (2 Sam. 1:15–16) that the Amalekite was lying about having killed Saul, but had good reason for executing him, anyhow, just as Solomon did well to execute Adonijah.[18] Luther was here analyzing motives in a legal and political frame. As a psychologist he could reconstruct Christ's strong arousal when tempted by Satan.[19] He understood Pilate's common-sense appraisal of his prisoner: "He's just a simple man [Pilate thought], probably just strayed out of the woods, a well-meaning, ordinary fellow."[20] The command to sacrifice Isaac affected Luther powerfully, because Abraham, he thought, must have had feelings similar to his own for his youngest, Martin. He not only knew how Abraham felt, but was also sure he had not dared inform Sarah of his intentions with their son.[21]

Just as great temptations went before great writing, Luther thought a competent reader had to know sufferings as well. He spoke most condescendingly of Jerome—how could a man who had lived in his favorable times possibly aspire to an understanding of that great sufferer Paul? "Jerome has a lot of quirks." He would have had to experience what Paul was talking about before he could have understood him. "Without the temptations of the devil, his violence and his tricks, we would not comprehend, either."[22] Luther's understanding of Abraham, David, Solomon, Paul, and others quite frankly arose from his identification with them. The students listening to the old professor lecturing on Genesis observed this method as applied to Noah.

Here was another of those instances where Moses "nodded," said Luther, for Genesis did not contain all he wanted his students to know, especially about Noah's activities before the flood. He could inform them that he had been a very busy man indeed. Luther detailed Noah's duties as "bishop of the church," as temporal ruler, and as paterfamilias.[23] He spoke most warmly on the charge of drunkenness which had been lodged against the patriarch.

Lyra [the great thirteenth-century interpreter] offers the excuse for Noah that he did not know the effects of wine, and took a little too much. But I don't think . . . Noah was ignorant of the nature of this drink. He had used it often in his family . . . I believe he occasionally outdid himself when drinking for relaxation.[24]

Luther refused to excuse Noah for this, but he assured his students that if he wanted to he could certainly do a better job than Lyra. He would say, for example,

> that a man heavy with years and exhausted by a multitude of daily tasks might be conquered by the wine he had become accustomed to. Wine conquers those more easily who are exhausted by labors or weighed down by years.

He was frankly incensed when Ham treated his father as senile. He enjoined his students "not to be offended when we see the saints fall, much less to gloat over the weakness of others . . . We are all one mass, and all of us born of one flesh."[25]

Being of one flesh with Noah permitted Luther to calculate that the old man had remained celibate until his mission began, only then to marry. By no means had he taken a wife out of lust—

> By divine command he accepted the girl, a little branch off the feminine stem, and begat three sons. It is written later on: "He found favor in the eyes of God." Else he who had abstained so long would have been able to abstain a little longer.[26]

It goes without saying that the reproaches Luther himself had suffered for drinking and for marrying contributed to his interpretation of Noah. It was Noah's faith, Luther knew, which enabled him

> to scorn the certainty of this world when it ridiculed him as a crazy old man. This faith commanded him to go right on with the building of the ark, which those giants ["There were giants in the earth in those days," Gen. 6:4] undoubtedly ridiculed as the height of stupidity. This faith so strengthed Noah that he stood alone against the judgment of all men.[27]

The professor was able to depict Noah's apparently crazy deeds in some detail and to recite the preachments of his detractors, concluding that

> It is useful to consider all this carefully, that we may be strengthened against the righteous outrage of the ungodly. The same things that happened to Noah are happening to us, too.[28]

All this embarrassingly total identification with Noah was not naive on Luther's part at all, but quite self-aware, even programmatic. He placed it before his students as an example for them to follow. He told them of events in the later life of Noah which were not in the Bible, saying, "Even if it is not recorded, it can be understood if we consider more carefully the deeds of our adversaries today."[29] Sectarians, he inferred, had plagued the patriarchs no less than the modern Christians!

Luther was sure it was impossible for anyone to comprehend scripture "unless it is brought home to him, i.e., unless he goes through the same experience."[30] Consequently, like a Renaissance painter, he dressed the patriarchs in sixteenth-century costume and set them down in Germany. Mount Horeb, he explained, "is a great mountain chain like our Thuringian or Bohemian Forest"; the wilderness through which Moses wandered, "like the plain between Wittenberg and Leipzig."[31] One summer's day when a distant thunderstorm approached, he required the boarders all to come out into the courtyard with him, the better to behold "coals of fire" in the clouds, and to appreciate Psalm 18.[32]

As popular author, Luther had taught the joy of reading and watched a literate populace develop in Germany during his lifetime. As interpreter, he began to make imaginative readers of his countrymen. His greatest influence, however, was in the humble (so it is often supposed) role of translator. The Bible carried Luther's example far beyond his homeland, imprinted his personal speech on the character of modern German. His theory of translation was of a piece with his philosophy of literature. If the text was to arouse genuine passion in the reader, then the translator like the interpreter must "bring it home." His freewheeling rejection of literalism was in harmony with his scorn for formularism, ceremony, and rules in every sphere. Mechanistic procedures were for him a sure sign that the substance was wanting—or not grasped by coldhearted pedants.

The Bible framed a very real universe for him. Events there recounted were utterly credible, awesomely immediate, and fraught with far-reaching significance. Since the original text had brought all this home to those who lived in its language, obviously it was up to him to produce equally genuine German. Following the rules and heeding the literal meaning might help—but then again it might not. He made famous the example of the Annunciation, "Hail Mary full of grace." In German, he maintained, you could talk about a barrel full of beer, all right, but not about a woman full of grace. He took mischievous delight in speculating about how pedants would tear their hair when he really translated it right, "Sweet Mary" (*du liebe Maria*). He doubted if there is any word in the sacred languages so expressive as German *lieb*.[33]

Did the archangel speak in a tongue blessed with such a beguiling adjective? Perhaps we, in a day when linguists have shown how interwoven are our thought processes with the language we speak, can appreciate Luther's rationale better than his contemporaries could.[34] They had the enlightened view we all know best from Huck Finn's effort to explain the various languages of the world to Nigger Jim. Huck's professorial show of cosmopolitan relativism was devastated by Jim's realistic: "Is a Frenchman a man, Huck? . . . Then why don't he talk like a man?"[35] It was Jim's view of language to which Luther accommodated the Bible. He makes all of them, from Moses to Paul, "talk like a man"—a man of the German Renaissance. He defended his practice with the notorious Lutheran verve, insisting that "translation must be free, retaining the sense, and conforming to the new wording while forgetting the old."[36] The most famous formulation of the doctrine was his statement that

> You do not have to ask the letter of the Latin alphabet how to talk German. You ask the mother at home, the children on the street, and the common man at the square, and translate accordingly. They understand you then, and know you are giving it to them straight.[37]

Such memorable formulations have led many to assume this was Luther's rule.

He detested rules. And he had tremendous appreciation for the unique perceptions and untranslatable idiom of ancient Hebrew.[38] He was always ready to commit quite un-German Hebraicisms where it seemed necessary for the reader to accept some Old Testament concept like "stumbling block."

God, what a great and troublesome task [he once sighed] to
force the Hebrew writers to speak German! They struggle
against forsaking their Hebrew culture and imitating German
barbarity, just like a nightingale forced to give up her exqui-
site song and imitate the detested monotone of the cuckoo.[39]

Like his emulator Tyndale, and with Tyndale the King James
scholars, he gladly enriched his native tongue with many an ancient Hebrew phrase.

Goethe was another German who did a great deal of translating. As son of the Enlightenment he formulated the problem
neatly:

There are two possibilities in translation. The one requires that
an author be brought over to us from his alien culture in such
a way that we can look upon him as one of our own. The
other makes rather the demand of us that we proceed over to
the foreigner and accustom ourselves to his life, ways of
speech, and culture.[40]

The great Bible translations have pursued both these goals at the
same time. The alien culture must be "brought over to us," but
the intent is not to accommodate the sacred text to our barbarian
ways. On the contrary, the Bible translation wished to change
our "life, ways of speech, and culture." How is it possible to
unite these conflicting goals? Luther claimed that, while knowing the language and its rules helps a lot, above all else the Holy
Ghost must assist.

Pedantic inability to fathom the linguistic feat did not in any
case prevent its coming to pass. Virtually every household in
Germany acquired the Hebrew classics in their modern vernacular. And the miracle—for had it not been thought impossible?—
was repeated throughout Europe. The practice of daily, family
Bible readings spread wherever the Bible went. Reading became
focal in the family structure of northern Europe, the hearth not
only for the Cotter's but also for the banker's Saturday Night.
This could not have occurred without the printing press, but it
was not the printing press brought it about. The source of the
miracle lay—as ever—in a gifted man's intellect and passion.

In one of his many novellas Thomas Mann pictures Moses as

not merely bringing down the tablets from Mount Sinai, but actually devising a written language in which to couch them. Similarly, it was the considered judgment of one of Luther's pupils that the doctor was the "father of the German language." The sobriquet stuck, and with good reason, but much to the consternation of language professors, who in their textbooks almost routinely caution that he did not, of course, "create German morphology and phonology."[41] His role in language history is, nonetheless, so very important that no discussion of his legacy to the German people would be complete without reference to it. Luther's was a mind of great energy, which drew together disparate historical developments. He "created" none of them, but out of their convergence did come something truly new.

In language history, two of the factors were that long-range growth of literacy we have talked about, and the economics of printing, which of course set a premium on generally understood, standard German. The flurry of pamphlet reading in the early 1520s, reinforced by the general familiarity with Luther's Bible, resulted in the normalization of German in accordance with his own middle German dialect. The standard modern language takes its beginnings there.

As chance would have it, Luther, the man who was actually turning out most of the printers' copy for nearly a generation, was especially favorably located in the motley patchwork of local dialects spoken by central Europe. Standard languages had already begun to emerge in some of the more compact nations like England and France. In the empire, the important norm was scribal usage in the imperial chancellery. At the time Luther translated his New Testament, the chancellery was in Meissen, under his own Frederick the Wise.[42] Saxony, moreover, had been populated relatively recently by Germans pressing eastward from the older dialect regions, so that the language here already offered a start toward the kind of compromise the printers needed among the various lands where they hoped to sell.

But normalization of usage, though important, was a minor matter compared with the creative germ of the language. In the Middle Ages German had not contained the vocabulary to permit a very refined level of intellectual or emotional discourse. The impulse whereby the words began to be evolved was a religious one. The German mystics had used the native stock of simple German to say things which had hitherto been couched in Latin. They wanted to show that religious concepts were intimate statements of the sort which any child must be able to utter. This kernel of mystic faith, that the highest truths are the simplest, reached its full flower in Martin Luther. His very first publication (1516) had been an edition of a well-loved mystic tract; his biblical scholarship sought the ultimate consequence of mystic, inward religiosity. The German public was quick to appreciate its implications and to participate in the religious discourse. Thus Luther's chief theological tenet was directly translatable into pamphlet and book sales, the mystics' conviction that religion is every individual's private, internal need being realized, through Luther's creativity and the new technology of print, on a broad, democratic base.

One long-range consequence was the passage into the vernacular of the great symbolic power which would eventually make it one of the world's chief poetic languages. This was most amusingly illustrated by a formal complaint lodged in 1539 by the Wardau town council against their pastor, John Reimann. They had suffered long from his righteous scolding, but when he began to hurl epithets from the pulpit, specifically, "lantern servants, stavemen, and torchbearers," that was too much. A generation earlier, these men (or their older cousins) would have been no more smitten by such biblical allusions than we are today. In the meantime, religious pluralism, literacy, and, above all, Bible reading had come to characterize protestant Germany. A new, highly compact symbolic language enabled writers and speakers to escape the cumbersome fetters of explicitness. The Wardau congregation immediately recognized the designations for those hirelings who had come to fetch Jesus from the Garden of Gethsemane. Reimann had told them,

> You are unthinking wretches, following self-serving leaders to do their shameful work for them. It is not in your interest. On the contrary. You are also committing a cruel act, terribly unworthy of you. It is a sin of immense, cosmic proportions.

He had said all that with "lantern servants, stavemen, torchbearers." Like a good flow chart, the new language was simple, succinct, and redundant. Symbolism was the Luther legacy with most far-reaching implications.[43]

The spate of little books which had made reading general in Germany could not pour on indefinitely. The positions had hardened. Public interest flagged. Bible reading, however, went on. The strange mixture of Old Hebrew and sixteenth-century German continued to characterize German literature for hundreds of years after Luther, and no doubt even today. The true blossoming of biblical language waited for that springtime of German letters, the early eighteenth century, when—for fascinating sociological reasons I will not discuss here—*every* single author of note was the son of a Lutheran pastor, with but one exception: the most passionately biblical of them all, Friedrich Gottlieb Klopstock. The author of Germany's major religious epic, Klopstock was the first to insist on the profound seriousness and religiosity of the poetic calling. He was a contemporary of Germany's first prolific and successful novelist, Christoph Martin Wieland, her first and greatest critic, Gotthold Ephraim Lessing, and the father of modern historiography, Johann Gottfried Herder, all pastors' sons deeply influenced by Luther, whose language they drew from his Bible to inspire a new, secular age.[44]

Reconciliation

We know more detail about Doctor Luther's last hours and "moment of bliss" than we know about the death of perhaps any other famous man. His passing was witnessed by trustworthy, articulate souls who regarded it as a turning point in history, of momentous importance. They refreshed one another's memory and long relived the experience with loved ones. They deemed it crucial for the world to know the circumstances, for a sudden or a violent end, with no time for prayer, would have impugned the divine approval of their master's life and work. Suicide indeed would have constituted Luther's own unequivocal rejection of all he had stood for—and rumors of his suicide had been circulating as much as a year before his death. An element of willfulness in the dying of Doctor Martinus cannot be denied, of course, consonant with the other ironies of his life.

His very longing for death had grown so imperious that he was finally going out to seek it impatiently and persistently, too restless to wait for its advent in his comfortable quarters in Wittenberg.

> It was not, my dear friends [Bugenhagen explained at the obsequies], only last night that Doctor Martinus began to die, but he had been dying for more than a year. He thought about death, preached about death, spoke of death, wrote of death . . . He called upon God frequently to remove him from this wicked world, the sooner the better, he was sick and tired of this life. He also prayed that he might not suffer long on the sickbed, if it pleased God.[1]

Bugenhagen saw the old man's restless shuttling to his homeland as the expression of his fervent longing for death there.[2] Other friends had observed how he was marking those passages in his Psalter concerning the promise of death, and they copied these out for their own benefit.[3]

When he had gone south the previous summer, he had thought he'd just stay there in his homeland until he died. Although he had let himself be persuaded to return to Wittenberg, the autumn had drawn him again into the hills of his childhood. That trip in November was followed by another at Christmas, ostensibly "that I may lie down in my coffin happily, having reconciled the dear lords of my land."[4] Again the loyal Melanchthon followed unwillingly along, his frail health forcing the two back to Wittenberg through one of the bitterest winters, and deep snow.[5] Toward the end of January, this time in response to an explicit request by the counts of Mansfeld for arbitration of their differences (until now, Luther seems to have been offering his services gratuitously), the doctor set out for his homeland one last time. It was during a proverbial January thaw; the rivers were rising and Kate was alarmed. This time their three sons went along.

> Dear Kate [Luther wrote two days after departure],
> We arrived in Halle today at eight, but did not continue on to Eisleben because a big Anabaptist [the Saale River] met us with waves and hunks of ice. She flooded the land and threatened to rebaptize us. We could not turn back home, because the Mulde was also high, so we must rest quietly here in Halle betwixt the waters—not that we are thirsty: we take refreshment and comfort in good Torgau beer and Rhenish wine, waiting to see whether the Saale will calm down . . . The devil resents us, and he is in the water—so better safe than sorry.[6]

Though death might be his quest, sudden death was abhorrent to the medieval mind. When the waters subsided and crossing the Saale became feasible, he mocked that the devil would certainly like to drown him and his three sons, together with Justus Jonas all at the same time.

An honor guard of 113 horse met the party at the Mansfeld border. Luther, weakened on the ferry, suffered a fainting spell in the coach, but upon arrival in Eisleben was revived by his favorite treatment, a rubdown with hot towels. He interpreted the attack as vindication of his mission, for, he said, the devil usually beset him on important occasions. His Germanic blend of taunting humor with dead seriousness remained characteristic of Luther until the end. He wrote,

> To my beloved wife, Catherine Luther, Mistress of the
> Doctor, of the Estate of Zülsdorf, of the Sow Market,
> and of whatever else she can master,
> Grace and peace in Christ, and my ancient love, impotent
> as I know it to be,
> Dear Kate,
> I was faint on the road close by Eisleben. It was my fault. But had you been there you'd have said the Jews were to blame, or their god. We had to pass through a village close by Eisleben where many Jews were dwelling—perhaps it was they blowing at me so hard. Right this minute here in Eisleben there are more than fifty Jewish residences. And it is a fact that when I passed that settlement such a cold blast came into the back of the coach and through my beret that I thought it would turn my brain to ice That probably aggravated my vertigo. But now I am, praise God, in good shape, except the pretty women are such a trial to me that I—have no problems with libidinousness whatsoever.[7]

Negotiations with the Mansfeld rulers—or, rather, with their legal counsels—consumed the next fortnight. Progress was good. Then, as is frequent in such proceedings, the talks became snagged on a remnant of stubborn disagreement. Luther slyly sent off instructions to Wittenberg for John Frederick to command his return. The ruse worked. On Valentine's Day of 1546 the old doctor actually succeeded in bringing the counts, long in a pout toward each other and not on speaking terms, to a fraternal reconciliation. Immensely proud of his accomplishment, he sent the good news off to Kate along with a package of trout from the local streams. A compact was signed on 16 February. Luther declared himself ready now to go home and give the worms a fine fat doctor to dine upon.[8] He had one day left to live.

With him during the final weeks had been only one of his old associates, Justus Jonas, now of Halle. Also present regularly was one of his older pupils, Michael Coelius, for he was pastor in Eisleben. Also native here was John Aurifaber, a young pupil who was to become famous as diligent compiler, translator, and free adapter of the *Table Talks*. These men all sensed the last moments of a uniquely grand figure in world history, and they were especially attentive to the eloquence of his pronouncements, "his high, dear words," as Jonas recalled.[9] The business at hand was indeed a most fitting epitome of his entire life. Here in the town of his birth the worldly rulers had enmeshed one another in legalistic trammels. Each had his troop of lawyers bent on exact justice, "suspecting poison in every syllable," Luther gibed. "You can call this disease we have contracted from the lawyers logomachy, or logomania."[10]

The formidable old negotiator relished his present role as mediator. His not to bother with the petty details of dispute, his but to hector the lawyers into what they, in his opinion, were most sedulously avoiding: agreement. He came to the sessions for only a few hours each morning, wrapped in his heavy fur-lined robes, a gold medallion around his neck and the doctor's beret on his head. No longer very robust, he had lost the sight in one eye to the cataract, but he was exceptionally quick-witted and still commanded the best ear for colloquial speech the world has ever known. He drew on an infinite repertory of proverbial wisdom. In that age when education revolved about debate, Doctor Martinus had held his own with the best, and still delighted in combining his great learning with the most grossly formulated practicality, all in that well-modulated, high-pitched voice.

The attentive Aurifaber took down certain of his metaphors for the finesse and flexibility desired at a bargaining table, e.g.,

If you want to pull a tree into the house, you don't grab it by the top. All the branches will catch at the door and jerk you back. Using force will just snap the branches. That's no way to pull a tree into the house. Here is the way you do it: you take hold of the trunk where you cut it down, then the branches will all bend together nicely, and you can pull it right in without any trouble.[11]

The folksy imagery disguised his source, but Luther was thinking about a passage from Aristotle, and the morning sessions kept reminding him of the same work. A few days later, Aurifaber overheard a conversation which pointed up the central irony in Luther's career. He had singled out the *Nicomachean Ethics* as Aristotle's greatest work. He especially appreciated Aristotle's concept of epikeia, that discretionary judgment we must use when applying general principle to specific cases. Lawyers, Luther knew, prefer formulaic, mechanistic administration of justice, "but what is a good magistrate, or a good prince? I say he is the living law. If he wants to act in accordance with the dead law and follow only what is in the books, then he'll make a lot of mistakes. That is why you have to have epikeia."

One of the lawyers quibbled. He did not advance his own opinion, but did quote a fourteenth-century authority, Baldus de Ubaldis, to the effect that "the man who makes arbitrary judgment is a beast, for he arrogates unto himself what were else left to the deliberation of many wise men."

"It is better for one man to be a beast," Luther retorted, "than for many men to be beasts."

Probably it was his friend Jonas who made bold to voice concern at this rash statement: "Herr Doctor, we are at this very moment being blamed for giving the laity power to make individual judgments about doctrine, because then they go ahead to arbitrate worldly affairs as well, so entangling their princes that no good comes of it. Everybody claims to be the man of 'reason.'"

But Luther remained firm. "We'll just have to see to it that a truly prudent person is at hand. You cannot dispense with epikeia."[12]

Epikeia, a concept which Luther had used during his entire professional life, had concerned him more and more after he cut himself loose from church authorities, until at last it grew into his most poetic, and perhaps his most important vision. He had encountered it first in the monastery as a quite specific provision for exceptions to canon law. One can still find an occasional scholarly treatise on epikeia in this sense, but Luther is never mentioned. I suppose this is because he devoted no special tract to the term. Nonetheless, he did develop epikeia more imagina-

tively than any other thinker. It became his recognition of inde-
terminancy in human affairs, and of the precious uniqueness in
each set of human circumstances—an insight which he always
expressed most aptly in imagery. Epikeia was Martin Luther's
final reconciliation of law with humanity in the business of the
world.

Aristotle had spoken of epikeia as a human quality exemplified
by flexibility in accommodating general, abstract law to the
specific case, or in ceding one's own strict rights in favor of set-
tling a dispute (hence Luther's metaphor of the tree in the
door). The church fathers, especially Thomas Aquinas and John
Gerson, elevated it to a stipulation as to when exceptions to
canon law are permissible; they specified just when one must
consult higher authority before invoking epikeia. Luther had
drawn on their interpretations during his years as Augustinian
vicar. When he became involved in temporal affairs from about
1520 on, epikeia was a frequent reference in his pleas for reasonable, equitable administration. His attempt to translate Paul's use
of the word in the Epistle to the Philippians had by this time
begun to broaden his understanding of the idea. He considered
Latin equivalents, *equitas, clementia, commoditas*, then confessed
he could find no better German word than *gelindickeyt*—
"gentleness":

> That is the virtue of accommodating oneself, of conforming to
> others and being like them, not trying to impose the standard
> and rule to which they must conform . . . Unyielding people,
> on the other hand, are the ungentle ones who make no excep-
> tions for others, but try to direct things according to their
> own way of thinking. They confuse everybody and are the
> cause of all strife and misery on earth. And then they claim
> they have done nothing except what was right! Even the pa-
> gans knew *summum jus summa injuria*.[13]

This Ciceronian aphorism, "extreme justice inflicts the greatest
wrong," was one of Luther's favorite quotations. Epikeia
shunned extremes.

He placed great value on experience in worldly affairs as our
best teacher of "gentleness," the essential quality in anyone entrusted with administering rules. This dimension of epikeia ex-

panded tremendously during the traumatic months of the peasants' uprisings in 1525, which seemed to fulfill, even to exceed all
the warnings from friend and enemy that Luther's resistance to
church authority would undermine all authority. Shaken, and
not yet fully appreciative of the power in the new pamphlet medium, he had indulged in unseemly outbursts against the peasants.
But the true horrors were yet to come: the German nobility exceeded the violence of Luther's language with their brutal atroci-
ties—indeed had already done so even while he was writing. He
was appalled by the indiscriminate slaughter and maiming.

"God demands epikeia, or equity in the laws," he declared,
"that we judge not according to the deed, but according to the
intention." Ignorant peasants had been drawn into mobs for a variety of extenuating reasons, and "true justice"—he was fond of
quoting Gregory—"is compassionate, false justice is vengeful."[14]
He had come to identify the classical Aristotelian concept of
epikeia with Christian charity. "Where the public peace is imperiled, let our queen and teacher, the moderator of the law who
bends it to mildness, be love." After a moment's reflection, he
added, "Of course, such moderation does call for heroic and singular men."[15]

He thought preachers, teachers, and lawyers should do all they
could to instill such courage, and by the late 1520s was setting an
example himself.[16] In a lecture on Deuteronomy 1:17, "The
judgment is God's," he pointed out,

> This verse is important for the civil magistracy as a comfort
> and admonition to the magistrate that he is not prosecuting his
> own ends, but divine ones, so that as an agent of God execut-
> ing a hallowed office he will all the more boldly make honest,
> straightforward judgments. Please note that by installing
> judges before he constituted laws God recommended epikeia
> to us. Judges are the living law, and superior to it . . . Into
> their hand is given both the law and the sword. This is to pre-
> vent applying the law in contravention of the law, as happens
> when silly people fix their gaze on the law, disregard the cir-
> cumstances of the case, and mouth: "Thus is it written, so be
> it."[17]

In his eagerness to embolden the magistrate to rely on his own
good judgment from case to case, Luther was encouraged both

by the prevailing doctrine of divine right and by the conscientious example of the Saxon sovereigns, Frederick the Wise, John, and even George—not to speak of John Frederick, groomed by Luther himself. Still, he was not unaware of the perils surrounding discretionary judgment in law.[18] He also agonized when his own attacks against legalism had come back to haunt him, even among his own pupils. At irritable moments in his later years he sometimes felt the strictest application of the law might be none too harsh.

Yet the importance of epikeia in his thinking continued to grow right up through those last February days in the town of his birth. It had become a major topic in the lectures on Genesis. A most characteristic passage began with the categorical statement that in the theological view—that is, insofar as he and his students were concerned—there was just no way of conceiving law except in connection with some man of good will giving thought to each individual application as it arises. Otherwise, the law will not be beneficial, but actually work woe. The old professor stated flatly, "A law which goes against love is not a law. Love is the mistress and the teacher of the law. She bids the law be silent in cases where following it without moderation might teach injustice instead of justice."

At this point in his delivery he cracked one of his favorite jokes about the proverbial new doctor who needs a fresh cemetery, the beginning diplomat who precipitates war, and the young theologian who populates hell—"Lacking experience, they do everything according to the rules."

The students looked up and smiled, but ducked assiduously back to their notes as the old doctor quickly followed up with the stern admonition: "So learn that peace and love must moderate and dispense all virtue and all law, just as Aristotle in the Fifth Book of his *Ethics* argues on epikeia."[19]

He was never at a loss for metaphors. Aristotle had made an obscure comparison of epikeia to a leaden measure used by stonemasons on the isle of Lesbos. Modern translators think it must have been some kind of flexible rod. Not so Luther, for whom "the Lesbian rule" was a synonym for epikeia. "That measure," he illustrated with a sketch on his slate, "reveals the fact that a tall building or a wall may be perpendicular from top to bottom even though individual stones here and there protrude beyond the plumb line." He also drew a tree to show how nature maintains an ideal trunk line despite interruptions by the branches. "A tree with knots sticking out is just as straight as a hewn timber."[20]

Of the kind of finagling necessary at Eisleben, he observed how "the birds fly straight to their goal, but the hunter sometimes has to go the long way around a mountain, or find a bridge, there being no other way."[21] Which represented epikeia in his mind, the circuitous path of the hunter, or the direct flight of the bird? Probably neither, but the acceptance of both as leading to the same goal in an appropriate way.

His entire life had been a rejection of rigidity. He even hooted at uniform spelling, and resisted the slightest formalism in matters that concerned him, such as the church.

> It is so easy for ceremony to grow into law [he brooded], and once the laws are laid down, they affect our conscience. They obscure and undermine the pure doctrine, especially when those who come after us are coldhearted, unlearned, and more interested in following the ceremony than in overcoming their own materialistic frame of mind.

How shall we take Doctor Luther's advice? Would he have us cast all regulations aside? Is there no fixed and unwavering guide for community or for individual?

A child of absolutistic times, he placed his trust in individual judgment, in the devoted father, in the experienced magistrate, and in the divinely appointed prince. It was up to them to correct failings as they arose, "not with laws, but by personal presence in accord with the will of God."[22] Did Luther, by making his concept of epikeia ultimately dependent on what seems to modern man an imponderable, remove his counsel from any court where modern problems are negotiated? We should not forget that for Luther, too, God was a remote imponderable. There came an epoch, beginning perhaps with the Industrial Revolution and certainly continuing into the twentieth century, when the Panglossian vision of a comprehensible world prevailed, governed by natural laws and peopled by rational beings. Imponderables now seemed irrelevant. Sensational feats of science and technology had made both nature and man appear tractable. But then physics, and shortly the biological sciences as well, uncovered a universe, and even in each of us a personal history, which clearly "pass human understanding." That is all, really, that Doctor Luther ever maintained about his own ultimate reality.

Biology has brought home to us the vast stretches of failure and pain out of which each rare, viable individual arises. Psychology reminds us of the measureless depths of unconscious being from which our thin surface cortex draws its moment of awareness. In the crisis of the late twentieth century we are awed by stark conflicts between the hasty works of human hands and that higher wisdom accumulated over the ages and faithfully recorded (as Doctor Luther held) in the bottom of every heart, or (as an evolutionist would put it) in a vast genetic pool of which any individual is the transitory creature.

Luther suffered a fainting spell at church. On the morning after the signing of a compact by the counts of Mansfeld, he did not join the others at the conference table as had been his wont, but rested on a little leather bed in his antechamber. From time to time he would arise and walk to and fro in prayer. He felt strong enough to go downstairs for the two main meals of the day. The company noted his musings and remembered them well. Twenty years, he said, was but a short interval. Yet it sufficed for the emptying of the world anytime man and woman should cease to come together in accordance with God's command. Little babes die by the thousands, he felt sure,

> but when I, Doctor Martinus, die at sixty-three, I don't think there'll be more than sixty or a hundred in the whole world who die with me . . . Well, all right, we old ones must live so long in order to look the devil in the ass.[23]

They asked him if they could expect to meet and recognize each other again in eternity. He, as usual, was loath to speculate on such subjects, but when pressed reminded them of Adam:

> He had never seen Eve in his whole life. He lay there asleep, and when he woke up he did not say, "Where do you come from?" or "What are you?" but, "Thou art flesh of my flesh

and bone of my bone." How did he know that? How did he know this woman was not sprung from out of the rocks?

Luther concluded that they would also know each other, "better than Adam did Eve."[24]

They had tired him with their questions. At eight o'clock he made his way back up the stairs to his room, where he lay down at a window to pray. His friends were unwilling to leave him alone, but spelled one another watching over him. When he complained of his heart, the solicitous Aurifaber remembered some unicorn horn (narwhal tusk) the countess had been accustomed to give her children for chest pains when he had been their tutor. He ran out to fetch some, and Jonas and Coelius went up to look after the beloved patient. They gave him his hot towel rub, and he said he felt better. Soon Count Albert of Mansfeld came, bringing the unicorn horn himself. He grated it and mixed some with wine. Given a spoonful of this remedy, Doctor Luther fell asleep about nine. An hour and a half later he awoke and, beholding his room occupied with anxious sentinels, urged them to go to bed. When they persisted in staying by him, he got up and went into the bedroom to be out of the night air. As he crossed the threshold he recited in Latin Psalm 31:5: "Into thy hands I commend my spirit. Thou hast redeemed me, Lord God of truth."

The featherbedding had been warmed for him. He gave his hand to each of his attendants in turn, and to his sons. Calling Jonas and Coelius by name, he asked them all to pray "for our Lord God and for his gospel, that it may fare well, for the council at Trent and the abominable pope do rage against it"— that general council of the church which had occupied so much of his time and thoughts for fifteen years had at last convened just a few weeks earlier.

The exhausted man slept for about two hours. Although the room was being kept heated, he awoke shortly after one o'clock feeling very cold, his heart anxiously aflutter. He said he thought he would never leave his birthplace again. He got up and returned to the antechamber, repeating that same little Latin formula as he crossed the threshhold, *In manus tuas commendo spiritum meum, redemisti me, domine Deus veritatis.* Presently he lay down on the little leather bed and was given a hot towel rub. He said it made him feel good to be kept warm. By this time a little crowd had accumulated, the host and his wife, the local count and countess with their physicians. Luther began to perspire. Coelius told him that this was a good sign, and he would soon be better. "Yes," Luther agreed. "It is the cold sweat of death. I'll give up the ghost now, for the illness increases." He began to pray:

O heavenly father, one God and father of our Lord Jesus Christ, thou God of all comfort, I thank thee that thou hast revealed thy dear son Jesus Christ to me, in whom I believe, whom I have preached and confessed, whom I have loved and lauded, whom the abominable pope and the godless defile, persecute, and blaspheme. I beg thee, my Lord Jesus Christ, to take my little soul. O heavenly father, though I must forsake this body and be torn from out of this life, I know for a certainty that I continue in thee and that none can tear me from thy hands.

He recited John 3:16, and Psalm 31:5, again in Latin.

Several of those keeping vigil possessed highly touted nostrums, in which they placed great faith. These were tried on Doctor Luther, but at about two o'clock he gasped three times, *In manus tuas commendo spiritum meum, redemisti me, domine Deus veritatis,* and answered no further queries. They shook him, rubbed his wrists with stimulants. Jonas called out to him loudly, "Reverend father, will you die steadfast in Christ, and in the doctrine you have preached?" All present thought they heard a perceptible "*Ja.*" He slept peacefully for about a quarter of an hour, so that some thought the crisis past. Others murmured that this was a sleep not to be trusted. Shortly his face grew ashen and, despite frantic efforts to revive him, he gave a deep sigh and moved no more.

It was between two and three o'clock in the morning of 18 February. Unseemly efforts were made to call, rub, and stimulate life back into the corpse. At four o'clock the remaining royalty and nobility of the district had arrived, and citizens of Eisleben were permitted to pass through the antechamber during the dawn hours to behold the earthly remains of Doctor Luther on the little leather bed. Later in the day he was washed and clad in a white gown, and the visits continued. In the meantime a great pewter coffin was being cast. The next afternoon (Friday), Doctor Luther was borne to church in it, followed solemnly by his sons, princes, counts, other nobility, and citizens. Here Justus Jonas, friend for thirty years, preached a funeral oration.[25]

From Jonas' perspective, Luther appeared first of all to be a genius who had employed his talents well. A powerful orator, an incomparable translator and writer who had "renewed the German language, so that German can again be spoken and written correctly."[26] Jonas recalled the depth and humility of Luther's intellect. He was most affected by how Luther had spent an entire year preparing for his death. Jonas wanted to impress on these listeners in Eisleben the grandeur of his personal association with Luther just in the past few months. He concluded his sermon with the contention that the death of such a man has to be received as a grave portent. It behooved Germany to search and cleanse its soul, to avert calamity. It was a simple sermon, quite in Luther's spirit. Jonas had not sought to mourn the death, but to edify the congregation.

On Saturday Pastor Coelius preached a well-organized sermon on Isaiah 57: "The righteous perisheth, and no man layeth it to heart." First he told something of Luther's background and accomplishments as the reformer of a corrupt church. Noting then the gossip already circulating about circumstances of the death, he gave his own detailed personal witness. As local pastor, Coelius enjoyed absolute credibility with the assemblage, and he took this opportunity to render his testimony publicly, for all to hear. Next, he raised the question which his flock might reasonably ask: why should God take Luther away just at the moment when his leadership seemed most urgently needed? This gave the pastor occasion to dwell comfortingly on the various kinds of benefit God accomplishes when he removes our loved ones from this life. In conclusion, Coelius expressed his belief that Luther's death must be understood as a grave admonition to the living that the time was at hand for their repentance and conversion.

The counts of Mansfeld had understandably hoped to bury their countryman here at his birthplace, but a sharply worded dispatch from the prince elector of Saxony (not lacking reference to the Mansfeld spat as cause of the dear man's death) demanded return of the body to Wittenberg. Accordingly, the coffin was lifted up immediately after Coelius' sermon and, amid song and weeping, borne out beyond the city gates, where a procession led by fifty-five mounted men set out across the gray, wintry countryside. Wherever the train passed through a village, church bells tolled out and the peasants came forth to accompany Doctor Luther on his last journey. When the city gates of Halle hove into view, a throng came out to receive him. The press in the narrow streets was such that it took hours to reach the Church of Our Lady, where the pall was greeted by strains of Luther's own hymn, *Aus tiefer Not schrei ich zu dir*. Sunday at dawn, beneath the deafening knell of all the church bells in Halle, and accompanied by the city council, the preachers, teachers, and schoolchildren, the procession departed. By noon it had reached John Frederick's border, where he and the dignitaries of his land waited in stately assemblage. The march which crossed the Elbe into Wittenberg on Monday was led by the prince elector and a tremendous troop of horse. The funeral car was followed by a coach carrying Kate and her entourage of ladies. Other members of the family strode solemnly along behind them. Then came the dignitaries of the university and the young noblemen who were studying there, then Chancellor Gregory Brück, the important theologians Philip Melanchthon, John Bugenhagen Pomeranus, Caspar Cruciger, and other university faculty and students, then the Wittenberg city council, other citizens, wives, and children. Thousands of mourners had by this time converged on Wittenberg. The great pewter coffin was at last laid in the castle church, where Doctor Luther was to be buried before his pulpit.

In what appeared to be an uncharacteristically short sermon for John Bugenhagen, but what were in fact only his characteristically prolix opening remarks, this old friend recalled how Luther had hoped for a gentle death and had been granted the wish. The main address was by Philip Melanchthon.

True to the humanist philosophy, Philip made a serious attempt to frame his mentor in a comprehensive historical context. In every epoch, he averred, beginning with Adam's, God has awakened his defenders of the faith. "Just as in a battle phalanx, whenever one member has been removed from the front line, another has stepped forward to take his place." Philip presented the conventional view of history, recalling how the Old Testament patriarchs, judges, kings, and prophets had been succeeded "by John the Baptist, by Christ himself, and the apostles. It is profitable and pleasant to contemplate this beautiful order and succession of supreme individuals on earth." In more recent times there came the church fathers and, although our "last, weakest age of the world is much more fragile than the earlier ones, God has always retained a few through whom he renews the doctrine of the church." Doctor Martinus, in Melanchthon's view, "should reasonably be counted in the number and sequence of these high, excellent people whom God has appointed and sent." The pure Christian gospel had been most clearly laid forth by five men, he felt: Isaiah, John the Baptist, Paul, Augustine, and Doctor Luther.[27]

Melanchthon now turned a substantial portion of his sermon to a defense of the harsh, coarse writings of the last of these, which he would "neither deny nor excuse, nor praise, but answer as Erasmus often did, 'God gave the world in these latter days, when grave and acute illness and failings prevail, a harsh, severe physician.'"[28] He freely granted that Luther had written too violently, but protested that the human being he had known in private was ever kind and gentle, never quarrelsome. In his description of Luther's personal attributes Philip for the first time waxed a bit fulsome, despite his obvious resolve to remain academic. Filial devotion, which had characterized his relationship to Luther for so much of his life, showed through when he confessed, "we are now entirely poor, wretched, forsaken orphans, who had a dear, noble man as our father, and are bereft."[29] Like the speakers before him, he closed with the sincere observation that the death of such a man has throughout history "often meant great punishment for posterity."[30]

It was natural for those so close to this illustrious figure to see his legacy, when they tried to assess it during the days immediately following his death, in the context of their own efforts to further the good. Even Melanchthon, clearly struggling to place his spiritual father in the largest possible perspective, also spoke exclusively in terms of church history. Of course, the "church" in his view encompassed much more of human experience than we are accustomed to allow it today. Luther himself, as the efforts of his last weeks testified, interpreted his task on earth very broadly. Found in his rooms after his death were certain notes jotted down sometime after the negotiations in Eisleben, which give us some idea of his thinking in this regard. They are held to be the last lines he wrote.

Those hours at the conference table had again brought the old debater face to face with the ultimate question: what is there in this world that we can rely upon? Are not all statements about human affairs made by humans themselves? And what a beggarly lot we humans are! We see things only as they relate to our tiny niche in time and place, so that our silly proclivity to utter general truths is invariably confuted by the experience of others whose world is different from ours. Even the Bible, so great a classic, must be interpreted in accordance with our limited experience, like any other literary monument. Who can understand even the Roman classics, he had wondered during his last hours in Eisleben.

None can comprehend Virgil in his *Bucolics* and *Georgics* who has not first been a herdsman or a farmer for five years. Furthermore, none comprehends Cicero in his letters who has less than twenty years' experience in a principality of some size. Let none think he has sufficiently tasted Holy Scripture unless he has governed the church with the prophets for a hundred years! Ah, great is the wonder—first of John Baptist, then of Christ, and third, of the apostles. Lay no hand on this divine *Aeneid*. Rather, fall down on your knees and worship at its footsteps. For we are truly beggars.[31]

We weak, dull instruments in God's ark and tabernacle, we lower lights and lanterns, we must help focus the gleam of the grand candles, and polish their globes. For lights both great and small adorn God's firmament, where lightning, hail, cloud, and storm wind execute his word and command.

JOHANNES MATHESIUS
(Luther's first protestant biographer)

EPILOGUE

A biography pure and simple must seem an unusual pebble cast among the towering crags of theological and historical scholarship about Martin Luther. His was a figure of such colossal importance for those disciplines, and they in turn so dominate Luther studies, that would-be biographies often turn out to be theological or historical chips themselves. As biographer, I have tried to offer no more than a characteristic impression of Doctor Luther. His personality may well have implications for current writers on those subjects, but it was not for me to argue such points.

In an earlier biography (of the German poet Wolfgang Goethe) I set forth my notions as to just what a biography ought to accomplish, and how. I followed the same principles in this book. In essence they amount to my assumption that biography seeks an authentic impression of life, of the same sort one receives from living men and women. No one comes before us as a résumé in chronological narrative, but as an individual characterized by a particular time of life. Biography must be best served when the writer can seize on his subject at an especially characteristic moment, if possible one at which a personality itself sensible of its own former epochs was able to come to terms with them. The mature Luther, looking back over his career, achieved a comprehensive vision of one man in his time. I have tried to pass it on.

Luther helped me to recognize that my understanding of the biographer's task is in fact embedded in a larger ideal of what studies in general should accomplish, and how. Luther's life is nearly a half millennium removed from ours, and his conceptions, strange at first, may guide us to a better perspective on our own. Today, for example, a bright era of science and scholarship is dedicated to a good life for all men and women on earth. This Luther would regard as an aspiration unique to our era. For him, learning was by no means a servant to the world, but a refuge from it. His was a traditional attitude shared by other reflective men. Albert Einstein, for example, looking back on his life, recalled the attraction of physics in this way:

> As a fairly precocious young fellow I became acutely aware of the vanity of hope and striving, which drives most men restlessly through life. I also perceived the cruelty of such effort, which hypocrisy and glittering words concealed more carefully in those days than they do now.

In "Notes" which might have been set down by Martin Luther four hundred years earlier, Einstein speaks of his initial resort to conventional religion, and how it had not withstood his youthfully critical scrutiny. "It is clear to me now," he goes on, "that the thus lost paradise of youth was a first attempt to free myself from the 'Merely Personal,' from an existence dominated by desires, hopes and primitive emotions." He never willingly spoke of these "merely personal" developments, and touched on them here solely by way of explaining the tremendous attraction studies held for him. Here he could flee to a harmonious sphere, to that beautiful order glimpsed by Kepler, Galileo, Newton—more: he had been called further to simplify and generalize those universal laws. Over the ages, this has probably been the goal of all sincere studies, the solace of that final oneness, not to be found in the world. I am sure it is also the ultimate appeal of biography.

What wonder if the physical sciences boast more impressive progress toward the common goal than humane studies can, which are still in a most primitive state? The "objects" of our investigations are not objects at all, but are themselves perceiving minds! Each has assimilated its different experiences in its own unique way. A humanist must renounce all intention of bringing them into harmony with his own mentality. This act of resignation, itself bitter enough, is only the beginning of humane studies. Their end is to apprehend remote and alien minds, to try to look out on the world in those strange, unaccustomed ways. This is not seeking harmony in the outer world at all, but is at best an attempt to expand the individual experience of it. I understand biography in this epistemic sense.

By that I mean biography places on the reader the impossible demand that he change his mind. It can be a reasonable demand only when the reward is proportionate. Doctor Luther's was a mind of exceptional power and devotion. Appreciation of his views can move us to sympathy with a sector of the human experience which we had thought to scorn. We must allow for the possibility that Luther's vital concerns were, at some human level, identical with our own.

In this rationale for biography I found a fairly clear obligation for the biographer. He is the one who is acquainted with both worlds, that of his subject and that of his reader. It is up to him to make the community of interests apparent. This, I think, is why each generation must write history anew, including the biographies. It would be too much to ask Doctor Luther to agree with posterity in every successive epoch, but we can ask that he at least recognize some of our problems—that is enough. I found a first reconciliation between Luther and industrial man on the subject of the law. As American society became complex, its regulation growing more crucial and at the same time more intricate, we at last equaled and perhaps even exceeded the labyrinthine involutions of the monstrous Renaissance officialdom that called itself the church. While Luther's life presented a wide range of themes, I naturally perceived those as dominant which my time and place can best comprehend, like the law.

For my era, I was not thus distorting Luther's essentially religious orientation. On the contrary, to present the man as merely religious in the current, often narrowly pious sense would have been a misrepresentation to my contemporaries. For his age religion was the all-embracing institution, by no means yet sequestered into its carefully defined pale. Perhaps for the twentieth century, law alone functions so universally as religion did in the sixteenth. Society subjects both of these institutions to human wisdom, even though both clearly transcend any society. Men are constantly tempted to enlist religion and law in the service of transitory conceptions of the good. This human tendency has changed little since the Renaissance. In his vigorous criticism of mere human understanding, and in his humbling the arrogance which ever characterizes the human mind, Martin Luther took his place among the classical thinkers of our civilization.

et mortuus vivit!

MELANCHTHON

Solomon is certainly right when in the last chapter of Ecclesiastes he says: "Of making many books there is no end; and much study is a weariness of the flesh," but this should be applied only to immature books by people like me who are not yet sufficiently learned and experienced. [Their books are] like stung fruit to be eaten by hogs under the trees before it is half ripe. I have these thirty years seen very many books which are no longer remembered or retained. Yet there have at no time been too many good books, nor are there now, and we do have from the Lord his certain commandment to search the scripture, likewise Saint Paul admonishes Timothy not to cease reading. Now such searching and reading is not possible except with pen in hand, that we may note down what particulars occur to us in reading, mark them, and retain them.

DOCTOR LUTHER, 1543

NOTES

ABBREVIATIONS FOR FREQUENTLY CITED WORKS

Quotations from Martin Luther are in my own translations from the Weimar edition:

WA   *D. Martin Luthers Werke: Kritische Gesamtausgabe.* 58 vols. Weimar: Böhlau, 1883– .

TR   *Tischreden.* 6 vols. Weimar: Böhlau, 1912–19.

WA Bible   *Die Deutsche Bibel.* 12 vols. Weimar: Böhlau, 1906–61.

WAB   *Briefwechsel.* 14 vols. Weimar: Böhlau, 1930– .

ARG   *Archiv für Reformationsgeschichte.* Gütersloh: Gerd Mann, 1903– .

CR   *Corpus Reformatorum.* 96 vols. Halle and Leipzig: Heinsius, 1834–1918.

KK   Julius Köstlin. *Martin Luther: Sein Leben und Schriften.* 5th ed., rev. by Gustav Kawerau. 2 vols. Berlin: Duncker, 1903.

Kolde   Theodor von Kolde. *Analecta Lutherana. Briefe und Aktenstücke zur Geschichte Luthers.* Gotha: Perthes, 1883.

Nuntia-turen   Walter Friedensburg, ed. *Nuntiaturberichte aus Deutschland. Erste Abtheilung 1533–1559.* Vol. 1: *Nuntiaturen des Vergerio 1533–1536.* Gotha: Perthes, 1892.

SVR   *Verein für Religionsgeschichte. Schriften.* Halle and Leipzig: Heinsius, 1883– .

Volz   Hans Volz, ed. *Urkunden und Aktenstücke zur Geschichte von Martin Luthers Schmalkaldischen Artikeln (1536–1574)*. Berlin: de Gruyter, 1957.

Walch   Johann Georg Walch, ed. *Dr. Martin Luthers sämtliche Schriften*. Rev. ed. 22 vols. Saint Louis: Concordia, 1881–1903.

NOTES

APPROACH FROM THE SOUTH

1. The letter of recommendation is quoted by Christian Heinrich Sixt, *Petrus Vergerius, päpstlicher Nuntius, katholischer Bischof und Vorkämpfer des Evangelium's. Eine reformationsgeschichtliche Biographie* (Braunschweig: Schwetschke, 1855), p. 9. Anne C. J. Schutte, *Pier Paolo Vergerio: The Making of an Italian Reformer* (Geneva: Droz, 1977), focuses on Vergerio's conversion. Our best treatment of the younger Vergerio is Walter Friedensburg's introduction to the *Nuntiaturen*, pp. 12–34.

2. TR 4, 650, 22.

3. Walch 16, 1889–90.

4. Various biographies offer accounts of the visit, but all appear to rely on KK 2, 370–76. Johannes Sembrzycki, "Der Nuntius Vergerio und seine Begegnung mit Luther im Jahre 1535," *Beilage zur Allgemeinen Zeitung* 1, 61 (12 March 1892), 1–3, also has nothing new to offer.

5. Spalatin's report is in CR 2, 982–89=No. 1364, dated 30 November. Also Walch 16, 1893–99. Irmgard Höss, *Georg Spalatin, 1484–1545: Ein Leben in der Zeit des Humanismus und der Reformation* (Weimar: Böhlau, 1956), judges that Vergerio was not granted his private audience with John Frederick until the next day. I believe she was misled by the date of Vergerio's written summary, requested by John Frederick (which she does not mention).

6. Vergerio's report is in *Nuntiaturen*, pp. 539–47, in Italian.

7. This is a letter to Duke Christoph of Württemberg, 29 February 1558, in *Briefwechsel zwischen Christoph, Herzog von Württemberg, und Petrus Paulus Vergerius*, ed. by Eduard von Kausler and Theodor Schott, Bibliothek des litterarischen Vereins in Stuttgart 124 (Tübingen: Hiersemann, 1875), 162.

8. Luther first recalls the Vergerio visit in a letter to Justus Jonas on 10 November (WAB 7, 322, 5–11), characterizing his own demeanor. On 3 December (WAB 7, 330, 8–16), he offers Melanchthon a snatch of the conversation. There is another recollection as late as February 1537 (WAB 8, 36, 32–33). At table, Vergerio is mentioned in March of 1536 (TR 3, 401, 19), May of 1540 (TR 4, 588, 24–25), and then perhaps nine years later (TR 5, 636, 24–32) Luther recalls that Vergerio agreed with him on a major point. Pomeranus's joke is TR 3, 362, 8–10.

9. The Wittenberg report is TR 5, 633–35. Melanchthon probably had access to the same source, and writes that Luther spoke "libere de Romana Tyrannide cum nuncio," but promises to give the whole story in person (CR 2, 973).

10. Sarpi wrote under a pseudonym, *Historia del Concilio Tridentino de Pietro Soave Polano*. I used the 4th ed., revised and corrected by the author (Geneva: Chouët [1660]), pp. 73–78.

INVITATION TO BREAKFAST

1. WAB 7, 172, 13–14 and WAB 7, 239, 10–12. My assumption that the barber who attended early on 7 November was Andreas Engelhard is conjecture. This is the barber most intimate with Luther, and most likely to speak jocularly with him. One of the wealthiest men in Wittenberg, Engelhard was a familiar presence in the Luther household (e.g., TR 3, 369, 25ff., and n. 3). Luther's beloved old barber Petrus had been exiled from Wittenberg the previous summer. Speaking against my conjecture is the fact that John Aurifaber, including this report in his supplement to Luther's works in 1566, followed his usual habit of supplying additional information (often covering his tracks by putting his addenda into Luther's own mouth), and called the barber Heinrich. A barber Heinrich is attested in

Wittenberg during Aurifaber's time with Luther a decade later, but we have no reason to think he was on the familiar terms which this scene requires. It does not do to follow Aurifaber too trustingly, just because he was on the spot during Luther's last years. Joseph Lortz, for example, in his great history of the Reformation, places Vergerio's visit to Wittenberg in 1533. While a papal nuncio did come to Wittenberg in that year, it was not Vergerio, nor did this nuncio see Luther. I can account for Lortz's error only by tracing it to Aurifaber, who also puts Vergerio in Wittenberg in 1533. Aurifaber just got his Italian nuncios mixed up, not having himself been in Wittenberg in the early 1530s.

2. TR 5, 633–34. For Luther's clothing see *Nuntiaturen*, p. 541.
3. Walch 16, 1891.
4. TR 2, 482, 6–8.
5. TR 5, 510, 19–30.
6. TR 3, 631, 1–3.
7. TR 4, 290, 18–21.
8. TR 5, 510, 6–7.
9. TR 4, 588, 24–25.
10. WAB 8, 36, 32–34.
11. *Nuntiaturen*, p. 541.
12. *Nuntiaturen*, p. 542.
13. Sarpi, pp. 73–78.
14. WAB 7, 330, 8–16; WAB 7, 322, 5–11; *Nuntiaturen*, p. 542; TR 3, 401, 16–17. Nicholas Schomberg is not so well known as Bishop Fisher, but one finds a note on him in Sebastian Giustinian, *Four Years at the Court of Henry VIII*, tr. by Rawdon Brown (London: Smith & Elder, 1854), pp. 61–62.
15. TR 5, 634, 8–21—these words are among the best attested at the meeting.
16. *Nuntiaturen*, p. 546; Sarpi, pp. 73–74; TR 5, 636, 24–32.
17. TR 5, 634, 23–32.
18. TR 5, 636, 31–32.
19. TR 5, 634, 33–36.
20. *Nuntiaturen*, pp. 541, 547.
21. TR 5, 635, 1–2.

THE CALM AFTER A STORM

1. *John M. Todd, Martin Luther. A Biographical Study* (New York: Paulist Press, 1972), p. 316 for the quotation beginning this chapter. Paul J. Reiter, *Martin Luther. Umwelt, Charakter und Psychose*, 2 vols. (Copenhagen: Levin & Munkegaard, 1940). Julius Köstlin=KK. Roland Bainton, the most affectionate of Luther's biographers, devoted scarcely one twentieth of his well-known *Here I Stand* (New York: Abingdon, 1950) to the last third of Luther's adult life. The popular Richard Friedenthal, *Martin Luther* (Munich: Piper, 1967) gave slightly more space to the man in his fifties, calling it "old age." After finishing my manuscript I read the posthumously published *Martin Luther in der Mitte seines Lebens* (Göttingen: Vandenhoeck & Ruprecht, 1979), by the grand old man of Luther studies in Germany, Heinrich Bornkamm. Here we have a most detailed study of Luther in his forties. It will be the standard reference for the important decade between Worms and Augsburg.
2. *Nuntiaturen*, pp. 540–41.
3. TR 6, 301, 16–18.
4. WAB 5, 316, 16–18.
5. TR 4, 489, 33–35.
6. WAB 5, 241, 82–87.
7. TR 2, 187, 3–5.
8. Gilbert Creighton, "When Did Renaissance Man Grow Old?" *Studies in the Renaissance* 14 (1967), 7–32, discusses the various errors moderns have made by failing to take into account the era's own concept of aging.
9. WAB 8, 291, 5–6, and 292, 18–21.
10. TR 4, 325, 22–24. In the six years 1530–35 he averaged over two publications a month (a bit higher than in the previous years). Some seventy to eighty letters per year from his pen have survived, but he must have written more. All this aside from the great Bible translation, which at last appeared in 1534 complete, although revision continued. Kurt Aland's *Hilfsbuch zum Lutherstudium*, 3rd ed. rev. (Witten: Luther-Verlag,

1970), pp. 647–69, lists the works chronologically. Omitting multiple editions, as well as separate sermons and lectures, one can abstract the following figures:

Year	Publications	Letters	Year	Publications	Letters
1530	46	172	1539	24	109
1531	27	116	1540	16	55
1532	27	86	1541	14	59
1533	18	79	1542	18	87
1534	22	79	1543	23	74
1535	21	87	1544	19	54
1536	12	94	1545	24	58
1537	31	53	1546	6	17
1538	19	66			

A fair generalization might be to say that the average of twenty publications per year remained constant until his death in February of 1546. For more detail, one might consult Alfred Dieck, "Luthers Schaffenskraft," *Luther* 27 (1956), 35–39.

11. WAB 7, 348–50 and n. 26 on p. 350.
12. WA 26, 530, 7–19.
13. WA 50, 109, 14–23. See also WA 38, 271, 2–8.
14. TR 5, 23–24.
15. WA 8, 685, 6–11. See also WAB 6, 355, 5–6, and WAB 5, 43–45.
16. TR 3, 512, 24–29.
17. TR 4, 397, 6–14.
18. KK 2, 255.
19. KK 2, 282.
20. WAB 7, 249, 3–13.
21. TR 5, 77–78, 10–13.
22. Kolde, p. 378, quotes the advice of a courier to George of Anhalt not to visit Luther in his home.

PARALIPOMENA AFTER PART ONE

TR 2, 197, 14–17.
TR 4, 306, 21–25.
TR 5, 121, 2–6.
TR 3, 434–35.

TR 4, 591, 18–20.
TR 5, 291, 11–12.
TR 2, 264, 16–19.
TR 3, 587, 2–4.

SONG AND DEVOTION

1. WA 54, 179, 11–12.
2. The strophes I translate here are WA 35, 560, 29–33 and 461, 9–12. The air is on p. 525. The editors say it "could be" by Luther.
3. WA 3, 549, 33–35.
4. TR 2, 518, 6–7; WA 19, 50.
5. WA 18, 123, 22–24.
6. WAB 7, 145, 9–19; TR 3, 371–72; TR 5, 130, 1–5; etc.
7. TR 1, 86, 11–12; TR 1, 490; TR 4, 32, 19–20; WAB 5, 639, 20.
8. TR 2, 11–12.
9. WAB 5, 639.
10. WAB 5, 321.
11. According to WA 35, 80.
12. John L. Nuelsen, *John Wesley and the German Hymn*, tr. by Theo Parry et al. (Keighley: Mantissa Press, 1972).
13. WA Bible 3, 125, 15.
14. WA 38, 358–59.
15. WA 38, 362–64.
16. WA 38, 372, 27–31.
17. WA 38, 373, 5.
18. WA 38, 373, 16–32.

SCHOLARSHIP

1. John M. Todd, *Reformation* (London: Barton, Longman & Todd, 1972), is representative. Todd is also a Luther biographer.
2. WA Bible 10/1, 100, 7–14.

3. Carl Krause, *Helius Eobanus Hessus. Sein Leben und seine Werke* (Gotha: Perthes, 1879).

4. WAB 8, 107, 12–13, 17–18, 20–24, and 107–8.

5. WA 31/1, 67, 9–10.

6. WA 31/1, 69, 8–10 and 69–70.

7. WA 31/1, 71, 3–7.

8. WA 31/1, 72, 5–14.

9. WA 31/1, 75, 1–5.

10. TR 2, 40, 22–27.

11. WA 31/1, 95–96.

12. WA Bible 3, 4, 18–19.

13. WA Bible, 3, lxii, 9 and 15–19.

14. TR 4, 323, 1–5.

15. WA Bible 3, 150, 13–16.

16. TR 3, 244, 12–16.

17. WA Bible 3, xxxix, 16–17.

18. WA Bible 3, xxx–xxxi.

19. WA 38, 10, 21–29.

20. WA 38, 13, 22–30.

21. In addition to the examples given above, one might look at verse 9 of this same psalm, or Psalm 118:27. There are numerous other examples.

22. WA 38, 16, 23.

23. This is from Melanchthon's preface to the (posthumous) edition of Luther's Latin works. I translate from Walch 14, 464.

24. TR 2, 346, 17–19.

25. TR 5, 183, 27.

26. Max Beyna, *Das moderne katholische Lutherbild* (Essen: Ludgerus, 1969), p. 84.

GLOSS

1. Johannes Mathesius, *Luthers Leben in Predigten*=Vol. 3 of his *Ausgewählte Werke*, ed. by Georg Loesche (Prague: Koch, 1898), p. 298.

2. WA 6, 329, 29–32.

3. WA 6, 331f.; WA 6, 330, b.

4. WA 6, 332, g.

5. WA 6, 336, 9–10, and e.

6. WA 6, 347, 22–26.

7. WA 8, 267, 7–11.

8. E.g., WA 14, 141–54.

9. TR 4, 18, 22–26.

10. WAB 5, 232, 18–23.

11. WAB 5, 235, b.

12. WAB 5, 235, f.

13. WAB 5, 235, g.

14. WAB 5, 235, k.

15. WAB 5, 235, m.

16. WAB 5, 235, q.

17. WAB 6, 117f.

18. TR 2, 120, 9–10.

19. TR 5, 311, 8–9.

20. There are two scholarly investigations of these episodes. Paul Zimmermann, "Der Streit Wolf Hornungs mit Kurfürst Joachim von Brandenburg und Luthers Beteiligung an demselben," *Zschr. für preussische Geschichte und Landeskunde* 20 (1883), 310–43; Rudolf von Jacobi, "Die Flucht der Kurfürstin Elisabeth von Brandenburg," *Hohenzollern Jahrbuch* 13 (1909), 155–96. Also see Hermann Kunst, *Evangelischer Glaube und politische Verantwortung. Martin Luther als politischer Berater* (Stuttgart: Evangelisches Verlagswerk, 1976), pp. 319–27.

ON BEHALF OF CHILDREN AND YOUTH

1. WAB 5, 286, 17–24.

2. WAB 5, 289, 1–2 and 20–24.

3. WAB 5, 290f., 5–44.

4. WA 51, 223, 22–27.

5. WAB 7, 163–64.

6. WA 51, 243, 31–35, and note.

7. TR 3, 353, 16–17.

8. WA 50, 452, 14–19.

9. WA 50, 452–53.

10. WA 50, 453, 19–24.

11. TR 4, 126, 7–8.

12. E.g., WA 38, 134, 18–19; WA 54, 186, 25–27.
13. WA 30/2, 547, 23–27.
14. WA 30/2, 549, 24–26.
15. WA 30/2, 561–62.
16. WA 30/2, 567, 22–35.
17. WA 30/2, 570–71.
18. WA 30/2, 574, 16–17.
19. WA 30/2, 575–76.
20. WA 30/2, 576, 32.
21. WA 30/2, 577, 21–31.
22. WA 30/2, 584, 18–20 and 27–31.
23. WA 30/2, 585–86.
24. WAB 5, 377–78.

THE GERMAN MACHIAVELLI

1. A recent treatment of Frederick is by Heinrich Bornkamm, "Kurfürst Friedrich der Weise," ARG 64 (1973), 79–85. Many volumes have gone to the subject of Luther and the state, not to speak of the immense detailed work evoked each time Luther is accused of, or credited with, influence on some current situation. Here are a few works with which the interested reader might begin. William A. Mueller, *Church and State in Luther and Calvin* (Nashville, Broadman, 1954); Luther H. Waring, *The Political Theories of Martin Luther* (Port Washington, N.Y., Kennikat, 1968); Walter Ellinger, *Luthers politisches Denken und Handeln* (Berlin: Evangelische Verlags-Anstalt, 1952); Gerd Fesser, various articles, of which the most accessible is "Luthers Stellung zur Obrigkeit, vornehmlich im Zeitraum von 1525 bis 1532," in *450 Jahre Reformation*, ed. by Leo Stern and Max Steinmetz (Berlin: Aufbau, 1967), a volume which contains other essays illuminating the subject from the Marxist angle; Walther von Loewenich, "Luthers Stellung zur Obrigkeit," in *Luther und die Obrigkeit*, ed. by Gunther Wolf (Darmstadt: Wissenschaftliche Buchgesellschaft, 1972), another volume with many relevant articles; and Heinz Horst Schrey, *Reich Gottes und die Welt: Die Lehre Luthers von den zwei Reichen* (Darmstadt: Wissenschaftliche Buchgesellschaft, 1969).
2. TR 5, 380, 6–17.

3. WA 51, 203–4.
4. WA 51, 204, 10–13.
5. WA 51, 204, 21–22.
6. WA 51, 214, 29–35.
7. WA 51, 217, 10–11.
8. TR 2, 509–10.
9. WA 51, 219, 24–26 and 249, 21–22.
10. WA 51, 220, 10–16.
11. WA 51, 205, 16–22.
12. WA 51, 226, 36–39.
13. WA 51, 236, 12–14.
14. WA 51, 237, 25–27.
15. WA 51, 240, 13–20.
16. WA 51, 258, 8–15.
17. WA 51, 212, 14–20.
18. WA 51, 245, 20–29.
19. TR 5, 496, 31–35. See also TR 5, 681, 35–37.
20. WA 51, 254, 9–12.
21. WA 51, 255, 15–19 and 35–39.
22. WA 51, 256, 26–31.
23. WA 51, 257, 5–7.
24. WA 51, 259, 19.
25. WA 51, 262, 31.
26. WA 51, 263, 24–26.
27. WA 51, 264, 2–5.
28. WA 51, 264, 10–14.

SATIRE

1. WA 38, 197, 17–21.
2. According to the article on the Mass in the *New Catholic Encyclopedia*.
3. Most notably in *On the Babylonian Captivity of the Church*, WA 6, 497–573, but also after that writing, e.g., in his dismissal of the silent mass, WA 18, 22–36.
4. WA 38, 185, 7–8.
5. WA 38, 185, 10.
6. WA 38, 188, 6–9.
7. WA 38, 188, 13–15.
8. WA 38, 189, 2–12.

9. WA 38, 190, 22 and 31.
10. WA 38, 197, 21–198, 2.
11. WA 38, 198, 17–23.
12. WA 38, 199, 3–5 and 12.
13. WA 38, 201, 3–9.
14. WA 38, 204–5.
15. WA 38, 207, 14–20.
16. WA 38, 227, 22–29.
17. WA 38, 292, 1–13.
18. The following three satires appeared anonymously, but there is general agreement that their style betrays Luther as the author.
19. WA 38, 284–89.
20. WA 50, 129, 18–22.
21. WA 50, 132–33.
22. WA 53, 404–5.
23. WA 38, 202, 16–27.
24. The editor of WA 38 takes some pains to make this point, p. 177. The translator for the modern English edition of *Luther's Works* (Philadelphia: Fortress, 1971), vol. 38, p. 144, faithfully relays the opinion.

PARALIPOMENA AFTER PART TWO

TR 4, 691, 26–29.
TR 4, 87, 27–34.
TR 5, 34–35.
TR 2, 503, 15–18.
TR 4, 414, 16–18.
TR 4, 232–33.

THE OMNIPRESENCE OF GOD

1. WAB 7, 327, 9–11. Also WAB 7, 290, 20–22 and WAB 7, 329, 7–8.
2. There are numerous treatments of the problem, all from a the-

ological angle, occasionally with some attention to political overtones. The standard works on the Lord's Supper, the issue closest at hand here, are: Walter Köhler, *Zwingli und Luther. Ihr Streit um das Abendmahl nach seinen politischen und religiösen Beziehungen*, 2 vols. (Leipzig, Heinsius, 1924), and Ernst Bizer, *Studien zur Geschichte des Abendmahlstreites im 16. Jahrhundert* (Gütersloh: Bertelsmann, 1940).

3. WA 38, 347, 2–6.

4. Walter Köhler, *Das Marburger Religionsgespräch 1529*, SVR 48 (1929), 57 and 105. Köhler's is the best of several attempts to reconstruct the Marburg meeting. Köhler also offers the various protocols, most of them in Latin (except when Zwingli archly renders a quotation in Greek, to be called to order by Luther, who insists on Latin or German—p. 102). My citations in the following are to these protocols, which I naturally offer in English. See also Köhler's own excellent reconstruction in German, which even makes allowance for Zwingli's Swiss dialect.

5. Luther expressly prefers the papist to the Zwinglian interpretation in WAB 6, 245, 17–20.

6. WA 26, 383, 22–35. Peter Meinhold, *Luthers Sprachphilosophie* (Berlin: Lutherisches Verlagshaus, 1958), makes considerable use of this passage, pp. 39–45.

7. Köhler (see my note 4 above), p. 93.

8. TR 5, 235–36.

9. TR 2, 112, 13–15.

10. WA 26, 333, 6–20.

11. WA 26, 339, 34–36.

12. WA 26, 345, 20–29.

13. WA 38, 204, 27.

14. Accounts of Bucer's activity may be found in Heinrich Bornkamm, *Martin Bucer's Bedeutung für die europäische Reformationsgeschichte*, SVR 169 (1952), and James M. Kittelson, "Martin Bucer and the Sacramentarian Controversy: The Origins of His Policy of Concord," ARG 64 (1973), 166–83. The latter is much influenced by Hans Baron, "Religion and Politics in the German Imperial Cities During the Reformation," *English Historical Review* 59 (1937), 405–13 and 615–33. See also Mark U. Edwards, Jr., *Luther and the False Brethren* (Stanford: Univ. Press, 1975), pp. 127–55.

15. WA 38, 298.

APPROACH FROM THE WEST

1. WAB 7, 379, 3–7.
2. WAB 7, 408, 23–26.
3. WAB 7, 354, 26–30.
4. Hans Baron, "Religion and Politics in the German Imperial Cities During the Reformation," see my note 14 of preceding chapter.
5. Walter Köhler, *Das Marburger Religionsgespräch 1529. Versuch einer Rekonstruktion.* SVR 148 (1929), 39.
6. See Roland Bainton's essay on Wibrandis Rosenblatt-Zell, the young widow who married John Oecolampadius and, upon his death, took Capito at the encouragement of Bucer. Capito died in 1541, and Elizabeth Bucer on her deathbed required her husband Martin and Wibrandis to marry. In *Gottesreich und Menschenreich. Ernst Staehelin zum 80. Geburtstag,* ed. by Max Geiger (Stuttgart: Helbing & Luchtenhahn, 1969), pp. 72–86.
7. WAB 2, 407, 71–72.
8. WAB 2, 410, 9–10.
9. WAB 2, 421, 16.
10. WAB 2, 430, 5, and 431, 15–16, 20–22, and 26–31.
11. James M. Kittelson, *Wolfgang Capito. From Humanist to Reformer* (Leiden: Brill, 1975).
12. WAB 7, 410, 9–14.
13. WAB 7, 413, 7–9.
14. CR 3, 73.
15. WA 29, 83, 20–25, and WA 23, 377, 1–18.
16. TR 3, 549, 5.
17. W. Koepchen, "Wittenberg in the Days of Luther," *Four Hundred Years. Comparative Essays on the Reformation of Dr. Martin Luther and Its Blessed Results,* 2nd ed. (St. Louis: Concordia, 1917), pp. 172–85; G. Krüger, "Wie sah die Stadt Wittenberg zu Luthers Lebzeiten aus," *Luther Jahrbuch* 15 (1933), 29–41.
18. TR 3, 269, 5–6.
19. WAB 7, 411, 12–14.
20. Walch 17, 2093–94. My account of this meeting is based on

three reports from the participants: Frederick Myconius to Veit Dietrich of 11 June, in Walch 17, 2090–98; John Bernardi's redaction of an account put together by the south German delegation after their return to Frankfurt, 2 to 5 June, in Walch 17, 2099–119; and the travel journal of one of the Augsburgers, Wolfgang Musculus, in Kolde, 216–30. These contemporary accounts are primarily concerned with setting forth the theological substance. There are various modern reconstructions, e.g., in biographies of Bucer. All fail to take into account what seems to me to be the major factor, Luther's own remarkable personality.

21. Walch 17, 2094—a remark by Myconius.
22. Walch 17, 2110—this from the south Germans' report.
23. Kolde, 227–28.
24. WAB 7, 382–83.
25. The time when he refused to see his son Hans for three days seems petty, but should be mentioned. It is not unlike his dealing with his former pupil Stephan Roth, who had become an important official in his home town of Zwickau. When Roth sided with the Zwickau city council against the town pastor, he found himself at outs with a pouting Luther. It seemed only the alienated pastor's good offices with Luther could effect the reconciliation. This was in the year before the Wittenberg Concord.

KNOCKING THE GRAND HEADS

1. TR 5, 380, 18–26.
2. TR 2, 455, 33–35.
3. TR 4, 309, 6.
4. KK 1, 643.
5. Walch 19, 380.
6. Walch 19, 382.
7. See the letter in which he introduces himself to Erasmus in 1519, WAB 1, 361–63.
8. As early as 1936, Herbert Schöffler called attention to the German reform as a generation movement, thus anticipating more recent theories on the sociology of intellectual movements like that by Thomas Kuhn. Schöffler's Reformation writings have been reissued in *Wirkungen der Reformation. Religions-*

sozialogische Folgerungen für England und Deutschland (Frank-furt: Klostermann, 1960).

9. Otto Vossler, "Herzog Georg der Bärtige und seine Ab-lehnung Luthers," *Historische Zeitschrift* 184 (1957), 272–91. Hans Scheible, "Fürsten auf dem Reichstag," in *Der Reichstag zu Worms von 1521* (Worms: Staatsarchiv), pp. 390–98, gives particular attention to George's reform activity. Both rely on Hans Becker, "Herzog Georg von Sachsen als kirchlicher und theologischer Schriftsteller," ARG 24 (1927), 161–269.

10. Walch 19, 353 and 357.

11. Walch 19, 372–74.

12. Walch 19, 364.

13. Walch 15, 1666.

14. WAB 2, 642, 15–16.

15. WAB 3, 4, 6–16 and 26.

16. WAB 3, 27, 12–21.

17. WA 11, 250, 15–20.

18. WA 11, 252, 12–14.

19. WA 11, 263, 7–11.

20. WA 11, 267, 1–6.

21. WA 11, 268, 1–8.

22. WA 11, 270, 22–26.

23. WA 11, 277, 28–30.

24. Vossler (see my n. 9 above), p. 19, n. 2.

25. WA 19, 254–56, and WA 30/2, 25.

26. WA 34, 135.

27. For evidence of this curious compromise, check WAB 6, 449, 6–7 and notes.

28. WAB 6, 450, 17–22.

29. George Rörer has left us notes of the sermon, WA 37, 577–82. We also have Luther's own recollections of it and the prayer afterward, in his letter to Chancellor Brück of about seven weeks later, WAB 7, 143–44.

30. WAB 7, 138, 16–21.

31. WAB 7, 139, 50–56.

32. WAB 7, 142, 10–24.

33. WAB 7, 146f., 14–25.

34. The word *Zorn* is used in this sense of (righteous) anger from the nineteenth century right on through the present, e.g., Her-mann Kunst, *Evangelischer Glaube und politische Verant-wortung* (Stuttgart: Evangelisches Verlagswerk, 1976), who

treats most of the conflicts dealt with in this chapter. American scholars have too often followed the German lead.

35. Jaroslav Pelikan, *Luther the Expositor* (St. Louis: Concordia, 1959), p. 37: "The finesse of Gene Tunney with the violence of Jack Dempsey." Here is truly one of those remarks which tell everything about the expositor (in this case, Pelikan), and nothing about the author being "interpreted."

36. WA 30/2, 68, 12–17.

37. E.g., WA 43, 46, 11.

38. TR 5, 461, 1–3. Friedrich Koldewey, *Heinz von Wolfenbüttel. Ein Zeitbild aus dem Jahrhundert der Reformation*, SVR 2 (1883), 10ff., is one of the many who tell this story.

39. WA 51, 462.

40. KK 2, 559.

41. WAB 9, 366, 20–23.

42. WA 51, 476–510.

43. WA 51, 537–44.

44. TR 4, 441–42.

45. TR 5, 497–98.

PRINT AND REPRINT

1. A tremendous amount has been written in recent decades on technology and society, much of it under the conviction that "the principal cause of everything connected with modernization is transformation of the world by technology"—Peter L. Berger and H. Kellner, *The Homeless Mind. Modernization and Consciousness* (New York: Random House, 1973), pp. 8–9. Other recent books to serve as an introduction are: Thomas Parke Hughes, *The Development of Western Technology Since 1500* (New York: Macmillan, 1964); R. A. Buchanan, *Technology and Social Progress* (New York: Oxford, 1965); Emmanuel G. Mesthene, ed., *Technology and Social Change* (Indianapolis: Bobbs-Merrill, 1967); Melvin Kranzberg and William Davenport, eds., *Technology and Culture* (New York: Schocken, 1972). The detailed argument specifically that the new technology of print transformed European culture has found its most recent advocate in Elizabeth Eisenstadt, *The Printing Press as an Agent of Change. Com-*

munications and Cultural Transformations in Early-Modern Europe, 2 vols. (Cambridge: Univ. Press, 1979). My critique of this view is forthcoming in the spring issue of *Michigan Germanic Studies* (1980) in an article entitled "Technology: Potter or Pot?"

2. T. F. Carter, *The Invention of Printing and Its Spread Westwards* (New York: Columbia Univ. Press, 1955); S. H. Steinberg, *Five Hundred Years of Printing* (New York: Criterion, 1959); Helmut Presser, *Das Buch vom Buch* (Bremen: Schünemann, 1962). A most helpful focus on the scrivener mentality is cast by H. J. Chaytor, *From Script to Print* (New York: October House, 1967).

3. Antonia McLean, *Humanism and the Rise of Science in Tudor England* (New York: Watson, 1972), p. 22. More recently, Hans Widmann has written on "Der koreanische Buchdruck und Gutenbergs Erfindung," *Gutenberg Jahrbuch* (1974), pp. 32–35.

4. Rolf Engelsing, *Analphabetentum und Lektüre* (Stuttgart: Metzler, 1973), p. 20. See also Friedrich Kapp, *Geschichte des deutschen Buchhandels bis in das siebzehnte Jahrhundert* (Leipzig: Börsenverein, 1886).

5. These figures were first worked out by Burckhardt, "Druck und Vertrieb der Werke Luthers," of which only the first installment appeared: "Die Jenaer Gesamtausgabe, 1553–70," *Zeitschr. für die historische Theologie* 32, NF 26 (1862), 456ff. See also Otto Clemen, *Die lutherische Reformation und der Buchdruck*, SVR 167 (1939), and Johannes Luther, "Der Wittenberger Buchdruck in seinem Übergang zur Reformationspresse," in *Lutherstudien zur vierten Jahrhundertfeier der Reformation* (Wittenberg, 1917), pp. 261–82. This is another subject on which much has been written. It is safe to say that the modern science of bibliography arises in large part from the centuries of scholarly effort with Luther's work, culminating at last in the Weimar edition.

6. WAB 2, 379, 5–8.

7. WA 2, 166, 1–11.

8. WA 10/3, 176, 2–5.

9. WA 17/2, 251, 5–10.

10. WA 17/2, 3–4.

11. WAB 3, 577.

12. WA Bible 2, 273.

13. WA Bible 8, 7, 21–22.

14. WA Bible 8, 8, 7.
15. WA Bible 8, 7, 24–26.
16. TR 5, 59, 8–10.
17. TR 2, 553–54.
18. TR 2, 17, 32, and WA 51, 547, 4, no doubt elsewhere as well.
19. TR 4, 431–32.
20. WA 30/3, 259.
21. WAB 5, 660, 9–10.

"THAT DAMNED CARDINAL"

1. There is no recent biography of Albert, but see J. May, *Der Kurfürst Cardinal und Erzbischof Albrecht II. von Mainz und Magdeburg . . . und seine Zeit,* 2 vols. (Munich: Jakob Franz'che Buchhandlung, 1865–75). Anton Philipp Brück has elucidated the early relationship with Luther, "Kardinal Albrecht von Brandenburg, Kurfürst und Erzbischof von Mainz," in *Der Reichstag zu Worms von 1521. Reichspolitik und Luthersache* (Worms: Staatsarchiv, 1971), pp. 257–70. For later years, see Hermann Kunst, *Evangelischer Glaube und politische Verantwortung* (Stuttgart: Evangelisches Verlagswerk, 1976), pp. 329–49.
2. A. Schulte, *Die Fugger in Rom 1495–1532* (Leipzig: Duncker & Humblot, 1904), vol. 1, p. 104, and vol. 2, pp. 93ff.
3. Walch has collected a number of such tales, 15, 333–81.
4. Walch 15, 301–33.
5. Hans Wolter, "Kardinal Albrecht von Mainz und die Anfänge der katholischen Reform," *Theologie und Philosophie* 51 (1976), 496–511, recommends Albert (in the best spirit of the Renaissance churchman) for his patronage of the arts.
6. WA 1, 65–69.
7. WAB 1, 114–15.
8. The 1960s saw a spate of publications on this issue. A good summary can be found in the third edition of a book by the scholar most responsible for airing the problem in the first place, Erwin Iserloh, *Luther zwischen Reform und Reformation. Der Thesenanschlag fand nicht statt* (Münster: Aschendorff, 1968). The most scholarly response from the Lutheran camp is probably that by Heinrich Bornkamm, *Thesen und Thesenanschlag Luthers. Geschehen und Bedeutung* (Berlin:

Töpelmann, 1967), but the issue also evoked argumentation, especially in the United States, of an obscurantist and authoritarian air which would have brought down the hearty derision of Doctor Martinus.

9. WA 1, 243–46 and 383–93.
10. WAB 2, 28, 34–39.
11. WAB 2, 54, 10–17 and 24–27.
12. KK 1, 738.
13. WA 18, 408–11, and 30/2, 391–412.
14. WA 23, 390–431.
15. WAB 7, 219, 95–100.
16. Kunst (see my n. 1, above), p. 341, says Luther "learned more details," but this seems pretty unlikely since Ludwig Rabe had been living with him for several months.
17. WAB 7, 368–71, and CR 3, 42.
18. WA 50, 395, 23–24.
19. WA 50, 396, 25–26.
20. WA 50, 397, 22–27.
21. WA 50, 399–400.
22. WA 50, 403, 5–8.
23. WA 50, 405, 32–35.
24. WA 50, 404, 23–28.
25. WA 50, 414, 8–9.
26. WA 50, 414, 33–415, 8.
27. WA 50, 430, 28–31.
28. WA 51, 138, 10.

IT *IS* THE DEVIL

1. KK 2, 290–91.
2. WAB 8, 185f., 40–42.
3. WAB 8, 353, 38–39.
4. WA 28, 329, 5–7.
5. TR 2, 527, 11–12.
6. TR 5, 87, 7–8.
7. WA Bible 3, xlii, 7–8.
8. TR 1, 153, 26–28.
9. KK 2, 516.
10. TR 4, 225, 14–24.

11. WA 30/2, 211, 29–39.
12. TR 4, 687, 12–14.
13. TR 2, 358, 13–15.
14. TR 1, 511, 32–33.
15. TR 5, 150, 26–27.
16. WAB 11, 287, 43–44.
17. TR 2, 25, 4–6.
18. TR 2, 435, 12.
19. TR 2, 19–20; TR 1, 483–84.
20. TR 2, 28–30.
21. TR 2, 420, 30–31.
22. TR 2, 114–16.
23. TR 2, 35, 25–27.
24. TR 2, 111–12.
25. TR 2, 116, 22–31.
26. TR 2, 159, 3–6.
27. TR 2, 131–32.
28. TR 1, 534–35.
29. TR 6, 93, 34–35.
30. TR 6, 215–16.
31. TR 1, 288–89.
32. TR 1, 62–63.
33. TR 1, 244–45.
34. WAB 6, 254, 6–9.
35. TR 1, 216, 6–11.
36. TR 1, 232–33.
37. WA 16, 130, 7–12.
38. TR 3, 651–52.
39. TR 5, 333–34.
40. TR 1, 493, 27–28.
41. TR 5, 328–29.
42. TR 5, 92, 8–10; TR 1, 86, 11–12.
43. WAB 12, 135, 3–28.
44. TR 2, 306, 8–14.
45. WAB 7, 336, 11–16. See also TR 3, 503, 21–23, and WAB 6, 386, 15–18.
46. WAB 10, 645, 12–26.
47. WAB 4, 625, 5–18.
48. TR 1, 95, 1–12.
49. WA 42, 17, 36–38, and 18, 21–22.
50. WA 18, 709, 21–22.
51. TR 5, 16, 10–25.

52. TR 2, 10, 23–28.
53. WA 45, 638, 34.
54. TR 1, 62, 8–9.
55. WA 36, 428, 2–11.
56. WA 40/2, 417, 18–418, 20.
57. WA 44, 429, 17–19.
58. WA 24, 632, 31–32, or WA 41, 675, 8, etc.

PARALIPOMENA AFTER PART THREE

WA 38, 340, 14–18.
TR 2, 585, 14–19.
WA 40/2, 329, 20–31.
TR 5, 329, 19–20.
TR 5, 368, 21–23.
TR 5, 586, 10–11.
TR 4, 195, 1–4.

THE TWO TESTAMENTS OF SCHMALKALDEN

1. Heinz Bluhm, *Martin Luther, Creative Translator* (St. Louis: Concordia, 1965).
2. J. F. Mozley, *William Tyndale* (New York: Macmillan, 1937), pp. 52–54, and Preserved Smith, *English Historical Review* (1921), p. 422, made this inference independently. Charles Harold Williams, *William Tyndale* (London: Nelson, 1969), pp. 16–17, regards the presence in Wittenberg as established. E. Gordon Rupp, *Six Makers of English Religion 1500–1700* (London: Hodder & Stoughton, 1957), p. 18, still did not, however.
3. *Urkunden und Aktenstücke zur Geschichte von Martin Luthers Schmalkaldischen Artikeln (1536–1574)*, ed. by Hans Volz (Berlin: de Gruyter, 1957), p. 16, lines 29–30.
4. WAB 7, 504, 9.
5. Volz 108, 11–12.

6. Walch 21b, 2136.
7. For a good documentation of these illnesses see Volz, p. 19, n. 7. Also Wilhelm Ebstein, *Dr. Martin Luthers Krankheiten und deren Einfluss auf seinen körperlichen und geistigen Zustand* (Stuttgart: Enke, 1908).
8. The request must have been made sometime in July or August of 1536. Volz 19, 7–13.
9. Volz 33; 76, 15; 79, 12. A photocopy of the manuscript is displayed in Karl Zangemeister's edition of *Die Schmalkaldischen Artikel vom Jahre 1537 nach D. Martin Luther's Autograph in der Universitätsbibliothek zu Heidelberg* (Heidelberg: Winter, 1886).
10. Volz 38, 11–21.
11. Volz 66–67.
12. Volz 35–37.
13. TR 3, 383, 9–11.
14. Volz 35, 34–39.
15. WAB 7, 540, 6–10.
16. CR 1, 1008; CR 2, 709; Volz 95, 1.
17. TR 5, 388–89.
18. Volz 93, 9–10. For a report of Melanchthon's gloomy outlook, Volz 94, 10–23. The "gross Pomeranian" is at Volz 105, 18, and n. 11.
19. Volz 99, 13–14, and 102, 306; WAB 8, 22–23.
20. Volz 112, 13; 96, n. 1; 112, 7–8; 111–12.
21. WAB 8, 40, 16–31, and Ebstein (see my note 7, above), pp. 20–21.
22. WAB 8, 35, 2–4. As to the inactivity in the first days, Volz 110, 6 and 111, 8–9.
23. TR 3, 587, 31–32; Volz 117, n. 2.
24. TR 3, 578, 10–12.
25. TR 5, 96, 10–13.
26. Volz 117–18.
27. TR 3, 388–89.
28. TR 5, 96, 21–22.
29. TR 3, 389–90.
30. WAB 8, 49, 1–9.
31. WAB 8, 47; TR 5, 97, 10–13.
32. Otto Clemen, "Luther in Schmalkalden 1537," ARG 31 (1934), 257.
33. TR 3, 393, 34–37.

34. WAB 8, 55–56.
35. TR 3, 394, 10–11.
36. TR 3, 394, 16–21.
37. H. Richard Tyler, "Neurological Disorders Seen in the Uremic Patient," *Archives of Internal Medicine* 126 (1970), 781–89.
38. Norman B. Levy, "Uremic Syndrome," *American Journal of Psychiatry* 130 (1973), 1159–60.
39. George F. Schreiner, "Mental and Personality Changes in the Uremic Syndrome," *Medical Annals of the District of Columbia* 26 (1957), 316–62. Worthy of mention because they do *not* draw personality implications from the uremic syndrome are a dissertation from the urological clinic of the University of Munich, Annemarie Halder, "Das Harnsteinleiden Martin Luthers" (Munich, 1969); and "Martin Luther: A Panel Postmortem," *Chicago Medicine* 69 (1966), 107–16.
40. *Zeitschrift für Kirchengeschichte* 4 (1881), 326.
41. KK 2, 395. One reads the charge against Luther in the historian best known for his ecumenism, Joseph Lortz, *Die Reformation in Deutschland,* 5th ed. (Fribourg: Herder, 1962), 2, 208–9.

LOSS OF A FRIEND

1. TR 4, 582, 21.
2. E. Thiele, "Denkwürdigkeiten aus dem Leben des Johann Agricola von Eisleben von ihm selbst aufgezeichnet," *Theologische Studien und Kritiken* 80 (1907), 253.
3. Thiele, ibid., p. 256.
4. Luther also made a collection of proverbs, which he never published. It is often remarked that there is little overlap between his and Agricola's work. This may reflect the collaborators' mutual awareness of the other's material. Perhaps Agricola's publication of his large collection then also made the printing of Luther's seem unnecessary (or unprofitable).
5. WAB 5, 145–51; WAB 4, 557–58.
6. WA 50, 23–39.
7. WAB 4, 40, 3; 55, 10–12; 45, 73–74.
8. WAB 4, 210–11 and 219–20.
9. TR 4, 97, 11–15.

10. The most recent telling of the tale is by Mark U. Edwards, Jr., *Luther and the False Brethren* (Stanford: Univ. Press, 1975), pp. 156–79. See also WA 50, 461–66 and WA 51, 425–28, as well as WA 39/1, 359, 418, and 486–87. Somewhat more sympathetic to Agricola is Gustav Kawerau, *Johann Agricola von Eisleben. Ein Beitrag zur Reformationsgeschichte* (Berlin: Hertz, 1881)—and, of course, Agricola's own account (my note 2 above). The most thorough treatment is that by Joachim Rogge, *Johann Agricolas Lutherverständnis unter besonderer Berücksichtigung des Antinomismus* (Berlin: Evangelische Verlagsanstalt, 1960), esp. pp. 132–210.
11. WA 6, 459, 1–4.
12. WA 16, 374, 19–21. See also WA 16, 371, 26.
13. TR 2, 583, 8–10 and 16–18; TR 6, 85, 9–14.
14. TR 3, 405, 6–12.
15. TR 4, 673, 7–14.
16. WA 50, 470, 32–33.
17. TR 3, 480–81.
18. WA 39/1, 344–45.
19. TR 3, 483, 19.
20. WAB 8, 186.
21. Thiele (my note 2 above), p. 259.
22. WAB 8, 346.
23. WAB 7, 342–43. Luther says this himself about his own remarks. The WA editors take the phrase "at table" to be intended figuratively, but I do not think that affects their significance.
24. WA 39/1, 571f., 10–14 and 1–15.
25. TR 4, 88, 4–6.
26. Quoted from Edwards (my note 10 above), p. 175.
27. TR 5, 40, 11. See Rogge (my note 10 above), pp. 200ff., for details.
28. WAB 11, 82, note.
29. TR 3, 660, 33–36.
30. TR 4, 433, 26–27.
31. WA 51, 432, 11–12.
32. TR 3, 661, 9–10.
33. TR 3, 405, 16.
34. TR 4, 635, 14–22.
35. WA 50, 474, 9–11 and 28–31; 475, 7–13, 16–18, and 23–26; 476, 15–20.

36. WA 50, 472, 11–12.
37. WA 50, 473, 6–13.
38. WA 50, 471, 23.
39. TR 2, 271, 23–31.
40. WA 11, 280, 17–18.
41. WA 51, 214, 14–20.
42. TR 2, 374, 17–18.

"LIKE A HORSE WITH BLINDERS ON"

1. Aurifaber's *Table Talks* are available in many editions, including Walch. Ernst Kroker made the earlier transmission accessible in the second section of WA (which I cite TR). For an early treatment of the problem, see Preserved Smith's dissertation, *Luther's Table Talk* (Columbia, 1907).

2. The old man Luther has never been of much interest to historians; he has been an embarrassment to Lutheran theologians. Averting one's eyes from the old reprobate, one drew excerpts from his *Table Talks* insofar as they might appear to support one's current hypothesis. The most notorious example of this kind was the attempt to reconstruct Luther's childhood from scattered phrases in the *Table Talks*. See Lewis W. Spitz, "Psychohistory and History: The Case of Young Man Luther," *Soundings* 56 (1973), 182–209. Literally thousands of pages have been written in the attempt to nail down the exact time and place of Luther's "Tower Experience," where he was supposed, all of a sudden flash, to have "discovered the gospel." See H. G. Haile, "The Great Martin Luther Spoof: Philological Limits to Knowledge," *Yale Review* 67 (1977), 236–46.

3. Modern scholars, on the other hand, have established the fact to their own satisfaction that Luther "broke" with the church during what they have styled "the Protestant Revolt" and dated around 1520. Therefore, just to cite one example from a book familiar to my reader, Hermann Kunst says he is "astonished" that Luther would appeal to "Catholic" prelates in Brandenburg during the Wolf Hornung affair—*Evangelischer Glaube und politische Verantwortung* (Stuttgart: Evangelisches Verlagswerk, 1976), Scholarly hypotheses soon pro-

duce a reality of their own, to which historical figures will be
good enough to conform.

4. WA 44, 112, 11ff.; WA 28, 609ff.
5. TR 2, 134, 4–12.
6. TR 1, 192–93.
7. WA 44, 111, 32–34.
8. WA 28, 609ff.
9. TR 3, 417, 26–28.
10. TR 3, 415–16.
11. TR 5, 254, 6–10.
12. WA 15, 46, 7–10; WA 15, 33, 9–10.
13. WA 47, 682, 22–23.
14. WA 47, 669, 13–14.
15. TR 4, 274, 13.
16. WA 37, 661, 22–24.
17. WA 47, 84, 18–20.
18. WA 8, 573–74.
19. TR 4, 440, 5–11.
20. Jean Wirth, "Sainte Anne est une Sorcière," *Bibliothèque
    d'Humanisme et Renaissance* 40 (1978), 449–80.
21. WA 36, 388, 28–32.
22. His recollections of that epoch in his life are voluminous. In-
    dexing them alone requires twenty-six pages in WA 58. Oddly
    enough, within that section, we find a heading entitled "Recol-
    lections of Cloister Life." This would belie the obvious fact
    that all the other references constitute recollections, too. We
    have no descriptions by Luther of his cloister life while he was
    living it, so far as I have been able to discover.
23. WA 28, 761, 17–19.
24. WA 26, 12, 12–13.
25. WA 47, 590, 16–20.
26. TR 5, 100, 3–7.
27. WA 33, 83, 20–26; WA 38, 148, 11–12; WA 45, 482, 16; WA
    46, 46, 5; WA 47, 99, 35–37; etc.
28. WA 33, 539, 20ff.
29. WA 51, 95, 7–9.
30. WA 40/3, 719, 20–22; WA 38, 148, 12–32; etc.
31. WA 51, 202, 24–33.
32. WAB 6, 378, 12–13 (top).
33. WA 16, 88, 35–37.
34. TR 3, 486, 9.

35. WA 26, 12, 7–14; WA 33, 561, 30–35; WA 34/2, 48, 31–34; WA 38, 160, 7–18; WA 40/2, 91–92; WA 47, 92, 9–13; WA 51, 113, 7–10; TR 2, 204, 42–44; etc.

36. WA 49, 529, 14–21; TR 4, 607, 4–6.

37. WA 38, 588, 30–38.

38. WA 40/1, 138, 1.

39. TR 5, 657, 4.

40. WA 50, 472, 31–37; see the many other references in WA 58, 8–13.

41. TR 4, 303, 10–18.

42. TR 4, 261, 2–6.

43. TR 1, 47, 23–24.

44. TR 6, 106–7.

45. References in WA 58, 27–28.

46. This is the main thesis of Hermann Steinlein, *Luthers Doktorat. Zum 400-jährigen Jubiläum desselben (18. und 19. Oktober 1912)* (Leipzig: Deichert, 1912).

47. WA 30/3, 386–87.

48. WA 30/3, 521, 7–10 and 522, 3–5.

49. WA 43, 513, 23–33.

50. TR 4, 25, 10–18.

51. TR 3, 564, 6–21.

52. TR 3, 656, 9–26.

53. TR 1, 601, 15–24.

54. WAB 3, 642, 33–36.

55. TR 3, 618, 15–17.

56. TR 5, 658, 1–3.

57. TR 3, 438–39.

58. TR 1, 216, 1–6.

59. TR 4, 587, 13–15.

60. TR 5, 215, 26–29.

61. TR 5, 656–57.

62. TR 1, 233, 9–10.

63. TR 5, 78, 5–14.

64. TR 1, 597, 29–35.

65. TR 1, 597–98.

66. WA 15, 214–15.

67. TR 4, 666, 15–18.

68. TR 5, 69, 18–24; TR 5, 65, 13–15.

69. The narrative above has drawn on TR 5, 68–73, with occasional additions from the Latin version of the same, TR 5, 65–68.

"NO SWEETER THING THAN LOVE OF WOMAN—MAY A MAN BE SO FORTUNATE"

1. TR 6, 265, 3–4.
2. WA 11, 395, 6–7.
3. WA 11, 400, 21.
4. TR 4, 89, 2–12.
5. TR 2, 427, 21–30.
6. WA 11, 398, 2–7.
7. Ernst Kroker, *Katharina von Bora* (Leipzig: Haberland, 1909), pp. 59ff. Kroker's remains the best biography, but it is out of date, and poor enough. The subject remains in the background; "the great reformer" is the real focus of interest.
8. WA 18, 275–76.
9. WAB 3, 474–75.
10. Kroker (my note 7 above), p. 127.
11. TR 4, 503, 20; WAB 3, 541, 8.
12. WAB 3, 635, 22–28.
13. TR 1, 69, 18–19.
14. TR 2, 649, 14.
15. TR 1, 17, 10–15.
16. WAB 3, 265, 9–30.
17. TR 3, 300–1.
18. TR 2, 526, 8–12.
19. TR 1, 512, 5–7.
20. TR 4, 137, 22.
21. TR 2, 634, 1–2.
22. TR 4, 503–4.
23. TR 4, 263, 4–6.
24. TR 4, 365, 5–7.
25. TR 2, 104, 17–20.
26. WAB 6, 271, 24–32.
27. TR 4, 700–1.
28. E.g., TR 4, 592, 19–24; TR 4, 704, 20–23. See Deborah Jean Voigt, "Martin Luther's Attitudes on Women as Reported in His *Tischreden*" (M.A. thesis: Urbana, 1976), pp. 27ff.
29. TR 4, 576, 18.
30. TR 2, 290, 13–16. Another instance of Cordatus' impatience with Kate's financial control is at TR 3, 307, 26–27.

31. TR 4, 503, 21.
32. TR 2, 300, 9–11.
33. TR 2, 305, 15–18.
34. WAB 7, 317, 14–17.
35. TR 4, 121, 15–19.
36. TR 4, 559, 15.
37. TR 2, 105, 11–19.
38. TR 2, 286, 26; TR 5, 229, 16–26.
39. TR 3, 25, 39–40.
40. WA 30/3, 205, 12–13.
41. WA 47, 318–20.
42. This question has been extensively discussed by those seeking to justify Luther's role in the bigamy of Philip of Hesse, e.g., Th. Brieger, "Luther und die Nebenehe des Landgrafen Philipp von Hessen," *Preussische Jahrbücher* 135 (1909), 35–49.
43. TR 4, 444, 20–27.
44. TR 4, 445, 5–7.
45. TR 3, 378, 9–23.
46. TR 2, 150, 21–24; TR 3, 217, 11–14; WA 38, 349, 23–26.
47. Some examples: TR 3, 3, 22–29; TR 4, 91, 43; TR 4, 408, 18–20.
48. TR 4, 592, 17–18.
49. TR 5, 276, 7.
50. TR 2, 75, 4; TR 4, 437, 5–9; WA 51, 248, 30–34.
51. TR 4, 408, 18–19.
52. WA 42, 282, 31–40.
53. TR 3, 446, 18–27.
54. WAB 9, 573, 27–28.
55. TR 1, 406, 23–25. See also Voigt (my note 28 above), pp. 83–84.
56. TR 5, 375, 21–29.
57. TR 2, 117, 15–16.
58. TR 4, 171, 23–25.
59. TR 4, 661, 2.
60. TR 5, 600, 8–10.
61. TR 5, 14, 32–33.
62. TR 2, 99, 22.
63. WA 51, 52, 9–11.
64. TR 2, 630, 5–6.
65. WA 31/1, 130, 7–17.
66. TR 5, 214, 18–35.

67. WAB 5, 84, 83–87.

68. TR 4, 346, 5–10.

69. TR 4, 424, 7–22.

70. TR 4, 184, 15–16.

71. William W. Rockwell, *Die Doppelehe des Landgrafen Philipp von Hessen* (Marburg: Elwert, 1904), p. 7.

72. WAB 8, 641–43.

73. Rockwell (my note 71 above), p. 153.

74. Rockwell, ibid., p. 159.

75. WAB 9, 162, 18–20 (a favorite Lutherism).

76. WAB 9, 134, 47.

77. Rockwell (my note 71 above), pp. 178 and 180. For some other interesting remarks by Luther on his own conduct in the Hesse affair, see WAB 9, 178, 24–26 and 33–38.

78. WAB 9, 137, 8–9.

79. TR 4, 655, 10–11 and notes 16–17.

80. WAB 9, 145, 40–41.

81. TR 4, 386, 21–22.

82. WA 53, 206, 15–18.

83. TR 5, 144, 17–19. Luther felt it his duty to pray against sinners, KK 2, 440.

84. TR 3, 447–48.

85. KK 2, 219.

86. TR 5, 123, 7–19.

87. My account is based on Luther's *Table Talks* as edited by Förstemann-Bindseil, and on CR 3, xvii–xviii (after column 1284).

88. WAB 9, 168, 1–6.

89. E.g., TR 5, 129, 31–33; TR 5, 244, 27.

SHALL WE RECEIVE GOOD AT THE HAND OF GOD AND SHALL WE NOT RECEIVE EVIL?

1. TR 5, 50, 18–51, 4.

2. TR 2, 322, 3–4.

3. TR 2, 636, 15–17.

4. WAB 8, 569, 17.

5. TR 5, 376, 17–22.

6. WAB 8, 328, 29–32.
7. TR 1, 404, 14.
8. WA 42, 322, 9–12.
9. TR 5, 21, 17–22.
10. TR 2, 291, 25–26.
11. TR 2, 524, 17–22.
12. TR 4, 282, 34.
13. TR 3, 10, 19–21.
14. WA 56, 449, 1–9.
15. WAB 11, 278, 1–2; WA 50, 447, 2–3; TR 5, 290, 5–6.
16. Hans Leiermann, "Der unjuristische Luther," *Luther Jahrbuch* 24 (1957), 69–85.
17. TR 4, 282, 20–30.
18. TR 4, 306–7.
19. WA 53, 524, 28–525, 7.
20. WAB 1, 21–22.
21. WA 54, 16–24. One of the more influential books on the subject argued in favor of various stages in Luther's attitude: Reinhold Lewin, *Luthers Stellung zu den Juden* (Berlin: Trowitzsch, 1911). It is a problem on which much has been written. Johannes Brosseder, *Luthers Stellung zu den Juden im Spiegel seiner Interpreten,* in *Beiträge zur ökumenischen Theologie* 8 (Munich: Hueber, 1972), offers a survey. The more recent C. Bernd Sucher, "Luthers Stellung ze den Juden. Eine Interpretation aus germanistischer Sicht," in *Bibliotheca Humanistica & Reformatorica* 23 (Nieuwkoop: de Graf, 1977), is of interest only as its subtitle might suggest.
22. TR 3, 370, 9–14.
23. WAB 8, 89–91.
24. TR 3, 442, 5–7.
25. TR 3, 442, 7–8.
26. TR 3, 600, 4–6.
27. TR 5, 166, 28–30.
28. TR 5, 167, 1–5.
29. WA 53, 520, 9–14, and 522, 1–6.
30. WA 53, 521, 23–27.
31. WA 53, 523–24.
32. WA 53, 524, 18–22.
33. WA 53, 541–42.
34. TR 5, 246–47.

35. WA 53, 414 and 574.
36. WA 54, 16.
37. WA 51, 196.
38. TR 5, 198–99.
39. WA 51, 587–88.
40. TR 2, 178, 5.
41. TR 4, 116, 11–12.
42. TR 4, 27, 22–27, and 81, 5–15.
43. TR 1, 436, 10–11. Luther's involvement in the persecution of the Anabaptists may be documented in his letter to Philip of Hesse, suggesting banishment, WAB 8, 324, 9; to John Frederick recommending punishment and recantation, WAB 8, 503–5; or requesting more severe punishment, WAB 8, 102–3, etc.
44. Compare WA 50, 11, 17, with WA 50, 34, 18–19.
45. TR 5, 127, 4, and TR 5, 300–1.
46. WAB 6, 46–47.
47. WA 38, 338, 5–8.
48. WA 54, 455, 26–32.
49. KK 2, 599.
50. WA 54, 198.
51. WA 54, 199.
52. WA 54, 221, 8–23.
53. WA 54, 200.
54. WAB 11, 94, 6.
55. KK 2, 602.
56. TR 5, 231, 11–16.
57. TR 3, 512, 20–30.
58. WAB 9, 222, 6–7.

TENTATIO TRISTITIAE THE SENSE OF THEOLOGY

1. TR 4, 6, 19.
2. TR 4, 37, 6–16.
3. TR 4, 25–26.
4. TR 3, 664, 17–23.
5. TR 1, 199, 27–201, 6.

6. WA 8, 574, 23.

7. Wilhelm Ebstein, *Dr. Martin Luthers Krankheiten und deren Einfluss auf seinen körperlichen und geistigen Zustand* (Stuttgart: Enke, 1908), p. 47, diagnosed a heart attack in the 1527 crisis. Paul Reiter, *Martin Luthers Umwelt, Charakter und Psychose*, 2 vols. (Copenhagen: Levin and Munksgaard, 1941), agrees. It is Reiter who provides the most thorough survey of Luther's illnesses with sharpest attention to depression, but the work is flawed by Reiter's invidious intent. The review of Reiter in *Ugeskrift for Laeger* 104 (1942), 70–74, suggests the 1527 attack may have been a touch of the bubonic plague.

8. WA 32, 2, 31–32, and 4, 16–19. See also WA 32, xvii–xxii.

9. TR 3, 438, 4–19.

10. TR 3, 341, 8–14.

11. This has been especially encouraged by remarks made by the old man, and by the interpreters' desire to extrapolate data for reconstructing Luther's youth. The tendency is most apparent among writers committed to theoretical systems, be they theological, as Heinrich Boehmer, *Luther im Lichte der neueren Forschung* (Leipzig: Teubner, 1968), or psychiatric, like Reiter and his follower Erik Erikson, *Young Man Luther* (New York: Norton, 1952).

12. TR 1, 240, 16.

13. TR 3, 51–52.

14. WA 47, 852, 8. Cp. WA 40/3, 674, 5.

15. TR 2, 22–23.

16. TR 3, 626, 5–6.

17. TR 3, 506, 30–31.

18. TR 3, 593, 1–10.

19. WAB 7, 66, 7ff.; TR 2, 64, 11–16; WAB 6, 387, 43–51.

20. TR 1, 239, 17–18.

21. TR 2, 441, 28, etc.

22. TR 5, 46, 27–29.

23. TR 2, 388ff.

24. WAB 6, 388–89.

25. TR 2, 441–42.

26. TR 3, 507, 8–16.

27. TR 1, 146, 11–31.

28. TR 2, 222, 19–23.

29. TR 4, 490, 24–491, 1.

30. TR 3, 476, 24–28.
31. TR 4, 19, 14–24.
32. WAB 8, 231f., 12–18.
33. TR 2, 239, 4–5 and 263, 32–33.
34. E.g., WAB 4, 274, 3–5 (bottom); WAB 4, 277, 12; WAB 4, 282, 6–9.
35. WA 41, 198, 2–4; WA 45, 86, 7–8; WA 22, 174, 29–30; TR 2, 582, 18–20; WAB 4, 289, 18–20; KK 2, 515f.
36. TR 3, 520, 31–35.
37. TR 4, 600, 20–28.
38. TR 3, 439, 7.
39. WA 8, 482, 27–483, 4. See also WA 23, 420, 25ff.
40. WA 38, 563, 11–16.
41. TR 1, 200, 17, and 241, 2.
42. See the entries WA 58, 57–61.
43. TR 1, 198, 4–5.
44. WA 44, 166, 22–29.
45. TR 5, 367, 17–20.
46. TR 2, 309, 5–6.

PARALIPOMENA AFTER PART FOUR

TR 5, 327, 3–5.
TR 4, 692, 10–22.
TR 3, 427, 22–26.
TR 2, 292, 19–20.
TR 4, 369, 5–10.
TR 4, 462, 5–8.
TR 5, 265, 31–33.

EXSPATIATUR ANIMI CAUSA

1. TR 5, 187–88.
2. TR 5, 189, 23–30.
3. TR 5, 193, 8ff. and 194, 22–27.

4. KK 2, 595.
5. WA 46, 177–78; WA 49, 278; WA 41, 471–72; WA 44, 666–67; WA 44, 156, 33–34, for various of Luther's remarks on the conditions in Wittenberg. See also the entries in WA 58, 153–54.
6. TR 5, 646, 7–13.
7. E.g., CR 5, 801.
8. WAB 11, 149–50.
9. WAB 7, 182, 40–42.
10. WAB 7, 160, 5–12.
11. E.g., TR 5, 660–61.
12. TR 4, 281, 5; TR 5, 660, 22.
13. CR 5, 313: Cruciger to Melanchthon.
14. TR 2, 407, 28–30.
15. TR 2, 189, 2–6.
16. Kolde, p. 416.
17. WAB 11, 164.
18. Georg Buchwald, "Luther-Kalendarium," SVR 47 (1929), 156: 7 August.
19. WA 49, 798, 28–30.
20. WA 49, 801, 3–5.
21. WA 49, 801, 25–30.
22. WA 49, 804, 7.
23. WA 51, 17, 30–34.
24. WA 51, 25–26.
25. WA 51, 36–37.
26. WA 44, 718–19.
27. See, for example, TR 3, 695, 16–17; TR 4, 30, 1–16; TR 5, 311–12.
28. WA 44, 813, 28–34.
29. TR 5, 311; TR 5, 329, 14–21; TR 5, 62, 4–12; TR 3, 476–77.
30. WA 44, 812, 9; 812, 23–26; 812, 38–39; and 813, 6–11.
31. WA 44, 813–14.
32. Relevant excerpts from Philip's correspondence in WAB 11, 191.
33. WAB 8, 79, 7.
34. WA 44, 825, 3–12.
35. TR 5, 188–89.
36. TR 5, 666, 3–11.
37. WA 51, 618–19; TR 4, 318, 13–16; WA 19, 225, 12–15.
38. TR 2, 579–80.

39. TR 3, 697–98.
40. TR 5, 413, 29–31.
41. TR 3, 358, 9; KK 2, 199 and 389.
42. WA 48, 33, 4–10.

THE LEGACY

1. WA 10, 23.
2. TR 3, 362–63.
3. TR 1, 203, 18–25.
4. TR 1, 203, 30–32.
5. TR 1, 330, 15–16.
6. WAB 3, 50, 24–25.
7. TR 1, 203–4.
8. TR 1, 417, 6–13; TR 2, 415, 14–18; TR 1, 474, 4–9.
9. TR 3, 23, 3–7; WA 25, 138, 4ff.
10. WA 42, 277, 13–14.
11. TR 1, 194, 1, and TR 1, 210, 9; TR 1, 206–7.
12. TR 1, 207, 3.
13. An excellent treatment of this whole subject constituted Heinrich Bornkamm's earliest work, *Luther und das alte Testament* (Tübingen: Mohr, 1948). See pp. 162ff.
14. TR 1, 354, 12–17.
15. I gave an overview of some of the scholarly treatments of Luther the interpreter in "Luther and Literacy," *PMLA* 71 (1976), 816–28. Probably the very best presentation is still the essay by Karl Holl, "Luthers Bedeutung für den Fortschritt der Auslegekunst," originally a lecture before the Prussian Academy of Sciences, 1920, and printed in his *Gesammelte Aufsätze zur Kirchengeschichte* 1 (Tübingen: Mohr, 1921), 414–50. The English reader with more patience might turn to Jaroslav Pelikan, *Luther the Expositor* (Philadelphia: Fortress, 1959).
16. WA 4, 333, 18.
17. TR 1, 136, 18–20.
18. TR 1, 364, 4–22.
19. TR 1, 350, 25–30.
20. TR 1, 333, 9–11.
21. TR 2, 635, 12.

22. WA 40/1, 634, 3–8.
23. WA 42, 377, 29ff.
24. WA 42, 378, 31–36.
25. WA 42, 380, 39–40; WA 42, 381, 30–31; WA 42, 382, 16–21.
26. WA 42, 279, 19ff. and 37–42.
27. WA 42, 281, 22–26.
28. WA 42, 299, 27–29.
29. WA 42, 416, 18–22.
30. TR 1, 472, 22–23.
31. WA 16, 333, 6–7 and WA 14, 546, 5–6.
32. TR 1, 341, 16–21.
33. WA 30/2, 638, 13ff.
34. The most influential work in this direction was the article by Benjamin Whorf, "The Relation of Habitual Thought and Behavior to Language," first printed in *Language, Culture and Personality* (New York, 1941), pp. 75–93, and reissued many times since.
35. Chapter 14, at the end.
36. Luther argued his views in his preface to the Old Testament of 1523 (WA Bible 8, 30ff.); in his *Summarien über die Psalmen* of 1531 (WA 38, 8–19); and, best-known, his *Sendbrief vom Dolmetschen* of 1530 (WA 30/2, 627–46). The quotation in my text is from a letter to Spalatin in 1523 (WAB 3, 220, 7–12). Also less well known are Luther's incisive words at table, TR 2, 648–49.
37. WA 30/2, 637, 17–22.
38. TR 2, 648–49.
39. WAB 4, 484, 14–18.
40. *Goethes Werke* (Stuttgart, 1906), 37, 22.
41. Adolf Bach, *Geschichte der deutschen Sprache*, 6th ed. (Heidelberg: Quelle & Meyer, 1965), p. 27.
42. Luther's explicit espousal of this norm is TR 2, 639–40. See Günter Feudel, "Luthers Ausspruch über seine Sprache . . . Ideal oder Wirklichkeit?" *Beiträge zur Geschichte der deutschen Sprache und Literatur* 92 (1970), 61–75.
43. WAB 8, 433–37.
44. One of those to demonstrate how Luther's language survived over the centuries was Gottfried Felix Merkel, beginning with his review of Arno Schirokauer's *Germanistische Studien* for *JEGP* 59 (1960), and then in later articles, especially "Vom Fortleben der Bibelsprache im 16. und 17. Jahrhundert," *Zeitschr. für deutsche Sprache* 23 (1967), 7–12.

RECONCILIATION

1. Walch 21b, 3404.
2. Walch 21b, 3421.
3. As, for example, Justus Jonas reports, Walch 21b, 3439.
4. WAB 11, 226, 17–18.
5. See the letter from Georg Major in Walch 21b, 3187.
6. WAB 11, 269, 5–14.
7. WAB 11, 275f., 1–15.
8. TR 6, 302, 12–14.
9. Walch 21b, 3439.
10. WAB 11, 285, 16–17.
11. TR 6, 295, 23–34.
12. TR 6, 345–46.
13. WA 10/2, 174, 13–19 and 178, 15–19.
14. E.g., TR 1, 546, 15.
15. WA 42, 503–4.
16. WA 25, 58–60 contains Luther's most extensive discussion of epikeia. It is in a lecture on the Epistles to Titus and Philemon.
17. WA 14, 554–55.
18. See the article on this subject by Haile in *Soundings* 61 (1978), esp. pp. 507ff.
19. WA 42, 505, 9–23.
20. TR 1, 255, 16–22, and note.
21. TR 2, 108, 1–3.
22. WAB 11, 132, 7–47.
23. WA 54, 488–89.
24. Walch 21b, 3384.
25. The account of Luther's dying is based on that by Jonas and Coelius, as published in Wittenberg and reproduced by Walch 21b, 3381–93. I take my account of the funeral procession from the same source.
26. Walch 21b, 3438.
27. Walch 21b, 3424–26.
28. Walch 21b, 3428.
29. Walch 21b, 3431.
30. Walch 21b, 3434.
31. TR 5, 317–18.

INDEX

Middle Europe in the 16ᵗʰ Century

DENMARK
Copenhagen

ENGLAND
London
Berlin
Wittenberg
POLAND
SAXONY
HOLY ROMAN EMPIRE
Paris
Nuremberg
Vienna
FRANCE
MAP
Mantua
Trieste
Rome

Weser R.

Eisen

Frankfurt
Main R.
Mainz
Worms
Neckar R.

--- Capito ⎫ routes to Wittenberg, 1536
—— Bucer ⎭
—·— Luther's route to Schmalkalden, 1537
········· Wanderings of Doctor Luther, 1545–46
▓▓ Ernestine ⎫ SAXONY
▒▒ Albertine ⎭
▨▨ Joint and mixed sovereignties

Rhine R.

Stuttgart

Strasbourg

morris